David Harbecke

Modernisation through Process

The Rise of the Court of Chancery in the European Perspective

Studien zur
europäischen Rechtsgeschichte

Veröffentlichungen des
Max-Planck-Instituts
für europäische Rechtsgeschichte
Frankfurt am Main

Band 309

Vittorio Klostermann
Frankfurt am Main
2018

David Harbecke

Modernisation through Process

The Rise of the Court of Chancery in the European Perspective

Vittorio Klostermann
Frankfurt am Main
2018

Bibliographische Information der Deutschen Nationalbibliothek
Die Deutsche Nationalbibliothek verzeichnet diese Publikation in der Deutschen Nationalbibliographie; detaillierte bibliographische Daten sind im Internet über *http://dnb.dnb.de* abrufbar.

Druck und Bindung: docupoint GmbH, Barleben
Typographie: Elmar Lixenfeld, Frankfurt am Main

Gedruckt auf Eos Werkdruck.
Alterungsbeständig ∞ ISO 9706 und PEFC-zertifiziert

Printed in Germany
ISSN 1610-6040
ISBN 978-3-465-04331-7

Contents

Acknowledgements

This book is based on my doctoral dissertation under the same title, which was written at the Max-Planck-Institute for European Legal History and submitted at the Johann Wolfgang Goethe University in Frankfurt.

I developed first ideas for this dissertation in summer 2012. The research on the primary sources took place in 2013. The thesis was finally successfully defended on 2 November 2015. With the exception of a few highly noteworthy publications, literature up to that date has been considered.

During the years 2012 to 2014, the financial support from the LOEWE Research Focus "Extrajudicial and Judicial Conflict Resolution" allowed me to focus all my efforts on the preparation of my dissertation. I would especially like to thank my supervisor Albrecht Cordes, who developed an immediate interest in my research topic and showed great support throughout all this time. As leader of my research group at the Max-Planck-Institute for European Legal History, Wim Decock has been an indispensable help in the process of writing this book – from discussing my very first ideas to commenting on the final manuscript. I would like to thank him for his incredible dedication to this project.

My understanding of English legal history was in no small part formed by John H. Langbein's phenomenal course on the History of the Common Law at Yale Law School. I am also especially grateful for Professor Langbein's critique of the first ideas I had developed for this dissertation. It has greatly helped me in finding my way through the scholarship on the Court of Chancery and its pitfalls.

This book would not have been possible without the incredible support of the Max-Planck-Institute for European Legal History. The staff at the institute was a source of invaluable help throughout the whole process of my dissertation – from identifying first sources to finally printing this book. The excellent academic contacts and the financial support from the institute facilitated extended research trips to Yale Law School and the National Archives of the United Kingdom in Kew. I would especially like to thank Thomas Duve, director at the institute, for not only providing me personally with incredibly helpful comments as an examiner of this dissertation but also for supporting a climate of open academic debate at the institute, from which I and many others greatly profited.

Special thanks also go to Katharina Isabel Schmidt, Yoan Hermstrüwer, Rafael van Damme, Paolo Astorri and Rita Vavra who not only offered critical comments on my ideas but also great friendship during all the highs and lows of the writing process.

Last but not least, I would like to thank my parents for the wonderful support provided throughout all my years of education and studies.

David Harbecke

Chapter I

Introduction

The existence of a separate equitable jurisdiction long remained a seemingly idiosyncratic feature of the common law tradition. It is a source of continuous fascination and irritation for common law students and continental legal historians alike. The Court of Chancery was not the only but by far the most prominent of the equitable courts. It thus came to dominate the development of the equitable jurisdiction in the English legal system and our understanding thereof.

Much has been said about the evolution of the Court of Chancery and yet the historical accounts have commonly failed to explain the reason for the singularity of the English development satisfactorily for the modern reader. It is my strong belief that recourse to legal theory carries the potential to facilitate a better understanding of a seemingly inscrutable late medieval phenomenon. The theorisation of the historical developments also opens the way towards comparisons to other legal systems – present and past – and thus provides links for both contemporary common lawyers and continental legal historians.

The dialogue between legal theory and legal history has often been neglected in the literature on the common law tradition. That is not necessarily due to ignorance or a lack of interest from capable scholars. It is rather the result of a conscious decision by numerous 20th century legal historians. This decision is best understood as a reaction to late 19th century scholarship. The classical legal historians of that period were deeply invested in offering a theoretical framework for the development of law through the centuries. A special focus lay on establishing the continuity of English legal instruments – from Anglo-Saxon times into the 19th century.[1] Many scholars thus uncritically transferred contemporary theory and doctrine to earlier periods without much respect for specific historical circumstances.[2]

1 See most prominently the works of *O. W. Holmes*, The Common Law (1881), Transaction Publishers, New Brunswick, NJ, 2005; *H. Adams et al.*, Essays in Anglo-Saxon Law (1876), Rothman, South Hackensack, NJ, 1972.

2 Also *M. J. Horwitz*, The Historical Contingency of the Role of History, Yale Law Journal, Volume 90 (1981), p. 1057–1059; *R. W. Gordon*, Critical Legal Histories, Stanford Law Review, Volume 57 (1984), p. 57–125; *D. Rabban*, The Historiography of the Common Law, Law and Society, Volume 28 (2003), p. 1161–1201, especially p. 1187–1188.

This undifferentiated and uncritical historiography has understandably given a bad name to combinations of legal theory and legal history. The reaction of many 20th century legal historians was to isolate their research from other areas of law and focus on its historical dimension instead.[3] This has allowed for a far better understanding of normative contexts through the course of history. On the other hand, however, it has also mostly banished the legal historians' perspective from the discussion of contemporary legal issues. That is especially regrettable since argumentation with history remains common and often lacks the contextualisation that could be offered by legal historians.

I will attempt to overcome this schism with regard to the specific case of the development of the separate equitable jurisdiction in the English Court of Chancery. The major part of this work will therefore be devoted to a thorough examination of the documentation from the early phase of the Court of Chancery. Based upon this study, however, I will then reflect my findings from the perspective of modern legal theory. The aim is twofold: First, I want to identify the concrete role of the Court of Chancery in the English legal system in its origin. Second, I aim to explain why the development of a separate equitable jurisdiction seemingly remained unique. Why did other European legal systems not develop a similar jurisdictional bifurcation and how did they address problems that the Court of Chancery addressed in England?

An early caveat is in order: Throughout the 14th and 15th the century, in which the Court of Chancery established itself as a central royal court, the term 'equity' was rarely used in proceedings before the court and never in relation to the court itself. During the timeframe under consideration, the Court of Chancery was instead commonly referred to as a 'court of conscience'. The respective meanings of equity and conscience and their usefulness for the understanding of the role of the court will be recurrent issues in the following chapters.

My examination will begin with an introduction to the history of the Court of Chancery (chapter II). This will include an identification of my research period and its relevance for the development of the bifurcated English legal system. I will then present an overview over the existing literature on the early phase of the court (chapter III) with a view to identifying neglected areas and delineating my own research. The next chapter will then be devoted to a presentation of the primary sources underlying my research (chapter IV). Based upon these sources,

3 This reproach was already foreshadowed by *F. W. Maitland*'s programmatic statement that legal history is history not law in: Why the History of English Law is not Written, in: H. A. L. Fisher (ed.), The Collected Papers of Frederic William Maitland, Cambridge University Press, Cambridge, Volume 1, 1911, p. 480–497, p. 491–494.

I will characterise the typical structure of the 15th century Chancery process from its opening to the final decree (chapter V). In order to illustrate the novelty of the Chancery process in the English legal system, I will constantly refer to corresponding stages in the established common law trial. The identification of the Chancery process will then allow a first comparison with contemporary Roman-canon law. I will discuss in how far the Chancery process originated in Roman-canon law procedure and thus exhibited ties to the legal developments on the European continent (chapter VI). Building upon the knowledge of the 15th century process, I will then identify central functions of the Court of Chancery in the developing English legal system with the help of modern legal theory (chapter VII). This will finally facilitate a comparison with supreme courts in surrounding jurisdictions that should answer the question whether the establishment of a separate jurisdiction in the Court of Chancery indeed constituted an idiosyncratic English development (chapter VIII).

Chapter II

A short history of the Court of Chancery

In this chapter, it is my aim to sketch out the historical context, in which my work, which will focus on the 15thcentury, is situated. The Court of Chancery existed as a separate institution from the 14th to the 19th century. The earlier history provides the background (1.) against which the court originally developed and thus marks the starting point for my explanations. As neither the formation nor the later role of the court can be adequately explained without recourse to the contemporary jurisdictional landscape, I will present the most important institutional developments between the 12th and 14th century in some detail. The later history, on the other hand, serves as a point of reference for the development which was set in motion during the period of my research.

For better orientation, I will differentiate five stages of development in the Court of Chancery. These stages are designed to allow a sensible positioning of my own research as well as to reflect far-ranging public perceptions of the court through time. The first stage will cover the institutional formation of the Court of Chancery (2.). I will then proceed to what I will call the expansion period of the court in the 15th and 16th century (3.). Since this period forms the basis for my research, I will limit myself to some facts that will underline the relevance of my research. I will then present the systematisation efforts in the 17th and 18th century (4.), which lead directly into the deterioration phase of the 18th and 19th century (5.). At last, I will address the fusion process in the second half of the 19th century (6.) that resulted in the institutional integration of the Court of Chancery and the common law courts and marks the end of the strict bifurcation of the English legal system.

1. Background

The formation of the Court of Chancery – like most developments in English constitutional history – is a result of pragmatic reaction rather than of systematic action. It can thus only be understood against the background of the existing medieval institutions for conflict resolution and their respective functions, developments and relationships. The period between the Norman Conquest of 1066 and the settlement of the Court of Chancery as a separate court in the late 14th century was characterised not only by a great variety of jurisdictions but also by a highly dynamic development of legal institutions.

1.1 Medieval legal pluralism

The late medieval English legal landscape was highly fragmented. What would eventually develop into a distinct and unified legal system was, at that stage, best characterised as a multitude of complementary and competing jurisdictions. There was certainly no shortage of institutions for conflict resolution. Most major power-holders – individuals, organisations or communities – adjudicated the conflicts of their vassals or members. In the countryside, conflicts were commonly resolved in local courts of tribal origin, such as the county courts and hundreds, or in manorial courts. In the more populated areas, markets, city councils and universities usually maintained self-governing courts.[1] A classification of these institutions from our modern perspective is almost impossible. Were these courts and tribunals performing public or private functions? Premodern institutions hardly allow for such differentiations. Even though the administrative control over the country by central authorities was comparatively advanced,[2] it did not allow for a comprehensive regulation of conflict resolution in the localities. Nevertheless, royal officers were often involved in the adjudication process and royal interests played an ever-greater role in the outcome.[3]

1.2 Ecclesiastical jurisdiction

The two centralised institutions of adjudication – the ecclesiastical courts and the courts of the common law – are much easier to classify, partly because they have essentially survived until today and have thus shaped our conceptions of legal institutions.

The ecclesiastical courts of the Roman-Catholic church had successfully monopolized a sizeable extent of conflict resolution in the late medieval

1 See also *J. H. Langbein / R. T. Lerner/B. P. Smith*, History of the Common Law – The Development of Anglo-American Legal Institutions, Aspen Publishers, New York, NY, 2009, p. 4.

2 Compare *R. C. van Caenegem*, The Birth of the English Common Law, Cambridge University Press, Cambridge, 2nd edition, 1988 (repr. 1989), p. 92–93, p. 107–110.

3 For a short discussion of the revenue dimension of local criminal adjudication, see *J. H. Langbein / R. T. Lerner / B. P. Smith*, History of the Common Law – The Development of Anglo-American Legal Institutions, p. 66–67, with reference to *F. W. Maitland*, Introduction, in: F. W. Maitland (ed.), Pleas of the Crown for the Country of Gloucester A. D. 1221, Macmillan, London, 1884, p. xxxiv. *R. C. van Caenegem*, The Birth of the English Common Law, p. 103–104, classifies the revenue dimension as insignificant in comparison to the royal household.

period – their jurisdiction extended far beyond matters we might be inclined to consider religious these days.[4] The church had been the first organisation to establish a court hierarchy in England. Judgments from the parish or diocesan level could be appealed in the archiepiscopal court or even in Rome. A prerequisite for any such structure is the existence of a written procedure. The ecclesiastical courts applied the procedure and substantive rules of the canon law as it had been collected and systematised in the European universities since the 12th century.[5] This systematic application of written law stood in marked contrast to the traditional domestic courts, which based their judgments on – mostly local – customs. The ecclesiastical courts were thus able to offer functioning and comprehensive institutions, procedures and substantive principles – a feat only much later achieved by English law.

1.3 Common law

The common law courts, on the other hand, had developed in Westminster from the 12th century onwards.[6] They represented the main institutional embodiment of growing royal control over conflict resolution. The two most important common law courts, the Court of Common Pleas and the King's Bench, originated in the *curia regis*, the king's council. Even in Anglo-Saxon times, the king had already provided residual justice in cases where local adjudication had failed or where royal interests were involved. This tradition lived on under Norman rule – the task of dispensing royal justice was then commonly fulfilled by the king and his chief advisors in the council. With the rising power of the central administration and its growing interference with local practices after the Conquest, recourse to the council became more and more common. The legalisation of originally administrative processes – like the enforcement of the king's peace and the settlement of land disputes – heavily contributed to this development. Adjudication by the council became impractical. The chief

4 *R. H. Helmholz,* The Oxford History of the Laws of England, Volume 1: The Canon Law and Ecclesiastical Jurisdiction from 597 to the 1640s, Oxford University Press, Oxford, 2004, offers a comprehensive portrayal of the application of Roman-canon law in the English church courts.

5 For a more detailed account of the universal foundations of the late medieval ecclesiastical jurisdiction, see *P. Prodi*, Eine Geschichte der Gerechtigkeit: Vom Recht Gottes zum modernen Rechtsstaat, C. H. Beck, Munich, 2003, transl. by A. Seemann, especially p. 48–81.

6 As in introduction into the formative period of the common law courts, *F. Pollock / F. W. Maitland,* The History of English Law before the Time of Edward I, Cambridge University Press, Cambridge, Volume 1 & 2, 2nd edition reissue, 1968, remains unrivalled.

advisors were powerful Norman feudal lords with an interest in politics rather than in administrative detail. The task of dispensing royal justice in most regular cases was thus – whether through explicit delegation or evolving custom – transferred to specialists of the administrative process: Clerks served as the new justices.

At the end of the 12th century, the Court of Common Pleas was the first common law court to grow out of the jurisdiction of the *curia regis*. It quickly became the preeminent medieval court as it monopolised the adjudication of land disputes – the very basis of feudal economy.[7] The Court of King's Bench retained – as its name would suggest – a closer proximity to the *curia regis* and commonly followed the royal household before its institution in Westminster in the 14th century. Even then, the king would eventually be involved in its high-profile decisions.[8] At the outset, King's Bench mostly adjudicated trespass cases before encroaching more and more strongly on the criminal jurisdiction of local courts.[9] The third major common law court, the Court of the Exchequer, grew out of the administrative department of the same name during the 12th century. As such, it was chiefly concerned with revenue issues.[10]

Just like the local jurisdictions, the common law courts adjudicated on the basis of unwritten customary rules. However, they offered manifest advantages to both the king and common litigants, which elevated them above local jurisdictions and guaranteed their expansion throughout the Middle Ages.

7 Chapter 17 of the Magna Carta of 1215 guaranteed a settled Court of Common Pleas for the adjudication of land disputes in Westminster – geographically and functionally removed from the *curia regis*. Since the aristocracy made King John (1199–1216) sign the Carta under duress, this can be seen as an early manifestation of (limited) judicial independence from the king, compare *J. H. Langbein / R. T. Lerner / B. P. Smith*, History of the Common Law – The Development of Anglo-American Legal Institutions, p. 123–124. The 800th anniversary of the signing of the Magna Carta has renewed popular interest in the classical document. For a comprehensive introduction, see *J. C. Holt*, Magna Charta, Cambridge University Press, Cambridge, 3rd edition, 2015 or R. Griffith-Hill / M. Jones (eds.), Magna Carta, Religion and the Rule of Law, Cambridge University Press, Cambridge, 2015.

8 *B. Wilkinson*, Constitutional History of Medieval England 1216–1399, Longmans, Green and Co., London, Volume 3, 1958, p. 153; *J. H. Langbein / R. T. Lerner / B. P. Smith*, History of the Common Law – The Development of Anglo-American Legal Institutions, p. 120.

9 *J. H. Langbein / R. T. Lerner / B. P. Smith*, History of the Common Law – The Development of Anglo-American Legal Institutions, p. 120.

10 Compare *P. Brand*, The Formation of the English Legal System, 1150–1400, in A. Padoa-Schioppa (ed.), Legislation and Justice, Clarendon Press, Oxford, 1997, p. 103–121, p. 112; *H. Langbein / R. T. Lerner / B. P. Smith*, History of the Common Law – The Development of Anglo-American Legal Institutions, p. 120–122.

While they provided royal oversight and influence over the resolution of substantial conflicts throughout the realm (for the king), they also offered greater predictability and superior enforceability mechanisms than local courts (for the litigants).

It would far exceed the scope of this work to provide a detailed picture of the common law at any stage during the late Middle Ages. I will therefore focus on the two most influential institutional developments in the medieval period – and also those most closely related to the rise of the Court of Chancery: the emergence of jury trial and the establishment of the writ system.

Both jury trial and writ system represent conscious efforts to bring conflict resolution in the periphery of the English countryside under greater central control. While both institutions have substantial earlier roots,[11] Henry II's (1154–1189) comprehensive judicial reforms initiated the decisive steps for their uniform countrywide recognition.

1.4 Jury trial

1.4.1 Assize of Clarendon

On behalf of "King Henry II with the assent of the archbishops, bishops, abbots, earls and barons of all England", the first article of the Assize of Clarendon from 1166 declares that "for the preservation of peace, and for the maintenance of justice, [...] inquiry shall be made throughout the several counties and throughout the several hundreds through twelve of the more lawful men of the hundred and through four of the more lawful men of each vill upon oath that they will speak the truth, whether there be in their hundred or vill any man accused or notoriously suspect of being a robber or murderer or thief, or any who is the receiver of robbers, murderers or thieves, since the lord king has been king".[12] The article clearly refers to what we would consider criminal proceedings. It furthermore describes a jury that decides – like the American Grand Jury these days – about the opening of a trial rather than about its outcome.[13] Nevertheless, the recognition of a criminal jury of accusation in the Assize of

11 See for a more detailed account *F. Pollock / F. W. Maitland,* The History of English Law before the Time of Edward I, Volume 1, p. 138–144 for the jury and p. 150–151 for writs.

12 Assize of Clarendon (1166), cited in D.C. Douglas / G.W. Greenaway (eds.), English Historical Documents, Volume 2: 1042–1189, Eyre & Spottiswoode, London, 1968, p. 408.

13 Compare *T. F. T. Plucknett,* A Concise History of the Common Law, Butterworth, London, 5th edition, 1956, p. 112.

Clarendon represents a crucial step on the way towards jury trial in all common law proceedings.[14]

1.4.2 Jury of Accusation

The jury of accusation was a reaction to the failings of the appeal of felony that had been the standard procedure for severe disruptions of the king's peace in the 12th century.[15] The appeal of felony was opened through the accusation of a victim or a close family member of the victim.[16] The mode of trial was commonly by battle.[17] Both these features naturally discouraged the effective sanctioning of crimes. The victim might not be able to accuse a powerful or violent perpetrator unharmed and might also fear the unpredictability of a battle.[18] By officialising the accusation procedure, the risks of prosecution were reduced.[19]

The jury of accusation was composed of twelve lawful men from the vicinity of the conflict. They assumed the role of witnesses rather than judges. The jury thus also introduced a fact-finding element into the criminal process that was suspiciously absent in the appeal of felony.[20] The inquiry under oath mentioned in the first article of the Assize took place before a royal justice, who would annually travel the different counties of the realm.[21] This process embodies two features that might be considered characteristic for English administration – the

14 Compare *J. H. Langbein / R. T. Lerner / B. P. Smith,* History of the Common Law – The Development of Anglo-American Legal Institutions, p. 41–42.

15 *T. F. T. Plucknett,* A Concise History of the Common Law, p. 117; *J. H. Langbein / R. T. Lerner / B. P. Smith,* History of the Common Law – The Development of Anglo-American Legal Institutions, p. 38.

16 *T. F. T. Plucknett,* A Concise History of the Common Law, p. 117; *J. H. Langbein / R. T. Lerner / B. P. Smith,* History of the Common Law – The Development of Anglo-American Legal Institutions, p. 32–33.

17 *F. Pollock / F. W. Maitland,* The History of English Law before the Time of Edward I, Volume 1, p. 466; *T. F. T. Plucknett,* A Concise History of the Common Law, p. 117.

18 The emergence of the inquisitorial procedure in Roman-canon law rested on a similar rationale. Compare *A. Krey,* Inquisitionsprozess, in: A. Cordes / H. Lück / D. Werkmüller (eds.), Handwörterbuch zur deutschen Rechtsgeschichte, Schmidt, Berlin, Volume 2, 2nd edition, 2012, col. 1243–1248.

19 However, they were not completely erased. Numerous Chancery petitions from the 14th and 15th century complain about the ineffectiveness and factual unavailability of common law remedies against a powerful or notorious defendant, see below chapter V, 2.5.1.

20 *J. H. Langbein / R. T. Lerner / B. P. Smith,* History of the Common Law – The Development of Anglo-American Legal Institutions, p. 33–34.

21 Assize of Clarendon (1166), article 5, cited in D. C. Douglas / G. W. Greenaway (eds.), English Historical Documents, Volume 2: 1042–1189, p. 408.

reliance on private cooperation for the fulfilment of public functions and their central control from Westminster. Once the accusation had been made and the justice had considered eventual points of law, the standard mode of proof was by ordeal.[22] The accused was put to tests of either water or fire. In medieval thinking, the final judgment over a person belonged to God. However, the articles of the Assize of Clarendon show certain safeguards against the unpredictability of the ordeals: they would not be invoked after a confession[23] and absolved suspects could be outlawed in the event of their notoriety within the community.[24] The jury of accusation already fulfilled an adjudicative role in so far as it would only present defendants who it deemed sufficiently suspicious or notorious.[25]

1.4.3 Abolition of ordeals

The adjudicative role of the jury became all the more important when clerical involvement in ordeals was sanctioned by the Fourth Lateran Council in 1215.[26] Without the proper invocation of a divine judgment, the ordeals lost their justification. They were now seen more and more for what they actually were: random inflictions of pain and suffering with no bearing on the question of guilt. The continued adjudication of criminal cases required the acknowledgement of a different mode of trial. The continental European answer to this dilemma was the strengthening of the role of the judge whose discretion was in turn restricted through strict evidentiary rules and appellate control.[27] The

22 The Assize of Clarendon, article 2, cited in D.C. Douglas / G.W. Greenaway (eds.), English Historical Documents, Volume 2: 1042–1189, p. 408, specifically ordered the ordeal of water. For an illustrative introduction into the different types of ordeals, see *T. F.T. Plucknett,* A Concise History of the Common Law, p. 113–115.

23 Assize of Clarendon, article 13, cited in D.C. Douglas / G.W. Greenaway (eds.), English Historical Documents, Volume 2: 1042–1189, p. 409.

24 Assize of Clarendon, article 14, cited in D.C. Douglas / G.W. Greenaway (eds.), English Historical Documents, Volume 2: 1042–1189, p. 409–410.

25 *R. D. Groot,* The Jury of Presentment before 1215, The American Journal of Legal History, Volume 26 (1982), p. 1–24, especially p. 10; *J. H. Langbein / R.T. Lerner / B. P. Smith,* History of the Common Law – The Development of Anglo-American Legal Institutions, p. 41–42.

26 Canon 18 of the decree reads: "No cleric may pronounce a sentence of death, or execute such a sentence, or be present at its execution. […] Neither shall anyone in judicial tests or ordeals by hot or cold water or hot iron bestow any blessing", cited in H. J. Schröder (ed.), Disciplinary Decrees of the General Councils – Text, Translation, and Commentary, Herder, St. Louis, Mo., 1937, p. 258.

27 *J. H. Langbein,* Torture and the Law of Proof – Europe and England in the Ancien Régime, The University of Chicago Press, Chicago, Il., 1977, p. 5–8.

English answer, however, was trial by jury. As an alternative to the ordeals, the introduction of jury trial can almost be characterised as natural. The group inquest had already been an established element of adjudication. More importantly, when compared with the ordeals, the jury was equally inscrutable and provided equally definite answers.[28] It could further be legitimised by its strong communitarian or representative element.[29] Nevertheless, putting the fate of a person into the hands of humans rather than in the hands of God marked a radical (theoretical) shift. This might explain why trial by jury originally arose as an option for the defendant.[30] The accused was asked whether he "put himself upon the country".[31] Soon enough,[32] however, the question represented nothing more than a fiction and the defendant was commonly "convinced" to accept trial by jury through a process that must be characterised as torturous.[33]

1.4.4 Rationale

As I have alluded to earlier, the idea of a group inquest in the form of a jury itself was not revolutionary. It was perfectly suited to the socio-economic conditions that were widely present in medieval England: A large part of the population formed small communities of several families, who lived and worked in closest vicinity.[34] Every member's actions would be widely known and every outsider would easily be recognised and met with suspicion. The royal administration exploited this knowledge from early on – be it for revenue or land demarcation purposes. Group inquests equally played a role in local courts. Property disputes were commonly settled on the basis of customary rights declared by the

28 Compare *T. F. T. Plucknett,* A Concise History of the Common Law, p. 125.

29 For a most insightful explanation for the introduction of jury trial, compare *F. Pollock / F. W. Maitland,* The History of English Law before the Time of Edward I, Volume 1, p. 622–625.

30 *J. H. Langbein,* Torture and the Law of Proof – Europe and England in the Ancien Régime, p. 75.

31 *T. F. T. Plucknett,* A Concise History of the Common Law, p. 125.

32 See the Statute of Westminster I 1275, c. 12, cited in *T. F. T. Plucknett,* A Concise History of the Common Law, p. 125: "notorious felons who are openly of evil fame and who refuse to put themselves upon inquests of felony at the suit of the King before his justices, shall be remanded to a hard and strong prison as befits those who refuse to abide by the common law of the land".

33 For a description of the practice that became known as "*peine forte et dure*" and the reasons for bearing them, see *J. H. Langbein,* Torture and the Law of Proof – Europe and England in the Ancien Régime, p. 74–77.

34 For the classical introduction to this topic, see *C. S. Orwin / C. S. Orwin,* The Open Fields, The Clarendon Press, Oxford, 3rd edition, 1967. Compare *J. H. Langbein / R. T. Lerner / B. P. Smith,* History of the Common Law – The Development of Anglo-American Legal Institutions, p. 13–17.

community. Compurgation, the oath on a party's testimony by twelve other men, was the standard mode of proof in what we would consider contractual disputes. Even before the Assize of Clarendon, the men of a community were held liable for crimes committed from within their group that were not presented to the local authorities.[35] Whereas all these group inquests clearly fulfilled witness rather than adjudicative functions, they had already been an essential part of the process of local conflict resolution before Henry II's judicial reforms.

In cases outside the criminal sphere, trial by jury developed similarly and concurrently. Contemporary justices and litigants did not distinguish between criminal trial on the one hand and civil trial on the other hand. They recognised a large number of different procedures with their respective remedies and rarely thought in more abstract categories. What we would classify as criminal and civil cases was usually adjudicated in the same local institutions. Differences in the procedures were the result of numerous practical decisions rather than of abstract classifications. The jury thus naturally assumed a large role in all proceedings under royal control.

The assize[36] of novel disseisin that laid down the procedure for possessory claims is most likely from the same year as the Assize of Clarendon. It stated that, in the case of proprietary disputes, a local jury would be summoned in order the answer the question of seisin and disseisin[37] before royal justices. The assize illustrates the role of the jury in the 12th century: It gave preliminary verdicts on specific factual issues rather than final judgments. The assize of novel disseisin also points to the further development of the trial. When a jury decides on the possession and dispossession in a purely possessory claim, it has effectively monopolised the decision about the facts of the case. Throughout the 13th century, the jury thus came to give final judgments in all common law matters.

35 This system of suretyship for the neighbours was called frankpledge. *F. Pollock / F. W. Maitland*, The History of English Law before the Time of Edward I, Volume 1, p. 140–144, provide a detailed account of its origins and emphasise its close relationship with the jury of accusation.

36 The word 'assize' probably derives from the French *s'assoir* (to sit down). In the context of medieval English law it acquired several important meanings. It first characterised meetings of councils or courts and then also enactments made at those meetings (compare Assize of Clarendon). When the group inquest of twelve men form the vicinity was regularised, it was again called an assize (compare assize of novel disseisin) and so were the courts held by travelling justices that oversaw these inquests (the so-called assize circuit). See *T. F. T. Plucknett*, A Concise History of the Common Law, p. 112.

37 This basically addressed the question whether someone was in possession or not at a certain time.

1.5 Writ system

The writ system represented an even more transparent centralisation effort. It played a central role in the absorption of jurisdiction over most important matters by the royal courts. I will briefly characterise how judicial writs developed and how they came to shape the common law jurisdiction.

1.5.1 Development

In its origin, the writ[38] was nothing more than a royal command – the standard means of the Norman kings for the administration of the periphery of the realm.[39]Although it might have been used for the resolution of conflicts through the personal intervention of the king, it had no distinctively judicial function.[40] A writ might have ordered a local sheriff to oversee the complete payment of taxes, the distribution of land or simply the termination of local conflicts. Regularly, the king issued a writ on the personal appeal of a (privileged) party to the *curia regis*.[41] The risks of such an approach are apparent. Parties could rush to the king and present matters purely from their own perspective. Other interested parties might only be informed when the writ was about to be enforced by royal officers. Naturally, these parties were encouraged to appeal newly to the king themselves. This was both time-consuming and costly and created confusion about the enforceability of contradictory writs.[42]

It would seem much more sensible to provide the parties with the opportunity of a hearing whenever they objected to the allegations causing the issuance of the writ. The writ *praecipe*, which can be found in the great medieval law book Glanvill[43] from the 1180s, indeed illustrates such a development.[44] It

38 'Writ' is simply a short form of 'writing'. In its original meaning, the term 'writ' could cover all kinds of documents.

39 *R. C. van Caenegem*, Royal Writs in England from the Conquest to Glanvill, Selden Society, London, 1959, p. 177–179.

40 *R. C. van Caenegem*, Royal Writs in England from the Conquest to Glanvill, p. 180–182.

41 *R. C. van Caenegem*, Royal Writs in England from the Conquest to Glanvill, p. 239.

42 *R. C. van Caenegem*, Royal Writs in England from the Conquest to Glanvill, p. 241–242.

43 For a comprehensive modern version, see G. D. G. Hall (ed.), The Treatise on the Laws and Customs of England Commonly Called Glanvill, Nelson, London, 1965.

44 The writ praecipe, however, must date back much further as exemplified by the (even more advanced) structure of writs newly introduced by Henry II. Compare *R. C. van Caenegem*, Royal Writs in England from the Conquest to Glanvill, p. 238.

did not yet shun the administrative character of the writ but rather added a simple safeguard. The recipient was still obliged to follow the orders set out in the writ. However, he received the additional option to be summoned and have an opportunity to answer to the allegations before enforcement. The originally purely administrative writ then included optional judicial summons.[45] This development was largely contemporaneous with and related to the establishment of the common law courts. Glanvill's writ *praecipe* could therefore still be answered either before the king himself or before his justices.[46]

When an answer to the royal justices turned out to be the habit rather than the exception, the royal scribes modulated the writ further.[47] Instead of first commanding execution, the writ immediately required the recipient to answer to the justices and show why (*ostensurus quare* – the term under which this form of writ is commonly addressed) he or she had acted as it was alleged in the complaint.[48] The originally administrative writ had become a purely judicial instrument of summons.[49] The writ also played a vital role in the expansion of royal conflict resolution. It became the standard means for the instigation of processes in the royal courts. Additionally, Henry II actively encouraged the procurement of writs by guaranteeing that no man needed to answer for his title to land without royal writ.[50] Since defendants could from then on object to local adjudication – or have local judgments overruled –, this guaranty effectively monopolised property litigation in the Court of Common Pleas. The writ of novel disseisin, which would start the assize proceedings,[51] proves the point: A jury could only be summoned once a royal writ had been obtained.[52] The writ

45 *R. C. van Caenegem*, Royal Writs in England from the Conquest to Glanvill, p. 243–247.

46 G. D. G. Hall (ed.), The Treatise on the Laws and Customs of England Commonly Called Glanvill, p. 5 (I, 6).

47 For the role of the royal scribes and their position in the royal administration, see *J. H. Langbein / R. T. Lerner / B. P. Smith*, History of the Common Law – The Development of Anglo-American Legal Institutions, p. 93–95.

48 *R. C. van Caenegem*, Royal Writs in England from the Conquest to Glanvill, p. 247–248.

49 *R. C. van Caenegem*, Royal Writs in England from the Conquest to Glanvill, p. 247.

50 *F. W. Maitland*, The Forms of Action at Common Law – A Course of Lectures, Cambridge University Press, Cambridge, 1909 (repr. 1968), p. 21, relying on Glanvill, reproduced in G. D. G. Hall (ed.), The Treatise on the Laws and Customs of England Commonly Called Glanvill, p. 148 (XII, 25). *R. C. van Caenegem*, Royal Writs in England from the Conquest to Glanvill, p. 224, rejects this thesis on the basis that evidence points to an earlier existence of that principle.

51 See above 1.4.4.

52 *F. Pollock / F. W. Maitland*, The History of English Law before the Time of Edward I, Volume 2, p. 48.

was an effective tool for – and thus a prime example of – the centralisation and judicialisation of conflict resolution.

1.5.2 Regularisation

Judicial summons are part of most legal systems. What made the writ system such a defining feature of the common law tradition was its function for the further proceedings. The earliest writs included individual commands. When, however, litigants appealed to the king and his justices more and more often, the content of the writs not only changed with regard to the summons.[53] The number of complaints required a professionalization of writ creation. The royal scribes in the administrative department of Chancery, who were responsible for the issuance of writs, thus began to regularise them. Common complaints – like trespass to property or dispossession – would initiate the issuance of a standard form writ. The sources suggest that writ creation in Chancery was, at the outset, a creative exercise. The scribes developed several dozens of different 'forms of action' and regularly adjusted the existing standard forms in order to broaden their scope.

The writs not only covered standard factual situations and their potential remedy but also the proceedings necessary to establish the claim. They thus differed in their summons procedures, their costs, their evidentiary rules, their modes of trial and their remedies. Once again, the writ of novel disseisin proves illustrative: In order to be restored to the possession of property, a claimant had to apply for the writ in Chancery. This set in motion the summoning of the aforementioned local assize of novel disseisin that would decide on the question of unlawful dispossession. The claimant did not have any alternative options for the establishment of the claim. These might only have been available under different forms of action. In contrast to novel disseisin – and as a further example –, the writ of debt long employed the arcade mode of compurgation as the single means for proof.

We naturally think of civil procedure as transsubstantive – as a single set of rules sufficiently flexible to provide adequate reactions to all contingent cases. The English development, however, was once again pragmatic and void of systematic aspirations. An assize of novel disseisin was an effective invocation of local knowledge and compurgation had been the standard mode of proof in cases of debt long before the introduction of standard form writs. The different writs developed individually depending on their history and the specific political, administrative and judicial context. Each writ effectively had its own

53 See above 1.5.1.

life[54] and while effective legal instruments like the jury were extended to other forms of actions, the actions nevertheless remained fundamentally distinct.

1.5.3 Stasis

The writ system might not have had such a distinct impact on the common law tradition if writ creation in (the administrative department of) Chancery had continued into the late Middle Ages. However, the creation of new writs in Chancery ceased and the *curia regis* became the responsible authority. It is not entirely clear why this happened but, given that the writs had proven such effective means of judicial centralisation, the potential of this tool might have become apparent. By reserving their judgment on the creation of new writs, the noblemen represented in the *curia* might have intended to limit the power of central administration and secure their own. Either way, the inherent innovative force of the continuous exchange between litigants and the writ-creating clerks in Chancery was gone. Towards the end of the 13th century, the creation of new writs vanished altogether and the further development was limited to the modification of existing forms of action. The question why exactly this happened has caused some controversy and it would exceed the scope of this short history on the medieval common law developments to discuss it in any more detail.[55] The juxtaposition of common law and Chancery procedure in chapter V, however, should shed some light on the question.

Despite the central role of the writ system in the common law and the usefulness of its narrative for the explanation of the further development of English legal history – most importantly with regard to the Court of Chancery –, we should not make the mistake to regard the writ as the only means to royal

54 The life metaphor is borrowed from Maitland whose vivid depiction merits a quote: "Our forms of action are not mere rubrics nor dead categories; they are not the outcome of a classificatory process that has been applied to pre-existing materials [note by the author: in contrast to the Roman-canon civil procedure]. They are institutes of the law; they are – we say it without scruple – living things. Each of them lives its own life, has its own adventures, enjoys a longer or shorter day of vigour, usefulness, popularity, and then sinks perhaps into a decrepit and friendless old age. A few are still-born, some are sterile, others live to see their children and children's children in high places. The struggle for life is keen among them and only the fittest survive", *F. Pollock / F. W. Maitland*, The History of English Law before the Time of Edward I, Volume 2, p. 561.

55 For suggestions, see *F. Pollock / F. W. Maitland*, The History of English Law before the Time of Edward I, Volume 1, p. 196; *G. O. Sayles*, Introduction, in: G. O. Sayles (ed.), Select Cases in the Court of King's Bench under Edward III, Selden Society, London, Volume 5, 1958, p. lxvii–lxx. For a short introduction, see *J. H. Langbein / R. T. Lerner / B. P. Smith*, History of the Common Law – The Development of Anglo-American Legal Institutions, p. 271–274.

judicial redress at any stage.[56] When the functions of the royal institutions were still largely undifferentiated, individual complaints could continuously be addressed first to the *curia regis* and then to parliament. Later, the King's Bench allowed the opening of procedures by individual bills under certain conditions and through the use of judicial fictions.[57]

Nevertheless, and despite the continuing presence of local and ecclesiastical jurisdictions, the common law – with its chief characteristics jury trial and writ system – had gained a dominant position in judicial conflict resolution by the end of the 13th century. It was against this background that the Court of Chancery developed in the 14th century.

2. Formation

2.1 Administration in Chancery

As mentioned earlier, Chancery was first and foremost an administrative department at that time. Central royal administration was only in its infancy. The feudal system of landholding and military service was still the basis for control over the English countryside. However, the king had already successfully established the Exchequer – chiefly concerned with revenue collection – and the Chancery as instruments of central government. As exemplified by the executive writs, Chancery's main task was the preparation of (royal) documents. For this purpose, it employed a growing body of professional scribes.[58] Considering the state of literacy in medieval England, these were typically recruited from a clerical background.[59] It should be noted that Chancery was not only concerned with direct royal orders but also with foreign relations and the documentation of important private agreements.[60] Although of less relevance for the further judicial development, these diplomatic and notarial functions constituted a large part of the workload and contributed to the expansion of Chancery staff.

56 This criticism has – correctly – been advanced against *F. W. Maitland*'s history of the common law, see *G. R. Elton*, F. W. Maitland, Weidenfeld and Nicolson, London, 1985, p. 40–41.

57 The 'Bill of Middlesex', which appealed to the territorial jurisdiction of the King's Bench, played a decisive role. For more, see *M. Blatcher*, The Court of King's Bench 1450–1550 – A Study in Self Help, Athlone Press, London, 1978, p. 111–124; *J. H. Langbein / R. T. Lerner / B. P. Smith*, History of the Common Law – The Development of Anglo-American Legal Institutions, p. 250–253.

58 Compare above 1.5.2.

59 *T. S. Haskett*, The Late Medieval Court of Chancery, Law and History Review, Volume 14 (1996), p. 245–313, p. 247–248.

60 On the latter, see *T. Haskett*, The Late Medieval Court of Chancery, Law and History Review, Volume 14 (1996), p. 245–313, p. 248.

Since Chancery originally documented royal orders, it naturally followed the king's household in its early stages. This rendered access to its resources, most notably for the issuance of writs, highly problematic. When the common law courts settled in Westminster, it was thus a practical necessity for Chancery to follow suit, even though many of its officials continued to travel with the royal household.

2.2 Office of the Lord Chancellor

The office of the Lord Chancellor predates the Chancery as an administrative institution. The Lord Chancellor was the original keeper of the king's seal from at least as early as the Norman Conquest. It was only when the need for documentation increased during centralisation efforts after the Conquest that he was equipped with a wider staff. In addition to his function as the head of Chancery, the Lord Chancellor was the king's chief advisor for non-military purposes. His role might be likened to that of a modern Prime Minister or a Secretary of State but in order to avoid the confusion of transferring modern concepts, we might simply classify him as the chief civil government official.

The post was originally held by influential notables of the realm. From the middle of the 13th century, however, the king habitually appointed either bishops or archbishops from the English dioceses. Thus, Chancery had been in the hand of distinguished clerics, long before we can identify the first evidence of a distinctive Court of Chancery in the 14th century.[61] The continuous appointment of (arch-) bishops as Lord Chancellors[62] until the chancellorship of Thomas More in 1529 was not the result of an official agreement between church and state. It was rather again a pragmatic understanding. It has been claimed that the medieval church bore the origins of what could be classified as a state[63] and it is indeed true that the administrative experience of the church and its personnel could be brought to fruitful use at a time when the English king

61 *T. S. Haskett* has compiled a list of Lord Chancellors from 1396 to 1532 that includes not only their occupation but also their education and thus will serve as an important reference point for discussions of their legal knowledge. See *T. S. Haskett*, The Late Medieval Court of Chancery, Law and History Review, Volume 14 (1996), p. 245–313, p. 311–313.

62 Given the medieval entanglement of secular and spiritual power, there are numerous earlier examples of bishops holding the office of Lord Chancellor. However, a continuous tradition was only established by the middle of the 13th century. Even then, secular notables became Lord Chancellor on rare occasions. For a complete list of Lord Chancellor since the Norman Conquest including the other offices held at the same time, see <www.dca.gov.uk/lcfr.htm>.

63 Compare *B. Tierney*, Religion, Law, and the Growth of Constitutional Thought, Cambridge University Press, Cambridge, 1982.

sought to establish a more effective central administration. The church itself, on the other hand, could not match its administrative structures and its moral authority with military power. It was thus constantly in danger to be overwhelmed by sheer secular force. The institutional arrangement in Chancery was mutually beneficial. It also provided the king with easier access to Rome and the church with easier access to the English king.

2.3 Common law jurisdiction

The first judicial business of Chancery was – as far as the limited research suggests[64] – unrelated to what has become known as its equitable jurisdiction. Just like the Exchequer, which developed a common law court of far greater significance and longevity,[65] Chancery came to decide conflicts directly related to its administrative function.[66] As such, it oversaw the execution of royal grants or of royally certified deeds. Perhaps even more significantly – and like many other medieval institutions, be it the church, the universities or other administrative departments – , it adjudicated conflicts involving its own personnel.[67] The corresponding proceedings employed the contemporary common law forms, language and procedures and thus lacked the distinctive features of the later Court of Chancery.[68] The related documents were furthermore kept entirely in Latin,[69] which has lead to the classification of this common law jurisdiction as the 'Latin side' of Chancery.[70]

64 *F. Metzger*, Das englische Kanzleigericht unter Kardinal Wolsey, Promotion an der Friedrich-Alexander-Universität Erlangen-Nürnberg, 1977, p. 52, claimed that no comprehensive study has been made on the medieval common law jurisdiction of Chancery. One of the more detailed accounts was provided by *A. D. Hargreaves*, Equity and the Latin Side of Chancery, Law Quarterly Review, Volume 68 (1952), p. 481–499.

65 See above 1.3.

66 *T. S. Haskett*, The Medieval English Court of Chancery, Law and History Review, Volume 14 (1996), p. 245–313, p. 248.

67 *T. S. Haskett*, The Medieval English Court of Chancery, Law and History Review, Volume 14 (1996), p. 245–313, p. 248.

68 For a more detailed account, see *G. Spence*, The Equitable Jurisdiction of the Court of Chancery, Lee and Blanchard, Philadelphia, Pa., Volume 1, 1846 (repr. 1981), p. 335–336.

69 In contrast to proceedings in Law French or English in what became known as the equitable jurisdiction or the 'English side', see below chapter IV.

70 *T. S. Haskett*, The Medieval English Court of Chancery, Law and History Review, Volume 14 (1996), p. 245–313, p. 248. *M. R. T. Macnair*, Equity and Conscience, Oxford Journal of Legal Studies, Volume 27 (2007), p. 659–681, p. 665–666, claimed that the Latin side should be further subdivided into three parts: "(a) the *officia brevium*, which issued common law writs, (b) the 'control of the Exchequer', which dealt with patents and inquisitions *post mortem* in relation to the

It has been suggested that the Court of Chancery grew organically out of this early common law jurisdiction.[71] Indeed, sessions of the 'Latin' side and the 'English' side seem to have taken place under essentially the same conditions and on the same days in the 14th and up to the 15th century.[72] Furthermore, experience in common law adjudication in Chancery – added to the Lord Chancellors' experience in ecclesiastical adjudication – might have contributed to their willingness to assume a greater role in royal conflict resolution. However, an over-emphasis of these early parallels is still at best misleading as it clouds the peculiarities of the 'English', later to be called equitable, jurisdiction of Chancery that dominated the further development of the common law tradition.

2.4 Extraordinary royal jurisdiction

As I have mentioned earlier, the practice of petitioning royal authority for justice in individual cases continued despite the establishment of the central common law courts.[73] The scope of the writs was limited and the machinery of common law justice remained generally erroneous. During the 14th century, petitions often seem to have been addressed to parliament but when it assumed a distinctly legislative function, they generally reverted back to the *curia regis*.[74] At the same time, the number of petitions increased again, possibly as a result of the fixation of the writ system. Although the contemporary advisers of the king would not have thought in these categories, we might characterise this development as a failed attempt to regularise and institutionalise royal justice. The reaction of the *curia regis*, however, was the same as it was two centuries earlier: a regularisation of the adjudication of the underlying conflicts in a specialised court – this time in Chancery. Petitions from the late 14th and the early 15th century were commonly addressed, apparently indifferently, to either the Lord Chancellor, the *curia regis*, or both.[75] At that time, the Court of

Crown's feudal tenants in chief and (c) the Latin side proper, which dealt with common law pleas". For the purposes of my further argumentation, it is only the purely adjudicative branch, the "Latin side proper" which is of further interest.

71 *A. D. Hargreaves*, Equity and the Latin Side of Chancery, Law Quarterly Review, Volume 68 (1952), p. 481–499, p. 499.

72 *P. Tucker*, The Early History of the Court of Chancery: A Comparative Study, The English Historical Review, Volume 115 (2000), p. 791–811, p. 808–809.

73 *F. Pollock*, The Transformation of Equity, in: P. Vinogradoff (ed.), Essays in Legal History, Oxford University Press, Oxford, 1913, p. 286–296, p. 291.

74 *T. F. T. Plucknett*, A Concise History of the Common Law, p. 179.

75 See also *W. P. Baildon*, Introduction, in: W. P. Baildon (ed.), Select Cases in Chancery A. D. 1364 to 1471, Selden Society, London, 1896, p. xvii; *S. F. C. Milsom*, Historical Foundations of the Common Law, Butterworths, London, 2nd

Chancery under the supervision of the Lord Chancellor must thus have already been recognisable as an institution distinct from the council, yet without exclusive jurisdiction. The fact that what became known as the equitable jurisdiction of the Court of Chancery was based on the extraordinary jurisdiction of first the king and then the *curia regis* also explains why a differentiation from the Latin side is fundamental, irrespective of exact contemporary practice or recognition.

2.5 Delegation

Why Chancery came to adjudicate these petitions can be explained rather easily: The Lord Chancellor was one of the most, if not the most influential member of the *curia regis* and had therefore already played an important role in its (semi-)judicial practice. The professional staff of Chancery was furthermore experienced with judicial tasks through the issuance of writs as well as common law adjudication and could thus prepare cases for decision in a comparatively efficient manner. Lastly, Chancery was situated in Westminster and could be accessed more easily than the council.

How exactly Chancery came to adjudicate the individual petitions is, on the other hand, not entirely clear. We have no evidence of an express delegation by either the council or the king. When parliament expressly endorsed Chancery jurisdiction in the late 14th century, it was for limited subject areas and apparently declaratory.[76] We can thus assume that the creation of a new institution was again the result of pragmatic reactions. Adjudication by Chancery might have originally been introduced as a practical fall back solution when the *curia regis* was abroad[77] but it must soon have turned out genuinely beneficial – for petitioners, who could expect accelerated and specialised conflict resolution, and for the council, which could focus its attention on political matters.[78] By the

edition, 1981, p. 82; *J. B. Post*, Equitable Resorts before 1450, in: E. W. Ives / A. H. Manchester (eds.), Law, Litigants, and the Legal Profession, Royal Historical Society, London, 1983, p. 68–79, p. 69.

76 See *G. Spence*, The Equitable Jurisdiction of the Court of Chancery, Volume 1, p. 344 with reference to specific legislation.

77 As suggested by *N. Pronay*, The Chancellor, the Chancery, and the Council at the End of the Fifteenth Century, in: H. Hearder / H. R. Loyn (eds.), British Government and Administration – Studies Presented to S. B. Chrimes, University of Wales Press, Cardiff, 1974, p. 87–103, p. 97.

78 *W. P. Baildon*, Introduction, in: W. P. Baildon (ed.), Select Cases in Chancery A. D. 1364 to 1471, p. xviii; *T. F. T. Plucknett*, A Concise History of the Common Law, p. 180.

second half of the 14th century, a routine to delegate standard petitions to Chancery was established.[79]

3. Expansion

The court only started to keep continuous records of its proceedings from the middle of the 16th century onwards. By that time, however, the Court of Chancery had long been established as one of the most important royal courts and the operation of royal adjudication would have been hardly imaginable without its contribution. My research aims to identify the role of the Court of Chancery in the emerging English legal system and the reasons for its rapid expansion. It must therefore address the time between the formation in the 14th century and the beginning of record-keeping in the 16th century.

3.1 Workload

The expansion of the Court of Chancery and its establishment as one of the most important royal courts must have taken place during this period. Given the limited availability of primary sources,[80] supporting this claim with concrete numbers has proven a difficult task. A study of the surviving petitions from this early phase has identified a yearly average of no more than 20 cases from 1387–1426, 136 cases from 1432–1443, 126 cases from 1456–1460, 243 cases from 1461–1466, 553 cases from 1475–1485, 571 cases from 1485–1500 and 605 cases from 1500–1515.[81] While these numbers speak of a considerable expansion throughout the 15th century – with a minor stabilisation in the middle of the century –, they must be treated carefully. Many surviving petitions are undated

79 The jurisdictions of Chancery and council, however, were not strictly delineated until much later in the 15th century, compare *N. Pronay*, The Chancellor, the Chancery, and the Council at the End of the Fifteenth Century, in: H. Hearder/ H. R. Loyn (eds.), British Government and Administration – Studies Presented to S. B. Chrimes, p. 87–103, 100.

80 For a complete discussion of the 15th century sources, see chapter V.

81 *N. Pronay*, The Chancellor, the Chancery, and the Council at the End of the Fifteenth Century, in: H. Hearder/H. R. Loyn (eds.), British Government and Administration – Studies Presented to S. B. Chrimes, p. 87–103, p. 88–89, challenging earlier assumptions by *M. E. Avery*, The History of the Equitable Jurisdiction of Chancery before 1460, Bulletin of the Institute of Historical Research, Volume 42 (1969), p. 129–144; *M. Beilby*, The Profits of Expertise: The Rise of the Civil Lawyers and Chancery Equity, in: M. Hicks (ed.), Profit, Piety and the Professions in Later Medieval England, Sutton, Gloucester, 1990, p. 72–90, revisited both studies critically. For the problems associated with all the samples employed in these studies, see below chapter IV.

and directed indistinctively to 'the Lord Chancellor' (without mentioning his name); they thus cannot be dated.[82] More importantly, significant evidence suggests that petitions could be addressed to the Lord Chancellor not only in writing but also orally at this early stage: The number of surviving documents related directly to proceedings in the Court of Chancery[83] far exceeds the number of petitions.[84] Generally, there is no sign of a systematic collection or documentation of petitions – substantive parts might simply be lost.

It might therefore be a hopeless endeavour to try to establish the exact number of cases or the specific chancellorships with the highest growth rates.[85] Nevertheless, the numbers support the general diagnosis of expansion that is further evidenced by legislative sources:

From as early as 1377, we can identify repeated attacks from the commons in parliament against the accumulation of judicial business first in both council and Chancery and then specifically in the Court of Chancery. They complain about a subversion of the ordinary courts of common law.[86] Given the personal overlap between parliamentarians and common lawyers and the urgency of the complaints, we might infer that genuine financial interests were at stake. The influence of the court on royal adjudication must have been – at least potentially – substantial.

3.2 Involvement of civil lawyers

As part of the professionalization process, the staff of Chancery was complemented with academically trained civil and canon lawyers from the second half of the 15th century onwards. These lawyers became known as the 'masters' in Chancery. In the judicial functions directly related to the work of the court, they replaced the clerks, whose main expertise had lain in administrative business.

82 *N. Pronay*, The Chancellor, the Chancery, and the Council at the End of the Fifteenth Century, in: H. Hearder/H. R. Loyn (eds.), British Government and Administration – Studies Presented to S. B. Chrimes, p. 87–103, p. 88, fn. 1.

83 For the specific form and function of writs in the process of the Court of Chancery as opposed to the common law process, see below chapter V, especially 2.4.4.

84 *P. Tucker*, The Early History of the Court of Chancery: A Comparative Study, The English Historical review, Volume 115 (2000), p. 791–811, p. 794.

85 Similarly *J. A. Guy*, The Development of Equitable Jurisdictions, 1450–1550, in: E. W. Ives/A. H. Manchester (eds.), Law, Litigants, and the Legal Profession, Royal Historical Society, London, 1983, p. 80–86, p. 83, n.6.

86 *D. M. Kerly*, An Historical Sketch of the Equitable Jurisdiction of the Court of Chancery, Cambridge University Press, Cambridge, 1890 (repr. 2011), p. 37–46, provided a complete account of the parliamentary complaints and their respective contents.

While the actual decision of cases remained exclusively with the Lord Chancellor, these civilians assumed a powerful role in the pre-trial process that has contributed strongly to speculation about the influence of civilian learning on the Court of Chancery.[87] This change in personnel further underlines two important developments: the recognition of a distinctively legal character of the Court of Chancery despite its existence outside of the ordinary course of the law and the need for institutional regularisation.

3.3 The Wolsey court

Both these developments have been called into question with regard to the chancellorship of Cardinal Wolsey (ca. 1475–1530; Lord Chancellor 1515–1529).[88] Wolsey had no legal university education.[89] In the bill of indictment that led to his execution after his fall from the King's grace in 1530, he was accused of subverting the relations between the common law and the prerogative courts (including the Court of Chancery) by extending the jurisdiction of the latter.[90] The Court of Chancery during his tenure has been described as a supervisory department for alternative dispute resolution rather than a court.[91] Indeed, Wolsey accepted a great number of bills into the Court of Chancery – with no apparent regard for eventual jurisdictional limits.[92] Despite this, he showed no distinctive interests in adjudicating matters of law. After the hearing or the exchange of documents, cases before the court were either decided

87 See below chapter VI.

88 *M. R. T. Macnair*, Equity and Conscience, Oxford Journal of Legal Studies, Volume 27 (2007), p. 659–681, p. 671, diagnosed that "the Chancery [...] lapsed into a sort of anti-law" and "that this continued after Wolsey" until "Egerton in the 1590s".

89 *F. Metzger*, Das englische Kanzleigericht unter Kardinal Wolsey, p. 7.

90 *J. H. Baker*, Introduction, in: J. H. Baker (ed.), The Reports of John Spelman, Selden Society, London, Volume 2, 1978, p. 79, cited from the bill: "Also, the said lord cardinal hath examined divers and many matters in the Chancery, after Judgment thereof given at the common law, in subversion of your [note by the author: the King's] laws; and made some persons restore again to the other party condemned, that they had in execution by virtue of the Judgment in the common law. Also, when matters have been near at judgment by process at your common law, the same lord cardinal hath not only given and sent injunctions to the parties, but also sent for your judges, and expressly by threats commanding them to defer judgment, to the evident subversion of your laws, if the judges would have so ceased".

91 Compare *M. R. T. Macnair*, Equity and Conscience, Oxford Journal of Legal Studies, Volume 27 (2007), p. 659–681, p. 670.

92 Compare *J. H. Baker*, Introduction, in: J. H. Baker (ed.), The Reports of John Spelman, Volume 2, p. 77.

without resort to legal argumentation or instead delegated to local nobleman for further negotiation.[93] The historical judgment on Wolsey is undoubtedly clouded by his eminent role in the political struggles between Henry VIII (1491–1547, reigning 1509–1547) and Rome. His fall from grace must be attributed to his failure to procure a settlement for Henry's marriage conflict rather than to his judicial work. At the same time, there is ample evidence to suggest that the allegations brought against him were not unfounded.[94] The appointment of Thomas More – the first in a long tradition of common lawyers – as his successor is furthermore illustrative for the wish to better the relations between the common law and the Court of Chancery.

4. Systematisation

"Equity is a roguish thing: for law we have a measure, know what to trust to; equity is according to the conscience of him that is Chancellor, and as that is larger or narrower, so is equity. 'Tis all one as if they should make the standard for the measure we call a foot, a Chancellor's foot; what an uncertain measure would this be? One Chancellor has a long foot, another a short foot, a third an indifferent foot: 'tis the same thing in a Chancellor's conscience."[95]

4.1 Discretion

Nothing has influenced the further development of the Court of Chancery more strongly than reaction to the allegation of uncertainty. With this famous quote, the common lawyer John Selden (1584–1654) summarized a common perception of the court at the beginning of the 17th century. The discharge of the Lord Chancellor's office by Wolsey left a lasting impression of unfettered discretion. Apart from restoring a collegial atmosphere, the installation of common lawyers as Lord Chancellors seems to have done little to change the perception of the

93 *M. R. T. Macnair*, Equity and Conscience, Oxford Journal of Legal Studies, Volume 27 (2007), p. 659–681, p. 670.

94 *J. H. Baker*, in: J. H. Baker (ed.), The Reports of John Spelman, Volume 2, p. 77, concluded that Wolsey "delighted in irritating lawyers" and "[l]ike most laymen, […] had supreme confidence in his own common sense". For a comprehensive and thus more nuanced account of Wolsey's judicial activities, see *F. Metzger*, Das englische Kanzleigericht unter Kardinal Wolsey, summarised in *F. Metzger*, The Last Phase of the Medieval Chancery, in: A. Harding (ed.), Law-Making and Law-Makers in British History – Papers Presented to the Edinburgh Legal History Conference 1977, Royal Historical Society, London, 1980, p. 79–89.

95 *J. Selden*, in: F. Pollock (ed.), Table Talk of John Selden, Quaritch, London, 1927, p. 43.

court by common lawyers throughout the 16th century. Concerns about the extent of the jurisdiction of the Court of Chancery and the certainty of its judgments became all the more pressing when it gained effective supremacy over the common law during the jurisdictional struggles at the beginning of the 17th century:

4.2 The Ellesmere / Coke debate

These disputes have been personified by the antagonistic figures of Lord Ellesmere (1540–1617), Lord Chancellor 1596–1617, and Edward Coke (1552–1634), Chief Justice of the Common Pleas 1606–1613 and of the King's Bench 1613–1616.[96] Due to jurisdictional uncertainties, parties to a conflict would often sue at both common law and the Court of Chancery. The outcome could eventually differ. The confrontation between Ellesmere and Coke then evolved around the practical question of imprisonment upon a decree from the Court of Chancery.[97] Judgments from Chancery typically imposed personal duties upon the parties.[98] Noncompliance was sanctioned with imprisonment. When litigants were imprisoned by Chancery despite having established their claim at common law, Coke ordered their release upon a writ of *habeas corpus*.[99] This undermined the effectiveness of Chancery adjudication. King James I (1566–1625, reigning 1603–1625) intervened and decreed that the Lord Chancellors "shall not hereafter desist to give [...] relief in equity (notwithstanding any proceedings at the common law [...])".[100] This clarification did not formally establish a specific court hierarchy but it assured that the Lord Chancellor would effectively have the last word. Soon after, the council relieved Coke of his

96 For example in *J. P. Dawson*, Coke and Ellesmere Disinterred: The Attack on the Chancery in 1616, Illinois Law Review, Volume 36 (1941/42), p. 127–152; *M. Fortier*, Equity and Ideas: Coke, Ellesmere, and James I, Renaissance Quarterly, Volume 51 (1998), p. 1255–1281.

97 The background to the dispute is explained by *J. H. Baker*, The Common Lawyers and the Chancery: 1616, The Irish Jurist, Volume 4 (1969), p. 368–392. A concise summary of the arguments is presented by *J. H. Langbein / R. T. Lerner / B. P. Smith*, History of the Common Law – The Development of Anglo-American Legal Institutions, p. 329–335.

98 For a detailed account of remedies in the Court of Chancery and their relationship with common law remedies, see below chapter V, 5.2.3.

99 The most famous example of this method is *Glanvile's Case* (1615) 72 Eng. Rep. 939. For a complete account (with commentary) of a series of trials at King's Bench and in the Court of Chancery culminating with the royal decree of 1616, see *D. Ibbetson*, The Earl of Oxford's Case (1615), in: C. Mitchell / P. Mitchell (eds.), Landmark Cases in Equity, Hart, Oxford, 2012, p. 1–32.

100 Decree of 18 July 1616, 21 Eng. Rep. 65.

duties.[101] In formulating the decree, King James relied on his monarchical right and duty to provide justice in the royal courts.[102] The royal right to organize the court system as well as to appoint and dismiss judges had indeed never been questioned. The common lawyers, however, were already emancipating themselves from direct royal interference. Coke himself had ruled that the common law was subject only to parliamentary modification but not to royal proclamations.[103] In this situation, James's decision in favour of the Court of Chancery was plausible. At the same time, it further entrenched the frontiers that would define the constitutional struggles in the course of the 17th century.

4.3 The English Revolution

The great history of revolution and restoration in the 17th century far exceeds the scope of this short introduction to the Court of Chancery. However, as the conflicts evolved around the limits of royal authority, the court system underwent significant reforms. Since it formalised extraordinary royal conflict resolution, the Court of Chancery had always been associated with royal prerogative powers.[104] The Long Parliament (1640–1648) swiftly abolished the other prerogative courts, most notably the Star Chamber, in an attempt to strengthen the common law and to limit royal influence on adjudication. Why the Court of Chancery avoided this destiny is not entirely clear. As shown by Selden's quote, the arguments for its abolition – subversion of the ordinary course of the law and arbitrariness – were ready at hand. Considering the central position of the court in the English legal system, it seems most likely that parliament wanted to avoid the difficult question of comprehensive reform and integration into the common law.[105] When parliament finally came around to suggest the abolition of the Court of Chancery during the Interregnum in 1653, it had lost the power to effectively enforce its resolution.[106]

101 See for an overview *T. P. Taswell-Langmead*, in: T. F.T. Plucknett (ed.), English Constitutional History – From the Teutonic Conquest to the Present Time, Sweet & Maxwell, London, 10th edition, 1946, p. 392–395; *J. H. Langbein / R. T. Lerner / B. P. Smith*, History of the Common Law – The Development of Anglo-American Legal Institutions, p. 335.

102 Compare Decree of 18 July 1616, 21 Eng. Rep. 65.

103 *Case of Proclamations* [1610] EWHC KB J22. Judgments such as this one have established the image of Coke as the founder of common law constitutionalism. It is hardly surprising that the equity jurisdiction of the Court of Chancery that he fought so vigorously was relegated to a defensive position as a result.

104 See chapter VIII below for a comparison with other emerging European prerogative courts.

105 The fusion experience confirms this scepticism, see below 6.

106 For a complete account, see *S. E. Prall*, Chancery Reform and the Puritan Revolution, American Journal of Legal History, Volume 6 (1962), p. 28–44.

4.4 Regularisation

The Court of Chancery thus survived both revolution and restoration. However, the constitutional monarchy was firmly established and the common lawyers were its profiteers and its safeguards.[107] Law reform, be it substantive or institutional, became the exclusive responsibility of parliament. The self-conception of the Lord Chancellors was forever altered.[108] Instead of actively curing the defects of the common law, they now sought to emulate it.[109] The Court of Chancery still adjudicated the same subject areas and employed the same procedures but it shed its comprehensive aspirations. Lord Nottingham (1621–1682, Lord Chancellor 1675–1682) is considered the father of modern equity law. By relying on earlier decisions and filling gaps between them, he devised a comprehensive system of substantive rules on trusts.[110] The shift from largely discretionary judging to the recognition of precedents was emphasised even more clearly by Lord Hardwicke (1690–1764, Lord Chancellor 1737–1756). In contrast to earlier Lord Chancellors, he explicitly saw himself bound by precedent.[111] Equally, the Lord Chancellors only accepted bills, which addressed matters that the court had dealt with before. The jurisdiction of the Court of Chancery thus acquired a settled character. It became possible to predict the judgments of the court with reasonable certainty. The comprehensive collection and availability of judgments in law reports from the beginning of the 18th century was another catalyst for systematisation.[112] In 1768, Blackstone, the great chronicler of English law, held that Selden's critique had been overcome.[113]

107 The opposition to unrestrained royal authority had encouraged cooperation between common lawyers and parliamentarians since the Middle Ages. The two groups were furthermore aligned through business interests and personal overlap. The role of Chief Justice Coke, who first sought to restrain royal authority as a judge and then advanced the same purpose as a Member of Parliament is illustrative. For more, see below chapter VII, 1.2.3.

108 *S. F. C. Milsom*, Historical Foundations of the Common Law, p. 95, found that "the development of equity, more than of any other body of doctrine, was the work of identifiable persons".

109 For this adaption, see *M. R. T. Macnair*, Arbitrary Chancellors and the Problem of Predictability, in: E. Koops/W. J. Zwalve (eds.), Law & Equity – Approaches in Roman Law and Common Law, p. 79–104.

110 See *D. E. C. Yale*'s comprehensive introduction on mortgages and trusts in equity in: D. E. C. Yale (ed.), Lord Nottingham's Chancery Cases, Selden Society, London, Volume 2, 1961, p. 7–207.

111 *Prowse v Abingdon* (1738), 25 Eng. Rep. 955, 957.

112 See also *J. H. Langbein/R. T. Lerner/B. P. Smith*, History of the Common Law – The Development of Anglo-American Legal Institutions, p. 353–354.

113 Referencing Selden's criticism *W. Blackstone*, Commentaries on the Laws of England, Clarendon Press, Oxford, Volume 3, 1768 (repr. 1966), p. 432, stated:

5. Deterioration

At the same time, greater systematisation came at a cost. Parliament had already identified long delays, excessive costs and corruption as key weaknesses when it moved to abolish the Court of Chancery in 1653.[114] The application of a highly-formalised and precedent-based mode of adjudication intensified these problems. The exchange of legal arguments and the writing of judgments based on precedent require more time than discretionary judging. The institutional design of the court further contributed to the deterioration of its image.

5.1 Personnel

Until the beginning of the 19th century, the Court of Chancery continuously relied on a single judge to adjudicate its complete caseload.[115] It was only when the Lord Chancellor was unavailable that the Master of the Rolls would judge in his stead.[116] Even for the characteristically short-staffed English legal system, the Chancellor's workload was immense. The functioning of the court therefore relied heavily on the preparatory work of the masters. They collected and compiled documents, prepared testimony and sighted precedents. In most cases, they also drafted the judgments that would be handed out by the Lord Chancellor.[117] As civilians, the masters were generally qualified for all of these tasks. However, the office of master quickly came to exhibit some characteristics that often coincide with the accumulation of power. Its corruption was

"Once more; it has been said that a court of equity is not bound by rules or precedent, but acts from the opinion of the judge, founded on the circumstance of every particular case. Whereas the system of our courts of equity is a laboured connected system, governed by established rules, and bound down by precedents, from which they do not depart, although the reason to some of them may perhaps be liable to objection".

114 *S. E. Prall*, Chancery Reform and the Puritan Revolution, American Journal of Legal History, Volume 6 (1962), p. 28–44, p. 28.

115 *S. F. C. Milsom*, Historical Foundations of the Common Law, p. 95.

116 Also for an introduction to the role of the Master of the Rolls, see *G. Spence*, The Equitable Jurisdiction of the Court of Chancery, Volume 1, p. 357–359.

117 In fact, a greater judicial interest from the Lord Chancellor was a cause of concern rather than a virtue. Lord Eldon (1751–1838; Lord Chancellor 1801–1806 and 1807–1827) was renowned for both his thoroughness and his slow pace. *J. Bentham* wrote a scathing attack on the jurisdiction of the Court of Chancery as well as on the Lord Chancellor personally, dubbing him "Lord Endless". See *J. Bentham*, Indications Respecting Lord Eldon, Including History of the Pending Judges'-Salary-Raising Matter, in: P. Schofield (ed.), Official Aptitude Maximized; Expenses Minimized, Clarendon Press, Oxford, 1993 (repr. 2008), p. 203–289.

notorious.[118] The office was shut off from outside competition. The number of masters was limited to eight, irrespective of a growing workload. The office itself was considered a proprietary interest. It was thus sold off rather than offered to the most qualified person. The fee system further encouraged corruption and delay. Masters were paid by the litigants for every single task they performed. Every document they created and every witness they heard thus increased their income from a case. Furthermore, the masters had to employ and finance their own assistant clerks. This naturally encouraged understaffing. It was only by the 19th century that these defects were addressed by parliament. Legislation in 1813 and 1842 introduced first one and then two more Vice-Chancellors, who would assist the Chancellor as judges.[119] The masters in the Court of Chancery were reduced to a fixed salary in 1833 before the permanent office of master was abolished altogether in 1852.[120] From then on, the Lord Chancellor had to rely on freelance personnel and the administrative clerks.[121]

5.2 Procedure

The common perception of the deterioration of the Court of Chancery can only be fully understood through knowledge of its procedure. I will address the origins of Chancery procedure as well as its state in the 15th century in the later parts of this book. The roots of the later decline will hopefully become visible. A detailed account of 18th and 19th century procedure, however, would exceed the scope of my work. At this stage, it should thus suffice to say that Chancery procedure was, from the very start, potentially more work-intensive than common law procedure.[122] The heavy reliance on documentation, the practice of questioning witnesses through pre-prepared interrogatories in the localities

118 See *M. Lobban*, Preparing for Fusion: Reforming the Nineteenth-Century Court of Chancery, Part I, Law and History Review, Volume 22 (2004), p. 389–427, especially 389–397.

119 Administration of Justice Act 1813, (53 Geo. III) c. 24.

120 Court of Chancery Procedure Act 1852, (15 & 16 Vict.) c. 86.

121 *M. Lobban*, Preparing for Fusion: Reforming the Nineteenth-Century Court of Chancery, Part II, Law and History Review, Volume 22 (2004), p. 565–599, p. 583; *H. Langbein / R. T. Lerner / B. P. Smith*, History of the Common Law – The Development of Anglo-American Legal Institutions, p. 369.

122 The alleged similarity to civil law procedure is telling. *J. P. Dawson*, A History of Lay Judges, Harvard University Press, Cambridge, Ma., 1960, p. 69–72, compared the size of the English and the French judiciary over time. In the 18th century, he counted 15 royal judges in England and 5000 royal judges in France. Even adjusted for population figures this suggests a ratio of almost 1 to 100. In England, on the other hand, the 'civilian' Court of Chancery only employed a single judge despite allegedly operating under a similar procedure.

and the possibility of multi-party litigation all carried the potential for delay. The efforts to systematise equity in the common law tradition aggravated these concerns while at the same time making them all the more visible. Since equity now effectively worked like the common law, it was also judged by the same standards. Common law procedure, on the other hand, had evolved substantially since the Middle Ages. Writ system and jury trial were still dominating factors but the former had become more flexible and the latter more strictly controlled. Additionally, the introduction of cross-examination had provided common law procedure with a much-admired truth-finding tool. At the same time when clearing the Court of Chancery of Selden's charges of uncertainty,[123] Blackstone therefore compared its procedure unfavourably with that of the common law.[124]

5.3 Public perception

Charles Dickens' fictional portrayal of the case *Jarndyce v Jarndyce* in his satirical novel *Bleak House* (1853) has come to represent the ultimate verdict on the Court of Chancery.[125] Despite its fictional character, it "epitomised" the reputation of the court in the 19th century.[126] Indeed, practitioners' accounts sounded scarily similar to Dickens' satirical observations.[127] The legal historian John P. Dawson

123 See above 4.4.

124 *W. Blackstone*, Commentaries on the Laws of England, Volume 3, p. 373–374.

125 A short quotation on delay and multi-party litigation should illustrate both Dickens' view of Chancery proceedings as well as the reason for the novel's success: "Jarndyce v. Jarndyce drones on. This scarecrow of a suit has, in course of time, become so complicated that no man alive knows what it means. The parties to it understand it least; but it has been observed that no two Chancery lawyers can talk about it for five minutes, without coming to a total disagreement as to all the premises. Innumerable children have been born into the cause; innumerable young people have married into it; innumerable old people have died out of it. Scores of people have deliriously found themselves made parties in Jarndyce v. Jarndyce, without knowing how or why; whole families have inherited legendary hatreds with the suit".

126 *J. H. Langbein / R. T. Lerner / B. P. Smith*, History of the Common Law – The Development of Anglo-American Legal Institutions, p. 362.

127 Echoing *C. Dickens*' assessment of the length of trials in the Court of Chancery a decade earlier, the lawyer *G. Spence* (for his prominent role in Chancery literature, see below chapter III, 1.2) observed that no man "as things now stand, can enter into a Chancery suit with any reasonable hope of being alive at the termination, if he has a determined adversary", quoted in *C. S. Christopher*, Progress in the Administration of Justice During the Victorian Period, Select Essays in Anglo-American Legal History, Little, Brown, and Company, Boston, Ma., Volume 1, 1907, p. 516–557, p. 529.

correctly assessed the image of the Court of Chancery by concluding that it was "[u]nfortunate [...] for the subsequent reputation of the Chancery [that] it was not abolished in 1641".[128] On the other hand, what other court can claim to have provided the central motivation for a novel by one of England's greatest writers? Dickens' contemporaries were hardly spoilt for choice when it came to efficient adjudication and a slightly less disastrous image might have cost the Court of Chancery its place in literary history.

6. Fusion

The aggravated criticism that was levelled against the Court of Chancery throughout the 19th century mandated a comprehensive reaction. I have already outlined the attempts to tackle the alleged corruption in the masters' offices. The reform attempts, however, went much further; they also extended to the procedural sphere. In 1852, a Chancery Commission consisting of experienced lawyers and judges from the court suggested to avail the Court of Chancery with instruments of common law procedure, most notably cross-examination.[129] The Chancery Procedure Act 1852[130] implemented this suggestion, thereby noticeably moving Chancery procedure in the direction of the common law.[131] At the same time, some procedural limitations of the common law were equally questioned. A Common Law Commission supplemented the work of the Chancery Commission. Based on its recommendations, the Common Law Procedure Act 1854 extended the range of remedies to include the traditionally equitable instruments of injunction and specific performance.[132] It furthermore provided the parties to a suit with a possibility to waive jury trial despite the existence of a factual dispute.[133] By de-monopolising the two jurisdictions of their key features, both reform efforts heavily diluted the distinction of common law and Chancery procedure.

128 *J. P. Dawson*, A History of Lay Judges, p. 170.

129 *First Report of Her Majesty's Commissioners Appointed to Inquire into the Process, Practice, and System of Pleading in the Court of Chancery*, Clowes and Sons, London, 1852. For an excellent overview over the legislation process, see *M. Lobban*, Preparing for Fusion: Reforming the Nineteenth-Century Court of Chancery, Part II, Law and History Review, Volume 22 (2004), p. 565–599.

130 Court of Chancery Procedure Act 1852, (15 & 16 Vict.) c. 86.

131 Explicitly so, sec. 31 Court of Chancery Procedure Act 1852, (15 & 16 Vict.) c. 86.

132 Common Law Procedure Act 1854, (17 & 18 Vict.) c. 125, especially secs. 79 for injunction and 68 for specific performance (*mandamus*).

133 Sec. 1 Common Law Procedure Act 1854, (17 & 18 Vict.) c. 125.

6.1 Resistance to fusion

What further justification was there, then, for the continued separate existence of common law courts and the Court of Chancery? Integration into a single jurisdiction naturally became a subject of discussion. The Chancery Commission, however, voted against the creation of a universal jurisdiction.[134] It considered it "obvious, on considering the different subject matters of which Courts of Law and Equity are ordinarily required to take cognizance, that there must be different modes of procedure".[135] Undoubtedly, the institutional separation between common law and equity courts was deeply entrenched in the mind of English lawyers.[136] Effectively, however, this separation served no discernable purpose – maybe apart from specialisation in out-dated procedures.[137] It rather serves as an excellent example of the problem of path-dependencies in institutional history.

The separate jurisdictions had not only become useless, they were also an important cost factor. Parties in common law proceedings regularly opened additional suits in the Court of Chancery in order to obtain the full range of remedies and gain access to wider procedural instruments.[138] The Lord Chancellors in turn often freed themselves from the task of deciding factual issues by sending them to a common law court for jury verdict.[139] Both practices increased the costs of the proceedings and delayed their solution. It was thus high time when another royal commission advocated the fusion of common law and equity courts in 1869.

134 *First Report of Her Majesty's Commissioners Appointed to Inquire into the Process, Practice, and System of Pleading in the Court of Chancery*, p. 2.

135 *First Report of Her Majesty's Commissioners Appointed to Inquire into the Process, Practice, and System of Pleading in the Court of Chancery*, p. 2.

136 Arguably, this is still the case today. For an introduction into this 'fusion fallacy' mindset, see *J. Dietrich*, Attempting Fusion: Professor Worthington's 'Equity' and Its Integration with the Common Law, Common Law World Review, Volume 34 (2005), p. 62–84, especially p. 64–67.

137 Even then, this would beg the question of the effectiveness of specialisation in such distinct and limited areas of the law like trusts, mortgages and corporations. A purely equitable lawsuit that would not require the input of a common lawyer was unthinkable either way.

138 For a description of the bill of discovery and its use in common law proceedings, see *J. Story*, Commentaries on Equity Jurisprudence, Little, Brown, and Company, Boston, Ma., Volume 2, 1877, p. 725–753.

139 This practice was described by *W. Blackstone*, Commentaries on the Laws of England, Clarendon Press, Oxford, Volume 3, 1768 (repr. 1966), p. 452; *J. H. Langbein / R. T. Lerner / B. P. Smith*, History of the Common Law – The Development of Anglo-American Legal Institutions, p. 375.

6.2 Judicature Acts

This so-called Judicature Commission laid the groundwork for a comprehensive overhaul of the English court system through the Judicature Acts of 1873 and 1875.[140] The fusion of common law and equity has – at least in theory – an institutional, a procedural and a substantive dimension.

6.2.1 Institutional fusion

Institutional fusion was the most visible but also possibly the easiest process. The three original common law courts of Common Pleas, Queen's Bench and Exchequer were integrated with the Court of Chancery and a common Court of Appeal into a single Supreme Court of Judicature. The name of the new court was somewhat misleading. The Judicial Committee of the House of Lords retained its position as a court of last resort with universal jurisdiction until its replacement with a new Supreme Court in 2005. What was called Supreme Court of Judicature by the 1873 and 1875 Acts instead became known as the High Court and the Court of Appeal respectively. The High Court was – after further reform in 1881 – divided into three divisions: Queen's Bench; Chancery; Probate, Divorce and Admiralty. The Queen's Bench effectively consolidated the three original common law courts, while the Chancery division retained the jurisdiction of the Court of Chancery. The Probate, Divorce and Admiralty division mainly integrated the earlier jurisdiction of the ecclesiastical courts of the Church of England into the secular court system.[141] Despite formal fusion, the traditional jurisdictional separations thus retained a reduced institutional significance.

6.2.2 Procedural fusion

The creation of a single civil procedure proved to be the more challenging task.[142] My analysis of Chancery and common law procedure in chapter V will show the fundamentally diverging assumptions underlying the two procedural regimes in their origins. While the procedural reforms culminating in the 1852 and 1854 Acts had already gone a long way in preparing the convergence of common law and Chancery procedure, integration still required a substantial

140 Supreme Court of Judicature Act 1873, (36 & 37 Vict.) c. 66; Supreme Court of Judicature Act 1875, (38 & 39 Vict.) c. 77.

141 Court of Probate Act 1857, (20 & 21 Vict.), c. 77; Matrimonial Causes Act 1857, (20 & 21 Vict.), c. 85.

142 The Court of Chancery had not dealt with criminal matters and the concept of a distinctive public law has long remained foreign to the common law tradition.

change of mentality. It is arguable that the invisible boundaries between common law and equity procedure impair adjudication up to this day.[143] The respective influence of common law and Chancery procedure on modern English civil procedure would surely justify its own comprehensive study. A brief mention of the direction of procedural reform must suffice at this point.

Interestingly – and in line with the more experimental character of its decentralised legal system – the United States saw earlier movements towards a unified civil procedure. The so-called Field Code of 1848 abolished the distinction between actions in common law and equity in the state of New York and served as a template for similar developments in other states.[144] With a view to contemporary American civil procedure, the American scholar Stephen N. Subrin has claimed that "equity conquered common law" procedure.[145] He mentioned multi-party litigation, expansive discovery, greater judicial discretion, a wider range of remedies, reliance on professional experts, documentation as well as disengagement of substance, procedure and remedy as incidents of equity dominance in the modern Federal Rules of Civil Procedure.[146] These procedural instruments are generally paralleled in English civil procedure today. Returning to the beginning of this chapter, it is also important to keep in mind that the two defining features of medieval common law – writ system and jury trial – have effectively been abandoned in the process of procedural reform: the introduction of a single – transsubstantive – action for all civil matters was the central

143 For a relatively recent example, consider *R v Secretary of State for Transport, ex parte Factortame Ltd* [1989] 2 WLR 997. The *Factortame* cases are most famous for defining the status of European Union law in the United Kingdom. Much of the initial adjudication, however, focused on the alleged impossibility to issue the originally equitable remedy of an injunction in traditionally common law-governed judicial review proceedings. The lack of precedent in this area can be considered a lasting result of the institutional separation between common law and equity.

144 *S. N. Subrin*, How Equity Conquered Common Law: The Federal Rules of Civil Procedure in Historical Perspective, University of Pennsylvania Law Review, Volume 135 (1987), p. 909–1002, p. 931–938; *K. Funk*, Equity Without Chancery: The Fusion of Law and Equity in the Field Code of Civil Procedure, New York 1846–76, The Journal of Legal History, Volume 36 (2015), p. 152–191.

145 *S. N. Subrin*, How Equity Conquered Common Law: The Federal Rules of Civil Procedure in Historical Perspective, University of Pennsylvania Law Review, Volume 135 (1987), p. 909–1002.

146 *S. N. Subrin*, How Equity Conquered Common Law: The Federal Rules of Civil Procedure in Historical Perspective, University of Pennsylvania Law Review, Volume 135 (1987), p. 909–1002, p. 923–924. For a recent and largely approving discussion of *S. N. Subrin*'s thesis, see *D. Rendleman*, The Triumph of Equity Revisited: The Stages of Equitable Discretion, Nevada Law Journal, Volume 15 (2015), p. 1397–1453.

feature of the 19th reforms and the disappearance of jury trial in civil matters has been a more gradual but equally distinctive development ever since.[147]

6.2.3 *Substantive fusion*

Whether the substantive law has undergone any serious attempt at fusion is doubtful and cannot be discussed in this context.[148] However, any student of contemporary English law will admit that the common law / equity distinction still has the potential to 'rule us from its grave'. While the origin of a rule in common law or equity makes little difference in most practical cases, the application of specifically equitable maxims, (apparently) randomly assigned to areas of the law by history, still bears the potential for serious irritation.[149] For legal historians concerned with the relevance of their work for contemporary lawyers, it is comforting to know that a work on the origins of the equitable jurisdiction of the Court of Chancery can, at the very least, contribute to the demystification of the common law / equity distinction.

147 The right to a civil jury in federal proceedings in the United States is guaranteed by the 7th amendment but rarely invoked. *M. Galanter*, The Vanishing Trial: An Examination of Trials and Related Matters in Federal and State Courts, Journal of Empirical Legal Studies, Volume 1 (2004), p. 459–570, p. 463, observed that the percentage of jury trials with respect to all proceedings started in federal courts in civil matters in 2002 was merely 1.2 per cent. In England, on the other hand, civil juries are merely available, on the application of one of the parties, in cases of fraud, libel, slander, malicious prosecution and false imprisonment, see sec. 69 (1) Senior Courts Act 1981, c. 54 by virtue of the Constitutional Reform Act 2005, c. 4.

148 For a well-argued affirmative statement, see *S. Worthington*, Equity, Oxford University Press, Oxford, 2nd edition, 2006.

149 The maxim that "he who comes to equity must come with clean hands" might be considered most (in)famous. For its origins and in the way of a scathing attack, see *Z. Chafee*, Coming Into Equity with Clean Hands, Michigan Law Review, Volume 47 (1949), p. 877–906.

Chapter III

Literature on the Court of Chancery

In contrast to its contemporary common law courts, the Court of Chancery during the late medieval and early modern period has long remained a somewhat neglected area of English legal history. In the last decades, however, the literature has expanded dramatically. Any attempt at summarising the relevant contributions therefore bears the risk of over-simplification and superficiality. I will nevertheless try to present a basic overview over existing materials for the purpose of delineating and justifying my own research interests.

It is my aim to gain insights into the specific function of the Court of Chancery in the development of the common law tradition. The term function might require further explanation in this context: The identification of the 'functions' of law in a given society has come under fatal attack from critical legal historians in the second half of the 20th century.[1] Much of this criticism is well-founded. Insofar as functionalism is identified with the idea of one-directional evolutionary progress and the assumption of simple causal relations between law and society, it is indeed indefensible. However, the question how specific conflicts are solved in different times and places and which role law has to play in this goes to the heart of comparative legal historical research. The identification of the functions of law in a given society offers an almost intuitive mechanism for comparisons. It facilitates the necessary abstraction from specific historical circumstances, which is necessary for a broader comparative legal history. As long as the classical pitfalls of functionalism are avoided, the identification of the functions of the law should have a lasting role to play in our understanding of legal systems.

I will thus attempt to combine a detailed presentation of contemporary sources with the identification of the functions of the late medieval Court of Chancery. On the one hand, this should offer a representative insight into the actual work of the court in its formative period. On the other hand, however, it should also allow for a theorization of the role of the court in that era.

I suggest that external and comparative perspectives on the historical findings would help to facilitate the identification of the function of the court. For the

1 For representative works of two of Critival Legal History's most eminent proponenents, see *M.J. Horwitz*, The Historical Contingency of the Role of History, Yale Law Journal, Volume 90 (1981), p. 1057–1059; *R.W. Gordon*, Critical Legal Histories, Stanford Law Review, Volume 57 (1984), p. 57–125.

purposes of my argument, the concrete content of both external and comparative perspectives also requires further clarification.

In the context of the early Court of Chancery, the external perspective should be understood with regard to other academic disciplines. Legal history as a hybrid subject necessarily transcends traditional boundaries. I will argue, however, that despite this comfortable starting position, much of the work on the Court of Chancery represents isolationist tendencies. A truly external perspective would integrate ideas from both other areas of law (like legal theory and legal philosophy) and other disciplines (like sociology or theology). All the aforementioned subjects and disciplines are commonly concerned with the identification and description of higher-order concepts. Their integration could thus arguably enhance the theorization of the function of the Court of Chancery. With regard to the existing literature, I will both draw out the limitations of internal perspectives as well as highlight the tentative attempts to integrate an external perspective.

A truly comparative perspective could furthermore support the theorization of the role of the Court of Chancery by questioning the singularity of the English development and putting it in perspective. With regard to the Court of Chancery, comparisons can be made at several distinguishable levels. Most intuitively, specific procedural or substantive rules can be juxtaposed with rules from other legal orders, systems or traditions. The object of such a comparison could be Roman law or canon law but also the common law itself. Additionally, however, the general role of the Court of Chancery can also be compared with the role of other courts inside and outside England and its function in the wider framework of adjudication can be compared with wholly different instruments from other legal systems that might serve similar functions. On these latter levels, the objects for comparison are indeed much harder to identify but their inclusion in return promises deeper insights into the role of the Court of Chancery. I will argue that the existing literature has focused almost exclusively on what I have called intuitive comparisons and thus neglected the suggested theorization.

Overall, I will show that the existing literature falls short of providing truly comprehensive external and comparative perspectives. Due to these limitations, the question about the function of the Court of Chancery for the development of the common law tradition has either been ignored or only been addressed superficially. Despite these shortcomings, the literature on the Court of Chancery has gradually expanded our understanding of the institution over the last 500 years. In light of this and for the purpose of clarification, I will divide the relevant contributions into four main categories. At first, I will present an overview over the practice-orientated literature that coincided with the existence of the court up to the end of the 19th century (1.). The second part covers the scholarship of classical legal historians at the end of the 19th and the beginning of the 20th century (2.). I will then proceed to a summary of 20th century institutional accounts that characteristically limited the scope of their examinations for a focus on historical accuracy (3.). At last, I will introduce the tradition of literature on moral theology in the Court of Chancery (4.). The works in each of these strands share certain chronological, ideological and methodological similarities. At the same time, these categories should be understood as neither conclusive nor mutually exclusive. The specific works mentioned in each category are chosen on the basis of their representative character and their popularity.[2]

1. The practice-oriented literature

Many of the early works on the Court of Chancery were compiled with the aim of providing a comprehensive overview of its equitable jurisdiction in the form of treatises. They were typically written both by and for practitioners. As a consequence, the focus of these works lay on the law 'as it was' rather than on systematization. When reference was made to the history of the Court of Chancery at all, it was usually for practical reasons. In a legal system deeply entangled in history through the case law method, the appeal to history served as justification for the existence of both legal norms and institutions.

Like modern day textbooks, the treatises structured and condensed the available knowledge for the purpose of simplifying access. The scope of these works varied dramatically. However, even the shorter manuals typically covered a broad range of procedural and substantive rules.

1.1 Early modern treatises

The late 16th century marked the starting point for treatises and tracts dedicated to the work of the Court of Chancery.[3] As the practical focus would suggest, these works typically offered little in the way of jurisprudential insights. I will therefore limit myself to present the two most influential works directly related with the work of the court exemplarily:

The Lord Chancellors themselves were the most distinguished practitioners associated with the Court of Chancery. It thus comes as little surprise that

2 For a more complete overview of literature on the early stages of the Court of Chancery, reference should be made to the bibliography.

3 *W. Holdsworth,* A History of English Law, Methuen, London, Volume 5, 3rd edition, 1945 (repr. 1966), p. 266–278; Volume 6, 2nd edition, 1937 (repr. 1966), p. 613–619, provided a complete account of the literature from the early modern period.

treatises that were attributed to their name became highly influential. This is especially true for Lord Ellesmere (1540–1617)[4] and Lord Nottingham (1621–1682),[5] possibly the two most famous Lord Chancellors of the early modern period.

The treatise *Certaine Observations Concerning the Office of the Lord Chancellor. Composed by the Right Honorable, and most Learned, Thomas Lord Ellesmere, late Lord Chancellor of England*[6] represents one of the first comprehensive works on the Court of Chancery. On the question of authorship, the English 20th century legal historian William Holdsworth (1871–1944) concluded that the available "evidence shows clearly that it was not written by [Ellesmere], though it is possible that he may have encouraged the author to write it".[7] This finding, however, had no bearing on the authority and the reception of the text before the 20th century. The treatise is divided into three main parts. The first part deals extensively with the origin of the office of the Lord Chancellor[8] and represents an illustrative example of the aforementioned authoritative appeal to history. The second part then addresses the institutional role and the powers of the Lord Chancellor, while the third part presents the substantive rules of Chancery. The content of the latter part is divided into several chapters addressing some of the most common subject matters in early Chancery litigation, namely lands and chattels in use or trust, copyholds and the rights of aliens.

4 Sir Thomas Egerton, Lord Chancellor 1596–1617, became most famous for his confrontation with Chief Justice Coke over the constitutional and institutional role of the Court of Chancery in relation to the common law courts. In 1616, he secured royal support for the supremacy of Chancery in cases of manifest conflict with the common law jurisdiction.

5 Heneage Finch, Lord Chancellor 1672–1682, is often seen as the father of modern equity law. Through the systematisation of existing equitable rules, he fundamentally shaped the following two hundred years of Chancery adjudication.

6 Certaine Observations Concerning the Office of the Lord Chancellor. Composed by the Right Honorable, and most Learned, Thomas Lord Ellesmere, late Lord Chancellor of England, Printed for Matthew Walbanck, Henry Twyford and John Place, London, 1651.

7 *W. Holdsworth,* A History of English Law, Volume 5, p. 272.

8 As *W. Zeydel,* American and British Law, The Quarterly Journal of the Library of Congress, Volume 21 (1964), p. 285–292, p. 287, eloquently pointed out, the passage traces the office of chancellor back to "its antiquity, its origin in similar form among Hebrews, Greeks, and Romans, its later appearance in Spain, the Netherlands, and France, and its development in England from the time of Edward the Confessor".

Lord Nottingham's complementary treatises *Manual of Chancery Practice* and *Prolegomena of Chancery and Equity*[9] serve as another excellent early example of the early modern practice-oriented literature. Before ascending to the role of Lord Chancellor, and quite possibly in preparation thereof,[10] Nottingham compiled both a programme for his work as well as a handbook for future reference. The *Manual of Chancery Practice* describes the procedure and the institutional framework of the Court of Chancery in the second half of the 17th century. The *Prolegomena of Chancery and Equity*, on the other hand, might best be characterised as a digest of cases offering a far-ranging introduction into the work of the court.[11] While the main focus of the *Prolegomena* lies on the presentation of substantive rules governing leases, trusts, mortgages and law merchant, the treatise also includes general principles of equity as well as a discussion of the available remedies. As might be inferred from this enumeration, the *Prolegomena of Chancery and Equity* lack both structure and focus. As such, they again represent a collection rather than a systematisation of Chancery practice.[12]

1.2 19th century treatises

The 19th century represents the great transition period for the institutional design of common law and equity courts in England. As such, it saw two comprehensive treatises on the Court of Chancery, which have formed our understanding of the court throughout and after the fusion process. What they have in common with the earlier literature is the perspective of the practitioner as well as their comprehensive approach. At the same time, they are characterised by a greater effort at systematisation and doctrinal reasoning. Furthermore, the justificatory element of the historical accounts, so visible in earlier literature, is mostly absent. The authors were driven by scientific standards rather than by self-interest in justifying the separate equitable jurisdiction.

9 Both are available in an edited edition by D. E. C. Yale: Lord Nottingham's 'Manual of Chancery Practice' and 'Prolegomena of Chancery and Equity', Cambridge University Press, Cambridge, 1965, (repr. 1986).

10 *D. E. C. Yale* in: D. E. C. Yale (ed.), Lord Nottingham's 'Manual of Chancery Practice' and 'Prolegomena of Chancery and Equity', p. 6.

11 *D. E. C. Yale* in: D. E. C. Yale (ed.), Lord Nottingham's 'Manual of Chancery Practice' and 'Prolegomena of Chancery and Equity', p. 76.

12 As *D. E. C. Yale* in: D. E. C. Yale (ed.), Lord Nottingham's 'Manual of Chancery Practice' and 'Prolegomena of Chancery and Equity', p. 77, suggested, this might very well be attributed to the fact that Lord Nottingham prepared the Prolegemena for his own use and not for publication.

The American Supreme Court Justice Joseph Story's (1779–1845) *Commentaries on Equity Jurisprudence*[13] have become one of the classics of equity literature through many editions. Before covering the contemporary rules, Story provided an introduction to the concept of equity and the history of the Court of Chancery. He saw English equity as being firmly grounded in but simultaneously exceeding the principles of ancient Roman law and early modern natural law.[14] His comparative account relied mostly on the accumulation of similar maxims and thus remains superficial. This locates his work in an early period of Chancery writing that mostly ignored external and comparative perspectives.

Story's history largely avoids concrete comments on the early phase of Chancery before the Reformation. This is understandable since the treatise was prepared contemporaneously with the publication of the first Chancery documents from the time before the reign of Henry VIII.[15] Story could not yet rely on these sources. Substantively, he divided the equitable rules into three jurisdictional categories: the concurrent, the exclusive and the auxiliary jurisdiction of Chancery. The difficulty of classifying substantive law into jurisdictional categories should be apparent. Due to the success of Story's account, this classification has become highly influential despite not serving any apparent practical purpose.

The Scottish lawyer George Spence (1787–1850) presented an equally impressive accumulation of information in *The Equitable Jurisdiction of the Court of Chancery*[16] from 1846/1850. His work, however, showed a stronger historical focus than Story's *Commentaries*. Spence was a barrister at Lincoln's Inn and regularly practiced at the Court of Chancery. Stretching over two volumes and more than 1700 pages, his work presented a final comprehensive attempt at a practice-oriented account of the procedural and substantive rules, and their respective origins, before the abolition of the court.[17] In the first volume, Spence

13 *J. Story,* Commentaries on Equity Jurisprudence, Little, Brown, and Company, Boston, Ma., Volume 1 & 2, 1877.

14 *J. Story,* Commentaries on Equity Jurisprudence, Volume 1, p. 1–28, especially p. 4–5; 9.

15 Calendars of the Proceedings in Chancery in the Reign of Queen Elizabeth, To Which are Prefixed Examples of Earlier Proceedings from the Reign of Richard the Second to that of Queen Elizabeth, Inclusive, Public Record Office, London, Volume 1, 1827; Volume 2, 1830.

16 *G. Spence,* The Equitable Jurisdiction of the Court of Chancery, Lee and Blanchard, Philadelphia, Pa., Volume 1, 1846 (repr. 1981); Volume 2, 1850 (repr. 1981).

17 The work was published shortly before concrete steps towards the fusion of equity and common law were taken. Following *F. W. Maitland*'s – admittedly circular – definition that "Equity now is that body of rules administered by our English Courts of justice, which, were it not for the operation of the Judicature

provided a general overview over English legal history from the Roman Conquest to the establishment of the Court of Chancery – an ambitious project, culminating in the delineation of the common law and the equitable jurisdiction. Given the accumulation of historical data and the absence of a narrative structure, the reader might agree with the author who himself admitted that "[i]n a work, the design of which is mainly practical, it may perhaps be considered that too much of historical detail has been introduced, and that some collateral subjects [...] might have been omitted".[18] But while the combination of practical guidance and historical aspirations comes at the cost of readability, the latter can be seen as laying the groundwork for later efforts of legal historians.[19]

Spence covered the jurisdiction of the court in its initial stages. Upon the examination of its origins, he continually referred to institutions and concepts pertaining to Roman law.[20] However, these references again often exhausted themselves in references to etymological or conceptual similarities.[21] The comparative perspective was at best superficial – not least because Spence ignored the practical application of these concepts. The second volume presented the contemporary state of equity law, addressing the main equitable doctrines of trust, mortgage and assignment in great detail.

1.3 Conclusion

All four aforementioned treatises reflected a narrow, internal perspective on the work of the court. This might be attributed to the authors' practical training and thinking. Most notably, all four works lacked noticeable attempts of abstraction. Generally, the discussions about the Court of Chancery remained practical and the role of the equitable jurisdiction in the developing English legal system was

Acts, would be administered only by those courts which would be known as courts of Equity", (*F. W. Maitland*, Equity – A Course of Lectures, Cambridge University Press, Cambridge, 1936 (repr. 1969), p. 1.) however, we can see the use of *G. Spence*'s jurisdictional and doctrinal accounts for the delineation of equity law up to the current day.

18 *G. Spence*, The Equitable Jurisdiction of the Court of Chancery, Volume 1, p. viii.

19 See below.

20 See for example *G. Spence*, The Equitable Jurisdiction of the Court of Chancery, Volume I, p. 410.

21 See, for example, the comparison between the office of the Lord Chancellor and that of the Roman Praetor. *G. Spence*, The Equitable Jurisdiction of the Court of Chancery, Volume I, p. 407–419. *H. S. Maine*, Ancient Law (1866), Transaction Publishers, New Brunswick, NJ, 2002, p. 64–72, elaborated on this idea with a view to the evolutional stages in the development of legal systems.

not discussed.[22] Comparative assessments were largely limited to references to Roman law maxims and institutions.

Overall, the accumulation of practical information in the treatises provides valuable insights into the everyday work of Chancery for legal historians until today. On the other hand, the accounts appear deeply rooted in the past and hardly provide transferable ideas for modern readers. The lack of effort exhibited in relation to conducting an investigation into the role of the Court of Chancery as an institution placed in a wider jurisprudential setting as well as its development throughout time was indeed a typical feature of the treatises.

As a result of the fusion of common law and equity courts in the wake of the Judicature Acts 1875/77, practical accounts of equity law ceased to be directly related to the Court of Chancery. Instead, practitioners were able to opt for textbooks focused on contemporary equity as an area of law. Literature on the Court of Chancery then became a matter for legal historians – a profession that rose to prominence in Anglo-American legal academia at just the same time.[23]

Duncan M. Kerly's (1863–1938) Cambridge dissertation *An historical sketch of the equity jurisdiction of the Court of Chancery*[24] from 1890 can be seen as a transitional work in this regard. While its focus remained narrow and strictly institutional, it was guided by an academic interest in the development of the court from its origins to the eventual fusion with the common law courts. This represents a first attempt at providing a broader institutional history.[25] The encyclopaedic approach and the inclusion of current equitable doctrine, however, were at the same time reminiscent of the earlier treatises.

22 In fact, the early modern thinking about the Court of Chancery seems to be dominated by the medieval ideas of St. German's Doctor and Student (T. F. T. Plucknett / J. L. Barton (eds.), St German's Doctor and Student (ca. 1523), Selden Society, London, 1974) while later continental European ideas about the relationship between law and equity were mostly ignored.

23 See below 2.

24 *D. M. Kerly,* An Historical Sketch of the Equitable Jurisdiction of the Court of Chancery, Cambridge University Press, Cambridge, 1890 (repr. 2011).

25 Referring to the first volume of *G. Spence*'s The Equitable Jurisdiction of the Court of Chancery (see above 1.1), *D. M. Kerly,* An Historical Sketch of the Equitable Jurisdiction of the Court of Chancery p. v, himself submitted that "these scattered fragments are, so far as I am aware, the only history of equity we have." While Spence might indeed be credited with an early attempt to investigate primary sources, *D. M. Kerly*'s statement reflects the narrow understanding of legal history that dates the subject's birth to the second half of the 19th century.

2. The classical common law legal history

The birth of common law legal history as an academic subject is conventionally associated with the second half of the 19th century.[26] As evidenced by the literature presented above, this is not to say that English lawyers in earlier times did not engage with the past. The precedent-based approach, mandated by the common law, arguably guarantees for most legal practice to be inherently backward-looking. However, it was only during the second half of the 19th century that common law legal history became a subject for academics.[27] The earlier work compiled by practitioners provides us with rich historical data but is, by far and large, decidedly anti-theoretical.[28] Classical common law legal historians understood legal history as an academic discipline: instead of merely collecting historical facts, they aimed to explain the evolution of the common law with scientifically recognised methods. Their examination of cultural and social – in other words external – causes for the development of the common law was also a call for recognition in the wider academic community.

2.1 The German Historical School

The surging interest in legal history as an academic endeavour was, in no small part, owed to the influence of the German Historical School. While Carl-Friedrich von Savigny (1779–1861) was read and quoted in England by the 1840s,[29] later academics actually familiarised themselves comprehensively with the work of the Historical School through personal contacts and years of study.[30]

26 Compare *J. Rose*, Studying the Past: the Nature and Development of Legal History as an Academic Discipline, The Journal of Legal History, Volume 31 (2010), p. 101–128.

27 It should be noted that the study of the common law as an academic discipline does not date back much further either. *J. Rose*, Studying the Past: the Nature and Development of Legal History as an Academic Discipline, The Journal of Legal History, Volume 31 (2010), pp. 101–128, provided an account of the almost contemporaneous development of history, common law and common law legal history as academic subjects.

28 For a programmatic account of the early common law legal history, see *F. W. Maitland*, Why the History of English Law is not Written, in: H. A. L. Fisher (ed.), The Collected Papers of Frederic William Maitland, Cambridge University Press, Cambridge, Volume 1, 1911, p. 480–497.

29 *G. Spence,* The Equitable Jurisdiction of the Court of Chancery, Volume 1, p. vi.

30 The personal and intellectual ties between the German Historical School and American as well as English scholars offer a formidable ground for further research. It would far exceed the scope of this work to characterise the relationship between German and Anglo-American legal thought at the end of the 19th century. *D. Rabban*, Law's History – American Legal Thought and the Trans-

The appeal was evident: The German Historical School had helped to redefine the concept of law in academic thinking and had even proven influential for contemporary political debates.

Not unlike the Historical School in Germany, early common law legal history was chiefly concerned with the origins and development of the doctrine relating to specific legal instruments. Underlying this kind of research was an evolutionary conception of law: the belief that modern law was shaped into its current form by a century-long process of societal and cultural, internal and external, influences.[31] By way of another parallel to the German scholarly tradition, some of the works in this tradition provide what today would have to be classified as a nationalist or even racialist narrative of Anglo-American legal culture.[32] Even Frederic Maitland (1850–1906), the 'father' of English legal history, against whom no such allegations can be made, thus could not help but to admit that "[w]e have all of us been nationalists of late".[33]

2.2 Maitland

Maitland himself did not write a specific history of the Court of Chancery. This decision might be related to his insight that to "acknowledge [...] the existence

atlantic Turn to History, Cambridge University Press, Cambridge, 2013, offered an early general account of the ties between German and American legal historians at the time.

31 For an introduction to the concept of evolution in law that explicitly references the contributions of *C. F. v. Savigny* and *O. W. Holmes*, see *E. D. Elliott*, The Evolutionary Tradition in Jurisprudence, Columbia Law Review, Volume 85 (1985), p. 38–94. *R. W. Gordon*, J. Willard Hurst and the Common Law Tradition in American Legal Historiography, Law and Society, Volume 10 (1975), p. 9–55, p. 14–16 also showed the evolutionary background to the studies of the American legal historians at the end of the 19th century. *M. J. Horwitz*, The Historical Contingency of the Role of History, Yale Law Journal, Volume 90 (1981), p. 1057–1059, p. 1058, concluded that "legal history was tied to various forms of evolutionism and Social Darwinism".

32 Compare *D. Rabban*, The Historiography of the Common Law, Law and Society, Volume 28 (2003), p. 1161–1201, especially 1187–1188, with reference to *O. W. Holmes*, The Common Law, Transaction Publishers, New Brunswick, NJ, 2005, for example p. 138.

33 *F. W. Maitland*, English Law and the Renaissance (with some Notes), Cambridge University Press, Cambridge, 1901, p. 2. *F. W. Maitland* went on to emphasise that "Cosmopolitanism can afford to await its turn". Following later debates about the focus of legal history, it seems remarkable how long it has taken for that vision to be realized. Additionally, it should be noted that *F. W. Maitland*, despite his deep interest in the German Historical School, was in no way uncritical in relation to its shortcomings. See *T. F. T. Plucknett*, Frederic William Maitland, New York University Law Review, Volume 26 (1951), p. 1–9, p. 3.

of equity as a system distinct from law would [... be] a belated, a reactionary measure".[34] Whereas earlier generations of writers had limited themselves to practical and isolated perspectives, Maitland was the first to identify, more generally, the numerous interplays between different normative orders in medieval and early modern England. While only covering the time before the establishment of the Court of Chancery, his seminal work *The History of English Law before the Time of Edward I* (together with Frederick Pollock)[35] thus established the roots of later equitable instruments such as the trust or the oral contract.[36] In particular, Maitland identified contemporary societal needs, described malfunctions in the common law and contrasted those with the interventionist role of ecclesiastical courts in medieval England.

Two of Maitland's lectures addressed the Court of Chancery more directly, albeit in less detail. *English Law and the Renaissance*[37] shedded light on the Court of Chancery's contribution to the absence of a reception of Roman law in the 16th century, whereas *Equity*[38] commenced with a short introduction to the early history of the court. The latter lecture reflected Maitland's interest in continental European influences by mentioning the canonical origins of Chancery procedure, while challenging the assumption that the medieval court borrowed considerably from Roman law. However, no substantial evidence was provided for either of those claims.

2.3 The American contribution

The turn to legal history as an academic subject in England coincided with the establishment of the modern American law school. The creation of full-time professorships allowed for a heightened degree of scholarly sophistication that ultimately facilitated cross-Atlantic exchange of insights and ideas. Interestingly, a number of American scholars were already involved in ascertaining the roots of the common law, when Maitland was still a lonely figure in English academia.

34 *F. W. Maitland*, Equity – A Course of Lectures, p. 21.
35 *F. Pollock / F. W. Maitland*, The History of English Law before the Time of Edward I, Cambridge University Press, Cambridge, Volume 1 & 2, 2nd edition reissue, 1968.
36 The origins of the trust represent one of several topics, on which later legal historians have corrected *F. W. Maitland*. *R. H. Helmholz*, Views of trust and Treuhand, in: R. H. Helmholz / R. Zimmermann (eds.), Itinera fiduciae – Trust and Treuhand in historical perspective, Duncker & Humblot, Berlin, 1998, p. 27–44. This should, however, not diminish his pioneering role, which paved the way for all later research.
37 *F. W. Maitland*, English Law and the Renaissance (with some Notes). The lecture will be discussed in greater detail below in chapter VI.
38 *F. W. Maitland*, Equity – A Course of Lectures.

The geographical and mental distance from the origins of the common law might have contributed to an early interest in academic rather than practical questions. At the beginning, common law legal history can thus be considered as a shared Anglo-American project.[39]

Oliver W. Holmes (1841–1935), the later Supreme Court Justice, has been credited with breaking new ground for Chancery in his article *Early English Equity*[40].[41] Writing before Maitland, though in less detail, he traced the development of the doctrines of trust and contract in medieval England. Rejecting the idea of sudden and spontaneous innovations, he explained the long-standing interests behind the trust and their recognition in Germanic custom. Holmes then attempted to show the hardening of the common law rules that slowly forced both trusts and oral contracts out of the ordinary jurisdiction and into the more flexible jurisdictions of church and Chancery.

Christopher C. Langdell, then Dean of Harvard Law School, contributed *The Development of Equity Pleading from Canon Law Procedure*[42] to the debate. The article focused on the rules of pleading from both an evolutional and a comparative perspective and thus represented a classic example of the kind of common law legal history that was inspired by the German Historical School.

The approach taken by the late 19th century legal historians also opened up an opportunity for substantial debates on the origins of specific equitable instruments. James B. Ames' *The Origin of Uses and Trusts*[43] essentially represented a criticism of Holmes' *Early English Equity*. While acknowledging the Germanic 'Salman' or 'Treuhand' as the prototype for later uses and trusts,[44] Ames stressed the singularity of the English line of development. He strongly denied the alleged role of ecclesiastical courts in the early enforcement of uses.[45] Instead,

39 For an account of the relationship between English and American legal historians in this era with a focus on *F. W. Maitland*, see *D. Rabban*, From Maine to Maitland via America, Cambridge Law Journal, Volume 68 (2009), p. 410–435, p. 428–433.

40 *O. W. Holmes*, Early English Equity, in: Select Essays in Anglo-American Legal History, Little, Brown, and Company, Boston, Ma., Volume 2, 1908, p. 705–721.

41 See *W. T. Barbour*, Some Aspects of Fifteenth-Century Chancery, Harvard Law Review, Volume 31 (1918), p. 834–859, p. 834.

42 *C. C. Langdell*, The Development of Equity Pleading from Canon Law Procedure, in: Select Essays in Anglo-American Legal History, Little, Brown, and Company, Boston, Ma., Volume 2, 1908, p. 753–778.

43 *J. B. Ames*, The Origin of Uses and Trusts, in: Select Essays in Anglo-American Legal History, Little, Brown, and Company, Boston, Ma., Volume 2, 1908, p. 737–752.

44 *J. B. Ames*, The Origin of Uses and Trusts, in: Select Essays in Anglo-American Legal History, Volume 2, p. 737–752, p. 740.

45 *J. B. Ames*, The Origin of Uses and Trusts, in: Select Essays in Anglo-American

Ames stressed the moral dimension of practical cases that led the Lord Chancellors to enforce uses through the Court of Chancery.[46] Interestingly, the legal historians of this period largely ignored the question of a higher morality of the equitable jurisdiction of the Court of Chancery, which heavily attracted both earlier and later commentators on the history of the court. This was in accordance with the pragmatist approach that became popular in American scholarship of the late 19th and early 20th century. It further illustrates the strife for academic recognition.

2.4 Conclusion

The classical legal historians generally understood that the analysis of legal evolution requires both a comparative and an external perspective: Comparison with common law and canon law was equally prevalent in their work as the recognition of the importance of social and cultural phenomena for the development of law. While their knowledge of the sources remained highly eclectic, they thus already highlighted a potential direction for further research on the Court of Chancery.

The classical legal historians' insights into the respective origins of numerous Chancery rules in both medieval common and canon law constitute their main immediate contribution to Chancery literature. This recognition also laid the groundwork for later works on equitable instruments that could additionally rely on a greater knowledge of source material. William Barbour's *The History of Contract in Early English Equity*[47] and Alfred W. B. Simpson's *A History of the Common Law of Contract*[48] represent noteworthy examples in the area of contract

Legal History, Volume 2, p. 737–752, p. 740. *J. B. Ames* referred to the early case of *Horsmonger v Pympe*, in: W. P. Baildon (ed.), Select Cases in Chancery A. D. 1364 to 1471, Selden Society, London, 1896, p. 120 in order to support his claim. In this case, the beneficiary to a trust claimed a remedy against the trustee, submitting that he "cannot have any remedy by the law of the Holy Church, nor by the common law of the land". However, considering the regularity with which petitioners in Chancery claimed a lack of jurisdiction in other courts, this phrase might also have become a formality in an appeal to the auxiliary jurisdiction of Chancery.

46 *J. B. Ames*, The Origin of Uses and Trusts, in: Select Essays in Anglo-American Legal History, Volume 2, p. 737–752, p. 742–747. This idea is shared with the moral theological accounts presented below at 4.

47 *W. T. Barbour*, The History of Contract in Early English Equity, in: P. Vinogradoff (ed.), Oxford Studies in Social and Legal History, Clarendon Press, Oxford, Volume 4, 1914, p. 1–237.

48 *A. W. B. Simpson*, A History of the Common Law of Contract – The Rise of the Action of Assumpsit, Clarendon Press, Oxford, 1975.

law. On the other hand, it should not go unnoticed that many views expressed by the classical legal historians have remained controversial and that some have even been rebutted.[49] Their interest in establishing a wider theory sometimes collided with an insufficient knowledge of the sources. At the same time, they deserve credit for making common law legal history, and with it the history of the Court of Chancery, an academic discipline with (social) scientific aspirations.

3. The 20th century institutional accounts

Building on the foundations of classical legal history, research on the Court of Chancery in the 20th century became much more differentiated. However, we can identify some common trends: Many of the defining works shared a focus on the court as an institution within a wider legal landscape. They thus adopted, and often expanded, elements of the comparative approach. This is certainly true for the legal context in late medieval and early modern England. Much of the discussion has thus focused on relations between common law, ecclesiastical and equitable courts. On the other hand, wider normative contexts and foreign developments still remained underrepresented in the literature.

The 20th century accounts particularly profited from a wider availability and deeper understanding of primary sources. In fact, the edition and classification of sources had become the main occupation of legal historians by that time. This orientation towards source material often came with a rejection of jurisprudential or trans-disciplinary inquiries; an approach that was in line with Maitland's observation that legal history is history, not law.[50] At the same time, this approach also bore the risk of limiting the potential of legal history as an inherently trans-disciplinary subject.[51]

Most of the 20th century legal historians also rejected the ideological precepts espoused by their predecessors. This is especially noticeable in the complete

49 *J. H. Baker*, English Law and the Renaissance, The Cambridge Law Journal, Volume 44 (1985), p. 46–61 re-evaluated *F. W. Maitland*'s lecture on "Law and the Renaissance". *D. Rabban*, The Historiography of the Common Law, Law and Society, Volume 28 (2003), p. 1161–1201, provided a critical view on the historiography of the classical American legal histories with a focus on *O. W. Holmes*' most famous work, The Common Law.

50 *F. W. Maitland*, Why the History of English Law is not Written, in: H. A. L. Fisher (ed.), The Collected Papers of Frederic William Maitland, Volume 1, p. 480–497, p. 491–494.

51 Despite his generally well-meaning review of historicism, *C. Tomlins*, What is Left of the Law and Society Paradigm after Critique? Revisiting Gordon's "Critical Legal Histories", Law & Society Inquiry, Volume 37 (2012), p. 155–166, comes to the conclusion that the plurality, which was brought about by historicism, could leave legal history without direction or purpose.

absence of evolutionary ideas – certainly when understood in Darwinian terms as 'survival of the fittest' – that had been so heavily relied on by early legal historians.[52] The works thus represented a regression away from external perspectives.

3.1 Time periods

The decidedly historical perspective is visible in the works of three historians that were devoted to specific eras in the history of Chancery.

W. J. Jones examined *The Elizabethan Court Of Chancery.*[53] Focussing on the reign of Queen Elizabeth I. (1558–1603), he addressed the institutional design of the court, its procedure and its relation with other courts. The account is highly descriptive and largely void of theoretical aspirations. On the other hand, it represents a first attempt at formulating a comprehensive institutional history from a vast time-specific primary source material.

Franz Metzger's *Das englische Kanzleigericht unter Kardinal Wolsey,*[54] the only substantial German-language contribution to Chancery literature, is equally devoted to a specific era of the court. Contemporary sources identify Cardinal Wolsey as the most controversial Lord Chancellor of the early period of the court. While Metzger was concerned with writing an institutional history, he also attempted to trace the distinctiveness of Wolsey's chancellorship, which led to his fall from grace and, ultimately, his execution.[55] In addressing Wolsey's alleged judicial activism, Metzger cautiously opened the door for higher-order jurisprudential questions.

Timothy Haskett examined the earliest phase of the existence of the court as a separate institution in his article on *The Medieval English Court of Chancery.*[56] The first part mainly offered an introduction and evaluation of the secondary literature on the medieval court. In the second part, Haskett then presented a large sample of Chancery sources.[57] His analysis reflects historical interests.

52 See *R. W. Gordon*, Critical Legal Histories, Stanford Law Review, Vol. 36 (1984), p. 57–125, esp. 59–67, for one of the most critical and convincing rejections of 'evolutionary functionalism' in legal history. Also *R. W. Gordon*, Historicism in Legal Scholarship, Yale Law Journal, Volume 90 (1981), p. 1017–1024.

53 *W. J. Jones,* The Elizabethan Court of Chancery, Clarendon Press, Oxford, 1967.

54 *F. Metzger,* Das englische Kanzleigericht unter Kardinal Wolsey, Promotion an der Friedrich-Alexander-Universität Erlangen-Nürnberg, 1977.

55 See above chapter II, 3.3.

56 *T. S. Haskett,* The Medieval English Court of Chancery, Law and History Review Volume 14 (1996), p. 245–313.

57 For an explanation and a short critique of the sample, see below chapter IV, 3.

While it largely ignores questions of procedure and substantive law, it offers valuable insights into the demographic and economic situation of the litigants.

3.2 Comprehensive common law histories

Several works aimed at providing a general common law history also devoted chapters to the Court of Chancery. Given their aim, they all shared a broader perspective on the role of the court as existing in a wider legal framework. They thus advanced a comparative perspective with regard to English courts.

Theodore Plucknett's (1897–1965) chapter on Equity in *A Concise History of the Common Law*[58] focused on early equitable elements in medieval English law and the formative period of the Court of Chancery. With reference to late medieval legal terminology, he described equity as a "gloss written by later hands around an ancient and venerable text [the common law]".[59] Plucknett thus emphasised the importance of the dialectical relationship between equity and common law for the common law legal tradition. The institutional separation was portrayed as merely a "confusing" "accident [...] of history".[60]

In *Historical Foundations of the Common Law,*[61] S. F. C. Milson equally stressed the reciprocal relationship between the Court of Chancery and the common law courts. He thus identified Chancery's more immediate access to the parties through oath-taking and personal remedies as its decisive feature. For him, this presented the ideal supplementary to a largely impersonal common law procedure.

John Langbein's *History of the Common Law,*[62] on the other hand, credited the Court of Chancery with having had a much greater and more autonomous influence on the history of the common law legal tradition. As such, Langbein emphasised the role of Roman-canon law procedural thinking in Chancery. In particular, he portrayed the establishment of the court and its subsequent rise as having been facilitated by superior civilian methods of fact-finding and decision-making; both were considered necessary elements for the purpose of breaking up the inflexibility of late medieval common law. Equity procedure was also presented as a blueprint for later reforms during the fusion process and

58 *T. F. T. Plucknett,* A Concise History of the Common Law, Butterworth, London, 5th edition, 1956, p. 673–707.

59 *T. F. T. Plucknett,* A Concise History of the Common Law, p. 673.

60 *T. F. T. Plucknett,* A Concise History of the Common Law, p. 673.

61 *S. F. C. Milsom*, Historical Foundations of the Common Law, Butterworths, London, 2nd edition, 1981, p. 82–96.

62 *J. H. Langbein / R. T. Lerner / B. P. Smith,* History of the Common Law – The Development of Anglo-American Legal Institutions, Aspen Publishers, New York, NY, 2009.

consequently as a main foundation for modern Anglo-American civil procedure.[63]

John Baker, conversely, painted a very different picture in his *Oxford History of the Laws of England*.[64] The "influence of the civilians" was relegated to a small section in his already brief account of the Court of Chancery.[65] Baker acknowledged a civilian inspiration for the written procedure of Chancery but at the same time insisted that, in the court of conscience, "procedure was a servant rather than a master".[66] He also claimed that the Lord Chancellors adopted a "thoroughly English version of the Roman procedural tradition". This fundamental divergence on the question of Roman-canon law influence between two of the most eminent contemporary legal historians highlights the need for further research on the concrete roots of Chancery procedure.

3.3 Thematic accounts

Michael Macnair chose a specific thematic approach for one of the most recent and significant contributions to Chancery literature, *The Law of Proof in Early Modern Equity*.[67] Relying mostly on 17th and 18th century sources, he carefully outlined the law of proof in the Court of Chancery and compared it, step by step, with the corresponding rules in common law and canon law. This method arguably afforded a much better understanding of the similarities of the different legal orders than the more broad-brushed accounts of the classical legal historians. Macnair consciously avoided speculation about the origins of Chancery rules and instead demonstrated great parallels between Chancery and Roman-canon law procedure in the area of proof in the 17th and 18th century.

Given the variety of literature presented, the aforementioned works might be seen as defying categorisation under the single heading of institutional accounts. However, I would suggest that they all limit themselves to questions of institutional design and procedural law. Accounts of substantive law, conversely, are suspiciously absent. Considering the scarcity of reasoned judgments contained in the available sources up to the 17th century, many of these researchers consciously rejected the idea of writing a history of substantive law in the early

63 The influence on this book will become apparent in later chapters.

64 *J. H. Baker*, The Oxford History of the Laws of England, Volume 6: 1483–1558, Oxford University Press, Oxford, 2003.

65 *J. Baker*, The Oxford History of the Laws of England, Volume 6: 1483–1558, p. 171–190.

66 *J. Baker*, The Oxford History of the Laws of England, Volume 6: 1483–1558, p. 180.

67 *M. R. T. Macnair*, The Law of Proof in Early Modern Equity, Duncker & Humblot, Berlin, 1999.

Court of Chancery. It is only recently that Neil Jones has overcome this limitation with several works on early modern trust law.[68] Jones shares the institutional accounts' focus on primary sources as well as their historical perspective, thereby proving their compatibility with an accurate assessment of contemporary substantive law. At the same time, however, he also adopts the internal perspective that is characteristic for the institutional accounts. It seems legitimate to suggest that this perspective is in no small part owed to the fact that – as trained lawyers or historians – many 20th century scholars were (naturally) hesitant to engage with external perspectives on the work of the court. This challenge, then, has only been taken on by a much smaller group of scholars – as of yet mostly in the area of law and religion.

4. Moral theology and the Court of Chancery

There can be no doubt that the label 'Court of Conscience' for the early Court of Chancery was meaningful. The long line of bishops in the office of Lord Chancellor up to the Reformation unquestionably left an impression on the work of the court.[69] It is doubtful whether contemporaries of the early Court of Chancery clearly differentiated between legal and theological normativities. The concept of a single universal normative order regulating all aspects of life was only just making way for a higher degree of differentiation during the formative period of the Court of Chancery.[70] In light of this, the question as to whether the early Lord Chancellors themselves arrived at their decisions on the basis of their religious education and beliefs is a natural one for Chancery literature.

4.1 St. German

Accordingly, this question is also a central theme of the first substantive work on the Court of Chancery. Christopher St. German's (1460–1540) *Doctor and Student*[71] presented a justification for both the common law and the extraordi-

68 Perhaps most notably *N. Jones*, Trusts in England after the Statute of Uses, in: R.H. Helmholz/R. Zimmermann (eds.), Itinera fiduciae – Trust and Treuhand in historical perspective, Duncker & Humblot, Berlin, 1998, p. 173–205; *N. Jones*, Wills, Trusts and Trusting from the Statute of Uses to Lord Nottingham, The Journal of Legal History, Volume 31 (2010), p. 273–298.

69 For an intensive discussion, see below, especially chapter V, 2.7.

70 Compare *P. Prodi*, Eine Geschichte der Gerechtigkeit: Vom Recht Gottes zum modernen Rechtsstaat, C.H. Beck, Munich, 2003, transl. by A. Seemann, who provided a comprehensive account of this development from a mostly continental European perspective.

71 Doctor and Student is available in several edited versions. The version referred to here is T.F.T. Plucknett/J.L. Barton (eds.), St. German's Doctor and Student,

nary jurisdiction of Chancery in the form of a Socratic dialogue between a doctor of divinity and a student of the common law.[72] Based on late medieval scholastic theology, especially that of the Parisian university chancellor Jean Gerson (1363–1429),[73] St. German advocated the enforcement of an objective concept of conscience in the Court of Chancery. In particular, he portrayed conscience as objectively discernable from divine will. In the tradition ofThomas Aquinas (ca. 1225–1274), the human capacity to perceive the relevant knowledge was based upon '*synderesis*', i. e. the "natural power or motive force of the rational soul" that is "moving and steering [the person] to good & abhorring evil".[74] In light of this, St. German proceeded to illustrate practical cases, in which only Chancery could provide a result in accordance with conscience – a practical theology reminiscent of late medieval and (early modern) confessional literature.[75]

Doctor and Student became extensively quoted not only in literature but also, in fact, by Lord Chancellors in their judgments.[76] While this can be attributed in part to its interesting discourse and excellent timing,[77] it should not go unnoticed that it helped to create an image of moral superiority of the Court of Chancery that was most useful in the face of jurisdictional competition.

Despite the success of *Doctor and Student*, the theological sources of Chancery decisions were not elaborated upon any further until the beginning of the 20th

Selden Society, London, 1974. It provides a comprehensive account of both the Latin and the English original versions.

72 The publication of Doctor and Student was followed by a replication (J. A. Guy (ed.), Christopher St German on Chancery and Statute, Selden Society, London, 1985, p. 99–105), which strongly rejected the interference of the Court of Chancery with the ordinary course of justice at common law. This replication shows that theological arguments were not simply accepted as authoritative but rather could be challenged by political or legal considerations.

73 For a detailed account of the parallels (or exact congruities) between *St. German* and *J. Gerson*, see *Z. Rueger*, Gerson's Concept of Equity and Christopher St. German, History of Political Thought, Volume 3 (1982), p. 1–30.

74 T. F. T. Plucknett / J. L. Barton (eds.), St. German's Doctor and Student, p. 81.

75 See also, *P. Vinogradoff*, Reason and Conscience in Sixteenth Century Jurisprudence, Law Quarterly Review, Volume 24 (1908), p. 373–384, p. 378.

76 See for example *The Earl of Oxford's Case*, 1 Chan. Rep. 1 (1615), p. 8, an early landmark case on the relationship between legal and equitable title that lead directly to the question of institutional competition between the Court of Chancery and the common law courts.

77 The first editions of Doctor and Student were published in 1523 (in Latin) and 1530 (in English) and thus right before the English Reformation. They reflect a conception of theology and law that must have been highly attractive to *Henry VIII* and his absolutist aspirations. *St. German* consequently became a staunch supporter and apologist of the king. Compare *J. L. Barton*, Introduction, in: T. F. T. Plucknett / J L. Barton (eds.), St. German's Doctor and Student, p. xii-xiv.

century. When systematisation became the key objective of Chancery lawyers from the 17th century onwards, *Doctor and Student*'s theological dimension lost its attraction, whereas its casuistic passages effectively gained precedential character. St. German's work was simply accepted as authoritative for the early Court of Chancery and as practically irrelevant for the later equity jurisprudence based upon the case law method.

4.2 Elaborations on St. German

In 1908, the Anglo-Russian historian Paul Vinogradoff (1854–1925) revisited the different versions of *Doctor and Student* for his article *Conscience and Reason*.[78] Inspired by Maitland's *English Law and the Renaissance*,[79] Vinogradoff in particular traced the alleged civilian roots of St. German's work on Chancery. In doing so, he identified *Doctor and Student*'s debt to scholastic philosophy and theology. Presenting several Year Book cases from the 15th and 16th century, Vinogradoff then proceeded to exemplify the practical application of the theoretical concept of conscience in the Court of Chancery. It should be noted that the sample of cases is minimal and designed to suit his argumentation – the insight into the application of moral theological thought in the Court of Chancery was thus limited.

Helmut Coing (1912–2000)'s *English Equity and the Denunciatio Evangelica of the Canon Law*,[80] in turn, went further than any other work in identifying the exact origin of the Court of Chancery. Coing highlighted numerous parallels between the work of the court and the *Denunciatio Evangelica* – a supplementary procedure of canon law that was substantively based on conscience and reason.[81] His article shared many parallels with the aforementioned institutional accounts, especially in its comparative perspective. However, the choice of

78 *P. Vinogradoff*, Reason and Conscience in Sixteenth Century Jurisprudence, Law Quarterly Review, Volume 24 (1908), p. 373–384.

79 See above 2.2. *P. Vinogradoff* and *F. W. Maitland* were close friends. It is sometimes claimed that it was the historian *P. Vinogradoff* who inspired the devotion to history in the lawyer *F. W. Maitland*. Compare *C. H. S. Fifoot*, Frederic William Maitland – A Life, Harvard University Press, Cambridge, Ma., 1971, especially p. 58–68.

80 *H. Coing*, English Equity and the Denunciatio Evangelica of the Canon Law, Law Quarterly Review, Volume 71 (1955), p. 223–241.

81 *H. Coing*, English Equity and the Denunciatio Evangelica of the Canon Law, Law Quarterly Review, Volume 71 (1955), p. 223–241, p. 229–231. For a more detailed account, see *W. Decock*, Theologians and Contract Law – The Moral Transformation of the Ius Commune (ca. 1500–1650), Martinus Nijhoff, Leiden, 2013, p. 88–101.

examples was highly selective, thus limiting the work's potential from the perspective of comparative institutionalism.[82] Coing also extended his thesis to substantive rules. The *Denunciatio Evangelica* was a private action for the correction of a sinner. It was based directly on scriptural authority.[83] It thus served the purpose of enforcing natural law, the understanding of which might have been largely in line with St. German's ideas of conscience in the Court of Chancery.

Dennis Klinck's *Conscience, Equity and the Court of Chancery in Early Modern England*[84] represents the most comprehensive recent attempt at identifying a theological motivation for Chancery adjudication. Klinck recognised the central role of conscience not only in the Court of Chancery but also in early modern English life. This led him to an etymological study of the evolving understanding of the concept of conscience.[85] St. German and his scholastic inspirations once again served as the starting point in this context. In marked contrast to earlier studies, Klinck did not limit himself to legal or theological sources. He also examined contemporary literature, private correspondences and political tracts in order to paint a complete picture of the objective understanding of conscience up to the 16th century. The later chapters then address the slow subjectivisation of the term conscience in the aftermath of the Reformation, which rendered it unsuitable as a legal principle guiding the adjudication of individual cases.

Generally, it needs to be borne in mind that many legal historians have not only shied away from examining moral theological roots of substantive Chancery rules but actively refuted any attempts at drawing parallels. A distinct lack of sources, apart from St. German's second-hand account, has allowed them to portray any such attempts as speculative history based on religious motivations rather than scientific interests. The later adoption of the case law method in Chancery might additionally have relegated questions as to the moral theological motivations of late medieval or early modern Chancellors to the academic sidelines.

Klinck, however, highlighted the potential for further research in an area that has long been neglected for its apparent lack of a legal dimension. His trans-

82 For a more differentiated assessment of *Coing*'s theses, see below chapter VI, 2.

83 St. Mathew 18, 15: "If your brother or sister sins, go and point out their fault, just between the two of you. If they listen to you, you have won them over. But if they will not listen, take one or two others along, so that every matter may be established by the testimony of two or three witnesses. If they still refuse to listen, tell it to the church; and if they refuse to listen to even the church, treat them as you would a pagan or a tax collector."

84 *D. Klinck*, Conscience, Equity and the Court of Chancery in Early Modern England, Ashgate, Farnham, 2010.

85 For a more detailed analysis, see my review <www.forhistiur.de/zitat/1306harbecke.htm>.

disciplinary approach is in line with recent developments in jurisprudence and legal history.[86] It suggests that the interplay of different normative orders in late medieval and early modern England holds the potential of providing a fruitful ground for a broader understanding of common law legal history that is compatible with both existing legal as well as extra-legal scholarship on normativity.[87] Ignoring important external factors like religion, especially during a time when the differentiation of law, religion and morality was still very much incomplete, bears the risk of getting caught within a limited internal perspective.

5. Conclusion

Overall, the literature on the Court of Chancery covers a broad range of interests. A combined reading of the secondary sources offers a fairly consistent image of the work of the court. At the same time, I hope to have shown that the existing scholarship fails to provide a comprehensive theorization of the function of the role of the Court of Chancery in its formation and expansion period. While all of the referenced works would deserve a separate assessment in this regard, I will limit myself to a short review of the four categories presented above.

The practice-oriented literature naturally forewent any attempt at theorising the role of the Court of Chancery. The respective authors instead focussed on providing a collection of facts about the actual work of the court. In particular, the structure of their works was characterized by an unsophisticated classification of cases into narrow categories of legal instruments. While the referenced 19th century treatises aimed beyond these limitations through a more systematic presentation of equity history and law, they arguably remained trapped in their practical aspirations. The internal perspective is characteristic for any practice-oriented account. The comparative element was furthermore limited to the most

86 For such developments in legal history, see for example *T. Duve*, European Legal History – Global Perspectives. Working Paper for the Colloquium European Normativity – Global Historical Perspectives, Max Planck Institute for European Legal History Research Paper Series 2013–06 (2012), especially p. 21–22. For a recent example of such a study on St. German, see *I. Williams*, Christopher St. German – Religion, Conscience and Law in Reformation England, in: M. Hill / R. H. Helmholz (eds.), Great Christian Jurists in English History, Cambridge University Press, Cambridge, 2017, p. 69–92.

87 For an example of a recent study on the role of the law of nature in the practical adjudication of English courts, see *R. H. Helmholz*, Natural Law in Court – A History of Legal Theory in Practice, Harvard University Press, Cambridge, Ma., 2015.

intuitive comparisons to procedural and substantive rules of common law and Roman law.

The classical common law legal historians took the most courageous steps towards an integration of external, extra-legal, perspectives. They adjusted to the intellectual climate of the time by incorporating evolutionary ideas into their legal history. This led them to actively search for re-emerging patterns in the history of the common law tradition. The ambition to engage with ideas of the other natural and social sciences was palpable. At the same time, and quite possibly relatedly, the classical legal historians were also strongly driven by what could be considered ideological considerations, i. e. the establishment of a dominance of Germanic roots in the common law or its economic superiority.[88] However, even to the extent that this pitfall was avoided, their works generally lacked the truly comparative perspective that I have advocated for the identification of the function of the Court of Chancery. For once, the focus on national narratives generally impeded a look at other legal systems. Additionally, the works commonly addressed specific equitable instruments rather than the institution Court of Chancery as such. The natural objects of comparison were thus Germanic or canon law legal instruments rather than courts or legal systems.

The focus on source analysis in the 20th century institutional accounts has contributed greatly to increased historical accuracy. However, this also cut off ties to other social sciences and even to other legal sub-disciplines. Many accounts consciously rejected the transfer of late medieval or early modern English concepts to other time periods or places. They effectively proclaimed an isolated and idiosyncratic legal history, thereby risking the ability to engage in both a wider legal and an inter-disciplinary discourse. In a similar vein, the 20th century institutional accounts have been widely successful in establishing the role of the Court of Chancery in relation to common law and ecclesiastical courts and thus shown the merits of a comparative method. Instead of applying these insights for a theorisation of the role of the Court of Chancery that addresses its function from a comparative perspective, however, the institutional accounts in question have stopped at refining what I have called intuitive comparisons.

The examination of a moral theological dimension of Chancery adjudication represents the integration of an external perspective. In particular, the more recent works in this category advocated a wide understanding of normativity that holds the potential for inspiring further inter-disciplinary approaches. As of now, the inter-disciplinary dialogue in this context is limited to law and theology

88 See *D. Rabban*, The Historiography of the Common Law, Law and Society, Volume 28 (2003), p. 1161–1201, especially 1186–1190.

and is thus still in its infancy. Additionally, the interesting comparative question as to whether the relationship of law and theology in the Court of Chancery might be considered distinctly English has not yet been addressed.

The identification of limitations in the secondary literature must not be understood as an undifferentiated criticism. The literature often reflects an understandable focus on individual interests and expertise. Equally, I will not be able to address all the limitations highlighted in this chapter within this book. However, I hope to have shown that the identification of the specific function of the Court of Chancery in the development of the common law tradition merits further attention.

Chapter IV

Sources

For the purpose of presenting the typical features of the late medieval Chancery process, I will rely chiefly on 15th centuries sources.This is for both practical and theoretical reasons. Surviving sources from the first decades of the Court of Chancery in the second half of the 14th century are scarce.[1] Additionally, the jurisdiction of the court in this era was deeply intertwined with and hardly distinguishable from that of the council (*curia regis*).[2] With regard to the 16thcentury, a detailed examination of Chancery sources under the influential Chancellorship of Cardinal Wolsey has already been published.[3] The end of his chancellorship in 1529 and the designation of Thomas More, the first common lawyer in the office, then, already marked the end of the early phase of Chancery.[4] By that time, the Court of Chancery was institutionally fully established and performing an indispensable function in royal conflict resolution. As shown by Wolsey's fall from Henry VIII's grace, even severe discontent with the officeholder could not challenge the authority of the institution *per se* anymore. It was thus arguably the 15th century that saw the Court of Chancery establish its autonomy and thus shaped the role of the early Court of Chancery within the English legal system. In the following chapters, I will nevertheless provide continuous reference to typical features of the earlier and the later Chancery process in order to highlight developments and integrate the findings of existing literature.

My identification of the 15th century process relies on Chancery documentation both in manuscript form as well as in edited form. It furthermore integrates the finding of earlier samples and several late medieval Year Book reports. In the following, I will present the existing manuscripts (1.), editions (2) and samples (3.) before characterising the documentation underlying my own research (4.). At last, I will address the role of Year Book reports for Chancery research (5.).

1 See below 1.
2 Compare above chapter II, 2.
3 *F. Metzger*, Das englische Kanzleigericht unter Kardinal Wolsey, Promotion an der Friedrich-Alexander-Universität Erlangen-Nürnberg, 1977.
4 See above chapter II, 3.3.

1. Manuscripts

The complete (discovered) documentation of the Court of Chancery is kept at the National Archives in Kew, London. It includes court proceedings from as early as the reign of Richard II (1377–1399) until the abolition of the court in 1875. The archival history of the late medieval files in particular is largely unknown. According to the information of the National Archives, the documents were once kept at the Six Clerks Office before being transferred to the Tower of London from where they were integrated into the Public Record Office at some stage after 1827.[5]

1.1 State of documentation

The late medieval documents (up to 1558) are kept under the reference *C 1: Court of Chancery: Six Clerks Office: Early Proceedings, Richard II to Philip and Mary.*[6] They have been divided into 1522 larger files. These files form the basis of my own research as well as of all earlier original work on the medieval Court of Chancery. The overall number of documents in the files is unknown but previous estimates have put the number of cases before 1500 at 90,000.[7] It is thus hardly surprising that no complete study of the late medieval sources has ever been undertaken and that most of the files have never been studied thoroughly. However, it is not only the sheer volume of the material that has hindered a closer examination of the majority of the files.[8] Many documents clearly show their 600-year history. Most of the records from before the second

5 Compare the catalogue of the National Archives at <discovery.nationalarchives.gov.uk/SearchUI/details?Uri=C3564>. The time at the Tower of London is confirmed by the Calendars of the Proceedings in Chancery in the Reign of Queen Elizabeth, To Which are Prefixed Examples of Earlier Proceedings from the Reign of Richard the Second to that of Queen Elizabeth, Inclusive, Public Record Office, London, Volume 1, 1827, which include a reference to "the originals in the tower" on their front-page.

6 Following the classification of the National Archives, reference to specific documents is made to category/file/document (e.g. C 1/1/1). A large part of the files (currently C 1/1 – C 1/456) has lately been digitalised by members of the Anglo-American Legal Tradition project of the University of Houston Law Center. The image files are available at <aalt.law.uh.edu/ChanPro.html>.

7 *T.S. Haskett*, The Presentation of Cases in Medieval Chancery Bills, in: W.M. Gordon / T.D. Fergus (eds.), Legal History in the Making – Proceedings of the Ninth Legal History Conference, Glasgow, 1989, Hambledon Press, London, 1991, p. 11–28, p. 11.

8 Also *T.S. Haskett*, The Presentation of Cases in Medieval Chancery Bills, in: W.M. Gordon / T.D. Fergus (eds.), Legal History in the Making – Proceedings oft he Ninth Legal History Conference, Glasgow, 1989, p. 11–28, p. 11.

half of the 15th century are written in Law French – an originally Norman language that was introduced by the Norman elite after the conquest and represented the standard language of the royal courts at the time.[9] Furthermore, the handwriting, which is of varying readability anyway, has partly become illegible due to environmental influences. A significant part of documents is furthermore incomplete or rendered useless through holes and missing pieces. Arguably, the number of preserved documents at least reduces the significance of such losses.

1.2 Content

Earlier scholars might also have been discouraged from a closer examination of the sources by the types of documents that were preserved from the late middle ages. Up to about 1440, the documentation consists exclusively of so-called bills – petitions from individuals for adjudication of a specified issue.[10] Only a small number of these bills include short court decrees on their backside – usually setting a hearing or dismissing the claim and only occasionally providing a complete decision. Several new types of documents supplementing the bills appear from 1440 onwards. These include the defendants' answers to the original bill as well as further party correspondence in the form of replications and rejoinders. A look through the files also offers a smaller number of witness depositions and procedural writs.[11]

1.3 Dating and order

In the absence of dated decrees or the mentioning of a specific date in the bills, most documents cannot be dated conclusively. The bills can merely be arranged chronologically by the name of the Lord Chancellor to whom they were addressed. For most documents,[12] the National Archives have thus relied on the chronology of the Lord Chancellors when ordering the files. Within a Chancellorship, the records have been arranged according to the first letter of

9 For an introduction, see *J. H. Baker*, Manual of Law French, Avebury, Letchworth, 1979.

10 A detailed examination of these bills will be provided in the following chapter, see below chapter V, 2.

11 All these procedural instances will be explained below in some detail, chapter V.

12 Some bills that address the Lord Chancellor impersonally cannot be classified in this manner and have thus apparently been left in the vicinity of the cases they were found with. The special case of the first three files – referenced as C 1/1, C 1/2 and C 1/3 – will be discussed below, 2.

the first plaintiff's surname.[13] It was only from 1544 onwards – and thus after my immediate research period – that final and interim decisions were recorded systematically in the so-called Entry books.[14]

The late medieval sources thus provide an insight into the everyday business of the late medieval Court of Chancery that is almost exclusively shaped by the litigants' perspective. This naturally complicates research on the work of the court as an institution.[15] On a more positive note, however, the documents offer an interesting and unusual view from the demand side of the proceedings. The available body of sources effectively facilitates a bottom-up reconstruction of the late medieval Chancery process.

2. Editions

Considering the state of the original documents, it is hardly surprising that much of the secondary work on the Court of Chancery has relied exclusively on printed editions of the sources. However, only a comparatively small share of late medieval Chancery documentation has actually been edited and printed. Research on the late medieval Court of Chancery has thus remained highly dependent upon two 19th century projects:[16] the Record Commission's *Calendars of the Proceedings in Chancery in the Reign of Queen Elizabeth, To Which are Prefixed Examples of Earlier Proceedings from the Reign of Richard the Second to that of Queen Elizabeth*[17] (hereinafter: *Calendars*) and the Selden Society's *Select Cases in Chancery* (hereinafter: *Select Cases*).[18]

13 See <discovery.nationalarchives.gov.uk/SearchUI/details?Uri=C3564>.

14 The Entry books can also be found in the National Archives under the reference C 33.

15 It is thus understandable that earlier legal historians much preferred the common law Year Books that provide party pleadings as well as court opinions as research objects.

16 Apart from these two larger projects, some additional primary sources have been edited and printed on a case-by-case basis. See for example *L. O. Pike*, Common Law and Conscience in the Ancient Court of Chancery, in: Select Essays in Anglo-American Legal History, Little, Brown, and Company, Boston, Ma., Volume 2, 1908, p. 722–736; Some Proceedings in Chancery under Wolsey, Bulletin of the Institute of Historical Research, Volume 8 (1931), p. 17–20.

17 Calendars of the Proceedings in Chancery in the Reign of Queen Elizabeth, To Which are Prefixed Examples of Earlier Proceedings from the Reign of Richard the Second to that of Queen Elizabeth, Inclusive, Public Record Office, London, Volume 1 & 2, 1827.

18 W. P. Baildon (ed.), Select Cases in Chancery A. D. 1364 to 1471, Selden Society, London, 1896, p. 87.

2.1 Calendars of the Proceedings in Chancery

The cases printed in the *Calendars* were supposed to provide an introduction to a first comprehensive index of early Chancery proceedings.[19] They have been edited by the English Public Record Office on the initiative of the House of Commons between 1821 and 1827.[20] The documents chronologically cover proceedings from the reign of Richard II (1377–1399) to the reign of Elizabeth I (1558–1603). However, the Calendars include less than a dozen cases from the time after the reign of Henry VIII (1509–1547) – their focus thus clearly lies on the late medieval period. The first volume provided 131 and the second volume an additional 57 cases. Each of these cases is represented by a bill. A large number of cases from 1440 onwards was printed with additional documentation, most notably answers, replications or rejoinders. The editors translated the Law French of the original drafters into modern English, whereas originally English and Latin documents were merely transcribed.

2.2 Select Cases in Chancery

The *Select Cases* were edited by William P. Baildon for the Selden Society in the 1890s. As suggested by the subtitle of the collection, the sample included cases from 1364 to 1471. According to the editor, the volume offered a complete edition of the earliest file identifiable at the Public Record Office at the time[21] and a smaller number of selected cases. Overall, Baildon provided another 147 late medieval Chancery cases. The presentation was modelled closely after the *Calendars*: documents in Law French were translated into modern English and additional documents – other than the bills – were provided whenever available.

2.3 Case selection

The 19th century printed editions thus include more than 330 cases. They provide a most valuable introduction to the activities of the Court of Chancery in the late Middle Ages. Despite the relatively large number of cases, however, it seems advisable to avoid direct empirical conclusions from the available sample. The selection process for the *Calendars* remains a mystery. The *Calendars* themselves provide no information whatsoever. Baildon submitted that "we have no means of knowing what principle of selection was exercised", although the cases printed

19 Compare Calendars I, introduction.
20 Compare Calendars I, introduction.
21 The same file is now available at the National Archives under the reference C 1/3.

in the *Calendars* were of "very great interest and value",[22] thus possibly suggesting a selection on the basis of their importance for the development of the jurisdiction of the Court of Chancery. On my own revisitation of the *Calendars*, I have equally failed to identify any other (steady) chronological or thematic patterns.[23] Being aware of this problem with the *Calendars*, Baildon laid open his own selection process for the *Select Cases in Chancery*. He edited the complete earliest available file at the Public Record Office and complemented it with a smaller selection of cases he deemed interesting.[24] For the purpose of quantitative studies about the work of the court, this approach is obviously equally problematic. We have no information about the criteria for the original filing of Chancery documents that Baildon was confronted with but later filing efforts have identified thousands of other documents from the same time period. Taking these into account, Baildon's selection merely seems to represent another random sample. While the printed editions of primary sources thus provide a most valuable insight into the late medieval Court of Chancery process, they do not offer a representative impression of the practical work of the court.

3. Samples

Several scholars have tried to address this shortcoming by assembling what they considered representative samples from the late medieval sources.

3.1 Studies

In 1960, Margaret Avery undertook a first systematic attempt to identify the issues at the heart of late medieval Chancery suits and their development over time.[25] She thereby relied exclusively on bills from Essex and Kent before 1460. The problem of limiting the sample to rural areas was later exposed by Nicholas Pronay.[26] He counted the early Chancery bills from the National Archives

22 *W. P. Baildon*, in: Select Cases, p. xi.

23 The order in which the cases are presented suggests that the editors focused on certain subject areas for specific dates. As such, claims for *corpus cum causa* or injunctions as well as trust cases appear in noticeable accumulation over a certain timeframe. A look at the manuscripts shows that this accumulation does not represent a representative portrayal of the work of the court at the time.

24 *W. P. Baildon*, in: Select Cases, p. xii.

25 *M. E. Avery*, The History of the Equitable Jurisdiction of Chancery before 1460, Bulletin of the Institute of Historical Research, Volume 42 (1969), p. 129–144, table on p. 131.

26 *N. Pronay*, The Chancellor, the Chancery, and the Council at the End of the Fifteenth Century, in: H. Hearder / H. R. Loyn (eds.), British Government and Administration – Studies Presented to S. B. Chrimes, University of Wales Press, Cardiff, 1974, p. 87–103.

between 1387 and 1529 that were directly attributable to a certain chancellorship. When calculating the average yearly numbers of cases for each chancellorship, he found significant deviations from Avery's numbers. A closer look at the content of the bills showed that Avery's rural sample consisted mostly of property cases, whereas the great share of commercial cases from the larger cities had remained undiscovered.[27] A larger attempt to gain representative information about early Chancery proceedings was undertaken by Timothy Haskett and his team in the 1990s.[28] Haskett operated with a random selection of about 150 cases per year for seven sample periods (each covering between three and ten years) between 1417 and 1532. In contrast to earlier studies, he examined not only the number of cases and the substantive issues addressed but also what he calls the 'demography' of the court – gender, occupation and social status of the litigants. A similarly detailed analysis was undertaken by Franz Metzger with regard to the chancellorship of Cardinal Wolsey.[29] This study included all bills addressed to Wolsey that Metzger was able to identify from the primary sources. It thus avoids the problem of representativeness that the aforementioned samples were inherently faced with. On the other hand, the alleged uniqueness of Wolsey's chancellorship[30] calls for increased care before drawing conclusions about the general development of the Court of Chancery at the end of the Middle Ages.

3.2 Aims of the studies

Two basic questions are at the heart of all these research projects: How exactly did the caseload of the Court of Chancery develop and what issues were adjudicated? These two questions are generally linked by the hypothesis that it was the adjudication of specific issues that caused the overall expansion of the court in the late Middle Ages. Indeed, this hypothesis has sometimes unquestionably been taken for granted.[31] What should have immediately called it into

27 *M. Beilby*, The Profits of Expertise: The Rise of the Civil Lawyers and Chancery Equity, in: M. Hicks (ed.), Profit, Piety and the Professions in Later Medieval England, Sutton, Gloucester, 1990, p. 72–90, effectively reconciled both studies by explaining their different approaches and integrating undated bills that had been largely ignored by *N. Pronay*.

28 *T. S. Haskett*, The Late Medieval Court of Chancery, Law and History Review, Volume 14 (1996), p. 245–313, especially p. 280–313.

29 *F. Metzger*, Das englische Kanzleigericht unter Kardinal Wolsey, tables on p. 332–335.

30 See above chapter II, 3.3.

31 See for example *M. E. Avery*, The History of the Equitable Jurisdiction of Chancery before 1460, Bulletin of the Institute of Historical Research, Volume 42 (1969), p. 129–144.

question, however, is the sheer variety of issues the Court of Chancery dealt with and their non-systematic character. My identification of the functions of the late medieval Court of Chancery will thus stress the importance of its procedure – the common element of all suits.[32]

Nonetheless, it is the significant expansion of the Court of Chancery in the late medieval period that justifies a closer examination of its function within the wider legal system. That is why I have already assessed the available data on the workload of the Court of Chancery above in chapter II.[33] While all available material confirms a significant expansion of the workload of the court throughout the 15th century, the deviations in the different samples with regard to concrete numbers[34] or shorter time periods[35] mandate attention. They clearly speak of the problems that the scholars involved faced with regard to both the identification of suitable sources as well as their representative character.[36] At this stage, it should suffice to say that the respective samples present a varied – and potentially incompatible – picture of the substantive issues the Court of Chancery dealt with.

4. Selection of sources

4.1 Editions

My following assessment of the Chancery process will heavily rely on the sources printed in the *Calendars* and the *Select Cases* as well as those edited and printed

32 See below chapters V–VII.

33 My conclusions there depend on the samples presented above as well as on secondary sources.

34 Compare *F. Metzger*, Das englische Kanzleigericht unter Kardinal Wolsey, p. 332, and *N. Pronay*, The Chancellor, the Chancery, and the Council at the End of the Fifteenth Century, in: H. Hearder/H.R. Loyn (eds.), British Government and Administration – Studies Presented to S.B. Chrimes, p. 87–103, p. 89, who estimated the yearly average of cases under Cardinal Wolsey's chancellorship at 534 and 770 respectively – a deviation of 44 % despite a seemingly corresponding sample.

35 While *N. Pronay*, The Chancellor, the Chancery, and the Council at the End of the Fifteenth Century, in: H. Hearder/H.R. Loyn (eds.), British Government and Administration – Studies Presented to S.B. Chrimes, p. 87–103, p. 88–89 considered the Yorkist Period (1461–1485) the main expansion phase of the Court of Chancery, *M.E. Avery*, The History of the Equitable Jurisdiction of Chancery before 1460, Bulletin of the Institute of Historical Research, Volume 42 (1969), p. 129–144, situated the decisive developments in the Lancastrian period (before 1461).

36 For the fragmentary character of the documents preserved at the National Archives, see above 1.1.

individually. Despite their unrepresentative character, the overall regularity of the proceedings evidenced in the sources suggests their suitability for the reconstruction of the late medieval Chancery process. Taken together, the printed editions also cover Chancery proceedings for all chancellorships throughout the 15th century. It thus seems possible to identify and date developments in the 15th century Chancery process.

4.2 Manuscripts

I have compared the printed sources with the files held at the National Archives in Kew under the reference numbers C 1/1, C 1/2 and C 1/3. The vast majority of cases edited and printed in the 19th century collections has survived the changes of location and can be found in one of the aforementioned files.[37] Sometimes several versions of documents relating to the same case can be found[38] – suggesting revisions on the initiative of either the parties themselves or the clerks in Chancery.[39] In a few instances, additional documents, relating to a case in the *Calendars* or the *Select Cases of Chancery* but not printed therein, have been added to the archived files.[40]

While a focus on the edited sources carries the risk of ignoring exceptional cases, the selection seems sufficiently broad to allow an accurate portrayal of the standard 15th process. A random sighting of other files held at the National Archives under the reference C 1 has confirmed this impression. None of the documents showed significant procedural deviations from those to be found in the printed editions. I will identify the handful of cases, in which my sighting of the manuscripts provided additional information about the Chancery process. It is anyway highly doubtful whether the 15th century court felt legally bound by strict procedural rules at all. Characterising the standard process – rather than

37 References to cases in which I was unable to confirm the existence of the original file will include a respective note. Examples of such cases are *Sampson v Crewe* (1432–1443), Calendars I, p. xl; *Beauchamp v Norris* (1483–1495), Calendars I, p. cxii; *Fellow v Meke* (1528–1531), Calendars I, p. cxxvii.

38 Again, specific reference will be made to the respective versions.

39 A concrete analysis of revised files and a consideration of possible explanations can be found in *T. S. Haskett*, The Presentation of Cases in Medieval Chancery Bills, in: W. M. Gordon / T. D. Fergus (eds.), Legal History in the Making – Proceedings of the Ninth British Legal History Conference, Glasgow, 1989, p. 11–28.

40 I will take these documents into account when referring to the respective cases. Whether the editors consciously decided to leave out certain documents or were unaware of their existence remains unclear. For an example, see the numerous documents relating to the case *Babington v Gull* (1456–1460), Calendars I, p. lvi; additional documents in C 1/1/78–85c.

identifying singular exceptions – might thus represent the most helpful approach for understanding the late medieval Court of Chancery.

4.3 Samples

The quantitative analysis of the cases addressed to the court will play a minor role in my presentation of the Chancery process. Where, however, such an approach is necessary, I will rely on a critical reassessment of the available samples. While their often-unrepresentative character and their different objectives remain problematic,[41] they should provide sufficient information to promote my main aim of understanding the function of the late medieval Court of Chancery. Indeed, it seems currently impossible for an individual legal scholar to provide a better sample than the ones already available. While the catalogue of the National Archives provides the 'subject matter' of all the cases under the reference C 1, this information remains unsuitable for legal analysis. The reference to the subject matter is purely factual. It merely allows for a preliminary classification to a related field (for example property or commerce). The information might be of a certain interest for a social history but rarely provides insights into legal issues underlying the claims. A useful quantitative analysis would require the complete revisitation of the files by a group of scholars with clear research objectives based on the development of legal doctrine.

5. Year Books

Due to the limitations of the preserved sources, the litigants' perspective necessarily dominates accounts of the late medieval Court of Chancery. There is, however, one further source, which provides an initial impression of the court's involvement in the proceedings and its decisions. The Year Books effectively represent the forerunner of law reporting in the common law courts.[42] They were produced regularly between the later 13th and the earlier 16th century.[43] For the most part, they included transcriptions of pleadings

41 See above, 3.

42 *J. H. Langbein/R. T. Lerner/B. P. Smith,* History of the Common Law – The Development of Anglo-American Legal Institutions, Aspen Publishers, New York, NY, 2009, p. 179–180.

43 As an introduction to the history of Year Books, see *T. F. T. Plucknett,* A Concise History of the Common Law, Butterworth, London, 5th edition, 1956, p. 268–273.

before the common law courts.[44] Their origin has remained somewhat elusive. For many centuries, they were assumed to represent official court records.[45] Maitland, however, characterised them as student notes for educational purposes.[46]

Throughout the Year Books, cases heard in the Court of Chancery show up occasionally. Lately, W. H. Bryson has collected and edited the Chancery cases from the Year Books between 1325 and 1508.[47] Many of these cases follow the common law writ pattern and must thus be allocated to the Latin side of Chancery, which was adjudicating common law business.[48] Several others, however, clearly follow the standard – later to be termed equitable – Chancery process.[49] It is not entirely clear why these cases were occasionally included in the Year Books. Since generally the same lawyers acted in front of both common law courts and the Court of Chancery, Maitland's educational thesis might offer a clue. Aspiring lawyers would also need to learn about the Chancery process. Considering the vicinity of the courts in Westminster Hall, the inclusion was furthermore practical. As far as it offers additional insights, I will integrate the information from the Year Books into my following discussion of the late medieval Chancery process.

44 Due to the work of *D. Seipp*, the digitalised Year Book files can be searched and accessed through the homepage of the Boston University School of Law <www.bu.edu/phpbin/lawyearbooks/search.php>.

45 *J. H. Baker*, The Common Law Tradition – Lawyers, Books and the Law, Hambledon Press, London, 2000, p. 141.

46 *J. H. Baker*, The Common Law Tradition: Lawyers, Books and the Law, p. 145.

47 W. H. Bryson (ed.), Reports of Chancery in the Middle Ages (1325–1508), Dog Ear Publishing, Indianapolis, In., 2016.

48 W. H. Bryson (ed.), Reports of Chancery in the Middle Ages (1325–1508), p. 6. The search results at <www.bu.edu/phpbin/lawyearbooks/search.php> offer information about both the adjudicating body as well as the respective course of action (if applicable). The distinction between the common law and the extraordinary jurisdiction of the Court of Chancery at this stage, however, was notoriously unclear. See above chapter II, 2.3.

49 See J. H. Baker / S. F. C. Milsom (eds.), Sources of English Legal History – Private Law to 1750, Butterworths, London, 1986, S. 94–95; 98–99.

Chapter V

The Chancery process in the 15th century

1. Introduction

It will be my hypothesis that flexibility was the chief characteristic of the late medieval Court of Chancery process and a key aspect of its success.[1] It should thus be both impossible and undesirable to provide a complete portrayal of all the intricacies of the late medieval Chancery process. That is especially true for a work, which is chiefly concerned with the role of the court in the development of the English legal system. As the following discussion will show, Chancery procedure was created practically through the regular adjudication of cases rather than systematically. Already-established rules were dispensed when the resolution of individual cases required it. My aim is thus to provide a general illustration of the opportunities which the Court of Chancery process offered for late medieval litigants. Given the object of theorising the role of the Court of Chancery, my emphasis will firmly lie on a comparative analysis of the procedural developments rather than on presenting an exact image of the court's everyday business.

1.1 Research period

The development of Chancery procedure, however, could hardly be described as linear. Indeed, other authors have already identified two sharply distinct periods in the development of the Court of Chancery in the 15th century. Michael Macnair has suggested that we should distinguish between the first half of the 15th century, in which "the jurisdiction was developing but we know too little about it to be confident of its shape" and the second half, in which "Chancery's judicial staff were civilians or canonists and [...] the court began to have a perceptible shape as a jurisdiction".[2] Macnair based the distinction on the practical availability of sources on the one hand and on the professionalization of the staff on the other hand.[3]

1 See below chapter VII.

2 *M.R.T. Macnair*, Equity and Conscience, Oxford Journal of Legal Studies, Volume 27 (2007), p. 659–681, p. 670.

3 *N. Pronay*, The Chancellor, the Chancery, and the Council at the End of the Fifteenth Century, in: H. Hearder/H.R. Loyn (eds.), British Government and

The former ground for distinction is clearly sensible. It is from around the year 1440 that the original bills in the Chancery files are supplemented by answers, replications, rejoinders, witness testimony and sometimes even decrees. The reason for this probably lies in a shift from oral to written practice in the court.[4] How else the Chancery process differed between the first and the second half of the 15th century must remain a mystery. Given the absence of information, the Chancery process of the first half of the 15th century remains largely in the dark. That is also why my research mostly relies on cases from the second half of the 15th century.

The second ground for distinction, however, seems more questionable. The existing sources from the 15th century evidence a gradual evolvement rather than any abrupt changes. The canonists and civilians, who came to occupy the leading positions in the Court of Chancery, hardly caused a revolution. They rather exerted their influence on the process gradually through practical modifications. I will refer to this evolvement in the Chancery process throughout this chapter.

1.2 Structure

For the purpose of illustration, I will discuss the multiple stages of the process from initiation to execution with reference to the case of *Ardern v Ardern*.[5] I have selected this case as my main example for two reasons: First, it bears a strong resemblance to a trust constellation – seemingly the most common issue before Chancery at the time and certainly its most lasting legacy – and should thus evoke feelings of familiarity in most readers. Second, and more importantly, the process was documented thoroughly and can thus, to a great extent, be reconstructed through primary sources. The focus on an exemplary case obviously bears the risk of neglecting the variety of conflicts in the Court of Chancery. That is why *Ardern v Ardern* should rather be understood as a guide through the stages of the 15th century Chancery process than as an exemplary case. The following discussion will be oriented along the way of the documentation in *Ardern v Ardern*. Yet, this way will also provide ample opportunities for detours towards questions of a more theoretical nature (for example jurisdiction, conscience or extra-judicial conflict resolutions) as well as towards other types of cases (for example *corpus cum causa*, *certiorari* or injunction).

Administration – Studies Presented to S. B. Chrimes, University of Wales Press, Cardiff, 1974, p. 87–103, stressed the importance of the new personnel in the Court of Chancery even more decisively.

4 See below 2.4.1.

5 (1465/1466), Calendars I, p. lxiii.

1.3 Perspective

The limited source material effectively prescribes the perspective from which the late medieval materials can be assessed. Since the sources mostly consist of party-drafted documents, our understanding of the late medieval Court of Chancery is based on a view from the demand side of the proceedings. This might be considered an opportunity as much as it is a challenge. The parties might very well have presented a biased image of their respective disputes and their perspective might distort the reality of the 15th century process. On the other hand, however, the documents can help us to understand how litigants made use of the opportunities provided by the Chancery process and thereby potentially shaped its development. The last decades have witnessed a general shift in legal history from the study of institutions to the study of actors. The study of the late medieval Court of Chancery dissolves this antagonism by relying on the actors for the understanding of the institution.

1.4 Outlook

As outlined above, my presentation of the 15th century Chancery process will follow the documentation in the case of *Ardern v Ardern* – essentially from initiation to execution. As a first step, I will thus address the opening of Chancery proceedings through the plaintiff's bill (2.). This will be followed by a discussion of the further party documentation – in the form of answer, replication and rejoinder (further pleadings, 3.). My focus will then turn to the questions how the court sought to establish the truth of the matter (evidence, 3.) and how cases were finally resolved in or with the help of the Court of Chancery (determination, 4.). During each of these stages, I will continually compare the Chancery process with the contemporary process of the common law courts in order to identify reactions and innovations with a broader impact on the system of royal conflict resolution in late medieval England.

2. Bill

The bill functioned as the starting point for every suit in the late medieval Court of Chancery. By the middle of the 15th century, a certain canon of form for Chancery bills was established.[6] In order to fully understand the purpose of the

6 Also *T. S. Haskett*, The Presentation of Cases in Medieval Chancery Bills, in: W. M. Gordon / T. D. Fergus, Legal History in the Making – Proceedings of the Ninth British Legal History Conference, Glasgow, 1989, Hambledon Press, London, 1991, p. 11–28, p. 11.

bills, it will be necessary to identify their general structure. The plaintiff's bill in *Ardern v Ardern* will serve as a starting point.

> *Ardern v Ardern*[7]
> *To the most reverent Father in God and full noble and gracious lord the Archbishop of York and Chancellor of England.*
> *Beseechs meekly your humble servant and orator Walter Ardern esquire, that where one John Ardern his younger brother piteously and lamentably to him complaining, saying that where it was so that he had no living to live upon like a gentleman but upon your said beseecher, desiring him to make a grant by deed unto the said John for time of his life of a manor in the shire of Worcester called Pedmore, your said beseecher, having pity of his said brother and by mediation of one Agnes Middelmore and Richard son to the same Agnes, enfeoffed*[8] *the said John Ardern in and of the said manor to have him time of his life, and that feoffment, notwithstanding it was fully conditioned and agreed between the said John Ardern and your said beseecher that the same John should take no profits of the said manor during the life of your said beseecher, but after his death to enter and occupy time of his life, and to this intent the deed was delivered to the said Agnes and Richard by your said beseecher safely to keep during his life, and then immediately after his death the said Agnes to deliver the deed to the said John Ardern to the intent abovesaid. And now gracious lord the said Agnes and Richard contrary to the said agreement for favour which they owed to the said John have delivered to the same John the said deed of feoffment, whereupon he has entered into the said manor and put out your said beseecher, and will not suffer him to take a penny of the rent nor would not this three year and more, contrary to his said agreement and contrary to all right and conscience, to the great hurt of your said beseecher without your good and gracious lordship onto him showed in this behalf. Wherefore please it your said good and gracious lordship the promises to consider and how your said beseecher may have no remedy in this case by the course of the common law, to grant a writ subpoena to be direct to the said John Ardern and Richard Middelmore commanding them to appear before the king in his Chancery at the XVth of Easter next coming upon pain of CC. li. to answer to the promises, and to do and receive there as faith right and good conscience requiring in this behalf, for the love of God and in the way of charity.*
> *Plegii de prosequendo*
> *William Levyng de Bromwicham in County Staffordshire yoman*
> *Thomas Comeplane de eadam yoman*[9]

Before examining the bill as a legal instrument for the opening of a Chancery process, I will quickly recapitulate the basic facts for the purpose of clarification.

7 (1465/1466), Calendars I, p. lxxii. For the purpose of readability, I have adjusted the orthography to modern English.

8 A feoffment in English feudal law was effectively a transfer of freehold land. Compare W. Jowitt / C. Walsh (eds.), The Dictionary of English Law, Sweet & Maxwell, London, Volume 1, 1959, p. 795.

9 The *plegii de prosequendo* – pledges for the prosecution – have not been added to the transcriptions in the Calendars. Since the declaration of sureties was a routine matter in the second half of the 15th century, the words in the declaration were mostly abbreviated. I have completed the words in order to allow for a better understanding.

The name of the case carries within it the promise of great family drama. The plaintiff Walter was the older of the two brothers who were parties to the dispute. His habit of disposing over manors in Worcester suggests that he might have been the (sole) heir to a respectable fortune. His younger brother John, on the other hand, seems to have been the victim of primogeniture and thus a man of less fortunate circumstances. Understandably, Walter took pity in John's continuous laments about his living conditions, which even forbade him to live the life of a respectable English gentleman. It should not be forgotten that the following events are presented from Walter's perspective. Walter thus agreed to transfer the title to the manor in Worcester to his younger brother. Most conveniently, however, the full effect of the transfer was only to take effect upon Walter's death: The profits from the land should remain with Walter until then. Agnes and Richard Middelmore were effectively designated as executors for this promise and were therefore also entrusted with the title deeds. The elaborate construction can only be properly understood as a circumvention of feudal inheritance rules.[10] The elaboration, however, proved worthless when John decided that he was no longer to wait for his brother's timely demise and that it was time to finally start living like a gentleman. Conniving with the Middelmores, who owed him a favour, he took possession first of the title deed and then of the Worcester manor. Walter, our generous benefactor, was thus left without both possession of and profits from the land. An appeal to the Lord Chancellor represented his only hope for justice.

2.1 Structure of the bill

Ardern v Ardern exemplifies the typical structure of 15th century Chancery bills. My examination of the Chancery process will follow the topics addressed in the bill step-by-step in an attempt to characterise the main issues concerning the opening of proceedings in the late medieval Court of Chancery. The bill commenced with the obligatory address (2.2) to the Lord Chancellor, before presenting the parties to the proceedings in the opening (2.3) of the bill. The main part of the bill was then reserved for the plaintiff's presentation of the problem (2.4) to the court. Walter Ardern's bill also addressed the fundamental medieval issue of jurisdiction (2.5) in passing. The final sentence then included the plaintiff's request for process (2.6) in the form of a subpoena and an appeal to

10 For a short introduction to typical feudal inheritance rules in medieval England, see below chapter VII, 1.4.1. A more differentiated introduction to feudal property law generally and inheritance rules specifically was provided by *J. H. Baker*, An Introduction to English Legal History, Butterworths, London, 4th edition, 2002, p. 223–297, especially p. 259–279.

conscience as the ground for relief (2.7). At the end of the bill, the plaintiff presented two sureties (2.8) for the potential costs and damages that might result from wrongful accusations. Under each of the aforementioned headings, I will provide additional examples from other cases in order to facilitate a full understanding of the first stage of the Chancery process. At the end of this subchapter, I will then try to identify the original drafters of the bills (2.9).

2.2 Address

The bill in *Ardern v Ardern* was addressed to George Neville (ca. 1432–1476; Lord Chancellor 1460–1467) in both of his functions as Archbishop of York and Lord Chancellor of England. The mentioning of both roles was typical for late medieval bills. Bills, which addressed the Lord Chancellor exclusively, were also fairly frequent in the first decades of the Court of Chancery.[11] Since the reference to the clerical post of the Lord Chancellor also represents the easiest way of dating Chancery bills, however, the reason for the absence of an address to the clerical role remain largely in the dark. This absence might, for the most part, coincide with the infrequent periods, in which secular officials held the chancellorship.[12]

From today's perspective, with the knowledge of later developments, it is the role of the Lord Chancellor that shaped the history of the equitable jurisdiction in the Court of Chancery. The continuity of the court's history overshadows the early involvement of clerical office holders. But we should be careful to project our hindsight knowledge on the plaintiffs in the medieval Court of Chancery. There is simply no indication that the clerical role of the Lord Chancellor was merely a negligible by-product and its mention a sheer courtesy. Two important caveats should be borne in mind.

First, the process of the differentiation of distinctive social spheres was merely at its very beginning in the late Middle Ages.[13] While law, religion and morality

11 See for example *Lavender v Hilton* (1383–1386), Select Cases, p. 1; *Brampton v. Seymour* (1383–1386), Select Cases, p. 2; *Horsmonger v Pecham* (undated), Select Cases, p. 120; *Fryday v West* (undated), Select Cases, p. 123.

12 For example the chancellorships of Robert de Thorpe (1371–1372), John Knyvet (1372–1377), Richard le Scrope (1378–1379; 1381–1382), Michael de la Pole (1383–1386), John de Scarle (1399–1401), Thomas Beaufort (1410–1412), Richard Neville (1454–1455). Dates taken from W. P. Baildon (ed.), Select Cases in Chancery A. D. 1364 to 1471, Selden Society, London, 1896, List of Chancellors.

13 The differentiation of law and religion was elaborated meticulously by *P. Prodi*, Eine Geschichte der Gerechtigkeit: Vom Recht Gottes zum modernen Rechtsstaat, C. H. Beck, Munich, 2003, transl. by A. Seemann.

were identified as separate normative orders, contemporaries accepted and possibly even expected communication between the diverging normativities.[14] While the common law was already firmly established as a secular system of social control – albeit not without a moral dimension –,[15] the purely secular character of the Court of Chancery might not have been equally well established in the minds of the petitioners.[16] On the contrary, the combination of both secular and spiritual authority in the person of the Lord Chancellor might have been an attractive feature for litigants trying to navigate the different challenges posed by economic pressures on the one hand and diverging secular and spiritual normative orders on the other hand.

Second, the dual role of the Lord Chancellors as bishops might have raised concrete expectations on behalf of the petitioners. Walter Ardern asked the Lord Chancellor to act "for the love of God and in the way of charity". In the deeply devout society of late medieval England,[17] such a wish must not necessarily raise concrete implications – it could just as well be the formal invocation of a communally shared self-conception. The fact that it was addressed to one of the public figureheads of the church in England, however, could also suggest that the plaintiffs expected a decision somehow compatible with the (moral) standards of the church. Whether this expectation was indeed met or not is the central question of the literature on Chancery and moral theology.[18]

2.3 Opening

The 15th century bills typically start with an appeal to the Lord Chancellor to take note of the case.[19] The regularity of form in the Chancery bills is underlined

14 For an introduction, see *H.J. Berman*, Law and Revolution – The Formation of the Western Legal Tradition, Harvard University Press, Cambridge, Ma., 1983, especially p. 273–275.

15 See *N. Doe*, Fundamental Authority in Late Medieval English Law, Cambridge University Press, Cambridge, 1990, p. 132–154. It also seems important to remember that the role of clerics in the formation of the common law was hardly less influential than their role in the formation of the Court of Chancery. A closer examination of their general role in Norman nation-building was provided by *A. Boureau*, La Loi du Royaume – Les Moines, le Droit et la Construction de la Nation Anglaise (XIe-XIIIe siècles), Les Belles Lettres, Paris, 2001.

16 Equally, the distinction between office and office holder is a typical feature of modern associations, hardly adaptable to the context of the late English feudal system.

17 For an early modern account, see *M. Fortier*, The Culture of Equity in Early Modern England, Ashgate, Farnham, 2005.

18 See the overview above, chapter III, 4., with references.

19 *T.S. Haskett*, The Presentation of Cases in Medieval Chancery Bills, in: W.M. Gordon/T.D. Fergus, Legal History in the Making – Proceedings of the Ninth

by the reoccurrence of certain typical phrases at the outset of the bill. The formula "beseechs meekly", which appeared in *Ardern v Ardern*, and its French pendant "*supplie humblement*"[20] represent the most common examples. Luckily for identification purposes, the introductory formula is immediately followed by the plaintiff's name.

The plaintiffs commonly associated themselves with subservient attributes. Walter Ardern referred to himself as the Lord Chancellor's "humble servant". The hierarchical character of the medieval society suggests that such invocations should be understood as mere etiquette – or at best as a formal acknowledgement of the Lord Chancellor's power. More interestingly, many early petitioners additionally described themselves as "poor".[21] In this context, the attribute "poor" must usually refer rather to the current position of the petitioner as a victim of unfortunate circumstances than to actual poverty. This can be concluded not only from the matters in dispute but also from the occupation or rank of the petitioners, which often followed the mentioning of their names. This information additionally allows for interesting insights into the accessibility of the court and the class structure underlying it. Studies on the demography of the court have revealed that the 15th century court was most commonly frequented by lay gentry, esquires and knights, ecclesiastical office holders and tradesmen.[22] The name of the defendant was generally mentioned in connection with his or her alleged actions – mostly also at the very beginning. The occupation or rank of the defendant was provided whenever it revealed relevant information with regard to the case. In *Ardern v Ardern*, the only relevant information about the defendant from the plaintiff's point of view was the fact that he was his brother. From all we know, this might also have been John's only 'occupation'.

British Legal History Conference, Glasgow, 1989, p. 11–28, p. 12, addressed the first part of the bill under the self-explanatory Latin title of *incipit*.

20 See for early examples *van der Mere v Merchants of Gascony* (1386–1388), Select Cases, p. 3; *Milner v Brambre* (1388), Select Cases, p. 8; *Bond v Bond* (1410–1412), Select Cases, p. 100.

21 See for example *Tregoys v Earl of Warwick* (1388–1396), Calendars I, p. ii; *Bief v Dyer* (1377–1399), Calendars I, p. xi; *Raulyn v Bugules* (1396–1399), Select Cases, p. 23.

22 Relying on his own sample, see above chapter IV, 3, *T. S. Haskett*, The Medieval English Court of Chancery, Law and History Review, Volume 14 (1996), p. 245–313, p. 290, found that 43% of the parties in Chancery proceedings were of lay rank, whereas 28% held an ecclesiastical office and 21% were tradesmen. *T. S. Haskett* described the further distribution in the main category of lay rank as follows: 34% esquire, 23% knight, 18% gentleman, 7% yeoman, 5% husbandman, 5% urban citizen, 4% servant.

2.4 Problem

The description of the problem underlying the dispute was the key element of the respective bills. It provided the plaintiffs with the opportunity to present the facts from their own perspective, allowing them to set the subject matter and thereby the agenda for the further proceedings. From our modern-day perspective, this part of the bill looks thoroughly unspectacular. Describing the situation underlying the conflict between the parties in factual terms is a prerequisite for opening proceedings in both the common law as well as the civil law tradition. It might very well be described as an intuitive first step for a process of conflict resolution. However, what is most familiar or intuitive to us was a mark of distinction within the system of late medieval royal courts. The relationship between the common law writ system and the individually initiated bill in Chancery might provide a key to understanding the function of the Court of Chancery. Before elaborating on the differences to the contemporary common law process, I will return to the case of *Ardern v Ardern*.

2.4.1 Canon

The presentation of the problem in *Ardern v Ardern* followed a common pattern, which was identified by Timothy Haskett in his address to the Ninth British Legal History Conference in 1989.[23] Haskett subdivided the plaintiff's recollection of facts into three parts: recital, problem and conclusion. The recital described the circumstances of the case, usually including the plaintiff's original intention. Walter Ardern thus presented the scheme under which he originally intended his brother to receive the title to the Worcester manor. This included references to his motivation as well as to the exact design of the scheme and the parties involved. The problem then recalled the concrete events that lead to the emergence of the dispute, often the subversion of the original plan by the other party. In *Ardern v Ardern*, the conflict arose because John took possession of both the title deeds and the Worcester manor prematurely. At last, the conclusion portrayed the state in which the plaintiffs found themselves as a result of the aforementioned problem. Walter Ardern explained that he lost possession of the manor and was deprived of the profits from the land for three years.

The existence of a canon for formulating the factual issues in Chancery bills might have simplified their processing within the court. It also allowed for the relative brevity of the bills. This was certainly true for some standard issues of

23 *T. S. Haskett*, The Presentation of Cases in Medieval Chancery Bills, in: W. M. Gordon / T. D. Fergus, Legal History in the Making – Proceedings of the Ninth British Legal History Conference, Glasgow, 1989, p. 11–28, p. 12–13.

adjudication in the Court of Chancery. The numerous use cases lend themselves perfectly to the aforementioned three-partite structure. A use agreement was set up; its purpose was then subverted, commonly by the feoffees, which in turn left the intended beneficiary in a miserable situation.[24] The structure also suited what we might call contract formality cases in the late medieval Court of Chancery. The parties made a contractual agreement that was formalised by the exchange of bonds. After the exchange had been performed, one party refused to return the bond and claimed (double) performance, which left the other party vulnerable to common law judgment.[25] Statements of facts including recital, problem and conclusion can also be found in the *corpus cum causa* bills, in which the plaintiffs demand a writ to order their release from imprisonment by other public authorities. Such cases became more and more frequent in the second half of the 15th century.[26]

For other cases, however, this structure was less suited and the impression provided by the sources is that the drafters simply took a practical approach to the presentation of their problem. Cases of violent assault, in which the common law machinery failed to provide effective protection despite the availability of suitable (trespass) writs, were a common occurrence in the early Court of Chancery until the first half of the 15th century. Since plaintiff and defendant in these cases regularly lacked any pre-existing relationship, the bills immediately addressed what Haskett termed the problem.[27]

I have classified the above-mentioned cases according to the main issue underlying the dispute. What the steady reoccurrence of each of these classes might tell us is that such bills were commonly accepted for adjudication in the Court of Chancery. Obviously, later bills would be modelled after earlier successful petitions on a similar issue. When looking through the preserved sources in the light of our hindsight knowledge, we quickly identify recurring patterns. In fact, there can be no doubt that regularity ensued quickly once knowledge of the recognition of a certain instrument by the Court of Chancery

24 As examples for such use cases, in which the facts are presented in this three-partite structure, see *Wakeryng v Bayle* (1456–1460), Calendars I, p. lvii; *Tryppe v Chevin* (1483–1485), Calendars I, p. cxvi; *Peverell v Huse* (1492–1493), Calendars I, p. cxxii. The latter case is an appeal for an injunction against proceedings at common law that follows from the subversion of a use.

25 See *Brampton v Seymour* (1386), Select Cases, p. 2.

26 See for example *Howard v Sheriffs of London* (1467–1473), Calendars I, p. lxxxviii; *Foster v Sheriff of Kent* (1467–1473), Calendars I, p. lxxxix; *Kirkeman v Sheriffs of London* (1470), Calendars I, p. xci.

27 See for example *Bokelond v Bount* (1394), Select Cases, p. 12; *Pykworth v Sambroke* (1407), Select Cases, p. 87; *Beaufort v Puncherdon* (1410–1412), Select Cases, S. 97.

spread. Unfortunately, we lack the complete documentation of the earliest Chancery proceedings that would allow us to trace the establishment of a canon for a certain constellation of facts. Indeed, from all we know, this canon might originally have formed through oral petitions relying on guidance by the Chancery staff.[28] The recognition of this problem, however, leads us to the question of the originality of Chancery bills.

2.4.2 Variety

In no way was recourse to the early Court of Chancery limited to those most common classes of cases. Between hundreds of use, contract formation or trespass cases, we also find many other and often highly individual fact constellations. They represented – from the plaintiff's perspective – the expectation that the Court of Chancery could be addressed as a court of extraordinary jurisdiction in case of any failure of justice. This is what rendered the court manifestly distinct from the common law courts operating under the writ system. A few practical examples are in order:

In *Babington v Gull*,[29] the plaintiff was the executor of his mother's will. According to the conditions of this will, he had provided the defendant, who was a local priest, with a substantial amount of money that was to be used for the founding and operation of a chantry in his mother's home parish. The bill claims that, despite complete payment, no action had yet been taken by the defendant. Doctrinally, a parallel to the use cases can be established: The plaintiff asked for the enforcement of a promise, thus imposing what became to be known as a fiduciary duty on the defendant. It seems, however, unlikely that such an analogy caused the address to the Court of Chancery. The plaintiff's appeal probably had a simpler reason: As we will see when considering the available remedies in the royal courts, the common law courts were at this stage – irrespective of the question of recognition of oral promises – unable to order specific performance.[30]

The plaintiff in *Damico v Burdican*[31] was an Italian weaver, who had settled in Westminster with the King's permission in order to teach his trade. He claims to have been arrested on forged trespass allegations – possibly from concerned

28 For the existance of oral petitions before the 1440s, see *N. Pronay*, The Chancellor, the Chancery, and the Council at the End of the Fifteenth Century, in: H. Hearder/H. R. Loyn (eds.), British Government and Administration – Studies Presented to S. B. Chrimes, p. 87–103, p. 89, especially fn. 2.

29 (1458), Calendars I, p. lvi.

30 See below 5.2.3.3.

31 (1474–1480), Calendars I, p. ciii.

competitors – on one of his first visits to the city. Without any local support, he was unable to raise funds for bail and legal representation from prison. Damico thus feared conviction at common law. He appealed to the Court of Chancery to order his release (through a writ of *corpus cum causa*),[32] so that he could organise his defence. The case differs from the regular *corpus cum causa* cases in that the plaintiff did not contest the legitimacy of his imprisonment under common law. He rather contended that the regular process of the common law failed under the specific circumstances because of his status as a foreigner. With its staff of Latin-speaking civil lawyers and its diplomatic experience, the Chancery indeed became the natural addressee for continental European merchants and craftsmen with legal problems in England.[33]

The case of *Blank v Lynde*[34] was initiated by a doctor who treated the infected eye of the defendant's child. The child consequently lost his eyesight. The defendant had therefore originally sued the plaintiff in the sheriff's court. They had, however, not pressed for proceedings as long as the plaintiff was in the country. Once he had moved abroad, they tried to obtain damages from one of his sureties in the original common law action. The plaintiff claimed that he treated the child according to best medical practice and that it was the child's own behaviour – the rubbing of his eyes – that caused the deterioration. He also condemned the pursuance of the suit at a time when the defendants knew of his absence. The case raises several interesting legal issues. For one, it shows that medical treatment was already recognised as trespass to the person in late medieval common law. However, the case itself does not allow any conclusions on the legal approach to competent treatment or the effects of consent – the contested issues of contemporary medical law. It is also unclear whether Blank appealed to the Court of Chancery for *certiorari* (because of the legal intricacies of the case that required review by a higher court)[35] or simply because of his absence and the untimeliness of the original suit. Either way, the bill provides another illustration of the variety of cases the Court of Chancery was faced with in the 15th century.

32 See below 2.6.2.

33 Compare *N. Pronay*, The Chancellor, the Chancery, and the Council at the End of the Fifteenth Century, in: H. Hearder/H. R. Loyn (eds.), British Government and Administration – Studies Presented to S. B. Chrimes, p. 87–103, S. 96. With reference to staple town legislation, *N. Pronay* named the Lord Chancellor the "guardian of aliens". For more information, see below chapter VII, 1.4.3.

34 (1493–1500), Calendars I, p. cxxiv.

35 For a short introduction, see below 2.6.2.

2.4.3 *Conclusion*

Thousands of other cases could be presented. This selection, however, should suffice to provide an impression of the remarkable variety of cases in the late medieval Court of Chancery. From a legal perspective, the only thing all these cases have in common is the plaintiff's subjective impression of a failure of the regular course of justice. They confirm the historical classification of the court as an institution of extraordinary, and *vis-à-vis* the common law also extra-legal, jurisdiction. The most important conclusion to be drawn from an examination of the facts in late medieval bills is not the existence of a certain canon for their presentation but the simple fact that virtually every problem could be addressed. Despite the otherwise formulaic character of the bills, this happened in simple factual terms. The problems were generally presented in an untechnical language without excessive recourse to legal vocabulary.

2.4.4 *Common law comparison*

In order to understand the effect of this opportunity for fact presentation, I suggest a comparison with the standard way of opening a suit at common law at the time, the writ. This requires a preliminary clarification: The bill for Chancery proceedings was a document drafted by the plaintiffs themselves according to the circumstances of their case.[36] The writ, on the other hand, was an official document issued by the Chancery upon the application of the plaintiff. It would thus be more intuitive to compare the Chancery bill with the original application for a writ as both represent the requisite first steps for the opening of a suit by the plaintiff. This approach, however, would ignore the function of the respective actions for the further process. The application for a writ to initiate common law proceedings was generally a mere formality.[37] The plaintiff – usually represented by a lawyer – would approach the Chancery in order to ask for a specific writ, pay for it and have it issued immediately. The further proceedings were then modelled exclusively after the terms of the writ. The facts of the case could only be addressed in as far as the writ allowed for their presentation through the admissible methods of proof. In contrast, the bill

36 Scholars have provided different accounts with regard to the question who actually wrote the late medieval Chancery bills, see below 2.9. That question, however, is irrelevant for the purpose of this discussion. There can be no doubt that the parties at the very least instructed the actual writers.

37 The action (for trespass) on the case required far greater involvement of the plaintiff at the drafting stage. However, its extension to numerous areas of civil law, most importantly contract and tort, represented a later development.

remained at the centre of Chancery proceedings. As we will see,[38] the defendant had to answer to every single allegation brought forward in the bill and the witnesses were inquired accordingly. Within the framework of a standardised procedure, it was the substance of the factual claim rather than a specific procedure that dominated the process. It thus seems legitimate to compare writ and bill as the defining elements for the further course of common law and Court of Chancery proceedings, respectively.

I have already described the emergence of the writ system and its central role for the development of the common law.[39] My focus will now turn to the content of the writs. It is difficult to assess how many different writs were available at any given time during the Middle Ages. Older writs were rarely explicitly rejected; their application rather phased out slowly.[40] It has been estimated that about 40 different writs were in regular use by the 15th century, when the creation of new writs had long ceased.[41] Despite their differences, the so-called original writs – that would open common law proceedings – all shared the same function: They laid out the specific procedure applicable to the case.

Maitland drew up an illustrative list of the procedural features that were typically determined by the respective writ: At the pre-trial stage, these included the terms of summons, the necessity of security, the empanelment of an assize, the effect of the defendant's contumaciousness and the provisional treatment of disputed persons or property. During the immediate trial, the incidents covered included nonattendance or delay, the modes of proof, the admission of warrantors and the role of pleading. At the post-trial phase, the choice of the writ also prescribed the available remedies, the modes of execution and the effects of noncompliance.[42] It was a typical feature of pre-modern English procedure (and indeed of the writ system) that abstractions were avoided in favour of enumerations. What Maitland's collection of incidents nevertheless shows is that effectively every step of the process was determined by the respective writ.

While the writs covered a variety of factual situations, they generally showed a common approach to the presentation of facts. This amounted to nothing more than a standardised account of the typical behaviour justifying the respective

38 See below, especially 3.1.5.

39 See above, chapter II, 1.5.

40 *F. Pollock / F. W. Maitland*, The History of English Law before the Time of Edward I, Cambridge University Press, Cambridge, Volume 2, 2nd edition reissue, 1968, p. 561–564.

41 Compare *F. Pollock / F. W. Maitland*, The History of English Law before the Time of Edward I, Volume 2, p. 564–567.

42 *F. Pollock / F. W. Maitland*, The History of English Law before the Time of Edward I, Volume 2, p. 568.

claim.[43] Thus, the writ would merely allege that A owed something to B and kept it away from him or her[44] or that A 'broke the close' of B.[45] The writs were only individualised insofar as they stated the parties' names and the contested property, sums etc.

One significant exception to this model warrants attention – especially in the light of later developments. The action of trespass on the case allowed the plaintiff to state his special 'case' in the writ.[46] Originally, actions on the case were restricted to non-forcible trespass constellations.[47] A wide-ranging transformation, however, set in in the 16th century, when actions for assumpsit and ejectment developed out of the action on the case.[48] It was thus mainly through this action on the case that trespass became synonymous with any wrong.[49] The application of the writ was extended to virtually all areas of private law, most notably the whole realm of contract and tort.[50] This can be seen as the origin of a transsubstantive common law procedure.[51]

2.4.5 *Chancery's relief*

An examination of the Court of Chancery can hardly be expected to provide answers to the question why the common law remained caught in a largely inflexible writ system throughout the late Middle Ages.[52] The advanced explanations – for example fear of judicial discretion, limitation of royal jurisdiction and judicial conservatism –[53] all merit attention. The limited source

43 *J. H. Baker*, An Introduction to English Legal History, p. 62. For an impression of some selected writs, mostly in the original Latin, see *F. W. Maitland*, The Forms of Action at Common Law – A Course of Lectures, Cambridge University Press, Cambridge, 1909 (repr. 1968), p. 68–75.

44 Action for debt, see *F. W. Maitland*, The Forms of Action at Common Law – A Course of Lectures, p. 71.

45 Action for trespass to land, see *F. W. Maitland*, The Forms of Action at Common Law – A Course of Lectures, p. 72.

46 *J. H. Baker*, An Introduction to English Legal History, p. 62.

47 *J. H. Baker*, An Introduction to English Legal History, p. 62–63.

48 Compare *F. W. Maitland*, The Forms of Action at Common Law – A Course of Lectures, especially the illustration on p. 44.

49 *J. H. Baker*, An Introduction to English Legal History, p. 67.

50 *J. H. Langbein / R. T. Lerner / B. P. Smith*, History of the Common Law – The Development of Anglo-American Legal Institutions, Aspen Publishers, New York, NY, 2009, p. 104.

51 For interesting parallel developments in Roman and English common law in this regard, see *R. Zimmermann*, The Law of Obligations – Roman Foundations of the Civilian Tradition, Juta & Co., Cape Town, 1990, S. 908–914.

52 Compare above chapter II, 1.5.3.

53 For these suggestions, see *F. Pollock / F. W. Maitland*, The History of English Law before the Time of Edward I, Volume 1, p. 196; *G. O. Sayles*, Introduction, in:

material condemns any researcher on the Court of Chancery to address this question from the perspective of the litigants. What the bills suggest is that the late medieval plaintiffs had no reason to demand immediate flexibilisation from the common law. Royal administration provided them with an – at the very least – equally effective institution for conflict resolution under the control of one of the highest authorities of the realm in the Court of Chancery, where they could present their problems irrespective of the intricacies of the common law writ system. This constellation was not necessarily efficient but the evidence available suggests that it was workable. As we have seen, the Court of Chancery had developed gradually out of the extraordinary jurisdiction of the king. The concomitant professionalization might have lowered the public pressure for reforms in the common law. Viewed from this perspective, the static nature of the common law writ system and the expansion of the bill jurisdiction of the Court of Chancery might even be characterised as mutually reinforcing rather than as causal developments.

The comparison with the writ illustrates the basic characteristic of the bill procedure in the Court of Chancery: its openness for the presentation of any contingent issue. The exact formulation of Chancery bills is merely of secondary importance for an assessment of the function of the court. What matters most is not how plaintiffs presented their cases but the fact that they got the opportunity to present their cases in the first place.

2.5 Jurisdiction

After the presentation of the facts, the bill in *Ardern v Ardern* turned to a central legal issue. Addressing the Lord Chancellor personally again, Walter Ardern submitted that he "may have no remedy in this case by the course of the common law". This constituted a reference to the problem of jurisdiction. While explicitly invoking the jurisdiction of the Court of Chancery, the statement may also have represented an implicit recognition of the precedence of the common law. Walter correctly claimed that the breach of an oral promise could not be addressed effectively by the common law. The establishment of a fiduciary relationship and its enforcement lay outside the established procedures offered by the common law writ system. As Walter's statement suggested, his desired remedy was incompatible with the machinery of the common law. There was simply no available course of action. The plaintiff thus made a brief but

G. O. Sayles (ed.), Select Cases in the Court of King's Bench under Edward III Selden Society, London, 1958, Volume 5, p. lxvii-lxx. The debate is reflected in *J. H. Langbein / R. T. Lerner / B. P. Smith*, History of the Common Law – The Development of Anglo-American Legal Institutions, p. 271–274.

convincing case for the involvement of the Court of Chancery. But what role did such invocations of jurisdiction play for the work of the late medieval court? How was the general relationship between the common law and the Court of Chancery at the time? And how are these questions reflected in the bills?

2.5.1 Common law jurisdiction

A look through the sources provides numerous other references to the issue of common law jurisdiction – some of them substantially more explicit than the brief mention in *Ardern v Ardern*. In the early case of *Pykworth v Sambroke*,[54] the plaintiff alleged that the defendants had entered his lands, assaulted his tenants and seized his chattels. Such disturbances of the king's peace were a central area of common law intervention. Actions for trespass to land, battery and detinue would have been readily available to the plaintiff. Why was it, then, that Pykworth turned to the extraordinary jurisdiction of the Lord Chancellor in the Court of Chancery? The bill itself provides the explanation. According to Pykworth, the defendants were "notorious and common extortioners and oppressors of the people in their country". The situation was such "that he [could] not well undertake to pursue a remedy for his said grievances at common law". Pykworth thus doubted the effectiveness of common law remedies because of the power and reputation of the defendants. The bills that asked the Court of Chancery to intervene because of an alleged failure or ineffectiveness of the common law are heavily represented in the Chancery documentation of the late 14th and the early 15th century.[55] They almost disappear by the 1450s. At the same time, the rate of cases complaining of violent behaviour also dropped significantly.[56] It has been suggested that this development coincided with the gradual establishment of the extraordinary jurisdiction over criminal matters in the Court of Star Chamber.[57]

54 (1386–1411), Select Cases, p. 87.

55 For such examples, see *Qwyncy v Landasdale* (1432–1443), Calendars I, p. xxxii; *Abbot of Burton v Stanley* (1432–1443), Calendars I, p. xxxiii; *Trewonwall v Bodrugan* (1450–1454), Calendars I, p. xlvii. For the existence of a similar remedy under canon law, see *R. Perruso*, The iuramentum perhorrescentiae under Canon Law – An Influence on the Development of Early Chancery Jurisdiction?, Comparative Legal History, Volume 3 (2015), p. 2–37.

56 Compare *T. S. Haskett*, The Late Medieval Court of Chancery, Law and History Review, Volume 14 (1996), p. 245–313, p. 296.

57 *W. Holdsworth*, A History of English Law, Methuen, London, Volume 1, 7th edition, 1956, p. 408–409; also *J. H. Langbein / R. T. Lerner / B. P. Smith*, History of the Common Law – The Development of Anglo-American Legal Institutions, p. 281–282.

In *Haryngton v Haryngton*,[58] the plaintiff had been successfully sued at common law upon a bond, which he had issued many years before. This bond guaranteed the payment of an annuity of 20 marks to a knight in his service. The executors of the knight had brought the suit. The plaintiff claimed that the said knight had left his service and switched sides to his enemies long before his death. Upon this, the lord had stopped the yearly payments. The common law courts, however, could not recognise this change of circumstances as an existing bond was considered sufficient and irrefutable evidence of a payment obligation.[59] Complaining about the lack of remedy by the common law, the plaintiff thus asked the Lord Chancellor to intervene "as good faith and conscience [...] require" and thus to assume jurisdiction. *Haryngton v Haryngton* represents an early but typical example of strict formalism preventing the address of central factual issues at common law.[60] From this perspective, the case resembles *Ardern v Ardern* in that the recognised documental evidence prevented effective truth-finding.[61] The very different developments of contract and trust cases in the further development of English law – one being reintegrated into the common law through the action of assumpsit,[62]while the other remained a central element of the equitable jurisdiction of the Court of Chancery – justify a specific mention.

2.5.2 Common law precedence

I have already described the escalation of jurisdictional conflicts between the common law, represented by Chief Justice Coke, and the Court of Chancery, represented by Lord Ellesmere, at the beginning of the 16th century.[63] Indeed, occasional complaints about the appropriation of jurisdiction by the Court of Chancery date back to the 14th century.[64] That should not lead to the premature

58 (1432–1443), Calendars I, p. xxxiv.

59 *A. W. B. Simpson*, A History of the Common Law of Contract – The Rise of the Action of Assumpsit, Clarendon Press, Oxford, 1975, p. 88–112, especially S. 99.

60 A similar case also represents one of *St. German*'s central examples for the need of a separate court of conscience, T. F. T. Plucknett / J L. Barton (eds.), St. German's Doctor and Student, Selden Society, London, 1974, p. 77–79.

61 The contractual character of early trust agreements was already identified by *F. W. Maitland*, Equity – A Course of Lectures, Cambridge University Press, Cambridge, 1936 (repr. 1969), p. 110.

62 For a comprehensive history of the common law of contract, see *A. W. B. Simpson*, A History of the Common Law of Contract – The Rise of the Action of Assumpsit.

63 The conflict was best described by *M. Fortier*, Equity and Ideas: Coke, Ellesmere, and James I, Renaissance Quarterly, Volume 51 (1998), p. 1255–1281.

64 Compare the parliamentary petitions against the jurisdiction of the Lord Chancellor, which appear from the first year of the reign of Richard II (1377),

conclusion that the relationship between the courts and the actors involved was unregulated and continuously disputed.

The continuous references to common law jurisdiction reflect a general acceptance of common law precedence and of the subsidiarity of the Court of Chancery. Plaintiffs in the Court of Chancery saw the need to actively justify their choice of forum. Irrespective of their desire to have their case heard in the Court of Chancery, they formally paid respect to common law jurisdiction. The maxim that "equity follows the law" became one of the best-known principles of English law in the early modern period.[65] David Yale speculated that it was introduced into the English legal discourse by St. German's Doctor and Student.[66] Indeed, St. German specifically mentioned that "equity follows the law" in his discussion of Aristotelian equity.[67] However, no evidence exists for the explicit use of this formula in the late Middle Ages. The later acceptance of the maxim might even constitute an incident of post-rationalisation upon Doctor and Student.[68] Either way, the formal deference to common law jurisdiction, as exemplified in the 15th century cases, was already in line with the maxim.

The approach taken by the plaintiffs sits uneasily with our modern understanding of – strictly delineated and usually exclusive – jurisdiction. While they formally recognised the precedence of the common law, they practically undermined it. The jurisdiction of the Court of Chancery was invoked not only when no common law course of action was available, as was the case in *Ardern v Ardern*, but also when the remedies provided by the common law were considered ineffective, as in *Pykworth v Martin*, or when the plaintiffs could not advance their arguments, as in *Haryngton v Haryngton*. Practically, any actual or alleged failures of the regular process of law from the plaintiffs' perspective would be

quoted and explained in *D. M. Kerly*, An Historical Sketch of the Equitable Jurisdiction of the Court of Chancery, Cambridge University Press, Cambridge, 1890 (repr. 2011), p. 37–46.

65 Compare *D. E. C. Yale* in: D. E. C. Yale (ed.), Lord Nottingham's 'Manual of Chancery Practice' and 'Prolegomena of Chancery and Equity', Cambridge University Press, Cambridge, 1965, (repr. 1986), p. 200–204.

66 *D. E. C. Yale*, Introduction, in: D. E. C. Yale (ed.), Lord Nottingham's Chancery Cases, Selden Society, London, Volume 1, 1957, p. lii, fn. 2.

67 T. F. T. Plucknett / J L. Barton (eds.), St. German's Doctor and Student, S. 97.

68 It has been claimed that Doctor and Student was, at the time of its publication, an intellectual exercise rather than a practice report. See also *J. Getzler*, Patterns of Fusion, in: P. Birks (ed.), The Classification of Obligations, Clarendon, Oxford, 1997, p. 157–192, p. 178; *J. H. Langbein / R. T. Lerner / B. P. Smith*, History of the Common Law – The Development of Anglo-American Legal Institutions, p. 318. For the reception of Doctor and Student in Court of Chancery practice, see above chapter III, 4.1.

addressed in Chancery bills. In the absence of late medieval judgments, we naturally do not know whether the court actually accepted these bills for adjudication. The steady reoccurrence of trespass, use and contract cases, however, suggests that arguments like the ones presented above were commonly accepted. As far as we can tell from the bills, the Court of Chancery of the late Middle Ages operated with largely unrestricted discretion in relation to jurisdictional matters.

The potential for the escalation of jurisdictional conflicts under these conditions is tangible. The English lawyers, however, found a typically practical avoidance strategy. It was a second maxim that guided the way out of the conflict: "equity acts *in personam*".[69] Decisions in the Court of Chancery thus did not impose or articulate any general standard of law; they merely decided a single case upon the examination of the parties. This can hardly be seen as anything more than a fiction. The regularisation of Chancery adjudication effectively created a body of law similar to the common law.[70] Additionally, decisions in the Court of Chancery could pre-empt judgments at common law.[71] Seemingly, however, the fiction provided a workable solution. Throughout most of the 15th century, relations between the common law courts and the Court of Chancery were mostly amicable with both common law judges and lawyers regularly attending Chancery proceedings.[72]

2.5.3 Local jurisdiction

In light of the diverse legal landscape of medieval England, it would be problematic to consider the question of jurisdiction exclusively in relation with the common law. The relationship to local courts posed comparatively few problems. While some bills complained about proceedings in local courts or their impossibility,[73] plaintiffs apparently did not see the need to justify the

69 For the importance of this maxim, see *D. E. C. Yale* in: D. E. C. Yale (ed.), Lord Nottingham's 'Manual of Chancery Practice' and 'Prolegomena of Chancery and Equity', p. 17; *S. F. C. Milsom*, Historical Foundations of the Common Law, S. 90. *D. E. C. Yale* also identified an early reference in *Godwyne v Profyt* (after 1393), Select Cases, p. 48.

70 See above chapter II, 4.4.

71 Compare *E. G. Henderson*, Legal Rights to Land in the Early Chancery, American Journal of Legal History, Volume 26 (1982), S. 97–122, S. 98, who likened the effect of a possessory order from the Court of Chancery to a judgment at common law.

72 *J. H. Langbein / R. T. Lerner / B. P. Smith*, History of the Common Law – The Development of Anglo-American Legal Institutions, p. 312.

73 For mentions of local courts, see for example *Abbot of Peterborough v Semark* (1407), Select Cases, p. 85; *Trewonwall v Bodrugan* (1450–1454), Calenders I, p. xlviii; *Gody v Harry* (1465–1483), Calendars I, p. lviii.

involvement of the Court of Chancery in such cases specifically. The relationship between local courts and the Court of Chancery seems to have been of a strongly hierarchical rather than of a competitive character. The bills effectively presupposed a supervisory function of the Court of Chancery over local adjudication. It seems advisable to keep the lack of differentiation of state functions in the late Middle Ages in mind. An uneasy comparison with contemporary roles would characterise the Lord Chancellor not only as a judge but also as a minister of justice.[74] An oversight function over local courts might thus also have been grounded in the administrative functions of Chancery.[75]

2.5.4 Ecclesiastical jurisdiction

The relationship to the second centralised system of adjudication, the ecclesiastical jurisdiction, was fraught with considerably more difficulties. This is not the place to address the frequently recurring disputes between secular and spiritual jurisdictions, which arose all across Europe during the Middle Ages. In order to understand the position of the Court of Chancery, it should suffice to remember the core claims of the church. Ecclesiastical jurisdiction was invoked *ratione personarum* and *ratione materiae* – based on the status of the parties and the subject matter.[76] The former most notably included the exclusive jurisdiction over clergy – not only as a privilege but also as a compulsory duty.[77] The latter included the sacraments, including marriage, testaments, church property and tithes, pledges of faith and grave sins.[78]

For the English context, Richard Helmholz has presented an instructive introduction to the practical scope of the ecclesiastical jurisdiction in the face of competition from the royal courts.[79] The personal jurisdiction of ecclesiastical

74 Indeed, administrative functions like the appointment of judges or oversight over the court system were performed by the Lord Chancellor until the abolition of the office.

75 For a brief introduction to Chancery's procedural instruments for control over lower courts, see below 2.6.2.

76 *H.J. Berman*, Law and Revolution – The Formation of the Western Legal Tradition, p. 222.

77 *H.J. Berman*, Law and Revolution – The Formation of the Western Legal Tradition, p. 222.

78 *H.J. Berman*, Law and Revolution – The Formation of the Western Legal Tradition, p. 222.

79 *R. H. Helmholz*, The Oxford History of the Laws of England, Volume 1: The Canon Law and Ecclesiastical Jurisdiction from 567 to the 1640s, Oxford University Press, Oxford, 2004, especially p. 206–236.

courts over clergy was never accepted in civil cases in England.[80] Apparently the issue was not even raised in the notorious conflict between Henry II and Thomas Becket (1118–1170) over the Constitutions of Clarendon, which originally also foresaw jurisdiction over clergy in criminal matters.[81] This is also the only finding on personal jurisdiction that is compatible with evidence from the late medieval Chancery bills. The cases involving clergy on one or both sides are innumerable. In Timothy Haskett's sample of cases, 28 per cent of the identifiable parties to Chancery litigation held ecclesiastical offices.[82] While Haskett warns that clergy might be overrepresented in the sample because members of less prestigious professions could have withheld information on their occupations,[83] the great share clearly suggests the lack of any barrier of access. The question that imposes itself upon a look through the cases and the statistics is rather why the Court of Chancery was so attractive to clerical parties. A look at some bills, in which the alternative ecclesiastical jurisdiction was mentioned, might provide insights.

The case of *Middelton v Dean of Wimborne Minster*[84] provides a good representation of the constraints the ecclesiastical jurisdiction was faced with in medieval England. The plaintiff, the parson of a local church, and the defendant, the dean of the minster, were engaged in a dispute over tithes obligations for a newly developed piece of land. Claiming a common right to the tenth of all corn growing in the designated area, the plaintiff sued the Dean of the Minster, who had himself already collected the tithes, in the consistory court of the Bishop of Salisbury. Since Wimborne Minster was a royal chapel, a writ of prohibition was issued from the Chancery against the proceedings in an ecclesiastical court. The plaintiff then appealed to the Court of Chancery

80 *R. H. Helmholz*, Canon Law as a Means of Legal Integration in the Development of English Law, in: H. Scholler (ed.), Die Bedeutung des kanonischen Rechts für die Entwicklung einheitlicher Rechtsprinzipien, Nomos, Baden-Baden, 1996, p. 49–68, p. 53; *R. H. Helmholz,* The Oxford History of the Laws of England, Volume 1: The Canon Law and Ecclesiastical Jurisdiction from 567 to the 1640s, p. 315. *R. H. Helmholz* also referred to a decision of the Roman Rota, which characterised the English practice as a "wholly invalid practice under canon law" (*Decisiones antiquae sacre Romanae Rotae* (1509), no. 840). This finding, however, seems to have had no impact.

81 *H. J. Berman*, Law and Revolution – The Formation of the Western Legal Tradition, p. 263.

82 *T. S. Haskett*, The Late Medieval Court of Chancery, Law and History Review, Volume 14 (1996), p. 245–313, p. 290. The sample is presented above in chapter IV, 3.

83 *T. Haskett*, The Late Medieval Court of Chancery, Law and History Review, Volume 14 (1996), p. 245–313, p. 290.

84 (1364), Select Cases, p. 103.

instead. *Middelton v Dean of Wimborne Minster* shows the strong position of the royal courts in relation to the ecclesiastical courts. From what we can tell, the plaintiff simply had to accept the royal writ of prohibition and continue his suit in a royal court. That is despite the fact that a classical subject matter establishing ecclesiastical jurisdiction – tithes – was at issue. The mere possibility that the tithes duty could be owed to a royal chapel provided sufficient reason for exclusive royal jurisdiction. In light of the factual power relations, the plaintiff seems to have been left with no other choice than proceeding in the Court of Chancery.[85]

Sharp v Temper[86] represents another dispute over tithes. The plaintiff, the prior of a hospital, was sued for the payment of tithes by the parish church in an ecclesiastical court. He contended that the founder of the hospital had concluded an agreement with one of the defendant's predecessors and obtained a deed freeing the hospital from all future tithe duty. However, instead of defending his claim in the ecclesiastical court, he sued the defendants in the Court of Chancery. The wording of the bill made it very clear that a judgment in the ecclesiastical court was still outstanding.[87] In contrast to *Middelton v Dean of Wimborne Minster*, a challenge to the subject matter jurisdiction of the ecclesiastical courts in this case would have been entirely unfounded. Obtaining a writ of prohibition was thus impossible. In fact, the plaintiff did not even advance an argument why he could not await the judgment of the spiritual court. We might simply assume that he considered the church courts sympathetic towards the imposition of tithe duties. The appeal to the Court of Chancery can be seen as an exercise in forum shopping. Surviving evidence, including answer, replication and rejoinder from the parties, shows that the court actually entertained the suit.

2.5.5 Clergy in the Court of Chancery

Royal jurisdiction thus might have provided clergy with an opportunity to avoid foreseeable judgments in ecclesiastical courts, possibly even those predetermined by the church's hierarchical structure. The Court of Chancery was the royal court of choice for clergy for two reasons: First, the issues arising within a church context – most notably tithes duties – could not be addressed through traditional common law writs. Second, a closer look at the Court of Chancery will reveal a practical proximity to the church courts. The judge was himself a bishop with

85 There was, of course, no common law action available for (non-statutory) tithes claims. Thus, the Court of Chancery provided the only available royal forum.

86 (1461–1467), Calendars I, p. lxiii.

87 Compare the wording of the bill: "if so be that your said suppliants be convicted in the said spiritual court", Calendars I, p. lxiii (p. lxiv).

experience in ecclesiastical adjudication and the procedure of the Court of Chancery showed numerous similarities to canon law procedure.[88]

2.5.6 *Threat to ecclesiastical jurisdiction*

All this suggests that the late medieval Court of Chancery practically undermined the subject matter jurisdiction of the ecclesiastical courts in important areas such as testaments, church property and pledges of faith. As we have seen, decisions on tithes were also challenged in the Court of Chancery or even exclusively reserved for royal jurisdiction. While this should not be understood as a general challenge on the subject-matter jurisdiction of church courts, it must have effectively rendered church authority questionable. When asking why the Court of Chancery would accept tithe or other church property cases for adjudication, we should not overlook the economic dimension. There was quite simply a lot of money involved. Regarding other subject matter jurisdictions claimed by the ecclesiastical courts, the appropriation of jurisdiction by the Court of Chancery was subtler but potentially even more menacing. The use[89] effectively became an instrument of succession upon death and thus an alternative to testaments.[90] At the same time, the recognition of oral promises[91] encroached upon the ecclesiastical jurisdiction over pledges of faith.

Given the personal overlap, it seems unlikely that the Court of Chancery ever intended to launch a concerted attack on the ecclesiastical jurisdiction.[92] A look at the cases, however, presents an image of largely unfettered judicial discretion – not only but also – in jurisdictional matters. The practice of the court seems to have been in line with Lord Chancellor Morton's quote "no one departs from the Court of Chancery without a remedy".[93] The establishment of such a

88 This will be discussed intensively below, chapter VI.

89 See for a deeper discussion chapter VII, 1.4.1 below.

90 For jurisdictional competition over wills, see *J. Biancalana*, Testamentary Cases in Fifteenth-Century Chancery, The Legal History Review, Volume 76 (2008), p. 283–306, especially p. 304–306.

91 See for a deeper discussion chapter VII, 1.4.2 below.

92 The same might not be said for the common law. *R. H. Helmholz*, The Oxford History of the Laws of England, Volume 1: The Canon Law and Ecclesiastical Jurisdiction from 567 to the 1640s, p. 231–234, described how the common law courts 'wrestled' away ecclesiastical jurisdiction over contracts, defamation and testamentary debts from the church courts at the end of the 15th century by a creative reinterpretation of the Statute of Praemunire (1392–1393; 16 Ric. II, c. 5). This allowed plaintiffs to open a suit against proceedings in spiritual courts directly in the King's Bench. The often-ineffective writ of prohibition could be avoided.

93 "*Nullus recedat a Curia Cancellaria sine remedio*", (1489) Y. B. 4 Hen. VII, Hil., fol. 4, pl. 8.

powerful royal institution for conflict resolution necessarily came at the cost of other jurisdictions.[94]

2.5.7 *Failure of justice*

The study of the 15th century sources paints a clear picture: Plaintiffs originally addressed the Court of Chancery whenever they felt that they could not obtain justice in the regular course of the law – be it in common law or ecclesiastical courts. The concrete reasons for the appeal to the Lord Chancellor were manifold. Whether the regular courts did not allow the opening of proceedings, the introduction of certain arguments or evidence or whether they failed to enforce their judgments was irrelevant.[95] What mattered was the perception of a failure in the regular course of justice. While the concrete view of the Court of Chancery largely remains in the dark in the absence of reasoned decisions, the advancement of the cases to the further stages of trial suggests that the court perceived the scope of its jurisdiction accordingly.

The problem of such an open-ended approach is evident. The extensive use of jurisdictional discretion can come at the cost of all other courts. It was arguably only the practical involvement of common lawyers in the Court of Chancery that postponed the outbreak of an open conflict between the two jurisdictions.[96] It should not be overlooked, however, that the comprehensive jurisdictional ambitions of the court were in line with its origins in the residual jurisdiction of the king. Throughout the Middle Ages, the king considered himself the ultimate guarantor of justice. Not only did he claim the power to intervene in individual cases, he also asserted a corresponding responsibility.[97] This understanding of the role of the sovereign was by no means restricted to England. It is commonly traced back to Roman law models.[98] The engagement with the Roman law sources in the late Middle Ages led both secular leaders across Europe and the church to claim a general jurisdiction in cases of a failure of justice (*ex defectu justitiae*).[99] Ecclesiastical jurisdiction *ex defectu justitiae* was never acknowledged

94 For the loss of business in the ecclesiastical courts before the Reformation, see *R. H. Helmholz*, The Oxford History of the Laws of England, Volume 1: The Canon Law and Ecclesiastical Jurisdiction from 567 to the 1640s, p. 231–236.

95 Compare also *S. F. C. Milsom*, Historical Foundations of the Common Law, Butterworths, London, 2nd edition, 1981, p. 84–85.

96 See below 5.2.1.3.

97 Compare also above chapter II, 2.4.

98 Compare *R. H. Helmholz*, The Spirit of Classical Canon Law, University of Georgia Press, Athens, Ga., 1996, p. 121–123, who referred to *Justinian*'s Cod. 3.14.1.

99 For an introduction, see *R. H. Helmholz*, The Spirit of Classical Canon Law, p. 116–144.

in England.[100] On the contrary, the Norman kings had monopolised jurisdiction over failures of justice and thereby further strengthened their role *vis-à-vis* the church. In the course of its institution, the powers and responsibilities of the extraordinary jurisdiction of the king were then delegated (albeit not conclusively) to the Court of Chancery.[101] Its jurisdiction can thus be understood as an exercise of the royal prerogative to intervene when the regular course of justice failed.

2.6 Request for process

Having claimed the jurisdiction of the Court of Chancery, Walter Ardern proceeded to ask the Lord Chancellor "to grant a writ subpoena to be direct[ed] to [the defendants] commanding them to appear before the king in his Chancery at the XVth of Easter next coming upon pain of CC. li. to answer to the promises". His request for action was clearly procedural rather than substantive. Instead of asking for an order for possession or the reimbursement of profits, Walter pleaded for an examination of his brother in Chancery. That request was merely preliminary but it emphasises the dominance of procedure in the medieval Court of Chancery.

2.6.1 Subpoena

The request for a subpoena was a common feature of most Chancery bills.[102] The issuance of a subpoena represented the first official involvement of the court – through its masters[103] – in the proceedings. It was directed to the defendant in the form of a writ. The writ of subpoena must be distinguished from the original writs for the opening proceedings at common law: It included nothing more than a judicial summons and a threat of penalty in case of defiance.[104] In how far this penalty was ever enforced remains open. No such evidence can be found in the late medieval files.[105] It was nevertheless advisable to adhere to the summons since the court employed local sheriffs for their enforcement.[106] The subpoena

100 *R. H. Helmholz*, The Spirit of Classical Canon Law, p. 137–138.
101 See above chapter II, 2.5.
102 For alternatives, see below 2.6.2.
103 Compare for the early 16th century, *F. Metzger*, Das englische Kanzleigericht unter Kardinal Wolsey, Promotion an der Friedrich-Alexander-Universität Erlangen-Nürnberg, 1977, S. 93.
104 Also *J. H. Baker*, An Introduction to English Legal History, p. 103.
105 Also *F. Metzger*, Das englische Kanzleigericht unter Kardinal Wolsey, S. 95.
106 The continued presence of the parties in Westminster could then be guaranteed by their imprisonment, see *F. Metzger*, Das englische Kanzleigericht unter Kardinal Wolsey, S. 95.

in *Ardern v Ardern* has not been preserved with the litigation documents. Since writs of subpoena were issued in a standard form, however, we can refer to John Baker's specimen for an examination of the content.[107]

Some issues spring to mind on an examination of the standard writ. Perhaps most importantly, the defendants were apparently left in the dark about the cause of the proceedings. While they were surely aware of the conflicts they were currently involved in, the exact complaint was kept from them. The subpoena might have been issued with a copy of the original bill but the words of the form ("matters that shall then be charged against you") suggest that they were not. Less opportunity for preparation might have simplified the later examination. The neutral formulation also provides the impression of inquisitorial proceedings. Furthermore, the high penalty for non-appearance must have been included for reasons of deterrence only. In fact, it was never enforced; the defendant was instead subjected to proceedings for contempt.[108]

The subpoena was by far the most common but not the only process request in the late medieval Chancery bills. Requests for *corpus cum causa*, *certiorari* and injunction also show up continuously throughout the documentation.[109] While they played a much smaller role in Chancery practice, they provide an interesting insight into the court's oversight function for the developing English legal system.

2.6.2 *Corpus cum causa, certiorari and injunction*

A writ of *corpus cum causa*,[110] when issued, removed a case from a local jurisdiction and set a hearing in the Court of Chancery. It was requested by plaintiffs, who were kept in local custody without an immediate remedy.[111]

107 *"The king to C. D., esquire, greeting. For certain causes set forth before us in our Chancery, we firmly enjoining command you that, laying aside all other things and all excuses whatsoever, you be in your own person before us in our said Chancery in three weeks from Michaelmas day next following, wheresoever we may then be, to answer there upon those matters that shall then be charged against you, and further to do and receive whatever our said court shall award in that behalf. And this in no wise omit, upon pain of one hundred pounds. And have there then this writ."*, from *J. H. Baker*, An Introduction to English Legal History, p. 551.

108 *J. H. Baker*, An Introduction to English Legal History, p. 103.

109 Just like the subpoena, all three writs can be categorised as so-called 'bench' or 'prerogative' writs, which – in contrast to 'original' writs for the opening of common law suits – were issued by judges in the course of the proceedings.

110 For examples of *corpus cum causa* cases, see *Howard v Sheriffs of London* (1467–1473), Calendars I, p. lxxxviii; *Foster v Sheriff of Kent* (1467–1473), Calendars I, p. lxxxix; *Kirkeman v Sheriffs of London* (1470), Calendars I, p. xci.

111 Compare *J. H. Baker*, The Oxford History of the Laws of England, Volume 6: 1483–1558, Oxford University Press, Oxford, 2003, p. 188.

Corpus cum causa thus allowed a review of the legitimacy of detention.[112] A writ of *certiorari*[113] served a similar supervisory function. It was applicable not when the plaintiffs were imprisoned but when they were otherwise involved in litigation in other courts. The writ directed the usually local courts to 'inform' the Court of Chancery of the suit, which was then to be continued in Westminster.[114] The only function of an injunction[115] in the context of a process request in Chancery was to stop an on-going prosecution at common law.[116] It was applied for by plaintiffs who considered themselves unjustly involved in common law proceedings. Injunctions were issued as preliminary procedural orders to allow for a hearing and as final remedy restraining the parties from pursuing their case in another court indefinitely.[117]

2.6.3 Common law instruments

As shown by this summary, the Court of Chancery had valuable instruments for oversight and control over other courts at its hand. And the plaintiffs, at least from the second half of the 15th century onwards, encouraged their use. At the same time, the effect of the aforementioned writs should not be overestimated. Only a small proportion of Chancery cases concerned the issuance of writs of *corpus cum causa*, *certiorari* or injunctions.[118] *Habeas corpus* and *certiorari* were furthermore equally available to the common law courts.[119] They thus facilitated the centralisation of conflict resolution in the royal courts generally rather than the rise of the Court of Chancery specifically. The injunction to stay proceedings at common law, on the other hand, was a potentially powerful

112 For a short introduction to the role of *corpus cum causa* in the development of the writ of *habeas corpus*, see *J. H. Baker*, An Introduction to English Legal History, p. 146–147.

113 For examples of *certiorari* cases, see *Stokker v Colyns* (1474–1475), Calendars I, p. xcv; *Bowman v Fote* (1474–1480), Calendars I, p. ci; *Vele v Parsons* (1485–1486), Calendars I, p. cxix.

114 Compare *J. H. Baker*, The Oxford History of the Laws of England, Volume 6: 1483–1558, p. 188–189.

115 For examples of requests for an injunction, see *Astel v Causton* (1481–1482), Calendars I, p. cviii; *Edyall v Hunston* (1484), Calendars I, cxiii; *Peverell v Huse* (1486–1493), Calendars I, p. cxxii.

116 Compare *J. H. Baker*, The Oxford History of the Laws of England, Volume 6: 1483–1558, p. 189.

117 The remedy of injunction will be described below 5.2.3.4.

118 Also *J. H. Baker*, The Oxford History of the Laws of England, Volume 6: 1483–1558, p. 189.

119 Compare *J. H. Baker*, An Introduction to English Legal History, p. 146–147; p. 148–150.

instrument for the regulation of jurisdiction between the royal courts. However, the common law courts had their own methods of exercising control over jurisdiction. Writs of prohibition were issued against local, ecclesiastical and lower equity courts. Why none was ever directed towards the Court of Chancery,[120] even in times of direct confrontation between the courts,[121] remains an open question that might perhaps best be explained with its political power.

Either way, the main procedural writ in the Court of Chancery was the subpoena. It was the subpoena that allowed for the creative element of Chancery bills and thereby for the most significant expansion of the court's jurisdiction.

2.7 Grounds for relief

2.7.1 Absence of 'law'

Anyone seeking relief from a court of law nowadays would do so relying on a specific legal claim or right. Such a claim usually rests on legislation or, at least in the common law tradition, on precedent. Eventually, it might also be grounded in custom. Given the scarcity of legislation and the pre-nascent state of a system of precedent, we might expect late medieval plaintiffs in the Court of Chancery to ground their appeals on claims based on custom. A look through the bills, however, shows that they rarely invoked anything like a customary right.[122] In fact, we hardly find any legal terminology or argumentation at all in the bills. The absence of a clear designation of the legal claim is not necessarily surprising. Even today, it is the task of the judge to find the law applicable to the circumstances of the case – *iura novit curia*.

The plaintiff in *Ardern v Ardern*, however, actually designated the grounds for relief, which he deemed decisive in the Court of Chancery. Discerning them

120 At least as far as we know. Compare *C. M. Gray*, The Boundaries of the Equitable Function, The American Journal of Legal History, Volume 20 (1976), p. 192–226, p. 197.

121 Chief Justice Coke instead issued writs of *habeas corpus* on behalf of plaintiffs, who were imprisoned on default of Chancery judgments. See *J. H. Baker*, The Common Lawyers and the Chancery: 1616, The Irish Jurist, Volume 4 (1969), p. 368–392, especially p. 374–379; *J. H. Langbein / R. T. Lerner / B. P. Smith*, History of the Common Law – The Development of Anglo-American Legal Institutions, p. 330– 331.

122 If at all, customs were usually mentioned in relation with the circumstances of the case (what I have above called recital, see 2.4) rather than with the request for relief. Compare *Sharp v Temper* (1461–1467), Calendars I, p. lxiii, p. lxiv: "long consuetudo aforre rehersid".

from the bill simply requires some detachment from our modern concept of law as rights and duties. Walter Ardern expected the defendants to receive what "faith right and good conscience requir[e] in this behalf" – "for the love of God and in the way of charity". The latter quote represents a formula employed at the end of most late medieval Chancery bills. Whether it carried any independent meaning is unclear. As we will see, any potential programmatic aspect is best understood in the context of conscience.

2.7.2 *Prevalence of conscience*

The plea to act as "good conscience requires" was much less common than the final appeal to charity but it appears throughout Chancery bills from the second half of the 15th century.[123] The importance of the concept of conscience for all cases in the late medieval Court of Chancery is illustrated best by two other sources: For one, the requirement to act in accordance with conscience was mentioned repeatedly in the pleadings in front of the Court of Chancery, which were recorded in the Year Books.[124] Most tellingly, however, contemporaries commonly referred to the Court of Chancery as the Court of Conscience.[125]

What was the meaning of conscience in the late medieval Court of Chancery? The aforementioned sources do not provide us with a definite answer. Conscience was constantly referred to but never elaborated or even defined. The possibility that it meant nothing but nice words should not be dismissed all too easily. After all, John Selden (1584–1654) – a good century later – would famously proclaim that "one Chancellor has a long foot, another a short foot, a third an indifferent foot. 'T is the same thing in the Chancellor's conscience".[126] However, the polemical nature of the quote should be apparent. Selden relied on a purely subjective understanding of conscience. Such an understanding would indeed hardly have imposed any restrictions on the Lord

123 See for example *Bale v Marchall* (1456), Select Cases, p. 143; *Kylwyth v Bothrygan* (ca. 1464), Select Cases, p. 151; *Richard v Herry* (1465–1467), Select Cases, p. 154.

124 (1459) Y. B. 37 Hen. VI, Hill. f. 13, pl. 3; (1460) Y. B. 39 Hen. VI, Mich. f. 26, pl. 36; (1465) Y. B. 5 Edw. IV, Mich. f. 7, pl. 17. For further references, see *A. W. B. Simpson*, A History of the Common Law of Contract – The Rise of the Action of Assumpsit, p. 397, fn. 6.

125 In the case of *Horsmonger v Pecham* (1386–1486; no reference to chancellorship), Select Cases, p. 120, p. 121, the plaintiff appealed to the Lord Chancellor to order the defendants to come before him "in the King's Chancery, which is the Court of Conscience". In (1460) Y. B. 39 Hen. VI, Mich. f. 26, pl. 36, council for both, the plaintiff and the defendant, addressed the Court of Chancery as the Court of Conscience.

126 F. Pollock (ed.), Table Talk of John Selden, Quaritch, London, 1927, p. 43.

Chancellor's discretion. Dennis Klinck, however, has impressively outlined the changing meaning of the term conscience in the early modern period.[127] Relying on legal as well as theological, political and literary sources, he identified a subjectivization of the term from the 16th century onwards, concomitant with reformatory thought. Klinck's account of the late medieval meaning of conscience on the other hand stressed its objective dimension.[128]

The words of the bill in *Ardern v Ardern* were clearly compatible with this understanding. The Lord Chancellor was supposed to act as conscience "requires".[129] This suggests that conscience set certain objective standards, which had to be respected even by one of the highest authorities of the land. What exactly this objective notion of conscience required, however, still demands closer examination. Two distinguishable explanations – a substantive and a procedural one – have emerged from earlier studies that looked beyond the legal records of the Court of Chancery.

2.7.3 *Substantive understanding*

Many scholars view conscience as a guiding principle for substantive decisions in individual Chancery cases.[130] Klinck did not explicitly embrace this position. However, his book almost presupposed it, when it identified the changing understanding of conscience with regard to the Court of Chancery. Klinck's study provides the most elaborate and also the most recent attempt of an identification of the late medieval meaning of conscience. Since original Chancery documentation does not offer any additional insights, I will thus heavily rely on his findings.

In the absence of evidence from the Court of Chancery, Klinck reverted to a famous case from the Exchequer for a late medieval definition of conscience from a legal context.[131] Chief Justice Fortescue (ca. 1394–1480) stated that the

127 *D. Klinck*, Conscience, Equity and the Court of Chancery in Early Modern England, Ashgate, Farnham, 2010. Compare also *J. Carroll*, The Role of Guilt in the Formation of Modern Society – England 1350–1800, The British Journal of Sociology, Volume 32 (1981), p. 459–503, on the corresponding role of guilt.

128 *D. Klinck*, Conscience, Equity and the Court of Chancery in Early Modern England, p. 15–40. *A. Hudson*, Conscience as the Organising Concept of Equity, Canadian Journal of Comparative and Contemporary Law, Volume 2 (2016), p. 261–299, even identifies the objectivity of conscience as the basis of English equity law.

129 *D. Klinck*, Conscience, Equity and the Court of Chancery in Early Modern England, p. 17, drew the same conclusion from other cases.

130 This is mostly the case for the literature that I have classified under the heading 'Moral theology and Chancery' above, see chapter III, 4.

131 (1453), cited in: M. C. Klingelsmith (ed.), Statham's Abridgment of the Law (ca. 1490), The Lawbook Exchange, Clark, NJ, Volume 1, 2007, p. 392.

parties were "not arguing the law in this case, but the conscience". Just as Chancery sometimes decided cases at common law,[132] so the Exchequer could occasionally employ Chancery procedure.[133] Fortescue then provided a general account of his understanding of conscience: "'[C]onscience' comes of *con* and *sciosis*. And so together they make 'to know with God' to wit: to know the will of God as near as one reasonably can. For a man can have land by our law, and by conscience he shall be damned". The quote provides two immediate implications: First, the judge in a court of conscience should follow god's will as far as he can.[134] Second, adjudication in conscience was, in theory, focused as much on the salvation of the defendant as on providing a remedy for the plaintiff.[135]

How, then, could 'God's will' possibly have been discerned for adjudication in the Court of Chancery? Authoritatively speaking, the Lord Chancellors of the 15th century as distinguished clerics must have seemed supremely suited for the task. It is a very real possibility that they simply relied on their own moral judgment, defined by years in ecclesiastical service and rendered authoritative by their political and spiritual power, in the process of adjudication. However, the challenge to draw practical implications from a higher (natural) law was one that dominated most aspects of life in the devout society of late medieval England. Therefore, instructions for the application of 'God's will' to practical life existed in the form of the *summae confessorum*. These must have been either well known to – or at least readily available for – any bishop at the time.[136] The *summae* provided the reader with a religiously informed morality for almost all aspects of

132 See above chapter II, 2.3.

133 M. C. Klingelsmith (ed.), Statham's Abridgment of the Law, Volume I, p. 393–394, fn. 33.

134 *D. Klinck*, Conscience, Equity and the Court of Chancery in Early Modern England, p. 17, seems to have suggested that the judge should discern God's will personally. The contemporary understanding, however, was that the judge in the external forum should follow the authorities on conscience rather than interpret God's will himself. This also explains why literature on the *forum internum* was mostly dedicated to judges in the *forum externum*.

135 See *A. W. B. Simpson*, A History of the Common Law of Contract – The Rise of the Action of Assumpsit, p. 398–399, who also referred to (and wrongly referenced) the Year Book case (1489) 4 Hen. VII, Hill. f. 4, pl. 8, in which Lord Chancellor Morton found that a remedy should be granted because the defendant would otherwise "be damned to hell". According to Morton, "mak[ing] a remedy for such a thing [...] is well done according to the conscience".

136 *W. F. Cahill*, Development by the Medieval Canonists of the Concept of Equity, The Catholic Lawyer, Volume 7 (1961), p. 112–120, p. 119; *A. W. B. Simpson*, A History of the Common Law of Contract – The Rise of the Action of Assumpsit, p. 401; *D. Klinck*, Conscience, Equity and the Court of Chancery in Early Modern England, p. 25.

daily life in casuistic style.[137] As Thomas Tentler put it, "[t]hey taught, in their massive encyclopaedic way, that morality was definable; that human authorities could define it; that all men were responsible for knowing and practicing it [and] that those who did not were guilty".[138] Thus, a precedential body of substantive rules based on the principle of conscience was readily available for application by late medieval Lord Chancellors. Whether they actively applied these rules, whether their judgment was consciously or subconsciously influenced by them or whether they tended to follow more worldly interests altogether, cannot be answered definitely in the absence of documental evidence. However, the concurrence of the self-designation of the Court of Chancery as a court of conscience and the existence of a casuistic literature of conscience can hardly be attributed to mere coincidence. The Lord Chancellors must – at the very least – have encouraged the association.[139]

2.7.4 *Doctor and Student*

Those attributing a substantive dimension to conscience in the Court of Chancery have traditionally found support in St. German's *Doctor and Student*,[140] which sought to provide a "jurisprudential basis for equity"[141] in the 1520s.[142] I have already hinted at the substantial influence of *Doctor and Student* on the early modern Court of Chancery.[143] It should be noted, however, that St. German was a common lawyer with an apparent interest in theological concepts rather than an expert on or practitioner in the Court of Chancery.[144] While he continuously contrasted the solution to individual cases provided by both the

137 *T. N. Tentler*, The Summa for Confessors as an Instrument of Social Control, in: C. Trinkaus / H. A. Oberman (eds.), The Pursuit of Holiness in Late Medieval and Renaissance Religion, Brill, Leiden, 1974, p. 103–126, p. 122.

138 *T. N. Tentler*, The Summa for Confessors as an Instrument of Social Control, in: C. Trinkaus / Heiko A. Oberman (eds.), The Pursuit of Holiness in Late Medieval And Renaissance Religion, p. 103–126, p. 122–123.

139 For the possible advantages of this association, see below chapter VII, 2.1.

140 T. F. T. Plucknett / J. L. Barton (eds.), St. German's Doctor and Student.

141 *J. H. Langbein / R. T. Lerner / B. P. Smith*, History of the Common Law – The Development of Anglo-American Legal Institutions, p. 318.

142 *P. Vinogradoff*, Reason and Conscience in Sixteenth Century Jurisprudence, Law Quarterly Review, Volume 24 (1908), p. 373–384 and *H. Coing*, English Equity and the Denunciatio Evangelica of the Canon Law, Law Quarterly Review, Volume 71 (1955), p. 223–241, provide instructive examples for this approach.

143 See above chapter III, 4.1.

144 Compare *J. Getzler*, Patterns of Fusion, in: P. Birks (ed.), The Classification of Obligations, p. 157–192, p. 178.

common law and the Court of Chancery,[145] his theoretical analysis of the concept of conscience, remained mostly superficial.[146] At its core, *Doctor and Student* represented an attempt to prove the compatibility of the English common law courts with the demands of natural law and reason.

St. German's understanding of conscience has been characterised as distinctively medieval.[147] Its roots in medieval theological literature have been identified in detail.[148] Clearly advocating an objective understanding, St. German claimed that conscience always "must be grounded upon some law".[149] As the three admissible sources of law in this sense, he identified human law, the law of god and the law of reason.[150] In this context, the law of reason was understood as the "knowledge of eternal law in a rational creature",[151] while every well made human law, in turn, participated in the law of reason.[152]

St. German's concept of conscience was undoubtedly conducive to his task of presenting the common law of the land as compatible – or indeed largely congruent – with divine will and thus largely outside the sphere of ecclesiastical or royal intervention. In a time, in which tensions between the Roman church and the English state reached a high point and in which the English monarchy showed first tendencies of absolutism under Henry VIII, this understanding was clearly favourable to the established interests of the common lawyers. That, however, still leaves us with the question what *Doctor and Student* can tell us

145 In line with contemporary literature on conscience, *St. German* did not necessarily ask the common law courts to conform with the solutions mandated by natural law and applicable in the court of conscience. Instead, he acknowledged the different aims of the respective jurisdictions.

146 Similarly *D. Klinck*, Conscience, Equity and the Court of Chancery in Early Modern England, p. 58.

147 *D. Klinck*, Conscience, Equity and the Court of Chancery in Early Modern England, p. 51–52.

148 See *Z. Rueger*, Gerson's Concept of Equity and Christopher St. German, History of Political Thought, Volume 3 (1982), p. 1–30, who identified several word-by-word adoptions of *J. Gerson*'s writings.

149 T. F. T. Plucknett / J. L. Barton (eds.), St. German's Doctor and Student, p. 133.

150 "And therfore conscyence muste be orderyd by that human lawe / (as long as it remains in strength and forve) in every way as it muste be in the proper cases vpon the lawe of god / and ypon the lawe of reason", see T. F. T. Plucknett / J. L. Barton (eds.), St. German's Doctor and Student, p. 111.

151 T. F. T. Plucknett / J. L. Barton (eds.), St. German's Doctor and Student, p. 13; also quoted in *D. Klinck*, Conscience, Equity and the Court of Chancery in Early Modern England, Ashgate, Farnham, 2010, p. 56.

152 "And therfore in euery lawe posytyue well made is somwhat of the lawe of reason", see T. F. T. Plucknett / J. L. Barton (eds.), St. German's Doctor and Student, p. 27; also quoted in *D. Klinck*, Conscience, Equity and the Court of Chancery in Early Modern England, p. 56.

about the (medieval) Court of Chancery. Despite a revived interest in St. German's work by scholars interested in the history of the Court of Chancery in the last decades,[153] no satisfactory answer has been provided. Most recent studies indeed tend to question the assumption that St. German had anything noteworthy at all to say about the late medieval Court of Chancery.[154] As Klinck pointed out, it is not entirely sure which role St. German saw for conscience in the Court of Chancery specifically, even though he defended the need for a separate equitable jurisdiction.[155] St. German's characterisation of the Court of Chancery was purely casuistic and lacked the theoretical elaboration provided elsewhere in the book.[156] It hardly allows for anything more but the 'simple' conclusion that the Court of Chancery should step in where the application of the general human law would create injustice in the individual case or where a right mandated by the law of reason or the law of god is not provided for by the common law – in cases where the regular course of justice had failed.[157]

St. German's approach might have been sympathetic to both earlier and later Lord Chancellors. The imprecise designation of the court as a necessary element

153 See for example *J. L. Barton*'s introduction to T. F.T. Plucknett / J. L. Barton (eds.), St. German's Doctor and Student; *J. A. Guy*, Law, Equity and Conscience in Henrician Juristic Thought, in: A. Fox / J. A. Guy (eds.), Reassessing the Henrician Age – Humanism, Politics and Reform 1500–1550, Blackwell, Oxford, 1986, p. 179–220; *T. A. O. Endicott*, The Conscience of the King: Christopher St. German and Thomas More and the Development of English Equity, University of Toronto Faculty Law Review, Volume 47 (1989), p. 549–570; *S. K. Dobbins*, Equity: The Court of Conscience or the King's Command, the Dialogues of St. German and Hobbes Compared, Journal of Law and Religion, Volume 9 (1991), p. 113–149; *G. Behrens*, An Early Tudor Debate on the Relation between Law and Equity, Legal History, Volume 19 (1998), p. 143–161; *M. Fortier*, The Culture of Equity in Early Modern England, Ashgate, London, 2005, p. 59–86; *J. Getzler*, Patterns of Fusion, in: P. Birks (ed.), The Classification of Obligations, p. 157–192; *M. R. T. Macnair*, Equity and Conscience, Oxford Journal of Legal Studies, Volume 27 (2007), p. 659–681; *D. Klinck*, Conscience, Equity and the Court of Chancery in Early Modern England.

154 Compare *J. Getzler*, Patterns of Fusion, in: P. Birks (ed.), The Classification of Obligations, p. 157–192, p. 178; *J. H. Langbein / R. T. Lerner / B. P. Smith*, History of the Common Law – The Development of Anglo-American Legal Institutions, p. 318; *D. Klinck*, Conscience, Equity and the Court of Chancery in Early Modern England, p. 62; *M. R. T. Macnair*, Equity and Conscience, Oxford Journal of Legal Studies, Volume 27 (2007), p. 659–681, p. 662.

155 *D. Klinck*, Conscience, Equity and the Court of Chancery in Early Modern England, p. 62.

156 Compare *D. Klinck*, Conscience, Equity and the Court of Chancery in Early Modern England, p. 63–64.

157 T. F.T. Plucknett / J. L. Barton (eds.), St. German's Doctor and Student, p. 207–208. Also *D. Klinck*, Conscience, Equity and the Court of Chancery in Early Modern England, p. 63.

for the realisation of natural law in the English legal system and its corresponding removal from secular interference must have appealed to the expertise of the early episcopal Chancellors as well as to the interests of later common law Chancellors. Klinck went as far as to suggest that it left their jurisdictional discretion largely unchecked.[158]

Either way, St. German's explanations tell us little about the process of substantive decision-making in the court. *Doctor and Student*, in effect, provided little more than further proof of the centrality of conscience in late medieval legal and societal discourse. Neither Year Book pleadings nor Chancery bills provide any evidence that lawyers before the Court of Chancery or the judges themselves shared St. German's concrete understanding of conscience, which was clearly shaped by the interests of a common lawyer. The popularity of *Doctor and Student* in the early modern period carries the risk of retrospectively overemphasising its significance for the history of the late medieval Court of Chancery.

2.7.5 Procedural understanding

The procedural understanding of conscience has been advocated most vehemently by Michael Macnair.[159] According to Macnair, conscience in the Court of Chancery "did not mean primarily either the modern lay idea, or the "conscience" of Christopher St. German's exposition".[160] Instead it referred to "the judge's, and the defendant's, private knowledge of facts".[161] Macnair developed his argument from the well-known medieval maxim that the judge decides according to what is alleged and proved, not according to conscience.[162] The common law clearly operated under this maxim: The issuance of the original writ already prescribed the available arguments and methods of proof.

158 *D. Klinck*, Conscience, Equity and the Court of Chancery in Early Modern England, p. 63, considered this the "problem" of St. German's treatment of the Court of Chancery.

159 *M. R. T. Macnair*, Equity and Conscience, Oxford Journal of Legal Studies, Volume 27 (2007), p. 659–681. The same idea seems to underlie the understanding of conscience in *S. F. C. Milsom*, Historical Foundations of the Common Law, S. 90.

160 *M. R. T. Macnair*, Equity and Conscience, Oxford Journal of Legal Studies, Volume 27 (2007), p. 659–681, p. 659.

161 *M. R. T. Macnair*, Equity and Conscience, Oxford Journal of Legal Studies, Volume 27 (2007), p. 659–681, p. 659.

162 "*Iudex secundum allegata et probata non secundum conscientam iudicat*." For an elaboration on this concept, see *K. W. Nörr*, Zur Stellung des Richters im Gelehrten Prozeß der Frühzeit: Iudex secundum allegata non secundum conscientiam iudicat, C. H. Beck, Munich, 1967.

After the pleadings had identified a matter of fact to be tried in the further proceedings, the court was then bound to a strict system of admissible proofs for the establishment of that fact.[163] The judgment was then rendered on the basis of what was alleged during the pleadings and proved at trial; any further considerations were deemed irrelevant.

Macnair presented conscience in the Court of Chancery as the alternative to this approach. Conscience "meant knowledge or belief of legally relevant facts which were not appropriately pleaded and proved".[164] Most importantly, this included facts discovered through the examination of the defendant under oath, a method of proof which was unavailable at common law at the time.[165] Additionally, the Lord Chancellor could judge upon his own suspicions or private knowledge.[166] The exact procedures for proof available in the Court of Chancery and their relation to the common law process will be discussed below.[167] For now, this short introduction should suffice to understand Macnair's view. In short, matters in conscience were all those which could not be proved by the common law because of its structure and which instead could be proved by examining the defendant on oath.

As the further discussion of the function of the late medieval Court of Chancery for the English legal system will show, I could not agree more with Macnair's assumption that the development of the court rested on its procedure. The procedural understanding of conscience was also clearly prevalent in canonical writings in the late Middle Ages.[168] However, Macnair's case for identifying the use of the term conscience in Chancery exclusively with its procedure seems less convincing. Although admittedly advanced in a procedural context, some late medieval uses of conscience, which Macnair cites in order to

163 Also *M. R. T. Macnair*, Equity and Conscience, Oxford Journal of Legal Studies, Volume 27 (2007), p. 659–681, p. 673.

164 *M. R. T. Macnair*, Equity and Conscience, Oxford Journal of Legal Studies, Volume 27 (2007), p. 659–681, p. 674.

165 *M. R. T. Macnair*, Equity and Conscience, Oxford Journal of Legal Studies, Volume 27 (2007), p. 659–681, p. 676.

166 Compare *M. R. T. Macnair*, Equity and Conscience, Oxford Journal of Legal Studies, Volume 27 (2007), p. 659–681, p. 675. This was indeed a characteristic of superior courts throughout Europe at the time. Compare *M. Meccarelli*, Arbitrium – Un'aspetto sistematico degli ornamenti giuridici in età di diretto comune, Giuffrè, Milan, 1998.

167 See below 4.

168 Compare *W. Decock*, The Judge's Conscience and the Protection of the Criminal Defendant: Moral Safeguards against Judicial Arbitrariness, in: G. Martyn / A. Musson / H. Pihlamajäki (eds.), From the Judge's Arbitrium to the Legality Principle – Legislation as a Source of Law in Criminal Trials, Duncker & Humblot, Berlin, 2013, p. 69–94.

illustrate his point, might just as well be explained with the modern understanding of an individual moral judgment.[169] Moreover, Macnair largely ignored the well-proved evidence of a substantive understanding of conscience in late medieval England. His warning that we should not conflate the technical use of a term in legal sources with its "'ordinary natural' meaning" goes wrong, insofar as other writers have already identified the contemporary meaning of conscience in legal contexts.[170]

2.7.6 *Conclusion*

What seems clear from the medieval sources is that conscience carried a specific meaning in the late Middle Ages and that the invocation of conscience expressed an expectation of substantive justice. On the other hand, fulfilling these expectations would have been wholly impossible without the additional procedural instruments available to the Lord Chancellor in the Court of Chancery. Together, procedural possibilities and substantive expectations provided the practical ground for the ascent of adjudication in late medieval Court of Chancery. In a work such as this, relying on the surviving court documentation and focusing on legal evolution, the focus necessarily lies on procedure. Further studies of medieval theological ideas and their practical application, however, might provide additional insight into the moral justification behind the work of the late medieval Court of Chancery. Even then, however, the availability of a justiciable concept of conscience does not lead to the conclusion it was consciously and consistently followed by the Lord Chancellors – all the hard evidence available about the late medieval Court of Chancery remains quiet on the substantive implications of conscience.

169 This is certainly true for the two jury-cases *M. R. T. Macnair* cites in support of his argument. When a jury is instructed to use "*conscientia*" rather than certainty when making its decision or when it is supposed to "inform the conscience of the court" in one of the later cases, in which matters of fact in the Court of Chancery were sent to a common law jury, the use of the term conscience is compatible with the modern understanding as an individual moral judgment. For these examples, see *M. R. T. Macnair*, Equity and Conscience, Oxford Journal of Legal Studies, Volume 27 (2007), p. 659–681, p. 674; 675.

170 This distinguishes conscience from the other examples *M. R. T. Macnair* provides for his premise: fee simple, tenant in tail and felony. See *M. R. T. Macnair*, Equity and Conscience, Oxford Journal of Legal Studies, Volume 27 (2007), p. 659–681.

2.8 Sureties

The bill in *Ardern v Ardern* closes with two 'pledges for the prosecution'. It tells us nothing more than the name and the rank of the sureties. As yeoman, they should have been part of the gentility of Birmingham – landed middle-class.[171] A parliamentary statute from 1436 had stipulated that no subpoena should be issued before the plaintiff had provided a surety for possible damages and expenses.[172] The statute was itself a reaction to parliamentary complaints about false suits in the Court of Chancery, which allegedly caused harassment to innocent subjects of the king.[173] It has, however, been suggested that a practice of providing pledges for Chancery suits existed even before the statutory intervention.[174]

A look through the bills shows that sureties were provided in most but not nearly in all cases. We can only speculate whether suretyship could also be declared separately or whether the requirement was habitually ignored altogether. The large number of files renders it unlikely that all bills without 'pledges for the prosecution' were dismissed. By the end of the 16th century, the practice had disappeared altogether.[175]

The interesting factual questions arising from the duty to provide sureties are who stood as surety, why did they do so and for what claims. The latter can be answered rather easily from the words of the statute: A surety had to stand in for possible damages and expenses of the defendant, in case the claims could not be realised against the plaintiff. Damages could be awarded at the discretion of the Lord Chancellor for bringing false suits.[176] As to the status of the sureties, Timothy Haskett has found that they were typically of local gentility – Ardern

171 Compare *T. S. Haskett*, Conscience, Justice and Authority in the Late-Medieval English Court of Chancery, in: A. Musson (ed.), Expectations of the Law in the Middle Ages, Boydell Press, Woodbridge, 2001, p. 151–163, p. 154. As we will see in the further proceedings, this classification appears doubtful for at least one of Walter Ardern's sureties, who at the same time designated himself as Walter's servant. See below 4.1.2.

172 (1436) 15 Hen. VI, c. 4, quoted in: *P. M. McDermott*, Jurisdiction of the Court of Chancery to Award Damages, The Law Quarterly Review, Volume 109 (1992), p. 652–673, p. 654.

173 *D. M. Kerly*, An Historical Sketch of the Equitable Jurisdiction of the Court of Chancery, p. 39.

174 *T. S. Haskett*, Conscience, Justice and Authority in the Late-Medieval English Court of Chancery, in: A. Musson (ed.), Expectations oft he Law in the Middle Ages, p. 151–163, p. 154.

175 *P. M. McDermott*, Jurisdiction of the Court of Chancery to Award Damages, The Law Quarterly Review, Volume 109 (1992), p. 652–673, p. 654.

176 *D. M. Kerly*, An Historical Sketch of the Equitable Jurisdiction of the Court of Chancery, p. 39–40.

thus seemingly represented a typical case.[177] That leaves us with the question why sureties would provide their assistance to plaintiffs in the Court of Chancery.

The possible explanations are numerous. First, Haskett nicely explained that this kind of support served an economic function: In the trust-based society of late medieval England, the pledge constituted a favour that could be – and would have to be – returned.[178] Second, providing the pledge might have been a profitable business model, as suggested by the reappearance of some 'old common sureties' in the Chancery bills.[179] Last and most importantly, acting as a surety was apparently risk-free. No evidence exists for actual prosecutions of sureties in the Court of Chancery.[180] In effect, Haskett suggested that the sureties were nothing more than compurgators adding the weight of their personal authority to the complaint.[181] The search for sureties might have already discouraged plaintiffs with fabricated claims. However, numerous clearly fictitious pledges – by John Ro, William Do, John Est and William West – have been identified within the Chancery bills.[182]

In the end, the evidence suggests that the requirement to present sureties was not more than a formal safeguard against abuses of Chancery process, which could be dispensed if necessary.[183]

2.9 Drafters

As we have seen, the bills followed a fairly elaborated canon. Their drafting must thus have required some familiarity with Chancery procedure. It is inconceiv-

177 *T. S. Haskett*, Conscience, Justice and Authority in the Late-Medieval English Court of Chancery, in: A. Musson (ed.), Expectations of the Law in the Middle Ages, p. 151–163, p. 154.

178 *T. S. Haskett*, Conscience, Justice and Authority in the Late-Medieval English Court of Chancery, in: A. Musson (ed.), Expectations of the Law in the Middle Ages, p. 151–163, p. 155–156.

179 Compare *M. E Avery*, An Evaluation of the Effectiveness of the Court of Chancery under the Lancastrian Kings, The Law Quarterly Review, Volume 86 (1970), p. 84–97, S. 96.

180 *T. S. Haskett*, Conscience, Justice and Authority in the Late-Medieval English Court of Chancery, in: A. Musson (ed.), Expectations of the Law in the Middle Ages, p. 151–163, p. 155.

181 *T. S. Haskett*, Conscience, Justice and Authority in the Late-Medieval English Court of Chancery, in: A. Musson (ed.), Expectations of the Law in the Middle Ages, p. 151–163, p. 154.

182 See *M. E Avery*, An Evaluation of the Effectiveness of the Court of Chancery under the Lancastrian Kings, The Law Quarterly Review, Volume 86 (1970), p. 84–97, S. 96.

183 Although some evidence exists for attempts of strengthening the requirements for sureties in the 1470s, see *M. E Avery*, An Evaluation of the Effectiveness of the

able that the plaintiffs themselves – whether widows, craftsmen or gentry – drafted them. Margaret Avery has identified a bill,[184] which "is defective in both grammar and construction and has the individualism of a real cry from the heart"[185] but that merely represents the exception to the countless elaborated bills, some of which I have described above.

2.9.1 Chancery clerks

Who else, then, might have drafted the bills? Avery herself concluded from the regularity of the formulations and from the fact that petition and answer sometimes appear on the same document that they must be the product of Chancery clerks, who might have formalised informal or oral complaints.[186] Interestingly, *Ardern v Ardern* represents one of the rather few cases, in which bill, answer and replication were all enclosed in a single document.[187] However, the case documentation further also includes all three forms individually.[188] The differences between the individual forms and the summary document are merely orthographical. Why would Chancery clerks prepare the documents both separately and combined and why would they employ different orthography when doing so? The only satisfactory answer is that they merely summarised the original documents, which had been drafted elsewhere, for procedural purposes.

2.9.2 Country lawyers

The original bills, then, must have been prepared for the respective parties by specialists – in other words: lawyers. This is also the result of Timothy Haskett's study on the linguistic and orthographical characteristics of late medieval

Court of Chancery under the Lancastrian Kings, The Law Quarterly Review, Volume 86 (1970), p. 84–97, S. 96.

184 *Gros v Of Wight* (1407–1456), C 1/16/331; quoted in parts in: *M. E Avery*, An Evaluation of the Effectiveness of the Court of Chancery under the Lancastrian Kings, The Law Quarterly Review, Volume 86 (1970), p. 84–97, S. 93.

185 *M. E Avery*, An Evaluation of the Effectiveness of the Court of Chancery under the Lancastrian Kings, The Law Quarterly Review, Volume 86 (1970), p. 84–97, p. 85.

186 *M. E Avery*, An Evaluation of the Effectiveness of the Court of Chancery under the Lancastrian Kings, The Law Quarterly Review, Volume 86 (1970), p. 84–97, p. 85.

187 C 1/1/114.

188 The bill can be found in file C 1/1/115, the answer in C 1/1/116 and the replication in C 1/1/117 at the National Archives.

Chancery bills.[189] Haskett not only recognised the varying quality of handwriting that would have reflected badly on professional Chancery clerks.[190] He also identified distinctively local style, idioms and language throughout the Chancery bills.[191] The distinctive canon and the general uniformity of the bills suggest a professional training of these lawyers in Chancery or from Chancery scribes.[192] Considering the combination of central court knowledge and local idiom, these lawyers must have been travelling between Westminster and the periphery.[193] They thus remained both available for plaintiffs as well as competent before the court.

3. Further Pleadings

While the defendant was commonly forced to reply to the original bill by a judicial writ – most commonly a subpoena –, the pre-trial process in the Court of Chancery remained very much in the hand of the parties. The court did not proceed with its own investigations before the parties had exchanged their positions conclusively. The defendant provided an answer (3.1) to the original bill and further reactions and counter-reactions could be advanced in the way of replication and rejoinder (3.2).

Following the later practice of the Court of Chancery and the secondary literature, I will designate the exchange of bill, answer, replication and (sur-) rejoinder as pleadings. A caveat, however, is in order: the 'pleadings' in the Court of Chancery show few similarities to the pleadings at common law, from which the term has been borrowed. Whereas the process of pleading at common law involved the exchange of barristers in front of a judge with countless technical limitations and with the aim of preparing the case for jury trial, 'pleadings' in the Court of Chancery were largely free of technical restrictions and arguably aimless.

189 *T. S. Haskett*, Country Lawyers? The Composers of English Chancery Bills, in: P. Birks (ed.), The Life of the Law, Proceedings of the Tenth British Legal History Conference, Oxford, 1991, Hambledon Press, London, 1993, S. 9–23.

190 *T. S. Haskett*, Country Lawyers? The Composers of English Chancery Bills, in: P. Birks (ed.), The Life of the Law, Proceedings of the Tenth British Legal History Conference, Oxford, 1991, S. 9–23, p. 12.

191 *T. S. Haskett*, Country Lawyers? The Composers of English Chancery Bills, in: P. Birks (ed.), The Life of the Law, Proceedings of the Tenth British Legal History Conference, Oxford, 1991, S. 9–23, p. 12.

192 *T. S. Haskett*, Country Lawyers? The Composers of English Chancery Bills, in: P. Birks (ed.), The Life of the Law, Proceedings of the Tenth British Legal History Conference, Oxford, 1991, S. 9–23, p. 17; 20–21.

193 Compare *T. S. Haskett*, Country Lawyers? The Composers of English Chancery Bills, in: P. Birks (ed.), The Life of the Law, Proceedings of the Tenth British Legal History Conference, Oxford, 1991, S. 9–23, p. 23.

3.1 Answer

Written answers to the original bills appeared from about 1440 onwards.[194] This immediately raises the question how defendants reacted to allegations against them presented in the bills before that date. Leaving aside the improbable explanation that answers from the late 14th and early 15th century were collectively lost, our attention has to turn to the prevalence of orality in late medieval Chancery proceedings. There is little more difficult for a legal historian than speculating on the extent and the content of oral procedures in the absence of contemporary reports. However, the subpoenas show that defendants were made to answer allegations presented in the bills in the Court of Chancery at a certain time.[195] In all likelihood, the examination of the defendant was originally effected in open court and never put in writing. The transition to written answers was then not abrupt. We can find several mentions of oral examinations of the defendant throughout the 15th century.[196] References in cases, which provide complete documentation with bill, answer, replication and rejoinder show that defendants could answer the original bill in writing and still be examined orally afterwards.[197] This might have provided a helpful tool in the case of evasive answers; the practice was therefore later reserved for such cases.[198] What we can generally see is a movement from oral to written procedures in line with the overall development of Chancery practice towards formality.[199]

In addition to their status as a response to an earlier document, the relative recency of written answers for the period of my research might also explain why they show less structural similarities than bills. While some repeating patterns and standard phrases evolved throughout the course of the late 15th century, we cannot identify an established canon for answers in the Court of Chancery in the

194 The difficulty of dating Chancery documents and the quantity of the sources hardly allow for a more accurate assessment. The date is in line with suggestions made by *M. E. Avery*, The History of the Equitable Jurisdiction of Chancery before 1460, Bulletin of the Institute of Historical Research, Volume 42 (1969), p. 129–144, p. 129 (setting the date at 1440) and *T. S. Haskett*, The Late Medieval Court of Chancery, Law and History Review, Volume 14 (1996), p. 245–313, p. 281 (mid-fifteenth century).

195 See above 2.6.1.

196 References to oral examinations can be found in the written answers themselves, see for example *Sharp v Temper* (1461–1467), Calendars I, p. lxiii, as well as in the depositions, see *Cobbethorn v William* (1458), Calendars I, p. li.

197 See for example *Cobbethorn v William* (1458), Calendars I, p. li; *Ardern v Ardern* (1465/1466), Calendars I, p. lxxii.

198 *J. L. Barton*, Roman Law in England, in: Société d'Histoire des Droits de L'Antiquité (ed.), Ius Romanum Medii Aevi, Giuffrè, Milan, Volume 5, 13a, 1971, p. 61.

199 See above 2.4.

late medieval sources. This carries with it the practical problem that it is much more difficult to present a clear picture of the standard process than in the case of the bills. The absence of a clear canon might also constitute the main reason for the absence of a detailed analysis of the answer in earlier scholarship. If at all, scholars counted the answers in order to gain an impression on how far individual processes went within the Chancery system.[200]

Another reason for the lack of scholarly attention might lie in the difficulty to compare the answer to classical elements of common law proceedings. Whereas writ and bill leave room for functional comparisons intuitive to any common lawyer, the answer as an individual document is difficult to compare to a specific part of the common law process. A look through the secondary literature shows that only John Barton has tried to present a succinct overview over the function of answers in Chancery proceedings in comparison to common law pleadings.[201]

Despite the lack of a strict canon, certain topics reappear in many or all answers of my research sample. The case of *Ardern v Ardern* once again provides a good impression of a 15th century Chancery answer as it includes most of the themes commonly appearing in the sources. In line with the presentation of the bill, I will thus follow the structure of *Ardern v Ardern* for my examination of Chancery answers. The answer started with a formal opening (3.1.1) and the recollection (3.1.2) of the plaintiff's bill. The defendant then went on to allege the insufficiency (3.1.3) of the plaintiff's claim and to contest the court's jurisdiction (3.1.4) before presenting the facts (3.1.5) of the case from his own perspective and praying for the dismissal of the case with costs in the conclusion (3.1.6). It should, nevertheless, be kept in mind that other answers – even when addressing the same issues – might look manifestly different. I will provide some information about and references to other possible modes of presentation when discussing the respective parts of the answer in *Ardern v Ardern*. Finally, I will provide a functional comparison of the answer in Chancery and common law pleadings (3.1.7).

> *Ardern v Ardern*
> *This is the answer of John Ardern the younger brother to Walter Ardern esquire to the bill put against him by the same Walter*
> *First where the said Walter says in the said bill that the said John piteously and lamentably to him complaining says, that where it was so that he had no living to live upon like a gentleman but upon your said beseecher, desiring him to make a grant by*

200 For an example, see *F. Metzger,* Das englische Kanzleigericht unter Kardinal Wolsey, tables on p. 335.

201 See *J. L. Barton,* Roman Law in England, in: Société d'Histoire des Droits de L'Antiquité (ed.), Ius Romanum Medii Aevi, Volume 5, 13a, p. 57–59.

deed unto the said John for time of his life on a manor in the shire of Worcester called Pedmore, your said beseecher having pity of his said brother any by mediation of one Agnes Middelmore and Richard son to the same Agnes enfeoffed the said John Ardern in and of the said manor to have to him time of his life and that feoffment, notwithstanding it was fully conditioned and agreed between the said John Ardern and your said beseecher that the same John should take the profits of the same during the life of your said beseecher, but after his death to enter and occupy time of his life, and to this intent the deed was delivered to the said Agnes and Richard by your said beseecher safely to keep during his life and then immediately after his death the said Agnes to deliver the deed to the said John Ardern to the intent aforesaid.
Thereto the said John by protestation that the matter comprehended in the said bill is not sufficient to put him to answer to, and also that it appears by the matter comprehended in the said bill that the said Walter if his matter were true should and might have an action of detinue of the said deed at the common law. Nevertheless for his answer and true declaration in this matter he says that for the good service that he did to the said Walter in his household and in other diverse places continually by vii years and more before the said feoffment [was] made, and for the love that the said Walter had to him, he of his own free will enfeoffed the said John in the said manor by a deed sealed by the seal of the said Walter and so made a letter of attorney unto one Thomas Hert to deliver seisin in the name of the said Walter upon the said deed to the said John, by force of which a livery seisin was openly made to the said John of the said manor in the presence of lx. persons and more, the which estate was made to the use and profit of the said John, without that it was conditioned and agreed between the said Walter and John that the same John should take no profits of the said manor during the life of the said Walter, and without that the said deed was ever delivered to the said Agnes and Richard by the said Walter safely to keep during his life in the form as the said Walter has supposed by his said bill. All which matters he will be ready to prove as this court would award him to do. Wherefore he prays to be dismissed and that he may have his reasonable costs and damages according to the statute in such case provided.

Despite the (relative) length of the answer, the facts – as presented by John Ardern – are quickly summarised: Unsurprisingly, the defendant confirmed the drafting of the title deed but denied the suspensive condition, effectiveness from the plaintiff's death, which was set forth in the plaintiff's bill. The fact that he also claimed to be deserving of the transfer of the manor due to his relentless service to his brother might seem less relevant from a legal perspective than it might have been in a court of conscience. Bill and answer then differed fundamentally on the circumstances of the actual transfer of title deed and possession. Whereas Walter had claimed to have instructed Agnes Middelmore and her son Richard, John introduced a new middleman: He contended to have received possession from one Thomas Hert, who had allegedly carried a sealed letter of attorney from Walter. The transfer was then effected by a livery of seisin, the common law conveyancing ceremony guaranteeing the publicity of property transfers in medieval England. Walter's differing account was fully rejected.

3.1.1 Opening

Knowing the contents of the original bill, the opening in *Ardern v Ardern* does not provide us with much exciting information. The names and the occupations of the parties were provided once more. A similar approach was visible in most other answers. In addition to facilitating the attribution to the original bill, the opening also provided us with the first evidence about the defendant's awareness of the circumstances of the case. Since the subpoena issued upon the original bill did not provide any information about its cause,[202] the answer must have been prepared after the defendant had been confronted with the allegations in the bill. In all likelihood, it was the immediate result of the summons. Additionally, the address shows that the documents were prepared not merely for the knowledge of the court but also explicitly for the other party. This might remind us of the adversarial character of the common law pleadings.

3.1.2 Recollection

What followed in John Ardern's answer was an almost word-by-word reproduction of the facts as stated in Walter Ardern's bill. It may be questioned whether this part of the answer served any useful purpose. This impression is supported by a look through other cases. While the wealth of sources almost guarantees the existence of similar answers, I was unable to identify another document, in which the facts as stated in the bill were reproduced almost in their entirety without additional comments. When direct recollections from the bill were provided, they were usually immediately followed, fact for fact, by rebuttals.[203] Otherwise, the alleged facts were either summarised briefly in the defendants' (or their lawyers') own words[204] or neglected altogether.[205] This clearly suggests that the recollection – in whatever form – was no requirement for an answer.

3.1.3 Insufficiency

After these purely formal opening paragraphs, the substantive part of the answer began. John Ardern claimed that the matters advanced in his brother's bill were

202 See above 2.6.1.

203 Compare *Felbrigge v Damme* (1443–1454), Calendars II, p. xxiii; *Scales v Felbrigge* (1448–1449), Calendars II, p. xxvi; *Berkeley v Shrewsbury* (1465–1467), Calendars I, p. lxxvi.

204 See for example *Revelle v Gower* (1471), Select Cases, p. 155; *Vavasour v Chadworth* (1473), Calendars I, p. xciii; *King's College v Ovy* (1480–1482), Calendars I, p. cvi.

205 See for example *Stokker v Colyns* (1474–1475), Calendars I, p. xcv; *Slefeld v Grafton* (1475), Calendars I, p. xcvii; *Mayhewe v Gardener* (1476–1477), Calendars I, p. xcix.

"not sufficient to put him to answer". While the context provides no help for ascertaining the meaning of sufficiency and a grammatical interpretation would allow for a large variety of understandings, the defendant's intention can be deduced from the contemporary legal meaning of the term. A bill was insufficient when the facts as presented by the plaintiff did not support the claim advanced in the same bill.[206] This raises an immediate problem for an examination of bills and answers in the Court of Chancery: In the absence of evidence on substantive rules, we simply do not know what claims would be 'sufficient' in the 'court of conscience'.

A look through the answers does not provide any guidance. When insufficiency was alleged, it was usually in the same form visible in *Ardern v Ardern*: as a blank allegation without any further explanation. This might suggest that an allegation of insufficiency was a mere formality, quite possibly in order to prevent prejudication in case the court sided with the factual presentation of the plaintiff. Support for such a view can be found in other answers: We can find several documents, in which the defendants concretely challenged a bill on the ground that the allegations of the plaintiff, even if true, did not justify a claim. In these cases, they provided the specific reason why the facts as stated by the plaintiffs should not lead to a judgment in their favour.

In *Fitz Harry v Lyngen*,[207] the defendant – amongst other things – argued that he should not be held liable to a deed he signed when he was illiterate and misinformed about its content. The defendant in *Pickering v Tonge*,[208] a city clerk, was sued in order to return an obligation, which he kept in his records. In his answer to the plaintiff's bill, he claimed that he had no authority to release documents without the mayor's consent. The defendant in *Toty v Norton*,[209] another use case, even portrayed himself – without using the technical language – as a good-faith purchaser without notice. All three answers provided concrete reasons, which we would consider matters of substantive law, why the plaintiffs should not be awarded a remedy, even if their statement of facts was accepted by the court.

206 Compare for the Court of Chancery also *J. L. Barton*, Roman Law in England, in: Société d'Histoire des Droits de L'Antiquité (ed.), Ius Romanum Medii Aevi, Volume 5, 13a, p. 57, and for English ecclesiastical courts *R. H. Helmholz*, The Oxford History of the Laws of England, Volume 1: The Canon Law and Ecclesiastical Jurisdiction from 567 to the 1640s, p. 324. This definition is also in line with the modern use of insufficiency in law. Compare W. Jowitt / C. Walsh (eds.), The Dictionary of English Law, Volume 1, S. 985.

207 (1454–1455), Calendars I, p. xlviii.

208 (1446–1450), Calendars I, p. xliv.

209 (1461–1470), Calendars I, p. lxxxiii.

In the light of this, the question why defendants would have abstractly claimed insufficiency remains open. Perhaps, the allegation of insufficiency was really nothing more than a reminder for the judge to consider the validity of the claim in conscience. After all, Chancery procedure did not foresee negative consequences for what common lawyers called 'mispleading'. This followed from the character of the court as a court of conscience. Mere formalities should not interfere with larger considerations of justice.[210] It might be suggested that this provides a first impression of later obstructions allowed by the additional procedural possibilities in Chancery.[211]

The allegation of insufficiency was a standard feature of many but not all late 15th century cases. Some answers also exclusively addressed the facts of the bill,[212] whereas others – as seen above – claimed and explained 'legal' objections specifically.[213] John Barton has, at least indirectly, likened the claim of insufficiency to a demurrer at common law. When pleading a demurrer, the defendant in a common law suit submitted that he was not bound to answer because the allegations disclosed no valid ground for relief.[214] The parallel is obvious. However, the effects of a demurrer at common law and a claim of insufficiency in the Court of Chancery were fundamentally different. A demurrer at common law was taken as an admission of facts.[215] Pleading a demurrer thus carried the immediate risk of a judgment against the defendant in case the judge disagreed.[216] In the Court of Chancery, on the other hand, insufficiency was alleged routinely, while the defendants also presented the facts from their own perspective.[217] Additionally, it was possible to claim the insufficiency of only parts of the bill,[218] whereas the common law demurrer went against the entire

210 (1469) Y. B. 9 Edw. IV, Trin., f. 14, pl. 9. Identified but misquoted by *J. L. Barton*, Roman Law in England, in: Société d'Histoire des Droits de L'Antiquité (ed.), Ius Romanum Medii Aevi, Volume 5, 13a, p. 57.

211 For those, see above chapter II, 5.

212 See for example *Manyngham v Mervyn* (1472–1473), Calendars I, p. xci.

213 *Pickering v Tonge* (1446–1450), Calendars I, p. xliv; *Fitz Harry v Lyngen* (1454–1455), Calendars I, p. xlviii; *Toty v Norton* (1461–1470), Calendars I, p. lxxxiii.

214 *J. L. Barton*, Roman Law in England, in: Société d'Histoire des Droits de L'Antiquité (ed.), Ius Romanum Medii Aevi, Volume 5, 13a, p. 58.

215 *J. L. Barton*, Roman Law in England, in: Société d'Histoire des Droits de L'Antiquité (ed.), Ius Romanum Medii Aevi, Volume 5, 13a, p. 58.

216 *J. L. Barton*, Roman Law in England, in: Société d'Histoire des Droits de L'Antiquité (ed.), Ius Romanum Medii Aevi, Volume 5, 13a, p. 58.

217 This is true for most answers from the 15th century. For instructive examples, see *Ardern v Ardern* (1465/1466), Calendars I, p. lxxii; *Vavasour v Chadworth* (1473), Calendars I, p. xciii; *Mayhewe v Gardener* (1476/1477), Calendars I, p. xcix.

218 See above.

claim.[219] All these differences can again be explained by the maxim that mispleading should not prejudice the parties in a court of conscience.[220] Once more, the procedural rules of the Court of Chancery showed greater flexibility. The formalities of the common law were rejected and effectively substituted with broad judicial discretion. The advantage of this approach is obvious: A decision can be made with regard to all the circumstances of the case rather than on mere technicalities. On the other hand, such an inclusive approach provides enormous potential for delay once the parties exploit it.

3.1.4 Jurisdiction

John Ardern further claimed that "Walter if his matter were true should and might have an action of detinue of the said deed at the common law". Given the difficulties in delineating common law and Court of Chancery jurisdiction in the 15th century, which I have highlighted above,[221] it comes as no surprise that a defendant would raise the issue in his defence. In this particular case, however, the assertion of common law jurisdiction seems rather far-fetched. While Walter indeed asked for a return of the title deeds, he would have had no possibility to prove that they were still rightfully his in a common law action of detinue. The matter underlying his whole claim, the oral condition made on the transfer of the deed, could not be addressed at common law at all in the late Middle Ages. John Ardern's sketchy argument again underlines that almost any answer in the Court of Chancery could challenge the bill on the grounds of jurisdiction – if necessary with some creativity and / or insolence. As I have explained above, the line between common law and Chancery jurisdiction was at best fine and more realistically permeable.[222]

It should not be necessary to return to the grounds of jurisdictional disputes and to the assumption of responsibility by the Lord Chancellors. The arguments advanced in the answers generally followed the pattern I have identified above: The defendants regularly brought up alternative common law remedies and ecclesiastical subject-matter jurisdiction. A few instructive examples should suffice:

In *Arkendon v Starkey*,[223] the vicar of a local parish advanced a simple tithes claim against the defendant, who answered briefly that "the said matter is merely spiritual and the knowledge thereof belongs to the ordinary".

219 *J. L. Barton*, Roman Law in England, in: Société d'Histoire des Droits de L'Antiquité (ed.), Ius Romanum Medii Aevi, Volume 5, 13a, p. 58.
220 See above.
221 See 2.5.1.
222 See above 2.5.1–2.5.2.
223 (1442), Calendars I, p. xxxv.

Morton v Langley[224] represented an inner-ecclesiastical tithes conflict. The archdeacon of Norwich claimed tithes from local priests within his archdeaconry. Contesting again the jurisdiction of the Court of Chancery, the defendants replied that the matter was for a spiritual court to decide. Moreover, the case had long been pendant in ecclesiastical courts and was now on a final appeal before the Papal court in Rome. Interestingly, the replication of the plaintiff distinguished that while the ascertainment of the existence of a claim should be left to an ecclesiastical tribunal, restitution was a matter for conscience in the Court of Chancery. This again shows the difficulty in delineating the jurisdiction of the Court of Chancery from other courts.

The problems associated with the theoretical precedence of common law jurisdiction are perhaps best exemplified by the case of *Fitz Harry v Lyngen*.[225] The defendant proposed no less than five concrete alternative actions at common law for what was at its heart a straightforward trust case.

3.1.5 Facts

In *Ardern v Ardern*, the denials of sufficiency and jurisdiction were "nevertheless" followed by John Ardern's own representation of the facts underlying the claim. This shows again that an attack on the bill on substantive or jurisdictional grounds did not preclude the defendants from providing their own version of the events, which lead to the conflict.[226] The manner of fact presentation in the answer is immediately reminiscent of Walter's original bill. Facts were presented in general terms without recourse to artificial or legal language. Thus, what has been said about the bill is confirmed by the answer: It provided another opportunity to present all the facts of the case from the defendant's perspective. In contrast to the common law, we cannot find artificial technical restrictions. More importantly, the parties did not have to plead to a single-issue, which could then be decided by a jury.[227] Instead, they could challenge every single fact alleged by the other party.

This – together with the rule that 'mispleading' could not prejudice the parties – also naturally encouraged the contestation of as many of the facts as possible. *Ardern v Ardern* represented one of the many cases, in which the defendant provided a widely diverging, and thus effectively new, presentation of

224 (1467–1470), Calendars I, p. lxxxi.

225 (1454–1455), Calendars I, p. xlviii.

226 See above 3.1.3.

227 As was the case at common law, see *S. N. Subrin*, How Equity Conquered Common Law: The Federal Rules of Civil Procedure in Historical Perspective, University of Pennsylvania Law Review, Volume 135 (1987), S. 909–1002, S. 916.

the facts from his own perspective.[228] In other cases, the facts as presented in the bill were often addressed and rejected one-by-one.[229] Overall, the answer offered opportunities for the presentations of facts, which were as far-ranging as those in the original bill. It thus merely reflected the adequate and logical response to the structure of the bill.

One potential problem of a written answer – not necessarily visible in *Ardern v Ardern* – probably comes to the mind of every lawyer: the possibility of evading concrete answers to the alleged facts. It would be an exaggeration to say that evasion appears as a major problem from the study of the 15th century answers. In fact, the defendants' statements largely addressed the issues at hand – whether the defendants acted especially genuine or unscrupulous is hard to judge. Nevertheless, the problem of evasion later led to the adoption of a rule that an oral examination of the defendant could follow after three evasive written answers.[230] We do not have clear evidence of the practice of the court regarding evasion in the 15th century. However, the parallel existence of both written answers and oral examinations suggests that additional oral examination might have been used earlier and more flexibly.[231] This is also supported by John Ardern's statement that he would be ready to prove his account as the court awards him to do. Additionally, it should be kept in mind that even if defendants evaded concrete answers to the bill, the Court of Chancery was still equipped with further opportunities for fact-finding, most notably witness testimony and documentary evidence.[232] With these instruments, it was arguably better suited for fact-finding than the common law, which disqualified party testimony and limited the availability of witness testimony and documentary evidence as modes of proof.[233]

For an explanation of the historical background, see *T. F. T. Plucknett*, A Concise History of the Common Law, Butterworth, London, 5th edition, 1956, p. 399–418; *J. H. Langbein / R. T. Lerner / B. P. Smith*, History of the Common Law – The Development of Anglo-American Legal Institutions, p. 147–152.

228 See also *Fowler v Iwardby* (1466), Calendars I, p. lxviii; *Clyfford v Apulderfeld* (1481), Calendars I, p. cv; *King's College v Ovy* (1480–1482), Calendars I, p. cvi.

229 For examples, see *Sharp v Temper* (1461–1467), Calendars I, p. lxiii; *Berkeley v Shrewsbury* (1465–1467), Calendars I, p. lxxvi.

230 *J. L. Barton*, Roman Law in England, in: Société d'Histoire des Droits de L'Antiquité (ed.), Ius Romanum Medii Aevi, Volume 5, 13a, p. 61, fn. 213.

231 For the parallel application of written answer and oral examination, see *Cobbethorn v William* (1458), Calendars I, p. li.

232 See below 4.1 and 4.2. Compare also *J. H. Langbein / R. T. Lerner / B. P. Smith*, History of the Common Law – The Development of Anglo-American Legal Institutions, p. 290–292.

233 For an elaboration of Chancery and common law means of proof, see below 4.

A look through answers from the late 15th century shows one more interesting development. In line with a general movement towards formalisation, answers began to start with a statement claiming the general untruth of the bill, for example declaring that the defendant "knows no thing in the said bill to be true".[234] While the answers then went on to present the facts from the defendants' perspective, this must be seen as a general rejection of the factual claims in the bill. This might remind us of the general statement of insufficiency examined above. The statement did not fulfil an immediately identifiable purpose, as the actual factual arguments were yet to follow. However, another common law parallel comes to mind. According to common law procedure, the defendant had automatically conceded every factual allegation, which was not expressly contested during the pleadings.[235] The statement might thus have been an imported safeguard from the common law,[236] despite the existence of the mispleading rule in the Court of Chancery.[237]

3.1.6 Conclusion

At the end of his answer, John Ardern submitted that he would be ready to prove his allegations, that he "prays to be dismissed and that he may have his reasonable costs and damages according to the statute in such case provided". His conclusion thus advanced three distinctive points: his readiness to prove the facts as alleged in the answer, a request for the dismissal of the bill and a claim for costs and damages resulting from what he considered unjustified allegations. These three points reappeared in most closing statements of answers from the second half of the 15th century.[238] The proofs, which John Ardern promised to present, if questioned, could include his own oral examination,[239] witness testimony or documentary evidence such as the title deed.[240] It should furthermore come as no surprise that the defendant to a suit would ask for a dismissal of

234 Quoted from *King's College v Ovy* (1480–1482), Calendars I, p. cvi. For further cases claiming the 'untruth' of all matters alleged in the bill, see *Flykke v Banyard* (1483–1484), Calendars I, p. cxv; *Cullyer v Knyvett* (ca. 1536), Calendars I, p. cxxxvii.

235 Compare *J. L. Barton*, Roman Law in England, in: Société d'Histoire des Droits de L'Antiquité (ed.), Ius Romanum Medii Aevi, Volume 5, 13a, p. 57.

236 Similarly, *J. L. Barton*, Roman Law in England, in: Société d'Histoire des Droits de L'Antiquité (ed.), Ius Romanum Medii Aevi, Volume 5, 13a, p. 57.

237 See above 3.1.3.

238 For further examples, see *Lovell v Echard* (1456–1460), Calendars I, p. liv; *Sharp v Temper* (1461–1467), Calendars I, p. lxiii; *Manyngham v Mervyn* (1472–1473), Calendars I, p. xci.

239 See above 3.1, introduction.

240 For the available modes of proof, see below 4.

the claim. More interestingly, John Ardern also claimed damages and costs "according to the statute in such case provided". The statute John Ardern was relying on seems to have been passed in the reign of Richard II as a consequence of reoccurring parliamentary complaints about false suits in the Court of Chancery.[241] It endowed the Lord Chancellor with the power to award damages according to his discretion, whenever bills had proven untrue.[242]

3.1.7 Answer and common law pleading

As I have already cautioned above, the answer in Chancery proceedings does not lend itself to similarly compelling common law comparisons as the bill. Its function thus cannot simply be explained through the contemporary state of the common law. Nevertheless, some observations about its function in and for the process in the Court of Chancery might provide us with an interesting contrast to the common law – and thus with further reasons for the rise of the Court of Chancery despite the existence of a fully-operational royal system of law.

First of all, it should be recognised that the defendants had to provide the answer under oath.[243] It seems largely futile to speculate about the practical effect of an oath on the truthfulness of the answers. Some observations, however, can be drawn from the sources: A study of the answers generally does not provide examples, in which the defendant actively conceded the allegations made in the bill. The cases rather show a willingness to counter the allegations of the bill with the defendants' own narrative. It should be borne in mind, however, that countless cases do not provide any more documents than the

241 Also *P. M. McDermott*, Jurisdiction of the Court of Chancery to Award Damages, The Law Quarterly Review, Volume 109 (1992), p. 652–673, p. 654. For more information about parliamentary petitions against the jurisdiction of the Court of Chancery, see *D. M. Kerly*, An Historical Sketch of the Equitable Jurisdiction of the Court of Chancery, p. 37–46. The tradition of statutory intervention against reckless or forged lawsuits dates back to Roman law, compare *Justinian*'s Inst. 4.16.

242 (1393), 17 Ric. II, c. 6. The bill was quoted by *P. M. McDermott*, Jurisdiction of the Court of Chancery to Award Damages, The Law Quarterly Review, Volume 109 (1992), p. 652–673, p. 654: "For as much as People be compelled to come before the King's Council or in the Chancery by Writs grounded upon untrue Suggestions; that the Chancellor fort he Time being, presently after that such Suggestions be duly found and proved untrue, shall have Power to ordain and award Damages according to his Discretion, to him which is so troubled unduly, as afore said". As explained above, sureties later had to be provided to guarantee this claim, see 2.8.

243 See also *M. R. T. Macnair*, Equity and Conscience, Oxford Journal of Legal Studies, Volume 27 (2007), p. 659–681, p. 676, who also provided a good introduction into the additional fact-finding opportunities provided by this tool.

original bill. A confession might have lead to immediate judgment or settlement. In such a case, no need for further documentation would have arisen.

Evidence from the late 16th century, when the technicality of answers had already greatly increased, also appears contradictory. While Lord Chancellor Bromley (1530–1587; Lord Chancellor 1579–1587) complained of the recent practice of providing "lewd, libelling and slanderous speeches" rather than "directly to answer the contents of the bill",[244] petitioners apparently still envisioned that the oath would regularly lead to a confession of the defendant.[245] Arguments about an increased reliability of the answers through the necessity of an oath thus have to rely on the general effect of religious sanctions in the devout society of the late Middle Ages.[246] The threat of damnation must have provided a great incentive for confessing the truth to late medieval litigants.[247] Yet, the many cases in which bill and answer remained contradictory show the limited impact of the threat. It is hardly conceivable that all plaintiffs – after all, bills were not provided under oath – in these cases brought false allegations into the Court of Chancery, which were then contested truthfully by defendants under oath.

An immediate confession, however, was not the only way in which the answer of the defendant could contribute to fact-finding in the Court of Chancery. Even if the answers were formulated untruthfully or evasively, we should not underestimate their usefulness for the further proceedings. The answers were studied, considered and relied upon by both the court as well as the opposing parties. They could thus inform the questioning of witnesses or the defendants themselves. Equally, they could again be contested through revised arguments in the plaintiffs' replication. Even when disagreement about the facts remained, the answers thus still carried the potential for a better understanding of the facts underlying the case.

This tentative conclusion admittedly suggests a rather modest contribution to fact-finding. However, the advantages should become clear in a swift comparison with the role of party testimony at common law: There, the defendant could neither present a complete account of the facts from his perspective nor be

244 *Carew v Kinge* (1582), quoted from *W. J. Jones*, The Elizabethan Court of Chancery, Clarendon Press, Oxford, 1967, p. 216.

245 *D. Klinck*, Conscience, Equity and the Court of Chancery in Early Modern England, S. 99, with further references.

246 For a detailed examination of the role of the oath in the contemporary canonical process specifically, see *A. Fiori*, Il giuramento di innocenza nel processo canonico medievale – Storia e disciplina della purgatio canonica, Klostermann, Frankfurt/Main, 2013.

247 Compare also *J. H. Langbein/R. T. Lerner/B. P. Smith*, History of the Common Law – The Development of Anglo-American Legal Institutions, p. 290.

examined during the trial. The examination of the defendant was not recognised as a means of proof in any common law action.[248] This was most likely because of concerns about the parties' self-interest and of resulting perjury.[249] It was only at the pleading stage that factual allegations were exchanged between the parties (or rather their lawyers) but even then the requirement of single-issue pleading forced the parties to reduce their factual claim to a single yes-or-no issue decidable by a jury.[250] It should be clear that the defendants' answers in the Court of Chancery introduced a comparatively greater capacity for fact-finding into the Chancery process.

The initial picture sharpens: The common law inhibited effective fact-finding through technicalities created to safeguard the parties and to reduce judicial discretion. Procedure in the Court of Chancery, on the other hand, provided a greater openness. In the 15th century, it seemed to embody a superior fact-finding capacity. However, it already carried within it the potential for abuse – in this case through evasive or untrue answers.

3.2 Replication and rejoinder

The replication allowed the plaintiff to react to the defendant's answer, whereas the rejoinder represented the defendant's reaction to the plaintiff's replication. Both types of documents appear regularly in the Chancery sources from about the same time as the answers.[251] The extent of party exchange differed from case to case. Many cases were apparently processed after the bill or after the answer of the defendant.[252] However, written replications and rejoinders became a common feature of Chancery process after 1440. In many cases, the documentation extended only to the replication.[253] Typically, however, replication and

248 *M. R. T. Macnair*, The Law of Proof in Early Modern Equity, Duncker & Humblot, Berlin, 1999, p. 58.

249 Compare, *M. R. T. Macnair*, The Law of Proof in Early Modern Equity, p. 203–219.

250 Compare *J. H. Langbein / R. T. Lerner / B. P. Smith*, History of the Common Law – The Development of Anglo-American Legal Institutions, p. 274.

251 See above 3.1.

252 *M. R. T. Macnair*, Equity and Conscience, Oxford Journal of Legal Studies, Volume 27 (2007), p. 659–681, p. 676, claimed that roughly three quarters of cases in the Court of Chancery went no further than to the defendant's answer on oath in later days. The figure correlates with my impression from the sighting of 15th century sources.

253 In the case of *Ellowe v Taylor*, Calendars I, p. cxxix, no answer has been preserved, while a replication can be found in C 1/1/212. This clearly shows a gap in documentation. The absence of a rejoinder on the other hand, can easily be explained by the circumstance that the defendant had no additional information

rejoinder appear together in the files.[254] Interestingly, the exchange of documents between the litigants was not necessarily limited to these four documents. We also have evidence of several 15th or early 16th century cases, in which the plaintiff replied to the defendant's rejoinder with a surrejoinder.[255] It thus seems likely that the extent of the exchange between the parties was not strictly regulated. This is in line with the general policy of the 'court of conscience' not to inhibit effective fact-finding with mere technicalities.[256]

3.2.1 Structure

A first look through replications and rejoinders also shows that they hardly followed an established canon. In the second half of the 15th century, they typically showed even less consistency than the answers. The reason for this is to be found in the simple fact that they generally only addressed the contested facts, jurisdictional or substantive issues, which emerged from a juxtaposition of bill and answer. Otherwise, the structure and content of replications and rejoinders were highly reminiscent of the answer, in that substantive issues, jurisdiction and facts were sometimes advanced individually and sometimes collectively. The case of *Ardern v Ardern* should again serve to illustrate typical features and functions of a replication. Given the fact that the further proceedings do not mention a rejoinder and that the disputed issues seem well established from the existing party exchange, it is most likely that the case immediately proceeded to the stage of proof after the replication.

> *Ardern v Ardern*
> *This is the Replication of Walter Ardern esquire unto the Answer of John Ardern his brother made to the bill put by the said Walter into this court against the said John. The said Walter says that he of pity at the lamentable complaint of the said John his brother granted to the same John by a deed the manor of Pedmore for time of his life and caused seisin to be delivered thereby, and that it was faithfully conditioned and agreed between them at the sealing and livery of the said deed that the said Walter should during his life take the profits and the revenues of the same manor to his own use and*

to add to the answer. Examples for this include *Ardern v Ardern* (1465–1466), Calendars I, p. lxxii; *Berkeley v Shrewsbury* (1465–1467), Calendars I, lxxvi; *Morton v Langley* (1467–1470), Calendars I, p. lxxxi.

254 See for example *Sharp v Temper* (1461–1467), Calendars I, p. lxiii; *Fowler v Iwardby* (1466), Calendars I, p. lxviii; *Mayhewe v Gardener* (1467–1477), Calendars I, p. xcix.

255 See *Worsley v Bettiscombe* (1465–1467), Calendars II, p. xlv. Additionally, the database of the National Archives provides the cases of *Yonge v Lucas* (1401–1500), C 4/6/62; *Smeythe v Mordaunt* (1471–1550), C 4/24/182; *Colles v Thomas* (1489–1524), C 4/9/93.

256 See above 2.4.

that after the death of the same Walter the same John should take the profits of the said manor during his life, and that the deed should remain in mean hand according to the said agreement, supposing then to the said Walter that the said John could by the said deed nor livery of seisin take no profits of the said manor contrary to the agreement abovesaid. All which matters the said Walter is ready to prove verify and make good as this court will award, and prays that the said John may be ruled and compelled to take no profits of the said manor during the life of the said Walter, and also to recompense the said Walter of all manor issues and profits of the said manor taken by the said John contrary to his agreement abovesaid, as reason and good conscience require in this behalf.

After the standard opening sentence, Walter Ardern readdressed the facts underlying his claim. While not explicitly deviating from the original bill, the replication provided some clarification. As such, it becomes clear that Walter originally consented to John taking possession of the manor with immediate effect. The question of possession thus required no further examination. What remained contested were the profits from the land. In contrast to the original bill, in which he merely requested a preliminary procedural remedy in the form of the subpoena, Walter also explicitly asked for compensation for lost profits and an order precluding John from taking future profits from the land.

The replication furthermore provides us with the new information that Walter believed the retention of the title deed in the hands of the Middlemores would preclude John from taking profits from the land. Since, however, John effectively got into the possession of the title deed, this fact merely adds to explaining Walter's original motivation. It had no effect on further proceedings.

3.2.2 Fact presentation

Generally, the replication offered several options for the plaintiffs to react to the defendants' answers. They could just outright deny the defendants' account and more or less refer to their original statement;[257] they could clarify or specify their original allegations[258] or they could try to disprove the answer by addressing its facts point-by-point.[259] Theoretically, they could also drop their charges but that would not have required the drafting of a replication and thus was not documented. Walter Ardern's replication clearly fell into the category of clarification. Interestingly, it did not even mention John's significantly diverging statement of facts. The respective accounts of the two parties were, on the other hand, so fundamentally inconsistent that an argumentative challenge to the other party's position might have seemed futile.

257 See for example *Baker v Parson* (1465–1467), Calendars II, p. l.

258 For example *Ardern v Ardern* (1465/1466), Calendars I, p. lxxii; *Fowler v Iwardby* (1466), Calendars I, lxviii; *Stokker v Colyns* (1474–1475), Calendars I, p. xcv.

259 For example *Berkeley v Shrewsbury* (1465–1467), Calendars I, p. lxxvi.

3.2.3 *Effect of non-contestation*

Further insights into the Chancery process can also be gained from what Walter Ardern's replication did not address: as far as we can tell from the documentation, the plaintiff simply ignored the allegations of insufficiency and lack of jurisdiction advanced in the defendant's answer. The reason for this can hardly have lain in a lack of arguments. As we have seen above, the allegation of insufficiency was effectively a formality advanced in the absence of a clear substantive challenge to the bill and the reference to a common law action of detinue in this case was misplaced.[260] As the further proceedings in *Ardern v Ardern* will show, however, this neglect did not prejudice Walter. Clearly, these issues of law were left to the decision of the judge. Neither the substance of the claim nor the alternative jurisdiction was mentioned again; the case simply proceeded to the stage of proof. This example again confirms the rejection of common law concepts of formality in the Court of Chancery. The parties should not be prejudiced by technical rules and thus did not have to repeat what was evident anyway. The discrepancy to common law pleading is again remarkable.

Another question, which comes to mind in this context, is the effect of the non-contestation of relevant facts. The replications in my sample merely included general allegations of non-contestation, which appeared entirely unfounded and accordingly do not seem have had an effect on the further proceedings.[261] Otherwise, a party to Chancery proceedings was only negatively affected, when it could not provide a sensible factual account in reply to either bill or answer upon further examination.[262] However, we have no evidence for a procedural rule, which automatically qualified non-contestation as a confession in the 15th century – as was the case at common law.[263]

The absence of jurisdictional and substantive arguments in *Ardern v Ardern* should not make us believe that these issues were generally disregarded in replications and rejoinders. In fact, most of the serious claims advanced in the answers were first rejected in replications and then reinforced in rejoinders. Discussions about jurisdiction generally followed the arguments outlined in the context of the bill.[264] Arguments touching substantive rules were kept in the comparatively simple and moral rather than legal terminology characteristic of the late medieval Court of Chancery.[265]

260 See above 3.1.3.

261 *Stokker v Colyns* (1474–1475), Calendars I, p. xcv; *Slefeld v Grafton* (1475), Calendars I, p. xcvii.

262 *M. R. T. Macnair*, The Law of Proof in Early Modern Equity, p. 76.

263 *M. R. T. Macnair*, The Law of Proof in Early Modern Equity, p. 76.

264 See above 2.5.

265 For example *Sharp v Temper* (1461–1467), Calendars I, p. lxiii, in which the defendant rejoined that the acts of the plaintiff were "contrary to the law of God"

3.2.4 Departure from the bill

With reference to *Ardern v Ardern*, I have shown that the clarification of the facts in the original bill was a common feature of replications. However, it is a thin line between the clarification of old and the introduction of new facts. This raises the question how such a so-called 'departure' from the original bill was treated. The common law position in this regard was once again fairly clear: departure from the original pleadings was impossible and new facts required a new process under a separate writ. This only left the problem of identifying departure.

In the Court of Chancery, the case of *Mayhewe v Gardener*[266] provided an example for a possible departure. The plaintiff had originally complained about the state of his parish church, which required substantial investments on his behalf. For the decay of the building, he blamed his predecessor, who had died intestate and allegedly transferred his assets by deed to the defendant before his death. The plaintiff thus asked for compensation for his costs from the defendant. Contesting the claim, the defendant answered that he had received certain sums from the predecessor in return for a concrete sale and for the celebration of masses. In the replication, the plaintiff then alleged that the defendant had also earlier received title to property from the deceased priest. It is upon this assertion that the defendant, in his rejoinder, claims that the issues "newly and first alleged [in the] replication" were "as a new complaint departed from the original bill". Despite the existence of a decree in this case, it is unclear how the court reacted to this objection. The plaintiff was awarded compensation without further reference to the details of the case.

The case does not provide us with a definite statement on the rules for departure from the court. It does, however, allow for a tentative conclusion: While departure from the bill was argued by the defendant in an apparent parallel to the common law, the court was not overly concerned with the intricacies of identifying a departure in its aspiration to decide the case. This finding is in line with John Barton's assessment that, in contrast to the later practice of the court, plaintiffs "who are alleged to have fallen into this sin do not appear to have suffered from it".[267]

Overall, replication and rejoinder represented the consequential results of bill and answer. While they showed a less developed canon, they addressed the same

since no "Christian man should be discharged from keeping his commandments to God". See also above 2.4.3.

266 (1476–1477), Calendars I, p. xcix.

267 *J. L. Barton*, Roman Law in England, in: Société d'Histoire des Droits de L'Antiquité (ed.), Ius Romanum Medii Aevi, Volume 5, 13a, p. 57, fn. 192, with reference to *Sharp v Temper* (1461–1467), Calendars I, p. lxiii, in which, however, no decree was preserved.

issues and fulfilled the same functions, thereby offering opportunities for the litigants to present their case without artificial restrictions. In the second half of the 15th century, both replications and rejoinders were still generally brief and to the point. This seems to have changed dramatically within less than a century.[268]

3.2.5 Replication, rejoinder and common law pleadings

The back-and-forth exchange between the parties in bill, answer, replication and rejoinder is reminiscent of the common law pleadings documented from contemporary Year Books. That is why it is also generally referred to as Chancery pleading.[269] But while replication and rejoinder were clearly helpful for clarifying or identifying the disputed issues, their function needs to be delineated strictly from common law pleadings. Most importantly, they did not force the litigants to reduce the case to a single disputed issue. On the contrary, the parties had the opportunity to present all the circumstances of the case from a factual as well as a substantive perspective. Moreover, in doing so, they were not inhibited by technical rules about admission or mispleading. Just like bill and answer, replication and rejoinder thus exhibited all the aforementioned qualities and dangers of the Chancery process.

4. Evidence

As I have shown above, the pleadings in the late medieval Court of Chancery allowed for substantially greater party input than the common law process. The opportunity to present contingent cases broadened the scope of royal conflict resolution beyond the traditional common law actions and the restrictive bill jurisdiction otherwise available. As a result, the court was faced with a comparatively greater volume of information, which was not simply filtered through the application of technical rules. What did the Court of Chancery do with this information in order to reach a judgment? How could it verify the information provided by the litigants in the pleadings? These questions already hint at the possibility that the greater volume of information provided not only

268 *W. J. Jones*, The Elizabethan Court of Chancery, p. 220, spoke of the "grotesque proportions" and "absurd lengths" of replications and rejoinders in the second half of the 16th century. Most documents from the 15th century, on the other hand, are significantly shorter than bills and answers.

269 Compare for example *D. M. Kerly*, An Historical Sketch of the Equitable Jurisdiction of the Court of Chancery, p. 67; *W. J. Jones*, The Elizabethan Court of Chancery, p. 177; *J. L. Barton*, Roman Law in England, in: Société d'Histoire des Droits de L'Antiquité (ed.), Ius Romanum Medii Aevi, Volume 5, 13a, p. 57.

an opportunity but also a real challenge. Facilitating parties to 'make their case' in a royal court, automatically raises their expectations. The opportunity to present a case in its full scope would be worth relatively little if the information presented could not be processed somewhat efficiently. How did the Court of Chancery address the resulting challenge?

For the 15th century, these questions are difficult to answer. The sources do not provide a whole lot of information beyond the party pleadings. As mentioned above, no reasoned judgments, in which the court would elaborate its findings, are available. We do, however, have some evidence about how the court tried to verify the allegations advanced in the pleadings. Two types of evidence, which mirror our two most common contemporary methods of proof, can be found scattered between the party pleadings from the second half of the 15th century: the testimony of witnesses (4.1) and documentary evidence (4.2).

4.1 Witness testimony

In the absence of further source material, the role and extent of witness testimony throughout the 15th century is difficult to trace. From the second half of the 15th century, regular evidence of the examination of witnesses in the English periphery – and thus outside of the Court of Chancery – exists.[270] The Lord Chancellor instructed local notables through a writ of *dedimus potestatem* to examine potential witnesses on the basis of the pleadings. It was the well-documented practice of the court in the early modern period that witnesses from the vicinity of London testified before a master in Chancery, whereas a writ of *dedimus potestatem* was issued for the examination of witnesses from other regions.[271] While I have sighted only one deposition which was taken by the Master of the Rolls in Westminster in the 15th century,[272] this distinction probably dates back to the late medieval period. The fact that witness testimony taken upon a writ of *dedimus potestatem* was preserved in greater number might be explained by the documentary routines: The writ was sent to the respective

270 See for example *Cobbethorn v William* (1458), Calendars I, p. li; *Babington v Gull* (1458), Calendars I, p. liv (the depositions in this case were not printed in the Calendars, they can be found at the National Archives under C 1/1/85A); *Fowler v Iwardby* (1466), Calendars I, p. lxviii.

271 See also *J. P. Dawson*, A History of Lay Judges, Harvard University Press, Cambridge, Ma., 1960, p. 150; *W. J. Jones*, The Elizabethan Court of Chancery, p. 237–248.

272 *Mathew v Oxenbrigge* (1422–1461), Calendars I, p. lix. Since only interrogatories (see below 4.1.6) by the plaintiff and the deposition by Oxenbrigge have been preserved from this case, it is not entirely clear whether Oxenbrigge was the defendant or merely a witness in the proceedings.

location of the examination with the pleadings, which were afterwards returned together with the depositions of witnesses. All the documents were then kept in one bundle. Masters' reports of examinations, on the other hand, might either have been lost or communicated orally within the court. The complete absence of documentary evidence on witness testimony before 1440 might – in parallel to the answers of the defendants – be attributed to the early oral practice of the court.[273]

4.1.1 Writ of dedimus potestatem

As its name (Latin for 'we have given the power') would suggest, the essence of the writ of *dedimus potestatem* lay in the transfer of a judicial task – in this case, examination and oath-taking – to a private individual. The Court of Chancery not only issued the writ for the examination of witnesses but also for recording the answer of defendants. In the latter case, however, the defendant needed to establish one of several grounds for the non-appearance before the court in Westminster, such as old age or specific weather conditions. Evidence from the late 16th century suggests that these respective conditions could be matched rather easily. My sample only provides incidents of answers expressly following a writ of *dedimus potestatem* from the late 15th century.[274] This might be the result of a stricter policy of attendance in the early phase of the court. Earlier, however, additional statements of the parties, who often also attended the examinations, were sometimes returned together with the witness testimony.[275] Overall, a look through the 15th century sources suggests that the issuance of a writ of *dedimus potestatem* for the examination of either witnesses or parties or both in the periphery at the time was not subject to any effective restrictions. It was simply a matter of convenience.

It thus seems like the most sensible approach to again consider the information we can obtain from the sources. *Ardern v Ardern* provides several lengthy witness depositions upon a writ of *dedimus potestatem* together with some helpful background information on the course of the proceedings from the examiner. Given their length and their lack of clarity, I will guide through the

273 Compare *N. Pronay*, The Chancellor, the Chancery, and the Council at the End of the Fifteenth Century, in: H. Hearder / H. R. Loyn (eds.), British Government and Administration – Studies Presented to S. B. Chrimes, p. 87–103, p. 89, especially fn. 2.

274 See for example *Clyfford v Apulderfeld* (1481), Calendars I, p. cv; *Bailly v West* (1493–1500), Calendars I, p. cxxiv.

275 See for example *Cobbethorn v William* (1458), Calendars I, p. li; *Fowler v Iwardby* (1466), Calendars I, lxviii.

respective statements in *Ardern v Ardern* step-by-step before addressing forms of witness testimony in other cases.

The writ of *dedimus potestatem*, just like other procedural writs,[276] followed an established structure. Most importantly, it enumerated the existing documentation and instructed the prospective examiner about the issues at hand. Additionally, it generally set a certain date for the return of the writ to Chancery together with the depositions:

> *Ardern v Ardern*
> *Edward, for the grace of God, King of England and France and Lord of Ireland is greeting the dear abbot of Kenelworth.*
> *Because we would benefit of a greater certainty on and about the truth of a claim proposed in a certain petition in our Chancery by Walter Ardern against John Ardern and on and about the truth of the answer and the subsequent replication in respect of the facts and on and about every single article and circumstance of the claim, answer and replication; in order to then make justice in this procedure; we desire to confer upon you, on whose prudential wisdom we rely, the power and authority over the said parties to ascertain the truth and to examine the said articles and circumstances diligently.*
> *And therefore we appoint you, so that immediately, in light of the actual events, and the content of the said petition, answer and replication, which we sent you in separate forms from this one, and the matter, in virtue of your full intellect, you call in front of you on a certain date and place the same said parties and every other man that you would consider useful to ascertain the truth and examine them and register the testimony.*
> *And then you would return this form together with all the previously said documents, under deed, on the fifteenth next to come [15 June], the day of Saint Trinity, and then we will consider these examinations that you will have prepared in our Chancery.*
> *Signed in Westminster, the third of May in the sixth year of our reign.*[277]

John Zerdeley, the abbot of Kenelworth, was charged with the task of examining potential witnesses in the case of *Ardern v Ardern*. This choice was in line with the general policy of the court to delegate examinations in the periphery to local dignitaries – in the 15th century to gentry or distinguished churchmen.[278] As we will see from the following report, the examiners did not only question the witnesses and receive their oath but also summarise their statements. This task obviously left them with considerable power over the proceedings, the effect of which will be discussed below.

276 See above 2.6.

277 The writ – like any other late medieval writ – was issued in Latin and has not been translated in the Calendars. My translation is supposed to preserve the style of the late medieval writs without entirely sacrificing comprehensibility.

278 *J. P. Dawson*, A History of Lay Judges, p. 150.

4.1.2 Depositions of Witnesses

Ardern v Ardern

(1) Introduction by John Zerdeley

> *Be it remembered that Saturday next after the fest Corpus Christi, the sixth year of the reign of our sovereign lord King Edward IV, at Coventry before me John Zerdeley abbot of Kenelworth appeared the parties within written in their proper persons and the said Walter Ardern demanded by me the said abbot if he had brought any persons which could and would depose the matters contained in the bill of his complaint against his brother, which said he had ready two men which would depose for his party in the matter, that is to say William Levyng and William Hert, desiring me the abbot that they might be examined of the said matter.*

John Zerdeley first provided a helpful introduction to the circumstances of the examination. After mentioning its time and place, he also informed the court that both parties appeared in person. Walter Ardern, the plaintiff, was then asked to present witnesses in support of his bill. This already suggests that the responsibility to summon witnesses to an examination generally lay with the respective parties rather than the court. Walter Ardern presented William Levyng and William Hert for testimony.

(2) Testimony of William Levyng

> *The said William Levyng by himself, sworn upon a book to truly say, asked by me the said abbot where he dwelled, he said at Castle Bromwich, and that he was manual servant to the said Walter Ardern, and he said he was present when the deed & the letter of attorney of the manor of Pedmore with the appurtenances now in travers between his master & his brother were ensealed at his master's place at Logge, and he said that he heard Richard Middelmore say that his master & his brother were agreed that John his master's brother should take no profits of the said manor during the life of the said Walter, but if Walter would otherwise be pleased. And he said that the said Richard Middelmore read in his hearing a bill of the said matter before the said Walter Ardern & John Ardern, but he said he could not expressly say whether the said John agreed thereto, for he heard him not speak therein, and otherwise or further he cannot depose therein as he said.*

The first deposition came from William Levyng, one of Walter Ardern's servants. As all other depositions, it was provided under oath. Interestingly, William Levyng was also named on the bill as one of the plaintiff's sureties. His description as a yeoman in that document seems hardly compatible with the role of a servant as evidenced by the deposition. This double appearance raises additional doubts about the requirement to present sureties for claims in the late medieval Court of Chancery.[279] When the process went ahead after a servant had

279 Compare above, 2.8. A comprehensive introduction into the role of yeomen in the English society of the 16th century was presented by *M. Campbell*, The English Yeomen under Elizabeth and the Early Stuarts, Yale University Press, New Haven, Ct., 1942.

guaranteed for his master, the statutory duty to present sureties cannot have presented any meaningful barrier to access – at least for plaintiffs, whose personal wealth was beyond doubt. Regarding the content of the deposition, William Levyng effectively confirmed Walter Ardern's assertion that the agreement between himself and his brother included a condition reserving the profits from the manor to himself. However, Levyng also admitted not to have heard an express agreement to this condition by John Ardern.

(3) Testimony of William Hert

> *The foresaid William Hert by himself, sworn & demanded by me the said abbot where he dwelled, he said at Pedmore, and he said that he was manual servant to the said Walter Ardern when the aforesaid deed & letter of attorney of the said manor of Pedmore & was present when they were made and ensealed, and he said that diverse times he heard the foresaid John Ardern desire the said Walter his brother to give him some livelihood to live on, for the world was full casual. And he answered & said he should have if he [out]lived him. And the said William Hert said further, that he heard Richard Middelmore say that the said Walter Ardern & John his brother were accorded that the said John should take no profits of the said manor during the life of the said Walter, but if Walter would thereof be pleased. And further he said according in all thing to foresaid saying of the foresaid William Levyng.*

The second deposition came from William Hert, another one of Walter Ardern's servants. It will be unnecessary to speculate on the credibility of witnesses so clearly depending on one of the parties. After reiterating the motivation for the transfer of the title deed, William Hert fully supported William Levyng's account.

(4) Summary of the first meeting by John Zerdeley

> *At this day Walter brought no more witness touching this matter, and the said John excused him[self] that he brought no witnesses this day saying that he had but short warning of the keeping of this day at Coventry. Whereupon I the said abbot gave day over to the said parties to appear before me at Coventry the Saturday then next saying, and then to bring before me such & as much witnesses as they would.*

John Zerdeley then summarised the first day of examinations, stating that Walter Ardern brought no more than the two aforementioned witnesses. John Ardern, on the other hand, had not provided a single witness at the time, claiming that short notice prevented him from assembling potential testimony on his behalf. The abbot was apparently sympathetic to this claim and thus adjourned the examinations to the following Saturday.

(5) Summary of the second meeting by John Zerdeley

> *The which Saturday that is to say the Saturday next before the fifteenth of the Blessed Trinity both the said parties at Coventry appeared before me the said abbot, at which time the foresaid Walter Ardern brought no witness for his part to be examined, but he offered to deliver to me the said abbot diverse letters testimonials, but no person named in them than being there present, wherefore the said abbot advised the said Walter to*

> *have the said letters in the court of your Chancery and there to show them at fifteenth of the Trinity or after as soon as he might.*
> *Witness brought the said Saturday for the party of John Ardern: William Berkeley esquire. Rafe Syndale gentleman.*
> *The which witnesses severally examined if they were lettered, said that they were lettered, whereupon they were desired by me the said abbot to depose in writing under their seals such matters as they knew touching the promises in variance between the foresaid Walter Ardern & John his brother, and thereupon the said William Berkeley made and ensealed a bill which is annexed hereto, the matters contained in which when they were read to him he swore by his holy oath were just and true in all things. And the said Rafe Syndale in like wise made a bill and ensealed it which hereto also is annexed, the matters contained in which when they were read to him he swore by his holy oath were just and true in all things.*
> *And at the same Saturday Agnes Lucy, now called so (before called Middelmore) named in the promises, being at Worcester thirty miles from Coventry diseased with sickness that she in no wise might labour to be examined, having knowledge of this day appointed her between the said parties in the promises sent to me the said abbot a bill in writing by her ensealed, hereto also annexed, the matters in which contained the same Agnes before John Hill bringer of the same bill swear, and said as she would answer to God were just and true as the same John Hill swore before me.*
> *The said John Ardern the said day further offered to have delivered me the said Abbot diverse letters testimonials in the name of diverse persons absent there and not present to be examined, which letters I advised the said John to have in your foresaid Chancery to be showed at the foresaid fifteeth, or also after as he might.*
> *And other or more persons were not brought before me the said abbot by any of the said parties to be examined in the promises.*

What followed the first two depositions was a longer account of the events on the next Saturday from the abbot of Kenelworth. Both parties again appeared before the abbot in Coventry. This time, it was Walter Ardern who did not present any witnesses. Instead, he offered several letters, allegedly written by witnesses in support of his claim. The abbot directed him to forward those letters to the Court of Chancery. Since we do not have any evidence of such letters in the sources and since John Ardern later offered the same, it is unclear whether these letters ever existed or provided any substantial support for one of the parties. They might simply have been mentioned in order to impress the abbot with sheer numbers – a practice somewhat reminiscent of earlier proof by compurgation.

John Ardern, on the other hand, made more active use of the second day of examination by naming William Berkeley and Rafe Syndale as witnesses for the defence. Both were then asked by the abbot whether they were literate and, upon confirmation, requested to depose in writing. Their respective testimony was sealed and sworn to in the presence of the abbot before being forwarded to the Court of Chancery. It might be suggested that this procedure looks like anything but an active exercise in truth-seeking. The abbot did not make use of the actual presence of the witnesses by questioning them in detail or addressing potential contradictions. Instead, he provided them with an opportunity to frame the deposition on their own terms. It is evident that evasions cannot be prevented effectively under such a regime. Moreover, only the threat of eternal damnation promised some hope of discovering the truth. All this was equally confirmed by the first two depositions, which were drafted upon oral examinations but also represented mere summaries of statements made on the witnesses' own terms. This leaves the impression of an examiner (unwillingly) fulfilling his duty upon orders from the mighty Court of Chancery rather than actively supporting the proceedings.

At last, the abbot of Kenelworth received a message from Agnes Lucy (before called Agnes Middelmore), claiming she was sick and thus unable to attend the examination in Coventry. Instead, she sent a messenger to deliver her written testimony. From what we know from the pleadings, Agnes Lucy and her son Richard (who did not depose personally) seem like the most useful witnesses for ascertaining the truth of the litigants' respective claims. After all, they were potentially present during the agreement and allegedly assigned the task of keeping the title deed. The abbot's statement did not answer the interesting question of who summoned Agnes Lucy as a witness. Since she was not listed as one of the parties' witnesses, it might have been either the court (represented by the abbot) or both parties together.[280] The information that Agnes Lucy swore an oath to her statement before the messenger John Hill, who then, in turn, swore to this fact, before the abbot, suggests a rather lax practice of administering oaths. This hardly increases confidence in the reliability of witness testimony. The summary of events by the abbot of Kenelworth was then followed by a reproduction of the three depositions we were informed about earlier.

(6) Deposition of William Berkeley

> *This is the saying of William Berkeley Esquire for truth in the matter in debate between Walter Ardern and John Ardern his brother for the manor of Pedmore in the county of Worcester, that is to say, the said Walter at diverse times speaking with Richard Middelmore of the said matter examined him whether ever he knew any condition accord entente or agreement to be made in writing or by mouth rehearsed, that the said John should not enjoy nor take any profits of the said manor during the life of the said Walter, and thereto the said Richard for truth said that he never knew nor heard any condition accord entente or agreement expressed by the said John in word nor deed, but the said Richard Middelmore said that he moved such a condition and entente to have expressed between the said Walter and John which the said John openly there countered and disagreed. Also I examined John Middelmore which was at the livery of seisin of the said manor in the name of the said Walter unto the said John Ardern, whether then the said Walter declared or uttered unto him or to Thomas Harte any condition entente or accord of the foresaid of the foresaid livery of the said seisin which he for truth [...] to me,*

280 The latter option might draw support from the abbot's slightly ambiguous statement that Agnes Lucy had "knowledge of this day appointed her between the said parties in the promises", *Ardern v Ardern* (1465/1466), Calendars I, p. lxxii, lxxv.

neither the said Walter nor none other for him moved him of any manner such condition or entente. Also I examined one John Garnell, which by the command of the said Walter wrote the said deed of the said grant of the said manor, whether ever the said Walter moved him or expressed to him any condition entente or agreement as is aforesaid, and he said to me by great deliberation that the said Walter never expressed to him any condition entente or agreement as is aforesaid, nor he never before livery of seisin heard any such condition expressed nor moved. And that all these articles above rehearsed been good and true as I shall answer to God at the day of dome. In witness whereof to these promises I the said William have put my seal, and also before the said Abbot commissioners of promises examined to be true upon a book have made a faithful oath.

The study of William Berkeley's deposition immediately raises the question of his role in the proceedings. It becomes fairly clear from his account that he himself was not involved with or even attendant to the events, which led to the Chancery suit between the two brothers. His status as a useful witness was thus in doubt. By his own account, William Berkeley instead 'examined' several people directly involved in the events. From our modern perspective, this behaviour makes him look like counsel for the defendant rather than a witness. Indeed, his deposition of supportive witness testimony almost asks for comparisons to depositions in modern American discovery procedures, for which counsel examines the witnesses on record.[281] However, William Berkeley was clearly designated as a witness for the defendant. It was Berkeley rather than any of the actual witnesses, who swore an oath to the testimony. The advantage is obvious: Berkeley was merely reporting what he had been told and those who he had examined did not risk perjury. Why did the court accept this sort of second-hand account from central witnesses? In the absence of evidence, this question cannot be answered. The fact that Richard Middelmore could escape examination under oath nevertheless raises serious doubts about the effectiveness of the Chancery process.

The testimony collected by William Berkeley and summarised in his deposition does not seem entirely inconsistent with the depositions from Walter Ardern's servants. Whereas Walter's witnesses reported that Walter and Richard Middelmore had repeatedly communicated the condition, William Berkeley's deposition confirmed this communication but denied John Ardern's acceptance of the condition. Even the comparatively underdeveloped English contract doctrine of the late Middle Ages[282] required an agreement for the imposition

281 Parallels between discovery in the modern American civil trial and early modern English Chancery procedure have been identified by *S. N. Subrin*, How Equity Conquered Common Law: The Federal Rules of Civil Procedure in Historical Perspective, University of Pennsylvania Law Review, Volume 135 (1987), S. 909–1002.

282 For a detailed account, see *A. W. B. Simpson*, A History of the Common Law of Contract – The Rise of the Action of Assumpsit, p. 3–198.

of a condition.[283] Berkeley reports that both Richard Middelmore, the central witness to the agreement, and John Garnell, the drafter of the transfer deed, denied the existence of a condition reserving the profits from the land for Walter during his lifetime. The deposition then turns to the act of publicity, which completed the transfer of the manor: the livery of seisin. William Berkeley claims to have examined John Middelmore, Richard's brother, on the circumstances of the ceremony. John insisted that no condition had been mentioned before or during the livery of seisin. Walter's witnesses had not reported on that event at all.

(7) Deposition by Agnes Lucy

Worshipful and reverent father in God I recommend me onto you. Please it you to have in knowledge that I received by the hands of Richard Middelmore my son a deed with a letter of attorney and a bill in paper of the manor of Pedmore in the county of Worcester, the which deed with the said letter of attorney I delivered again by the will of Walter Ardern to John Middelmore & to John Ardern, to deliver to the same John Ardern livery and possession of and in the said manor of Pedmore according to the said deed, and after that the said John Ardern had livery and possession of the said manor he sent to me by John Middelmore my son the said evidence to keep to the said John Ardern behalf. And in witness hereof to this my writing I have put to my seal. Written at Saint Johns in Beddwardyn the seventh day of June.

Agnes Lucy's deposition draws a remarkably passive image of her role in the events leading up to the Chancery suit. As Walter Ardern's bill had alleged, Agnes Lucy confirmed to have received the deed and the letter of attorney. She then claimed to have handed them over to her son John Middelmore and to John Ardern, so that the livery of seisin could be effected. The deposition does not mention the exact instructions under which Agnes Lucy was acting. While she claimed to have forwarded the deed and the letter of attorney 'by will of Walter Ardern', we do not know how or when Walter Ardern might have expressed this will. The testimony did not even mention the existence of a possible condition. It is needless to say that all these questions could have been answered in the course of a real examination. Agnes Lucy's deposition from afar effectively represents another example of evasion. At last, Agnes Lucy confirmed that she was again in possession of the disputed documents – this time on behalf of John Ardern.

(8) Deposition by Rafe Syndale

[Submitted] that in the year and reign of our sovereign King Edward the Fourth after the conquest the sixth, in the month of July the Friday next after Saint Barnabas the Apostle,

283 The interesting legal question of the effect of a disagreement on a central condition on the validity of the contract as a whole could not be argued in the depositions, which only addressed matters of fact. The fact that none of the parties argued the point in the pleadings underlines the general absence of legal doctrine in the late medieval Court of Chancery.

> *that I Rafe Sydnall record and say that Thomas Harte, bailee of the lordship of Pedmore in Worcestor, and all the tenants of the said township, say they had never spoken of no condition at the seisin of the said manor by John Ardern taking, not before nor in the space of a year after, and that I the said Rafe Sydnall will record during my life, and that this is just and true that I have sworn upon a book before the abbot of Kenelworth and to this bill set my seal.*

With regard to his role in the proceedings, Rafe Syndale's testimony raises the same questions as William Berkeley's. Syndale reported that the other witnesses to the livery of seisin had also not heard of any condition regarding the profits of the land associated with the transfer of the manor from Walter to John Ardern. He thus confirmed William Berkeley's testimony.

After all, it is impossible to reconstruct the actual events leading to the family confrontation in *Ardern v Ardern* from the documentary evidence we have studied. What the depositions might suggest is that Walter and John Ardern – despite discussing the issue beforehand – never actually agreed on the handling of the profits from the manor of Pedmore. I will thus turn my attention away from the specific facts of the case to the general insights about proceedings in the late medieval Court of Chancery, which can be gained from the depositions in *Ardern v Ardern* as well as from other cases in my sample.

4.1.3 Inadequacy for truth-finding

The dominating impression of the study of the depositions is one of a painful inadequacy for truth-finding. Apart from Agnes Lucy, who sent a messenger, the witnesses only contributed what we would consider hearsay – what others had told them of the events or what they had overheard. Irrespective of the intentions of the witnesses, such knowledge must be qualified as inherently unreliable. Regarding the content of this hearsay, the witness testimony in *Ardern v Ardern* addressed the pre- and post-agreement stages in some detail, while providing little information on the actual agreement itself.

Most suspiciously, the Middelmores escaped the direct testimony under oath in front of the abbot and instead provided evasive statements transmitted by third parties. Whether their attendance would have made a difference is another question but the simple acceptance of their testimony looks tame in comparison to the later practice of bringing defaulting witnesses to Westminster under a subpoena.[284] The examination itself was neither inquisitorial nor adversarial. In fact, it was hardly an examination at all. Those witnesses who actually came forward could apparently tell their story free from critical scrutiny from either

284 See *W. J. Jones*, The Elizabethan Court of Chancery, p. 241.

the parties or the examiner. The limits of this approach for effective truth-finding are apparent.

4.1.4 Role of the examiner

In how far can this be attributed to the role of the examiner? We lack sufficient material for contrasting the interrogation techniques of private examiners in the periphery with court officials in Westminster.[285] Nevertheless, one can hardly help but sense a profound disinterest in the proceedings in the report of the abbot of Kenelworth. Once the literacy of the witnesses was established, they were asked to prepare written depositions and to send them to Chancery directly. The delegation of the examination in the writ of *dedimus potestatem* thus apparently led to further delegation.

In the face of limited judicial personnel in the Court of Chancery and long distances between Westminster and rural regions, the delegation of examinations to local figures of authority initially might have represented a sensible idea.[286] In fact, it might be suggested that it embodied two typical features of the English legal tradition: a focus on practicality and an element of lay-participation. At the very least, the examinations remained quick and cheap. However, *Ardern v Ardern* also shows that, in the absence of central control, such a privatisation of conflict resolution risked professional standards. It is hard to imagine that the Court of Chancery could put depositions in this form to effective use in decision-making.

4.1.5 Common law testimony

In light of the historical development, the criticism advanced against the practice of examining witnesses upon a writ of *dedimus potestatem* in the 15th century is admittedly harsh. After all, merely two and a half centuries had passed since the sudden abolition of the ordeals at the Fourth Lateran Council in 1215. More importantly, the common law did not allow for an examination of witnesses at

285 In the case of *Mathew v Oxenbrigge* (1422–1461), Calendars I, p. lix, the Master of the Rolls was equipped with a detailed list of questions (interrogatories, see below 4.1.6), which must have simplified the examination of the witness substantially.

286 It might, however, have raised the problem that power-holders re-entered the process through the backdoor. In cases, in which the Court of Chancery was consciously appealed to in order to escape local power relations, this might have posed a serious problem. Compare for example the case of *Pykworth v Sambroke* (1407), Select Cases, p. 87.

all before the second half of the 15th century.[287] The concept of the self-informing jury instead required the jurors to act in a double capacity as witnesses and decision-makers. Being from the vicinity of the parties, they were considered to know the background to the case before their empanelment.[288] What they had to rely on exclusively was the kind of hearsay that I have criticised above in the context of Chancery testimony. In the light of more sophisticated interrogation techniques, which were in regular application in English church courts,[289] however, the practice of letting witnesses depose freely before local dignitaries can hardly be qualified as innovative. Nevertheless, John Langbein considered the "procedures for obtaining and using testimony of parties and witnesses" "Chancery's greatest contribution to the ultimate shape of Anglo-American civil procedure".[290] I would suggest that the introduction of witness testimony in the 15th century Court of Chancery was a sensible idea, which was still far from realising its potential.

4.1.6 Interrogatories

Either way, the 15th century Chancery process required substantial reform with regard to witness testimony. A greater role for Chancery officials in examinations would have mandated an expansion of the judiciary. Despite continental European models, this solution was never seriously considered in England.[291] The private examiners themselves could hardly be required to investigate cases more deeply without remuneration. Moreover, they were lay people neither trained nor experienced in judicial investigations.[292] Thus the parties themselves

287 Compare *T. F. T. Plucknett*, A Concise History of the Common Law, p. 435. For an introduction to the role of jurors and witnesses in medieval common law trials, see *J. H. Langbein / R. T. Lerner / B. P. Smith*, History of the Common Law – The Development of Anglo-American Legal Institutions, p. 238–246.

288 See above chapter II, 1.4.4.

289 For a closer comparison of the Chancery process with the contemporary canon law process, see below chapter VI.

290 *J. H. Langbein / R. T. Lerner / B. P. Smith*, History of the Common Law – The Development of Anglo-American Legal Institutions, p. 289–290.

291 Also *J. P. Dawson*, A History of Lay Judges, p. 150.

292 That does not mean that the option of increasing the role of private examiners, by then called commissioners, was never considered. Lord Chancellor Wolsey established a practice of delegating not only the examinations but also the decisions to the examiners. As *M. R. T Macnair* put it, he effectively established the Court of Chancery as a department for the organisation of 'alternative dispute resolution' (*M. R. T. Macnair*, Equity and Conscience, Oxford Journal of Legal Studies, Volume 27 (2007), p. 659–681, p. 670). This approach was abandoned at the end of the 16th century.

reformed witness testimony in the Court of Chancery through the introduction of interrogatories. First precursors of this practice were clearly visible in the 15th century.

Interrogatories were lists of questions to be answered by witnesses or the other party and prepared by counsel. They represented a direct answer to the problem identified in *Ardern v Ardern*. Whereas the opportunity to depose freely on the basis of the pleadings allowed witnesses under oath to tell only that part of the story, which would not prejudice themselves or their allies, a concrete list of questions facilitated a deeper investigation of the issues at hand.

Delegating the responsibility to frame the questions to the respective parties also reduced the problem of the involvement of private examiners. The central advantage of interrogatories is clear: They required only a minimal use of royal resources.[293] The work was left with the parties to the conflict. However, the disadvantage is almost equally clear: The parties tried almost anything to extract as much helpful information as possible from the witnesses. And since their answers could hardly be predicted, the litigants' lawyers tried to cover any contingency with their questions.[294] Accordingly, the lists of questions grew longer and exceedingly complicated, as the drafters tried to pre-empt any eventuality.[295]

This was mostly an early modern development.[296] Examinations in the 15th century generally still followed the pattern identified in *Ardern v Ardern*. The Calendars, however, include one example of an interrogatory from the 15th century. The documentation of the case *Mathew v Oxenbrigge*[297] merely consists of an interrogatory and a corresponding testimony. Since we neither know about the background of the case through the pleadings nor have any evidence about the exact date,[298] I would be careful to draw any conclusions on the role of interrogatories in the 15th century Chancery process. For the purpose of identifying the functions of the Chancery process for the developing royal system of conflict resolution, however, it is the fact that interrogatories evolved

293 Compare *J. P. Dawson*, A History of Lay Judges, p. 151.

294 *W. Holdsworth*, A History of English Law, Methuen, London, Volume 9, 1925, p. 341.

295 Compare *W. Holdsworth*, A History of English Law, Volume 9, p. 341; *J. H. Langbein / R. T. Lerner / B. P. Smith*, History of the Common Law – The Development of Anglo-American Legal Institutions, p. 297.

296 See also *J. P. Dawson*, A History of Lay Judges, p. 150–152.

297 (1422–1461), Calendars I, p. lix.

298 The editor of the Calendars assigned the case to the (first) reign (1422–1461) of Henry VI (1421–1471) based on the handwriting, Calendars I, p. lix, fn. 1. The danger of such a classification should be evident.

as a practical solution to the problem of obtaining proof from witnesses that is important.

In *Mathew v Oxenbrigge*, the plaintiff John Mathew seemingly tried to establish a claim to property. He thus provided the Master of the Rolls in the Court of Chancery with a list of questions, which seemingly tried to identify a property chain through three consecutive transfers. John Oxenbrigge, either the witness or the defendant in this case,[299] then answered on all three points enumerated in the interrogatories – not without adding further discrediting information about the plaintiff. Irrespective of the exact date of the document, it can be seen as a typical – and still fairly brief – example of an early interrogatory.

In the later practice of the court, rules for admissible questions were established, Chancery staff checked their observance and the answers were kept secret from the parties until a fixed date of publication.[300] The developments from open testimony upon the pleadings over unrestricted interrogatories to regulated interrogatories were, once more, in line with the general trend towards formalisation in the Court of Chancery.

4.2 Documents

The second common means of proof in the late medieval Court of Chancery was documentary evidence. In light of the developing written procedure, it is hardly a surprise that the court put great trust in documents for the establishment or rejection of the parties' claims. In the available sources from the 15th century, we cannot find any evidence of the sophisticated handling of documents borrowed from Roman-canon law, which Michael Macnair identified for the early modern period.[301] Instead, the treatment of documentary evidence appears highly pragmatic.

4.2.1 Evidence in support of a claim

Most commonly, documents seem to have been provided by the plaintiffs in support of their claim. The evidence was ideally annexed to the original bill.[302]

299 See above, fn. 548.

300 For brief introductions on early modern rules on testimony, see *J. P. Dawson*, A History of Lay Judges, p. 150–159; *J. H. Langbein / R. T. Lerner / B. P. Smith*, History of the Common Law – The Development of Anglo-American Legal Institutions, p. 291–298. An extremely detailed analysis is provided by *M. R. T. Macnair*, The Law of Proof in Early Modern Equity, especially p. 165–184.

301 *M. R. T. Macnair*, The Law of Proof in Early Modern Equity, p. 131–164.

302 Compare the rejoinder of the defendant in *Sharp v Temper* (1461–1467), Calendars I, p. lxiii.

The sources, however, also provide alternative ways of introducing documentary evidence. In *Sharp v Temper*,[303] the plaintiff presented an earlier agreement between the parties' respective institutions about the tithes in dispute together with the replication. The defendant afterwards complained that the document should have been provided with the original bill. In the light of the general policy of the late medieval court not to prejudice the parties for mispleading,[304] it seems unlikely that this objection was granted. Another approach was taken in the case of *Fowler v Iwardby*.[305] Together with the witness deposition, we find a report, which details the documents the plaintiff brought in support of his claim. The source provides a summary of the plaintiff's argumentation similar to the abbot's report in *Ardern v Ardern*. The documents themselves, on the other hand, have not been preserved. It is unclear whether the plaintiff presented the documents for proof before a private examiner or in Chancery. What is clear, however, is that he introduced them after the stage of pleadings. This reemphasises the impression that the introduction of documents as evidence in the proceedings did not yet follow any restrictive rules and was rather a matter of convenience.

4.2.2 Bill of discovery

The cases, in which the parties introduced documents in support of their respective claims, need to be distinguished from suits for the obtainment of documents, which later became known as bills of discovery. A bill of discovery in the Court of Chancery "was a bill which asked no relief, but which simply sought [...] the discovery of deeds, or writings, or other things, in the possession or power of the defendant".[306] This was essentially an auxiliary procedure, which allowed for the obtainment of crucial evidence, which the opposite party refused to procure voluntarily. It became highly influential not only in support of suits in the Court of Chancery but also in support of common law proceedings.[307]

Early examples for proceedings aimed exclusively at the obtainment of certain documents can be found in the 15th century sources. In *Baker v Parson*,[308] the

303 (1461–1467), Calendars I, p. lxiii.

304 See above 3.1.3.

305 (1466), Calendars I, p. lxviii.

306 *J. Story*, Commentaries on Equity Jurisprudence as Administered in England and America, Little, Brown & Co., Boston, Ma., Volume 2, 12th edition, 1877, p. 727–728.

307 *J. Story*, Commentaries on Equity Jurisprudence as Administered in England and America, Volume 2, p. 727–728; *J. H. Langbein / R. T. Lerner / B. P. Smith*, History of the Common Law – The Development of Anglo-American Legal Institutions, p. 290.

308 (1465–1467), Calendars II, p. l.

plaintiff sued for the surrender of several "evidence and monuments" relating to his inheritance, which he expected in the possession of the defendants. Whether the bill was issued in support of a specific existing claim is unclear. The bill and the answers do not provide any evidence about pending court proceedings. The prerequisite that the defendant to a bill of discovery already had to be a party to the pending lawsuit[309] might have been introduced later. *Reed v Prior of Launceston*[310] provides another – fairly similar – 15th century example of a suit for the 'discovery' of documents. Interestingly, a decree dismissing the claim (yet without reasons) has been preserved.

4.2.3 Documentary evidence and the common law

In both aforementioned cases, the plaintiffs claimed that they had no remedy at common law since they "know [...] not the certainty nor contents of the said evidence and mònuments nor wherein they were contained, in bag, box or chest".[311] From a modern perspective, this argument sounds almost comic. It is, however, easily explained. The common law provided an action for the surrender of a certain thing to which the plaintiff could successfully claim a right in the form of detinue.[312] An action for the production of a thing, which was not clearly defined, was unthinkable in the restrictive framework of late medieval common law. Nevertheless, plaintiffs often had a vital interest in the obtainment of those documents, which were necessary for either establishing or proving their claim. The common law tendency to safeguard the defendant against self-incrimination – visible already in the impossibility of questioning the defendant – again inhibited serious attempts at truth-finding.[313] The Court of Chancery thus, once again, remedied a severe shortcoming of the overly technical common law.

309 *J. Story*, Commentaries on Equity Jurisprudence as Administered in England and America, Volume II, p. 734–742, see also the limited exceptions.

310 (1483–1484), Calendars I, p. cxiv.

311 *Reed v Prior of Launceston* (1483–1484), Calendars I, p. cxiv.

312 However, the remedy for detinue was regularly monetary damages. See *F. Pollock / F. W. Maitland*, The History of English Law before the Time of Edward I, Volume 2, p. 174.

313 For the origins and the status of the privilege against self-incrimination at common law and in the *ius commune*, see *J. H. Langbein*, The Historical Origins of the Privilege against Self-incrimination at Common Law, Michigan Law Review, Volume 92 (1994), p. 1047–1085; *R. H. Helmholz*, The Privilege and the Ius Commune, in: *R. H. Helmholz et al.*, The Privilege against Self-incrimination, University of Chicago Press, Chicago, Il., 1997, p. 17–46, as well as the other contributions in that book.

In the regular common law process, the introduction of documents for proof by the parties was also fraught with difficulties. This is not the place to engage with the evidentiary rules of the respective medieval causes of action but two (simplified) examples should underline the point: Establishing a contractual claim required the production of a formal deed and the discharge of a contractual duty required the same formalities as the original commitment.[314] Additional supporting or contradictory documents were simply inadmissible. With its lack of technical restrictions, the late medieval Court of Chancery offered an attractive alternative for parties seeking to establish contingent facts.

5. Determination

The title I have chosen for the final stage of the late medieval Chancery process is deliberately vague and might yet be too specific. Not nearly all proceedings in the late medieval Court of Chancery were brought to a final determination. The incomplete documentation does not allow for definite assertions about the actual outcome of most Chancery cases. Data from the 16th century, however, suggests that more than half of the suits opened in the Court of Chancery never progressed to a final hearing, let alone determination by the court.[315] Nothing in the 15th century samples hints at a higher share of decided cases. Indeed, we would impose ideals of certain decision-making from the classical period on the late medieval litigants if we assumed that even the plaintiffs regularly sought authoritative adjudication from the court. As mentioned earlier, the rugged late medieval legal landscape offered a large variety of means for conflict resolution or regulation: from royal and ecclesiastical courts over local tribunals to more traditional forms of arbitration. This image still ignores the extra-legal (and sometimes illegal) opportunities to influence the course of a given conflict. Despite its elevated position as a central part of the royal machinery, the Court of Chancery in the end was only one of many institutions for conflict resolution – and while its decisions could not be actively challenged they could certainly be circumvented. Thus, many conflicts, which at some stage entered the Court of Chancery, were nevertheless drawn out over generations and also fought in different jurisdictions.[316]

314 Compare *A. W. B. Simpson*, A History of the Common Law of Contract – The Rise of the Action of Assumpsit, p. 15–17.

315 *W. J. Jones*, The Elizabethan Court of Chancery, p. 286.

316 For a famous example of a multi-generational conflict from the 16th century, see the Shakespeare family's internal struggle over family property. The history of the case was summarised by *W. N. Knight*, Shakespeare's Court Case, Law and Critique, Volume 2 (1991), p. 103–112. Proceedings initiated by Shakespeare's father against his brother-in-law in the Court of Chancery were published in the Calendars, *Shakespeare v Lambert* (1578), Calendars I, p. cxlv. As *W. N. Knight*

What the available evidence suggests, however, is that the Court of Chancery not merely acquiesced in this role passively but rather actively encouraged the (extra-judicial) determination of cases outside the court or at its edges. As we will see, its procedure provided a variety of instruments, which supported the finding of amicable solutions. I will therefore discuss the opportunities for extra-judicial determinations (5.1) before turning to the judicial determination of cases in the Court of Chancery (5.2).

5.1 'Extra-judicial' determination

5.1.1 Evidence

If identifying decisions of the late medieval Court of Chancery already represents a daunting task in the absence of regularised reporting, what hope could there be of finding out about the prevalence of and the mechanisms behind the extra-judicial resolution of Chancery cases? Edward Powell has assembled a number of cases, which directly refer to earlier arbitration or seek compliance with settlement awards from other institutions.[317] Any further insights into extra-judicial negotiations or settlements, however, are limited. Most cases disappear from the records at some stage during the regular proceedings and with this they also generally disappear from our knowledge. It is mostly circumstantial evidence, which points to a substantial rate of out-of-court determinations to the Court of Chancery cases that appear on the records in their typically fragmented form.

Perhaps most tellingly – but also most questionably from a scientific perspective – inferences might be drawn from the later practice of the court. W. J. Jones has identified a great density of extra-judicial resolutions to Chancery suits for the Elizabethan period, in which the decree books already provided support for ascertaining the outcome of cases.[318] The general extent of the late medieval sources themselves provides further support for this thesis. Singular decrees announcing the decision of the court appear scattered throughout the files on the back of a limited number of bills.[319] Whether this was the practice of certain scribes or the result of specific requests from the parties, we would expect

explained, they were, at the very least, followed by common law proceedings and William's own suit in the Court of Chancery in 1599.

317 *E. Powell*, Arbitration and the Law in England in the Late Middle Ages, Transactions of the Royal Historical Society, Volume 33 (1983), p. 49–67, p. 64–66.

318 *W. J. Jones*, The Elizabethan Court of Chancery, p. 266–280.

319 For such examples, see *Duke of Gloucester v Ely* (1472–1473), Calendars I, p. xc; *Stokker v Colyns* (1474–1475), Calendars I, p. xcv; *Slefeld v Grafton* (1475), Calendars I, p. xcvii.

some sort of regularity if the suits in the Court of Chancery regularly came to an end through the decision of the Lord Chancellor upon the completed process outlined above. This consideration might also lead us to another hint: The cases disappear from the records indiscriminately at any stage of the proceedings. Some cases advanced only to the bill,[320] others to the answers,[321] others to replication or rejoinder,[322] others to the examination of witnesses[323] or to a final or interlocutory decree.[324] Now, this might very well be another incident of fragmentary document-keeping. It might also, however, suggest that cases disappeared from the record because parties came to a mutual understanding or otherwise lost interest in the pursuance of the suit.[325]

While the extent of the extra-judicial resolution of Chancery suits has to be assessed (and frankly, guessed) from such circumstantial evidence, we can luckily point to rare incidents of evidence of extra-judicial resolution for proof of its general existence. Most conveniently (and admittedly causing my selection), *Ardern v Ardern* provides exactly such evidence.[326] An entry on the record tells us about an "accord between the parties".[327]

> *Ardern v Ardern*
> *[Be it remembered] that Walter of Ardern and John his brother thus been agreed that Agnes Middelmore of Eggebason shall have in keeping a deed of the manor of Padmore with a letter of attorney according to the said deed until such time it be the will of Walter*

320 This is obviously the case for all cases preserved from before 1440. As has been discussed above, the reason for this probably lies in the oral character of the proceedings, see 3.1, introduction. For later cases, see for example *Haryngton v Haryngton* (1432–1443, possibly still in the oral period), Calendats I, p. xxiv; *Bettenham v Frogenhale* (1461–1467), Calendars I, p. lxii; *Penteney v Lovell* (1467–1485), Calendars II, p. lxix.

321 See for example *Pickering v Tonge* (1446–1450), Calendars I, p. xliv; *Lovell v Echard* (1456–1460), Calendars I, p. lix; *Clyfford v Apulderfeld* (1481), Calendars I, p. cv.

322 See for example *Furby v Martyn* (1460–1465), Calendars II, p. xl; *Berkeley v Shrewsbury* (1465–1467), Calendars I, p. lxxvi; *Morton v Langley* (1465–1467), Calendars I, p. lxxxi.

323 See for example *Babington v Gull* (1456–1460), Calendars I, p. lvi with additional documents in C 1/1/78–85c; *Toty v Norton* (1461–1470), Calendars I, p. lxxxiii; *Mors v Coke* (1484–1485), Calendars II, p. lxxv.

324 See for example *Michell v Marmyun* (1473), Calendars I, lxxxvii; *Neville (in Calendars: Archbishop of York) v Osborn* (1473), Calendars I, p. xciv; *King's College v Ovy* (1480–1482), Calendars I, p. cvi.

325 Also *T. S. Haskett*, Access to Grace – Bills, Justice, and Governance in England, 1300–1500, in: H. Millet (ed.), Suppliques et Requêtes – Le Gouvernement par la Grâce en Occident (XIIème à XVème Siècle), École française de Rome, Rome, 2003, p. 297–317, p. 312.

326 Another such example would be the case of *Fowler v Iwardby* (1466), Calendars I, p. lxviii.

327 *Ardern v Ardern* (1465/1466), Calendars I, p. lxxii, lxxvi.

of Ardern that she should deliver the deed with the letter of attorney to John of Ardern his brother, and that she have them at all times in keeping unto Walter of Ardern [...] until such time that it be his will that she should them deliver. And also it is the said Walter Ardern his will that if he deceases at any time that the said Agnes shall deliver them to the said John his brother without any other delay.

The source clearly states that Walter and John Ardern have 'been agreed'. Thus, our publically enacted family conflict was brought to an end by a mutual understanding. From the words of the agreement, the outcome looks like an unqualified success for the older brother. While the text of the agreement only addressed the technical issue of custody over deed and letter of attorney, it also implicitly resolved all other issues underlying the suit. Imposing a duty on Agnes Middelmore to hold the title deed and the letter of attorney at Walter's (albeit restricted) disposal only made sense when the proceeds of the land also belonged to Walter. The documents were at John's disposal before and could simply have remained there if the outcome had been in his favour. No implications can be drawn on the earlier proceeds, which John appropriated before the start of the trial. While abandoning the respective claim might have been Walter's contribution to the settlement agreement, they might also have given rise to further litigation. From the limited impression provided by the surviving documents, the outcome might seem somewhat surprising. In fact, Walter did not exactly succeed to present a very strong case. The respective pleadings seemed equally (un)convincing and the witnesses happily supported both sides' claims in equal numbers. We can only speculate what motivated John to agree to the cited agreement: whether the examination revealed internal motives, which did not translate to paper, or whether perhaps the personal authority of the older brother was too strong to withstand any longer.

Why was the agreement added to the official documentation of the case, so that it could be found in the court records? It does not take much creativity to suggest that it might be for the very same reason that settlement agreements today are kept in court records: for simplifying their enforcement. I will not address the effectiveness of the enforcement of judgments or decrees in late medieval England generally or in the Court of Chancery specifically.[328] This is not only for the lack of systematic documentation but also for the fact that this problem affected all courts and tribunals to different degrees.[329] Irrespective of actual enforcement, however, definite documentation from the Court of

328 *F. Metzger,* Das englische Kanzleigericht unter Kardinal Wolsey, p. 311–317, described the Chancery practice of execution through 'recognisances' in the early 16th century.

329 For a short introduction to the enforcement mechanisms of the common law and additional Chancery instruments, see *J. H. Baker,* An Introduction to English Legal History, p. 66–67; 104.

Chancery could prevent further litigation concerning the underlying issues. That might already have represented sufficient motivation for both the parties and the court to document the agreement officially. The agreement in *Ardern v Ardern* also did not constitute the only incidence of the court documenting facts for a later use. Indeed, further evidence suggests that the late medieval Court of Chancery partly assumed a notary-like function. As such, it was also asked to certify witness statements[330] for use in (potential) later proceedings. Further evidence shows that masters in Chancery regularly decreed the outcome of extra-judicial settlements.[331]

Why were so many cases in the Court of Chancery settled extra-judicially? I will argue that the court's procedures (5.1.2), the involvement of charismatic authorities (5.1.3) and the constant appeal to conscience (5.1.4) in the Court of Chancery encouraged settlement between the parties.

5.1.2 Procedural incentives

Apart from a few exceptional cases like *Ardern v Ardern*, the extra-judicial determination of cases clearly operated in 'the shadow of the law', so that it remains largely invisible for legal historians relying on documentary evidence for the description of past legal phenomena. The 'shadow of the law' analogy, however, also provides a second dimension: No shadow could exist in the absence of the original object. It is my argument[332] that the procedural framework of the Court of Chancery provided superior assistance to extra-judicial conflict resolution in comparison to the established medieval courts. A reassessment of Chancery procedure in the light of its usefulness for the extra-judicial determination of conflicts should prove the point.

I argue that the late medieval Chancery procedure (despite its many shortcomings) exhibited a greater openness for the introduction of arguments, superior truth-finding mechanisms and more rational decision-making procedures[333] than the regular courts of common law at the time. All three of these features – despite being part of what we would call the 'judicial' process – also

330 In *Earl of Oxford v Tyrell* (1493–1500), Calendars I, p. cxx, the plaintiff asked for the perpetuation of testimony from a moribund witness.

331 An early example can be found in the case of *Michell v Marmyun* (1473), Calendars I, p. lxxxvii. A regular practice was established by the 16th century. See *W. J. Jones*, The Elizabethan Court of Chancery, p. 288.

332 This quality of Chancery procedure has been identified (more abstractly) before, most impressively by *J. A. Guy*, The Development of Equitable Jurisdictions, 1450–1550, in: E. W. Ives / A. H. Manchester (eds.), Law, Litigants, and the Legal Profession, Royal Historical Society, London, 1983, p. 80–86, p. 84.

333 See also below chapter VII.

encouraged extra-judicial conflict resolution throughout the course of the proceedings. Underlying this assumption is the economic theory that the parties' main motivation for entering a trial is their 'optimism' to win it and that a clearer sense of the outcome will encourage settlements. Once the parties can assess a likely outcome, a settlement is mutually beneficial since the remaining judicial process merely increases the overall costs.[334]

The openness of the procedure included every party's opportunity to present all the facts underlying the dispute without technical limitations. By the second half of the 15th century, the written character of the proceedings additionally ensured that the respective depictions were documented and thus could be compared easily. This simple tool carried the potential for the parties to comprehend the foundations of each other's claims better. It might also have prevented misunderstandings between them. In contrast to common law pleadings, the exchange of the factual claims was not effected before the court in technical language and thus reserved for the understanding of professional lawyers. Knowing and understanding a plaintiff's claim might have encouraged a rationally minded defendant to settle before the costs increased or the conflict escalated further.[335] This could of course only be true when justified claims regularly led to favourable decisions.[336] Whether this was the case depended on the capacity of the court for effective truth-finding and decision-making.

I have already referred to the comparatively advanced truth-finding mechanisms of the late medieval Court of Chancery. The threat of eternal damnation in the event of perjury might have encouraged some defendants with a guilty conscience[337] to seek an extra-judicial determination of the dispute even before answering to the bill. In the event that they answered the bill evasively, the weaknesses of their argumentation might have been exposed, leading effectively to the same result. Conversely, a well-reasoned rebuttal under oath might have confronted plaintiffs with the hopelessness of their claims at a reasonably early stage and led them to abandon their suit. The overall transparency of the

334 Compare *R. A. Posner*, Economic Approach to Legal Procedure and Judicial Administration, Journal of Legal Studies, Volume 2 (1972), p. 399–458, especially p. 421–426. The study of the article in the context of a legal historical question immediately directs attention to the potential of an integration of economic and behavioural economic considerations for the understanding of historical institutions.

335 *R. A. Posner*, Economic Approach to Legal Procedure and Judicial Administration, Journal of Legal Studies, Volume 2 (1972), p. 399–458, p. 421.

336 Compare *R. A. Posner*, Economic Approach to Legal Procedure and Judicial Administration, Journal of Legal Studies, Volume 2 (1972), p. 399–458, p. 423.

337 For once, the term conscience is employed non-technically in its modern understanding.

direction of the trial was further supported by the opportunity to introduce a comparatively broad and unrestricted range of evidence, most importantly the testimony of witnesses. Ideally, this open approach should have exposed the strengths or weaknesses of the respective claims and thus led the parties to a common assessment of the prospects of success. From this, the path to a mutual agreement should have been relatively short.

The greater transparency as a result of Chancery's truth-finding mechanisms would, of course, have amounted to nothing in the case of entirely arbitrary decision-making. As long as a party with weaker arguments can hope for arbitrary decision-making in its favour, it will not agree to an unfavourable settlement. The uncertainty of Chancery decisions is one of its most famous features.[338] Nevertheless, and even in the absence of easily-identifiable substantive rules, the decision-making by the Lord Chancellor exhibited noticeable elements of reason, which minimised this danger. Generally, the Lord Chancellor represented a sufficiently far-removed instance for the resolution of typically local conflicts. He rarely had any stake in the actual outcome of cases and could thus decide independently. As we know, the official claim of the court was the operation as a court of conscience. In order to proclaim this motto believably, the decision had to be understandable in the context of the specific facts of the case. Even if we imputed more mundane motivations like securing or advancing the peace and thus royal control, the Lord Chancellor would have had good reason for comprehensible decision-making: arbitrariness would hardly have strengthened his position in the longer perspective. None of this guaranteed predictable outcomes in the late medieval Court of Chancery. It should, however, be remembered that this assessment, once again, rests on a contemporary comparison. In the common law courts, the juries generally deliberated behind a veil, no matter how reasonable their decisions might have been. This must have caused comparatively higher hopes for arbitrary decisions by parties with weaker arguments.

Taken together, the greater openness for the introduction of arguments, the superior truth-finding mechanisms and the more rational decision-making procedures allowed for better risk assessment regarding the outcome of a trial. Documenting the different stages of the process and spreading them over a certain period of time also provided the parties with time for reflection. A rationally-minded litigant should thus have been encouraged to reduce the costs of the conflict by an early settlement.

338 See *M. R. T. Macnair*, Arbitrary Chancellors and the Problem of Predictability, in: E. Koops/W. J. Zwalve (eds.), Law &Equity – Approaches in Roman Law and Common Law, p. 79–104; and above chapter II, 4.1.

Every attentive observer of modern civil procedure will recognise the aforementioned ideas – however novel in relation to the late medieval Court of Chancery – from discussions about the disappearance of civil trial in the United States since the second half of the 20th century.[339] Indeed, this is where the underlying assumptions stem from. A transfer of ideas from the modern civil trial to late medieval proceedings obviously risks falling into the trap of anachronism. However, in the absence of records explaining litigants' behaviour imputing rational behaviour seems like a sensible approach as long as potentially contradictory evidence is recognised.

While I have not discovered such evidence, a closer examination of the procedure offers a view on two additional reasons for the large presence of extra-judicial resolutions to Court of Chancery cases. These reasons deviate much further from our modern understanding of effective procedures but might nevertheless have had an even greater impact at the time: the use of charismatic authority and the appeal to conscience.

5.1.3 Charismatic authority

What do I mean by charismatic authority?[340] The involvement of a neutral third party is a common means for facilitating a settlement agreement between parties involved in a dispute. In the modern civil process, this role might even be assumed by a judge.[341] In that case, the authority of the third party commonly stems from expert knowledge of either alternative dispute resolution mechanisms or the rules governing the respective dispute. In the late medieval Court of

339 *J. H. Langbein*, The Disappearance of Civil Trial in the United States, Yale Law Journal, Volume 122 (2012), p. 522–572, especially p. 544–553. For the economic considerations underlying this 'rational' approach, see *R. A. Posner*, Economic Approach to Legal Procedure and Judicial Administration, Journal of Legal Studies, Volume 2 (1972), p. 399–458, especially p. 421–429.

340 The term 'charismatic authority' stems, of course, from *M. Weber*'s three-partite classification of types of authority – the other two types being traditional and legal authority (see *M. Weber*, Grundriss der Sozialökonomik, Volume 3: Wirtschaft und Gesellschaft, Mohr Siebeck, Tübingen, 1922, p. 122–176). That is not to say that the 'charismatic authority' referred to herein fits neatly into Weber's 'ideal-type'. Most importantly, the 'charisma' relied upon in this section does not necessarily constitute a mere character trait (compare *M. Weber*, Grudriss der Sozialökonomik, Volume 3: Wirtschaft und Gesellschaft, p. 140–141). It was just as well grounded in hereditary status or office and thus showed elements of the traditional and legal types of *M. Weber*'s classification.

341 Compare the German model of the 'Güterichter', a charitable or even equitable judge, who is supposed to encourage settlement through the means of alternative dispute resolution before the regular proceedings, para. 278 (5) Zivilprozessordnung (Civil Procedure Code).

Chancery, however, the professional expertise was often limited to the masters, who were commonly university-trained civil lawyers from the 1460s onwards.[342] Other key players, however, largely obtained their authority from their status and their societal influence – their charismatic authority.

This is most obviously true for the Lord Chancellor. Since hearings in the late medieval Court of Chancery were not reported, we have little knowledge of the respective Lord Chancellor's inclination to push the parties in the direction of a mutual agreement. Given the time constraints coming with the office, however, it seems unlikely that he had much patience for easily arbitrable suits. Rather than testing the patience and risking the wrath of one of the most powerful men in the country, the parties – in the absence of sheer desperation – might have preferred to concede an agreeable sum. On the other hand, the Lord Chancellor was admittedly so far removed from most of the parties to late medieval Chancery disputes that his personal authority might have played less of a role for litigants, who would quickly return to the English countryside after the end of the suit.

The same cannot be said about the examiners involved in the proceedings in the localities. These men were local dignitaries with much closer geographical and social ties to the parties. They could bring in their standing in the community, their economic power or any subtle means of persuasion in order to encourage settlements between the parties. Indeed, they had an additional egoistic interest in the early settlement of disputes: They otherwise had to file time-consuming reports of witness testimony for return to Westminster. And who would refuse the advice of one of the most-respected figures of the local community light-heartedly? The potential social sanctions must have been severe. Ample evidence for a heavy involvement of local dignitaries in extra-judicial conflict resolution exists from the Chancellorship of Cardinal Wolsey.[343] During this period, decisions were effectively outsourced to local commissions and merely decreed in the court on a regular basis.[344] The commissions were explicitly ordered to 'hear and end' the cases in the periphery.[345] This practice has prompted Michael Macnair to label the Court of Chancery under Wolsey a

342 For a closer study of the professional background of Chancery masters, see *N. Pronay*, The Chancellor, the Chancery, and the Council at the End of the Fifteenth Century, in: H. Hearder/H. R. Loyn (eds.), British Government and Administration – Studies Presented to S. B. Chrimes, p. 87–103, S. 90–92.

343 *F. Metzger*, Das englische Kanzleigericht unter Kardinal Wolsey, p. 112.

344 See for example the case of *Petite v Ardelow* (1518–1529), Some Proceedings in Chancery under Wolsey, Bulletin of the Institute of Historical Research, Volume 8 (1931), p. 17, in which the commission expressly suggested that the court should find in favour of the defendants.

345 *J. P. Dawson*, A History of Lay Judges, p. 164–167.

department for the supervision of alternative dispute resolution.[346] The sources from the 15th century do not provide clear evidence for earlier roots of this practice. The proliferated summaries of testimony actually show remarkable efforts at an objective presentation. As noted with regard to the case of *Ardern v Ardern*,[347] the examiners presented themselves so deliberately unengaged that we might even doubt their commitment. This might suggest a much more subdued (or merely subtle) influence of the examiners on the extra-judicial resolution of Chancery cases in the 15th century. But even if the examiners took a more restrained approach at the time, the seeds of the later development lay in the already established role of 'charismatic' laymen in the Chancery process.

5.1.4 Appeal to conscience

Franz Metzger mentioned on a passing note that a contested decree could not be in the interest of the Lord Chancellor, who was officially in the business of correcting consciences.[348] Irrespective of the exact understanding of the term conscience in the court at the time,[349] he certainly had a point. What could prove the successful correction of the parties' consciences better than an amicable agreement? Such an agreement, followed by the unforced correction of the original wrong, must have served as perfect evidence for the realisation and acceptance of originally unconscientious behaviour. The self-correction of the remorseful sinner is a timeless Christian ideal. The bible already proposed a three-step approach towards private conflict resolution: negotiation between parties as a first step, the involvement of third parties as a second step and resolution by officials as a last resort.[350] In this line of thinking, the judicial resolution of a private conflict was merely a subsidiary in the event of a breakdown of negotiations. Extra-judicial conflict resolution thus not only offered practical advantages but was also an end in itself in the late medieval court of conscience.

346 *M. R. T. Macnair*, Equity and Conscience, Oxford Journal of Legal Studies, Volume 27 (2007), p. 659–681, p. 670.

347 See above 4.1.4.

348 *F. Metzger*, Das englische Kanzleigericht unter Kardinal Wolsey, p. 111.

349 See above 2.7.

350 Compare Mt 18, 15–17, fn. 226. The *denunciatio evangelica* of the late medieval canon law was directly based on this bible verse. *H. Coing* famously saw the canonical *denunciatio evangelica* as the model for the Court of Chancery (*H. Coing*, English Equity and the Denunciatio Evangelica of the Canon Law, Law Quarterly Review, Volume 71 (1955), p. 223–241). I will discuss this thesis critically in the following chapter VI. It should nonetheless be noted that the prevalence of extra-judicial resolutions of Chancery cases supports *H. Coing*'s argument.

Conducive procedures, charismatic interventions, moral desirability – the institutional design of the late medieval Court of Chancery was clearly favourable towards the extra-judicial determination of cases. Compared with the common law's obscure decision-making process behind the veil of jury deliberations, this constituted a substantial competitive advantage.[351]

5.2 'Judicial' determination

The substantial role of extra-judicial conflict resolution in the late medieval Court of Chancery should not preclude a closer examination of the process of judicial conflict resolution. Despite the relative rarity of preserved court decisions, the sources from the late 15th century allow at least for some insight into the decision-making process. It was by this time that the decrees, which can be found on the back of some original bills, exhibited a recognisable structure. Earlier decrees merely consisted of a single short sentence granting or denying the claim.

In the absence of primary sources, it is obviously much more difficult to reconstruct the way in which the court arrived at its decisions than to analyse the decrees themselves. In order to highlight the differences in decision-making between the late medieval Court of Chancery and contemporary common law courts, I will nevertheless provide an impression of the decision-making process (5.2.1.) before analysing the content of the decrees (5.2.2.). At last, I will then examine the effect of the court's decisions by explaining its remedies and comparing them once more with those of the late medieval common law courts (5.2.3.).

5.2.1 Decision-making process

5.2.1.1 Publication

The final stage of the evidence-gathering process in the early modern Court of Chancery was the publication of its results.[352] This practice was a direct result of the secret obtainment of testimony. Parties and witnesses were examined upon the interrogatories in private. Simultaneous publication of all evidence guaranteed that no party was privileged by superior knowledge when answering,

351 *J.A. Guy*, The Development of Equitable Jurisdictions, 1450–1550, in: E.W. Ives/A.H. Manchester (eds.), Law, Litigants, and the Legal Profession, p. 80–86, p. 84, came to the same conclusion.

352 See *W.J. Jones*, The Elizabethan Court of Chancery, p. 248–250; *D.E.C. Yale*, Introduction, in: D.E.C. Yale (ed.), Lord Nottingham's 'Manual of Chancery Practice' and 'Prolegomena of Chancery and Equity', p. 60.

drawing up questions or preparing the further proceedings. A reconsideration of the abbot's report in *Ardern v Ardern* immediately exposes the absence of a similar practice in the 15th century. According to the report of the examiner, both parties were present during the examinations and effectively brought their witnesses with them.[353] They thus already knew the content of the testimony insofar as it was provided orally. Furthermore, the manner, in which testimony was taken, also eliminated the rationale behind publication. Since the witnesses were merely heard upon the content of the bill and not actively interrogated according to party-drafted questions,[354] the potential for surprise was significantly reduced. Despite making reference to the preceding steps of procedure, decrees from other 15th century cases do not mention publication either.[355]

5.2.1.2 Hearing

It is there, however, that we can find clear evidence of the existence of another well-documented early modern practice in the late medieval proceedings: the hearing before the decision. The decrees reduce the practice to a simple formula: the documentation from the proceedings was "read, heard and understood" in the Court of Chancery.[356] What was actually reported to have been read, heard and understood depended on the respective proceedings. It generally included all documents exchanged between the parties as well as any testimony or documented evidence. From what we know about the later practice, the hearing was a rather speedy and simple affair.[357] Counsel for the parties[358] would

353 See above 4.1.2.
354 Compare above 4.1.6.
355 See below 5.2.2.2.
356 *Revelle v Gower* (1471), Select Cases, p. 155. The exact wording could differ but the message generally remained the same. Similar examples include *Bodenham v Halle* (1456), Select Cases, p. 137; *Bale v Marchall* (1456), Select Cases, p. 143; *Stokker v Colyns* (1474–1475), Calendars I, p. xcv.
357 Also *D. E. C. Yale*, Introduction, in: D. E. C. Yale (ed.), Lord Nottingham's 'Manual of Chancery Practice' and 'Prolegomena of Chancery and Equity', p. 63.
358 The counsel for the parties in front of the Court of Chancery should not be confused with the 'country lawyers' (see *T. S. Haskett*, Country Lawyers? The Composers of English Chancery Bills, in: P. Birks (ed.), The Life of the Law, Proceedings of the Tenth British Legal History Conference, Oxford, 1991, S. 9–23), who drafted the original bills. As *F. Metzger* observed for the Wolsey court, the most eminent common lawyers of the country, the seargeants-at-law commonly acted as counsel in Chancery proceedings (*F. Metzger*, Das englische Kanzleigericht unter Kardinal Wolsey, p. 204–214a). Here, we can identify another reason for the relatively smooth relations between common lawyers and the Court of Chancery at the time. The court simply provided another lucrative source of income (compare also *J. H. Langbein / R. T. Lerner / B. P. Smith*,

provide brief opening statements, whereas the hearing was otherwise limited to a recitation (if necessary also abridged) of the existing documents.[359] Only 16th century sources directly speak of re-examinations of witnesses in the course of the hearings after unsatisfactory written testimony.[360]

Why then, were the parties summoned before the court, for such a mundane affair? The answer is probably simple. Decisions in the Court of Chancery were reserved for the Lord Chancellor. He thus needed to be aware of all the established facts of the case. The masters could set the process in motion, order appearances and meetings, collect the documents and oversee their legality but they could not make decisions (officially at least). As mentioned several times already, however, the office of Lord Chancellor also involved many other extra-judicial duties. The hearing thus relieved the Lord Chancellor of the time-consuming duty to study the documents in every single case. It guaranteed that the public involvement of the Lord Chancellor remained comparatively brief.

5.2.1.3 Deliberation

Legend has it that the most-gifted of early modern Lord Chancellors dictated their history-making decisions straight from the bench after the hearings.[361] Irrespective of the truth of these stories for the 17th century, the 15th century practice clearly was a different one. When matters remained disputed up to the very end of the proceedings, the hearing was generally followed by deliberations. Naturally, these deliberations were not documented. Given the presence of university-trained civil lawyers in Chancery at the end of the 15th century and their knowledge of the cases, it seems highly likely that they also exerted great influence on the decisions of the court. As they were mere subordinates of the Lord Chancellor, however, their contribution was never mentioned explicitly.

In contrast, independent participants in the decision-making process were explicitly referenced in some of the decrees. As such, the justices of the common

History of the Common Law – The Development of Anglo-American Legal Institutions, p. 312).

359 *D. E. C. Yale*, Introduction, in: D. E. C. Yale (ed.), Lord Nottingham's 'Manual of Chancery Practice' and 'Prolegomena of Chancery and Equity', p. 61–62.

360 *D. E. C. Yale*, Introduction, in: D. E. C. Yale (ed.), Lord Nottingham's 'Manual of Chancery Practice' and 'Prolegomena of Chancery and Equity', p. 62, fn. 1, with reference to *G. Norburie*, The Abuses and Remedies of Chancery, in: F. Hargrave (ed.), A Collection of Tracts Relative to the Law of England from Manuscripts, Lynch & Co. Dublin, 1787 (repr. 1982), p. 426–448, p. 441.

361 *D. E. C. Yale*, Introduction, in: D. E. C. Yale (ed.), Lord Nottingham's 'Manual of Chancery Practice' and 'Prolegomena of Chancery and Equity', p. 62, presented Lord Nottingham as the most famous example.

law[362] as well as other members of the *curia regis*[363] are mentioned separately or accumulatively throughout the sources. The involvement of the common law justices might be considered the most interesting piece of information. The willingness to cooperate evidenced by this reference must have been an important factor in the relatively smooth rise of the Court of Chancery in the late medieval period despite the existence of a fully established central jurisdiction in the form of the common law courts. At the time, the justices apparently had a real say in the decisions of the Court of Chancery. Their involvement must have diminished the impression of a potential threat posed by the expanding Court of Chancery. On the other hand, the Lord Chancellor, regularly an experienced cleric but yet a lay lawyer, must have profited from the justices' expertise – not only but also in matters of jurisdiction. As long as time constraints allowed for regular exchange, these deliberations thus created a real win-win situation. The involvement of other members of the *curia regis* is probably best explained by the incomplete separation of the Court of Chancery from the *curia regis* at the time.[364]

5.2.1.4 Drafting

After the deliberations, the decrees were prepared. It might very well be true that the statements on the back of the original bills, which indicate the changing hand-writing of Chancery staff, merely constituted a copy of the decree. Nevertheless, it seems unlikely that the Lord Chancellors framed the decrees personally. In the second half of the 15th century, the actual decision was usually condensed in a single sentence. As we will see, the rest of the decree more or less consisted of formulaic summaries of the proceedings. Their drafting was thus a purely administrative task.

5.2.1.5 Decision-making at common law

Common law trials outside London were conducted on a yearly basis under the supervision of travelling justices in the assizes. Given our knowledge about the late medieval Chancery process, this arrangement made remarkable sense: The Court of Chancery collected evidence in the periphery through local commissions that would send their findings back to London. The common law courts,

362 See for example *Bodenham v Halle* (1456), Select Cases, p. 137; *Bale v Marchall* (1456), Select Cases, p. 143; *Stokker v Colyns* (1474–1475), Calendars I, p. xcv.

363 *Bale v Marchall* (1456), Select Cases, p. 143.

364 See above chapter II, 2.5.

on the other hand, sent their justices to the periphery in order to tap the knowledge of the local population in the form of the jury.[365]

At the trial, the beginning of the proceedings also showed significant similarities to the Court of Chancery. The court read out the pleadings and identified the decisive issue, whereas counsel for the respective parties provided their version of the underlying facts.[366] Just like the Lord Chancellor in the Court of Chancery, the jurors had to be informed about the official pre-trial proceedings, which were mostly carried out between the parties and professional staff.[367] Compared to the Court of Chancery, where evidence had been documented and could thus be taken into account by the Lord Chancellor in the course of the deliberations, however, common law jurors operated on even more shaky ground when it came to discerning the truth of the respective claims.

The decision-making procedure in the 14th and at the beginning of the 15th century was clearly deficient. The common law provided no room for evidence outside the regular forms of action, most notably, it did not allow for the examination of witnesses. The ideal underlying this procedure was the self-informing jury, which knew "the constancy, inconstancy, and repute"[368] of everyone involved in the trial, since it convened 'twelve reputable men' from the vicinity. It is hardly surprising that this constellation led to the establishment of rather curious practices: Counsel often approached the prospective jurors in the final days before the trial, presented its evidence and argued its case. Perhaps more effectively, the parties often treated the decision-makers to lavish meals or offered other favours.[369] Criticism of the potential for corruption is futile but it should be observed that such a system of fact-finding theoretically required the existence of a close-knit society, in which people knew their neighbours.

The decline,[370] or perhaps even the realisation of the illusion, of such a society might have been a driving factor in the slow disappearance of the self-informing

365 Compare *F. Pollock / F. W. Maitland*, The History of English Law before the Time of Edward I, Volume 2, p. 627–628.

366 *J. Fortescue*, in: S. Lockwood (ed.), On the Laws and Governance of England, Cambridge University Press, Cambridge, 1997, p. 38.

367 *J. H. Baker*, Introduction, in: J. H. Baker (ed.), The Reports of John Spelman, Selden Society, London, Volume 2, 1978, p. 38, drew a wider analogy between the functions of the Lord Chancellor in the Court of Chancery and the jury at common law.

368 *J. Fortescue*, in: S. Lockwood (ed.), On the Laws and Governance of England, p. 40.

369 Compare *D. J. Seipp*, Jurors, Evidences and the Tempest of 1499, in: J. W. Cairns / G. McLeod (eds.), The Dearest Birth Right of the People of England – The Jury in the History of the Common Law, Hart, Oxford, 2002, p. 75–92, p. 82–85.

370 *J. H. Langbein / R. T. Lerner / B. P. Smith*, History of the Common Law – The Development of Anglo-American Legal Institutions, p. 224–227, suggested that

jury. By the latter half of the 15th century, we can find clear evidence of witness testimony at trial in the common law assizes.[371] The coincidence with the rise of the Court of Chancery, which I have been describing, may not be purely accidental. It might be the case that a few decades of Chancery practice had already proved the usefulness of witness testimony. Considering the illiteracy of a large part of the population, witness examination at common law was and always remained oral. Given the difficulties we have identified with regard to the written depositions in the Court of Chancery, it might even be suggested that the common law eclipsed its inspiration within a few decades regarding the effectiveness of the proceedings.

After the presentations, the jurors retreated for deliberations.[372] In the late medieval trial, the judge did not provide substantial instructions. In comparison with the Lord Chancellor, his role was extremely reduced. He was a mere presenter rather than the master of proceedings. Generally, the jurors returned their decision quickly to the court to 'certify the truth'.[373] Given their involvement in the affairs and the pre-trial influences, they had usually made up their mind months or at least days ago.

The gap in expertise when compared to the Court of Chancery is apparent. Whereas the Lord Chancellor deliberated with staff and skilled advisers about issues of law and fact, the jurors could merely provide their assessment of the facts. The decision-making process is easily criticised for its intransparency and lack of professionalism. Nevertheless, one cannot help but admit that it possessed one decisive quality, the absence of which later accelerated the Court of Chancery's demise: it was quick.

5.2.2 Decrees

The decrees proliferated on the back of some 15th century bills do not yet reveal a fully consistent structure or terminology.[374] However, they show sufficient similarities to identify typical traits. The variety of decrees requires the consid-

the Black Death caused a disintegration of traditional rural societies in the 14th century.

371 *J. Fortescue*, in: S. Lockwood (ed.), On the Laws and Governance of England, p. 38–39.

372 *J. Fortescue*, in: S. Lockwood (ed.), On the Laws and Governance of England, p. 39.

373 *J. Fortescue*, in: S. Lockwood (ed.), On the Laws and Governance of England, p. 39.

374 For the chancellorship of Cardinal Wolsey, *F. Metzger*, Das englische Kanzleigericht unter Kardinal Wolsey, p. 110, found that "formulation and structure" followed a "strict form" [translation by the author].

eration of several different examples in order to gain an understanding of their content. The structure of the examination here follows the fairly typical case of *Revelle v Gower.*[375] All decrees were written in Latin.

5.2.2.1 Opening

Following contemporary – but also modern – standards for official documents, the decrees generally commenced with a mention of the date, the court and the parties involved in the dispute. This was followed by an enumeration of the evidence, which the court considered in the case. Evidence, in this context, needs to be understood as the entirety of all documents being brought to the attention of the court. The bill, or petition, which opened the proceedings and framed the original allegations, was mentioned at the outset, whereas the further pleadings were enumerated in the following passages. If applicable, the decree also recounted witness testimony and documentary evidence.[376]

5.2.2.2 Alleged and proved

Effectively, the document outlined what was 'alleged and proved' (*allegata et probata*) in the course of the proceedings. The phrase *allegata et probata* was

375 As main reference point for the general structure of decrees in the second half of the 15th century, I will be using the case of *Revelle v Gower* (1471), Select Cases, p. 155. The decree reads as follows: "*Be it remembered that on the 12*th *day of February, 11 Edward IV, 1472, this petition, exhibited before us in our Chancery in the 10*th *year of our reign by the within-written William Revelle and Maude his wife and Robert Blound and Ele his wife, cousins and heirs of Alice Fleming, against Edward Gower, esquire, and the answer and replication made and had thereto between the parties aforesaid having been read, heard and understood with mature deliberation in the said Chancery by the venerable father, the Bishop of Bath and Wells, our Chancellor, and by the Court of Chancery: It was considered and adjudged that, inasmuch as the said Edward has sufficiently proved before us in the Chancery, that he purchased and bought the within-written manor of Hinton Pippard from the above-written Alice Thorp, to hold to himself, his heirs and assigns for ever, and satisfaction for the same manor was made by the aforesaid Edward to the said Alice. Therefore it was considered and adjudged by the aforesaid Chancellor and by the consideration of the Court aforesaid that the same Edward may have, continue, hold, enjoy, and possess the said manor of Hinton Pippard with the appurtenances, to himself, his heirs and assigns, for ever, according to the consideration and judgment aforesaid. And thereupon he is dismissed out of Court, quit and without day.*"

376 See for example *Stokker v Colyns* (1474–1475), Calendars I, p. xcv; *Slefeld v Grafton* (1475), Calendars I, p. xcvii; *Mayhewe v Gardener* (1476–1477), Calendars I, p. xcix. However, the depositions mentioned in the respective decrees have not been preserved with the pleadings.

commonly used in the decrees by the time of Wolsey's chancellorship.[377] It does, however, not appear regularly in my sample from the second half of the 15th century.[378] The enumeration of all applicable evidence nevertheless clearly shows that the principle that the court would generally decide on what was alleged and proved was already well-established.[379]

The formula *allegata et probata* originally stemmed from Roman law but it was in use throughout all English courts from the late Middle Ages.[380] It was not the formula but its meaning that differed significantly between the respective courts. The common law, most importantly, strictly restricted what could be alleged through its writ system and then limited what could be proved through restrictions upon the means of proof for different actions – it acted entirely *secundam allegata et probata*, in a way that was never paralleled in Roman-canon law.[381] In contrast, the Court of Chancery's approach was much more open-ended. First, the parties were free to allege whatever they considered an injustice. Then, proof could result from the examination of the defendant's conscience under oath and from the Lord Chancellor's impression thereof or his private knowledge.[382] Arguably, this constituted a significant deviation from the maxim that the judge could merely consider what had been alleged and proved. Indeed, the Latin maxim explicitly said that "the judge should act according to what is alleged and proved, not according to conscience"[383] and Lord Chancellor Stillington insisted that he decided "according to conscience and not according to allegations".[384]

The fact that the medieval Court of Chancery listed what had been alleged and proved in the decree should thus not be misunderstood to mean that it had acted in line with either common law or Roman-canon law expectations of deciding strictly *secundum allegata et probata, non secundum conscientiam*.

As outlined above, the decree then expressed that the court had 'read, heard, and understood' the evidence and, if applicable, considered it with the common law justices or other advisors.[385]

377 *F. Metzger*, Das englische Kanzleigericht unter Kardinal Wolsey, p. 110.

378 An exceptional mention can be found in the relatively late case of the *Earl of Oxford v Tyrell* (1493–1500), Calendars I, p. cxx.

379 See *M. R. T. Macnair*, The Law of Proof in Early Modern Equity, p. 46–54, for the adherence to Roman-canon law standards of what was alleged and proved in the early modern Court of Chancery.

380 Compare *M. R. T. Macnair*, The Law of Proof in Early Modern Equity, p. 46.

381 See above 4.

382 See above 3.1, introduction.

383 See again *K. W. Nörr*, Zur Stellung des Richters im Gelehrten Prozeß der Frühzeit: Iudex secundum allegata non secundum conscientiam iudicat.

384 (1469) Y. B. 9 Edw. IV, Trin., f. 14, pl. 9.

385 See above 5.2.1.3.

5.2.2.3 Type of decision

With all this background information documented, the decrees then turned to the actual decision on the case. All later decrees from the Court of Chancery included the programmatic statement 'it is decreed' (*decretum est*). The case of *Revelle v Gower*,[386] however, represented a noteworthy deviation from this pattern. Instead of *decretum*, the decision was merely introduced by the words 'considered and adjudged' (*consideratum et adjudicatum*). What is most remarkable about this terminological choice is the fact that the formula *consideratum est* was otherwise used in common law judgments throughout English legal history. A look through further cases shows that *consideratum*[387] on its own and in combination with *decretum*[388] were used indistinctively throughout the second half of the 15th century. The respective cases can neither be distinguished by time nor by their content. In the absence of any discernible differences, it seems likely that the use of *consideratum* alone and in combination with *decretum* in the sources was a result of terminological confusion rather than of substantive quality. I will therefore also continue to use the term decree despite its absence in a large share of decisions from the 15th century. It needs to be borne in mind that the distinction between the common law and the future equitable jurisdiction of the Court of Chancery was incomplete in the 15th century.[389] Furthermore, while the break with the common law process was highly influential in a practical dimension, the concept of an alternative equitable jurisdiction had not yet been fully developed and theorised.[390] It seems likely that nobody had cared about the substantive difference between judgment and decree.[391]

386 (1471), Select Cases, p. 155.

387 See for example *Bale v Marchall* (1456), Select Cases, p. 143; *Duke of Gloucester v Ely* (1472–1473), Calendars I, p. xc; *Astel v Causton* (1481–1482), Calendars I, p. cviii.

388 See for example *Slefeld v Grafton* (1475), Calendars I, p. xcvii; *Mayhewe v Gardener* (1476–1477), Calendars I, p. xcix; *Peverell v Huse* (1492–1493), Calendars I, p. cxxii.

389 See above chapter II, 2.3.

390 The fame associated with the original theorisation of the equitable dimension of the Court of Chancery is commonly attributed to *St. German's Doctor and Student* (see T. F.T. Plucknett / J. L. Barton (eds.), St. German's Doctor and Student). See for example *D. E. C. Yale*, Introduction to Edward Hake, in: D. E. C. Yale (ed.), Epieikeia: A Dialogue on Equity in Three Parts, Yale Law School Library Publications, New Haven, Ct., 1953, p. xiii.

391 The question whether there is a relevant difference in English law will have to remain unanswered. After all, the classical definition states that common law courts give judgments whereas courts of equity provide decrees.

5.2.2.4 Content

The substantive part of the decree was entirely dependant on the circumstances of the case. In *Revelle v Gower*,[392] for example, the court found that the defendant had received the property in question in the course of a valid transfer and could therefore enjoy the disputed property rights.[393] It thus declared both its finding and the resulting consequences. In line with the opportunity to present contingent cases, the decisions in 15th century Court of Chancery cases were extremely varied. The court might quickly dismiss the claim[394] or provide a long list of remedies.[395] What decisions in favour of the plaintiff generally had in common was that they ordered the defendants to perform or omit certain acts.[396] This admittedly opened a wide spectrum of possible determinations.

Decisions in favour of the defendant ended with an unequivocal dismissal ('quit and without day'), whereas those in favour of the plaintiff finished with the remedy. Interestingly, the 15th century decrees did not yet include a declaration as to the costs of the litigation.[397] We can only speculate that this important matter must have been documented elsewhere.

5.2.3 Remedy

The contingency of the original bills guaranteed that plaintiffs in the late medieval Court of Chancery would pursue a huge variety of more or less concrete targets through their suit. What remedies did the court provide for these appeals? The answer is simple and yet it must have felt truly liberating at the time. While the common law courts could merely offered a conclusive list of fixed remedies, the Court of Chancery had the power to order each party to perform or omit certain acts.

392 (1471), Select Cases, p. 155.

393 The decision in *Revelle v Gower*, (1471), Select Cases, p. 155, provides another interesting insight into the Court of Chancery process at the time. It states that the defendant sufficiently proved the transfer of property. This suggests that – in contrast to modern rules of procedure – the court did not clearly attribute the burden of proof to the party seeking to establish the claim. This might be seen as another incidence of a lack of formality.

394 See for example *Revelle v Gower* (1471), Select Cases, p. 155.

395 See for example *Bodenham v Halle* (1456), Select Cases, p. 137.

396 For the result of this policy, see below 5.2.3.

397 That is in contrast to early 16th century cases; see *F. Metzger,* Das englische Kanzleigericht unter Kardinal Wolsey, p. 110.

5.2.3.1 Scope

Admittedly, this definition covers such a broad range of potential remedies that it might be considered useless. The respective acts and omissions could occur in all areas of law, they could be directed to all parties to the suit and they could relate to singular, recurring or continuous events. However, the definition also highlights one important constraint: The Court of Chancery could only impose personal obligations. As explained in relation with its jurisdiction,[398] it acted strictly *in personam*. Consequently, it could not establish rights *in rem* and thus not dispose over legal title. It is the very essence of proprietary rights that they are enforceable against the whole world. The Court of Chancery, however, could merely bind the parties to the respective suit. That, at least, was the theory. Effectively, declaring that someone "*may have, continue, hold, enjoy, and possess* [property] *to himself, his heirs and assigns, for ever*"[399] vis-à-vis the previous titleholder comes awfully close to a proprietary right. In the absence of competing claims, it put the respective party in the same position as a legal titleholder with regard to the future enjoyment of the property. The distinction between decisions *in personam* and *in rem* was thus not nearly as clear-cut as the Court of Chancery would have us believe.[400]

5.2.3.2 Restriction

With the confinement to personal obligations comes the rejection of a concept of precedent.[401] At the outset – and this theory is very much supported by the evidence from the 15th century sources – the court was merely concerned with providing individual relief[402] rather than with the establishment of a normative order. That, of course, is not to say that the individual decisions were not lead by the practical application of a certain normative order.[403] Either way, the remedies provided by the Court of Chancery embodied a fascinating contradiction: The emphasis on the personal dimension hinted at modest aspirations whereas the scope of potential remedies – and their potential impact on the rest

398 See above 2.5.1.

399 *Revelle v Gower* (1471), Select Cases, p. 155.

400 See also *E. G. Henderson*, Legal Rights to Land in the Early Chancery, American Journal of Legal History, Volume 26 (1982), S. 97–122, S. 98; *J. H. Langbein / R. T. Lerner / B. P. Smith*, History of the Common Law – The Development of Anglo-American Legal Institutions, p. 286.

401 Also *F. Metzger*, Das englische Kanzleigericht unter Kardinal Wolsey, p. 304–305.

402 Or correcting individual consciences, if one believes in its claims of a higher motivation.

403 See the discussion above 2.7.

of society – was unlimited. It might be suggested that a court equipped with such unfettered discretion does rather well stressing its personal or moral rather than its legal or political ambitions in a time of institutional changes.

In the absence of practical examples, the results of the competence to order any act or omission are admittedly difficult to grasp. I will nevertheless not merely enumerate cases, in which defendants were ordered to honour trust agreements[404] or in which other authorities were ordered to release plaintiffs.[405] Instead, I will address three characteristic 'acts' ordered in the Court of Chancery, which have later shaped the understanding of equitable remedies: specific performance (5.2.3.3), injunction (5.2.3.4) and fiduciary relationships (5.2.3.4). This approach should, on the one hand, help to demonstrate the scope of the court's power. On the other hand, it should illustrate the resulting superior potential in comparison with the common law.

5.2.3.3 Specific performance

Specific performance, in this context, should be understood as an order by the court requiring a party to fulfil its specific obligations under a contract.[406] Everyone familiar with modern English common law will know about the continuous reluctance of the courts to grant this remedy.[407] While this reluctance has a long history, it was not an original feature of the common law. Studies on medieval common law have shown that some of the oldest common law actions effectively provided a form of specific performance.[408] By the time the writ system was fixed, however, these actions had gone out of use and the only available remedy for what we would classify as breach of contract was damages.[409]

404 See for example *Duke of Gloucester v Bishop of Ely* (1472–1473), Calendars I, p. xc; *Neville (in Calendars: Archbishop of York) v Osborn* (1473), Calendars I, p. xciv; *Tryppe v Chevyn* (1484), Calendars I, p. cxvi.

405 See for example *Michell v Marmyun* (1473), Calendars I, p. lxxxvii. In a number of other cases, no decrees have been preserved but evidence suggests that hearings were set, for example in *John v Wardens of the Shoemaker's Corporation* (1473–1474), Calendars I, p. xciv; *Damico v Burdican* (1474–1480), Calendars I, p. ciii; *Gyseberdson v Lieutenant of the Tower* (1474–1480); Calendars I, p. civ.

406 Compare W. Jowitt / C. Walsh (eds.), The Dictionary of English Law, Volume 2, p. 1662.

407 Compare W. Jowitt / C. Walsh (eds.), The Dictionary of English Law, Volume 2, p. 1662–1663.

408 *H. D. Hazeltine*, The Early History of English Equity, in: P. Vinogradoff (ed.), Essays in Legal History, Oxford University Press, Oxford, 1913, p. 261–285, p. 269–270; *T. F. T. Plucknett*, A Concise History of the Common Law, p. 678.

409 *A. W. B. Simpson*, A History of the Common Law of Contract – The Rise of the Action of Assumpsit, p. 596–598.

This is not the place to speculate about the reasons for this development.[410] It seems hardly likely that medieval common lawyers discussed modern rationales like 'efficient breach'.[411] It might, however, have been easier to execute monetary penalties than to police the performance of a specific contractual duty in the absence of a fully developed administrative state in the periphery. Either way, the common law did not provide specific performance by the 15th century, whereas the Court of Chancery did.[412] In a Year Book case from 1468, Lord Chancellor Stillington (1420–1491; Lord Chancellor 1465–1491) clearly stated that a plaintiff, who was "damaged by the non-performance of the promise […] will have a remedy [in the Court of Chancery]".[413] It might have been the political authority of the court that rendered the execution of a decree on specific performance more likely.

5.2.3.4 Injunction

The term injunction can generally cover any kind of court order to perform or refrain from a certain act.[414] As I have already described above, this was indeed what the Court of Chancery was capable of ordering. This broad definition, however, is of no help for describing a specific subclass of remedies. Chancery injunctions varied in their scope and in their duration.[415] I, however, want to focus on only one common class of injunction: the injunction to halt proceedings in other courts.

It should be obvious that such a tool in the hands of a royal court has the potential to subordinate all other courts. Plaintiffs continuously sought injunctions from the Court of Chancery against common law and ecclesiastical courts throughout the 15th century[416] and the decrees clearly show that the court

410 A possible explanation might lie in the early influence of Roman law. For an introduction, see *R. Zimmermann*, The Law of Obligations – Roman Foundations of the Civilian Tradition, p. 770–782. The English development is summarised on p. 776–791.

411 For a recent introduction, see *G. Klass*, Efficient Breach, in: G. Klass / G. Letsas / P. Saprai (eds.), The Philosophical Foundations of Contract Law, Oxford University Press, Oxford, 2014, p. 362–387.

412 *A. W. B. Simpson*, A History of the Common Law of Contract – The Rise of the Action of Assumpsit, p. 595–598.

413 (1468) Y. B. 8 Edw. IV, Pasch., pl. 11, f. 4.

414 W. Jowitt / C. Walsh (eds.), The Dictionary of English Law, Volume 2, S. 972.

415 For a complete overview over equitable injunctions from a 19th century perspective, see *J. Story*, Commentaries on Equity Jurisprudence, Volume 2, 1877, p. 55–162.

416 See for example *Astel v Causton* (1481–1482), Calendars I, p. cviii; *Edyall v Hunston* (1484), Calendars I, p. cxiii; *Peverell v Huse* (1486–1493), Calendars I, p. cxxii.

followed these motions.[417] The issue underlying the claim was then commonly resolved in the Court of Chancery.[418] Despite the fact that the case officially remained 'on hold' in the other court, Chancery thereby effectively seized jurisdiction. The common law courts had very little to oppose to Chancery injunctions. As I have already outlined above,[419] the writ of prohibition fulfilled a similar function with regard to the ecclesiastical courts but was never issued against the Court of Chancery.[420]

5.2.3.5 Fiduciary relationship

A fiduciary relationship can generally be found where one party is under an on-going legal duty to protect the other party's interests or to act to their benefit.[421] Of course, such a relationship can hardly be considered a remedy in itself. It rather carries the potential for a large variety of remedies and thus shows the capabilities of the Court of Chancery's decision-making. Whereas the late medieval common law was strictly committed to damages in the form of singular payments (and proprietary remedies),[422] the Court of Chancery characterised and supervised on-going relationships.

The most famous and also most frequent form of a fiduciary relationship in the late medieval Court of Chancery was the one between what we now call a trustee and a beneficiary. Although it does not fit neatly into the trust scheme, the case of *Ardern v Ardern*[423] proves as a useful example: Following the settlement agreement, John, the legal title holder, was under a lasting obligation to Walter, the beneficiary, to pass on the profits from the land. As can be seen from this case, the Court of Chancery controlled the adherence to such duties from the early days of its jurisdiction over uses. The 15th century sources do not yet provide evidence of a sophisticated bureaucracy for the supervision of accounts[424] and the effectiveness of remedies resulting from fiduciary relation-

417 See for example *Edyall v Hunston* (1484), Calendars I, p. cxiii.

418 See for example *Astel v Causton* (1481–1482), Calendars I, p. cviii.

419 See 2.5.4. For further information, see *C.M. Gray*, The Boundaries of the Equitable Function, The American Journal of Legal History, Volume 20 (1976), p. 192–226.

420 That, of course, would also have necessitated that Chancery issued a writ against its own court.

421 Compare W. Jowitt / C. Walsh (eds.), The Dictionary of English Law, Volume 1, p. 800.

422 For the development towards this position, see also *F. Pollock / F. W. Maitland*, The History of English Law before the Time of Edward I, Volume 2, p. 522–526.

423 (1465/1466), Calendars I, p. lxxii.

424 This, however, was already visible in the late 16th century Court of Chancery. See *W.J. Jones*, The Elizabethan Court of Chancery, p. 280–281.

ships might thus be questioned. Nevertheless, the court had already assumed the power to control personal obligations over a longer timeframe.

The aforementioned classes of remedies merely represent a small excerpt of the opportunities of the late medieval Court of Chancery. What I hope to have shown is that the imposition of personal obligations allowed for highly flexible remedies for every situation. Ordering any act or omission was the necessary consequence of the open-ended bill jurisdiction. The plaintiffs could only be entirely free to ask for help in contingent situations, when the court could provide a correspondingly contingent range of remedies.

5.2.3.6 Common law remedies

The difference to the late medieval common law could hardly be clearer. The writ system had limited the number and type of available remedies. With the exception of proprietary remedies, the writs typically foresaw monetary damages as the singular remedy. This certainly made sense from a contemporary perspective. Since the decision-maker, the jury, was effectively dismantled after the decision, the supervision or enforcement of other obligations would have had to fall to the courts, which lacked the necessary personnel. Nonetheless, the range of available remedies provides one more incident of evidence for the greater openness and flexibility of the Court of Chancery process in the 15th century.

Chapter VI

Roman-canon law origins of the Chancery process

Ever since Maitland's famous lecture on *Law and the Renaissance*[1] (and arguably even before)[2] one question has been the focal point of research on the Court of Chancery: In how far does the court represent a civil law element in the English legal system? Maitland saw the equity courts with their seemingly civilian procedure as an entry gate for a potential reception of civil law in 16th century England. His lecture then described how the common law – in contrast to local continental laws – resisted this potential 'threat'.

The question of the civilian character of the Court of Chancery is of immediate relevance for my studies. If the procedure I have described, and which I consider to be the basis for the rise of the Court of Chancery in the late Middle Ages, was of civil or Roman-canon law origin, the Court of Chancery would have effectively Romanised parts of royal conflict resolution. The process I have been describing would thus have to be understood as part of a broader European development.

We might generally distinguish the countless reflections on the issue into those emphasising either the typically English[3] or the civilian[4] origins of the Court of Chancery. Obviously, none of the accounts is as one-sided as this

1 *F. W. Maitland*, English Law and the Renaissance (with some Notes), Cambridge University Press, Cambridge, 1901.

2 See for example *C. C. Langdell*, The Development of Equity Pleading from Canon Law Procedure, in: Select Essays in Anglo-American Legal History, Little, Brown, and Company, Boston, Ma., Volume 2, 1908, p. 753–778 (originally published in 1877).

3 This group might include *W. Holdsworth*, The Reception of Roman Law in the Sixteenth Century, The Law Quarterly Review, Volume 28 (1912), p. 236–254; *W. Holdsworth*, A History of English Law, Methuen, London, Volume 4, 3rd edition 1945 (repr. 1966), p. 252–293; *T. F. T. Plucknett*, A Concise History of the Common Law, Butterworth, London, 5th edition, 1956, p. 673–707; *G. R. Elton*, F. W. Maitland, Weidenfeld and Nicolson, London, 1985, p. 79–88; *J. H. Baker*, The Oxford History of the Laws of England, Volume 6: 1483–1558, Oxford University Press, Oxford, 2003, p. 171–190.

4 We might consider *C. C. Langdell*, The Development of Equity Pleading from Canon Law Procedure, in: Select Essays in Anglo-American Legal History, Volume 2, p. 753–778; *J. L. Barton*, Roman Law in England, in: Société d'Histoire des Droits de L'Antiquité (ed.), Ius Romanum Medii Aevi, Giuffré, Milan, Volume 5, 13a, 1971, especially p. 65–66; *J. H. Langbein / R. T. Lerner / B. P. Smith*, History of the Common Law – The Development of Anglo-American

admittedly superficial classification would suggest. Indeed, contemporary identifications of the civil law-character of Chancery proceedings date back to the year 1415.[5] Some sort of civil law influence on the late medieval Court of Chancery is thus undeniable. My classification therefore relies on degrees of association rather than on fundamental opposites.

Most of the aforementioned studies relied on a broad knowledge of common law legal history for integrating the history of the Court of Chancery into their respective narratives of common law legal history. This helps to explain the continuing fascination with the question but condemns those accounts to a relatively high level of abstraction. They are thus only peripherally useful for ascertaining the immediate impact of Roman-canon or civil law on the development of Chancery procedure specifically.

For this objective, it will be necessary to rely on more specialised research. Two accounts, both clearly coming down on the civilian side of the former distinction, stand out for their concrete approach and their actual knowledge about Roman-canon law sources. The scope of their work and their methods, however, could hardly be more different.

The title already gives away the scope of Michael Macnair's *The Law of Proof in Early Modern Equity*:[6] The study was limited to the law of proof, from a common law perspective effectively matters of evidence, and it mainly relied on 17th and 18th century sources. It strictly followed a classical comparative approach. The evidentiary rules of equitable courts[7] were identified and compared with Roman-canon law procedure. Whenever parallels were identifiable, Macnair also provided insights into the respective common law regulations. Macnair's approach is undoubtedly highly commendable as a starting point to any further discussion about the relationship of equity and Roman-canon law procedure at any given time, yet his concrete study is only of limited help for this work. My research period predates Macnair's by more than a century and Macnair himself recognised some fundamental differences between early modern and late medieval Chancery proceedings. Indeed, he effectively characterised the law of proof described in his study as a 16th century development.[8]

Legal Institutions, Aspen Publishers, New York, NY, 2009, most notably p. 267–344, examples of this group.

5 See a parliamentary petition from 1415 in: *Rotuli Parliamentorum, ut et Petitiones, et Placita in Parliamento*, Volume IV, London, 1767, p. 84.

6 *M. R. T. Macnair*, The Law of Proof in Early Modern Equity, Duncker & Humblot, Berlin, 1999.

7 In contrast to this work, *M. R. T. Macnair*'s study is not restricted to the Court of Chancery but also covers the other 'equitable' courts.

8 *M. R. T. Macnair*, The Law of Proof in Early Modern Equity, S. 93.

Helmut Coing took a more courageous approach in his article on *English Equity and the Denunciatio Evangelica of the Canon Law.*[9] His comparative observations were meant to reinforce his central hypothesis: Adjudication in the Court of Chancery was – in both substance and procedure – modelled on the canonical *denunciatio evangelica*. The question of the origins of the Court of Chancery moves this study closer to my own period of research and its scope suggests a complete explanation for the origins of the Chancery process. However, the danger of Coing's approach should be obvious in the light of the limited primary sources: He concluded the existence of a definite transfer of ideas from what was merely incidental comparative evidence.

In the following, I will briefly address the relevance of Macnair's results for the late medieval process (1.) before examining Coing's hypothesis about the *demonstratio evangelica* in detail (2.). The larger part of this chapter will then be devoted to an immediate comparison of the late medieval Chancery process with the contemporary Roman-canon law (3.).

1. Early modern law of proof

Macnair based his conclusion "that [early modern] equity proof was a system which applied the general principles of the roman-canon law" on three grounds: direct citations (1.1), linguistic similarities (1.2) and the parallelism of the rules (1.3).[10] One can hardly fault this method for the general identification of parallels or connections between two legal orders. It thus seems advisable to look at the potential connections between the medieval Chancery and the Roman-canon law process from a similar perspective.

1.1 Citations

The evidence of direct citations from the learned laws in equity treatises or judgments is scant, even in Macnair's research period.[11] From the late medieval sources, I could not identify a single direct reference to Roman-canon or civil law or their famous protagonists in the arguments advanced before the Court of Chancery. This, however, largely corresponds with the practice in courts operating under Roman-canon law procedure across Europe. Given the practical and

9 *H. Coing*, English Equity and the Denunciatio Evangelica of the Canon Law, Law Quarterly Review, Volume 71 (1955), p. 223–241.

10 *M. R. T. Macnair*, The Law of Proof in Early Modern Equity, p. 289.

11 *M. R. T. Macnair*, The Law of Proof in Early Modern Equity, p. 292, hardly identified a handful of direct roman-canon law references or citations in his vast sample of sources from more than three centuries.

fact-focused approach shown in the pleadings, the absence of citations from the learned laws can hardly be considered a surprise anyway. The search for direct references or citations in the documents submitted by the litigants thus remains unsuccessful.

1.2 Linguistic similarities

The search for linguistic similarities yields almost equally disappointing results. I have consistently referred to the absence of technical – and thus also Roman-canon law – language in the pleadings.[12] A look through the decrees proves a little more helpful in this regard, if only because their language was also Latin. The original bill was called *petitio* as it was in Roman-canon law summary proceedings.[13] However, the terminology for the further pleadings was borrowed from the vocabulary of the common law courts (replication, rejoinder) rather than that of Roman-canon law. When reference was made to a common Roman-canon law maxim like *secundum allegata et probata*, its actual use seems to have contorted the Roman-canon law meaning significantly.[14] The parallels thus appear either incidental or even slightly amateurish. Macnair's impressive account of the parallel use of exceptions (*exceptiones*),[15] confessions (*confessiones*)[16] and presumptions (*praesumptiones*)[17] in Roman-canon law, English equity and even common law courts seems far removed from the practice in the late medieval Court of Chancery. In how far the century between Macnair's sources and my own made a terminological or a real substantive difference remains difficult to assess.

1.3 Parallel rules

This leaves us with Macnair's most elaborated ground for comparison: the parallelism of proof rules. In the absence of directly traceable influences between the legal orders, a systematic comparison of the respective rules indeed promises the greatest possible insights into their relationship. I will thus devote the third part of this chapter to a comparison of the 15th century process in the Court of Chancery as identified from my sources with the contemporary learned laws on

12 See above, especially chapter V, 2.4.
13 Compare *K. W. Nörr*, Römisch-Kanonisches Prozessrecht – Erkenntnisverfahren erster Instanz in civilibus, Springer, Berlin, 2012, p. 87.
14 See above chapter V, 5.2.2.2.
15 *M. R. T. Macnair*, The Law of Proof in Early Modern Equity, p. 185–230.
16 *M. R. T. Macnair*, The Law of Proof in Early Modern Equity, p. 54–90.
17 *M. R. T. Macnair*, The Law of Proof in Early Modern Equity, p. 267–275.

procedure. In relation to Macnair's work, however, the important question in how far his findings for the early modern period can help us to understand the late medieval Court of Chancery will be addressed immediately.

Disappointingly, the answer seems to be relatively little. The reason lies in the degree of sophistication of the early modern laws of proof evidenced by Macnair's study. I have constantly referred to the process of legalisation in the Court of Chancery.[18] By the 17th century, the detail of regulations for evidentiary problems was immense whereas we have no documentary evidence of such questions even being discussed in the 15th century Court of Chancery.

One important caveat needs to be kept in mind: We might simply lack more detailed knowledge about the medieval procedural rules due to the limitation of the sources. Complaints (or exceptions as the Roman-canon lawyers would say) against the evidentiary submissions of the other party might have been handled orally. A Year Book case on the typical Chancery constellation of relief from a contractual obligation under deed in the absence of a formal acquittance reinforces the need for caution.[19] In this case, the Lord Chancellor seemed to suggest that relief from Chancery in such cases required the proof of two witnesses – a standard civilian requirement,[20] which otherwise did not appear in contemporary Chancery documentation at all. In the light of this, it seems doubtful whether such evidentiary rules were strictly followed in the late medieval Court of Chancery. The technicalities involved with the Roman-canon law system of half- and full-proofs were probably incompatible with the work of the 15th century court.[21]

All this should not suggest that a radical breach occurred in the Court of Chancery between the late medieval and the early modern period. The development from the largely unregulated medieval procedure to Macnair's early modern law of proof must have been an evolutionary process rather than a revolution. Despite the growing criticism about the Lord Chancellor's discretion,[22] we have no evidence of clean breaks or systematic reform attempts. The civilian-trained Chancellors and masters in the Court of Chancery from the last quarter of the 15th century onwards might already have resorted to their knowledge of Roman-canon law procedure when the necessity arose. The introduction of interrogatories as a reaction to the unworkable system of lay

18 See above chapter II, 4. but also chapter V, for example 4.1.

19 (1482), Y. B. 22 Edw. IV, Pasch.,pl. 18, f. 6.

20 For the two-witness rule, see *K. W. Nörr*, Römisch-Kanonisches Prozessrecht – Erkenntnisverfahren erster Instanz in civilibus, p. 153, with further references.

21 For an introduction to the system of proofs, see *K. W. Nörr*, Römisch-Kanonisches Prozessrecht – Erkenntnisverfahren erster Instanz in civilibus, p. 190–191.

22 See above chapter II, 3.3–4.1.

witness examination might be considered an illustrative example.[23] However, to our best knowledge, based on the study of the late medieval files, there was no systematic 'law' of proof and thus there could also be no parallelism to Roman-canon law.

2. Denunciatio evangelica

Helmut Coing's *English Equity and the Denunciatio Evangelica of the Canon Law*[24] can be qualified as a reaction to his own dissatisfaction with the vagueness of earlier attempts to identify Roman-canon law roots of the Court of Chancery. Whereas those scholars had suggested an "indirect reception",[25] the adoption of "current ideas"[26] or the carrying over of "the principles and theories of the ecclesiastical court",[27] Coing sought a more concrete explanation.[28] He thus advanced the hypothesis that what became known as the equitable jurisdiction of the Court of Chancery was originally modelled upon the canonical procedure of the *denunciatio evangelica*.[29] Coing referenced Luigi De Luca[30] as an earlier proponent of the same hypothesis, who had failed to elaborate it in any more detail.[31]

23 See above chapter V, 4.1.6. For the use of interrogatories in roman-canon law procedure, see *K. W. Nörr*, Römisch-Kanonisches Prozessrecht – Erkenntnisverfahren erster Instanz in civilibus, p. 142.

24 *H. Coing*, English Equity and the Denunciatio Evangelica of the Canon Law, Law Quarterly Review, Volume 71 (1955), p. 223–241.

25 *P. Vinogradoff*, Reason and Conscience in Sixteenth Century Jurisprudence, Law Quarterly Review, Volume 24 (1908), p. 373–384, p. 379.

26 *W. Holdsworth*, A History of English Law, Methuen, London, Volume 5, 3rd edition 1945 (repr. 1966), p. 216.

27 *W. T. Barbour*, The History of Contract in Early English Equity, in: P. Vinogradoff (ed.), Oxford Studies in Social and Legal History, Clarendon Press, Oxford, Volume 4, 1914, p. 1–237, p. 163.

28 All three authors were explicitly quoted and referenced by *H. Coing*, English Equity and the Denunciatio Evangelica of the Canon Law, Law Quarterly Review, Volume 71 (1955), p. 223–241, p. 224–225.

29 For a brief introduction, see above chapter II, 4.2.

30 *L. De Luca*, Aequitas Canonica ed Equity Inglese alla Luce del Pensiero di C. Saint Germain, Ephemerides Iuris Canonici, Volume 3 (1947), p. 46–66. *L. De Luca*'s thesis built almost entirely on *Doctor and Student*, which modern scholarship has often dismissed as an accurate portrayal of the work of the early modern Court of Chancery. For a deeper analysis, see above chapter V, 2.7.4.

31 *H. Coing*, English Equity and the Denunciatio Evangelica of the Canon Law, Law Quarterly Review, Volume 71 (1955), p. 223–241, p. 225.

2.1 Prerogative origin

Before engaging with Coing's arguments, one caveat seems in order. The idea that the jurisdiction of the Court of Chancery could be directly based upon Roman-canonical procedure might appear incompatible with my account of the roots of the jurisdiction in the extra-ordinary jurisdiction of the king in matters of grace. Coing clearly recognised the prerogative origins of the court.[32] However, he believed that the adoption of the principles of the *denunciatio evangelica* in the medieval Court of Chancery gave "new legal shape to an existing jurisdiction".[33] His argument thus sought to explain the rise of the court from an extra-legal obscurity to a central institution of royal judicial conflict resolution rather than its institutional birth. The *denunciatio evangelica* had been fully developed by Roman-canon law jurists in the 13th century.[34] It was thus theoretically available for adoption by learned lawyers in the developing Court of Chancery of the 14th and 15th century.

A good part of Coing's article was devoted to an explanation of the late medieval *denunciatio evangelica* with a view to identifying similarities to the contemporary Court of Chancery. Coing's knowledge of the details of Roman-canon law procedure undoubtedly far exceeds my own. My critique of his thesis will therefore be limited to his understanding and presentation of the late medieval Court of Chancery.[35] For a final assessment, however, it would be most useful to know more about the prevalence and practice of the *demonstratio evangelica* in late medieval England. In the following, I will adapt the structure of Coing's article by discussing its three overlapping, yet distinguishable topics from a comparative perspective: jurisdiction (2.2), substance (2.3) and procedure (2.4).

32 *H. Coing*, English Equity and the Denunciatio Evangelica of the Canon Law, Law Quarterly Review, Volume 71 (1955), p. 223–241, p. 238.

33 *H. Coing*, English Equity and the Denunciatio Evangelica of the Canon Law, Law Quarterly Review, Volume 71 (1955), p. 223–241, p. 238.

34 *H. Coing*, English Equity and the Denunciatio Evangelica of the Canon Law, Law Quarterly Review, Volume 71 (1955), p. 223–241, p. 231.

35 For more information about the denunciatio evangelica, reference should be made to the comprehensive secondary literature. See for example, *C. Lefebvre*, Gratien et les origins de la 'denunciatio evangelica' en droit canonique, Ephemerides iuris canonici, Volume 6 (1950), p. 60–93; *P. Bellini*, 'Denunciatio Evangelica' e 'Denunciatio Iudicialis Privata' – Un Capitolo di Storia Disciplinare della Chiesa, Giuffrè, Milan, 1986; *G. Herouschek / D. Müller*, Die Ursprünge der Denunziation im Kanonischen Recht, in: H. Lück / B. Schildt (eds.), Recht – Idee – Geschichte – Beiträge zur Rechts- und Ideengeschichte für Rolf Lieberwirth anläßlich seines 80. Geburtstages, Böhlau, Cologne, 2000, p. 3–24; *W. Decock*, Moral Theologians and Contract Law – The Moral Transformation of the Ius Commune, Martinus Nijhoff, Leiden, 2013, p. 88–101.

2.2 Jurisdiction

2.2.1 Supplementary character

Coing's hypothesis of a parallelism between the *denunciatio evangelica* and the Court of Chancery seems to rely heavily on their supplementary character.[36] While the Court of Chancery supplemented the self-restrictive jurisdiction of the English common law courts, the *denunciatio evangelica* generally served to complement the jurisdiction of secular as well as spiritual courts. Indeed, the parallels in the relationship towards these other jurisdictions were striking.

Both the Court of Chancery and the *denunciatio evangelica* relied on the pre-existence of a relatively well-defined system of laws, which left (more or less respectively) gaps at its periphery – chiefly towards the realm of morality. Their continued toleration by a well-established professional elite in the supplemented jurisdictions was furthermore facilitated by a common tool: the operation under a fiction of non-interference. Both the Court of Chancery and the *denunciatio evangelica* professed to merely engage in matters of sin and conscience. Their self-proclaimed target was targeted conflict resolution by individual correction rather than principled adjudication.[37] As mentioned before, the maxim 'equity acts *in personam*' was hardly more than a clever denigration of the court's actual power.[38] However, the emphasis on the conscience-corrective function was much stronger in the case of the *denunciatio evangelica* – probably not least because it lacked the royal institutional support of Chancery.

Coing's claims, however, obviously went much further. He identified a number of jurisdictional grounds upon which both the Court of Chancery and the *denunciatio evangelica* would grant relief. Quoting the theologian Panormitanus (1386–1445), he contended that the *denunciatio evangelica* was available for the following five reasons: *defectu iustitiae* (failure of justice), *crimen notorium and de sui natura ecclesiasticum* (notorious and ecclesiastical crimes), *ratione pacis* (breaking of the peace), *iuramenti* (oaths) and *obligatio naturalis* (natural obligations unenforceable in regular courts).[39]

36 *H. Coing*, English Equity and the Denunciatio Evangelica of the Canon Law, Law Quarterly Review, Volume 71 (1955), p. 223–241, p. 230.

37 For the importance of fraternal correction in the *demonstratio evangelica*, compare *H. Coing*, English Equity and the Denunciatio Evangelica of the Canon Law, Law Quarterly Review, Volume 71 (1955), p. 223–241, p. 231.

38 See above chapter V, 2.5.2.

39 *H. Coing*, English Equity and the Denunciatio Evangelica of the Canon Law, Law Quarterly Review, Volume 71 (1955), p. 223–241, p. 230.

2.2.2 *Ecclesiastical crimes*

Coing did not address all of these grounds separately or in detail but mostly instead focused on failures of justice and natural obligations. It nevertheless seems worthwhile to consider briefly in how far each of these reasons facilitated access to the medieval Court of Chancery. In relation to ecclesiastical crimes, Coing mentioned the appearance of sorcery and witchcraft cases in Chancery.[40] However, while the supernatural frequently found its way into the late medieval court, the matters underlying the dispute were typically of a civil rather than of a criminal origin.[41]

2.2.3 *Breaking of the peace*

From our modern perspective, a similar distinction may also prove useful in 'breaking of the peace' cases.[42] These cases appear frequently in the Court of Chancery of the 14th and early 15th century.[43] While commonly complaining about concrete financial loss or mutilations, the bills also stressed the power of the defendant and the inability of the common law to deal with these outrages. The procedure might thus be considered a private enforcement mechanism for criminal sanctions.[44] The breaking of the peace could therefore arguably be addressed in the Court of Chancery. However, as suggested earlier, this group of cases disappeared almost entirely from the Court of Chancery within the course of the 15th century, most likely with the ascent of the Court of Star Chamber.[45]

40 *H. Coing*, English Equity and the Denunciatio Evangelica of the Canon Law, Law Quarterly Review, Volume 71 (1955), p. 223–241, p. 233.

41 As such, plaintiffs appealed for an injunction on continued sorcery (see *W. T. Barbour*, Some Aspects of Fifteenth-Century Chancery, Harvard Law Review, Volume 31 (1918), p. 834–859, p. 853) or demanded restitution for loss during the services of a necromancer (see *Anlaby v Croke* (1485–1486), Calendars I, p. cxix).

42 The 'breaking of the peace' largely corresponds with the German concept of 'Landfriedensbruch'. For an introduction, see *A. Roth*, Landfriedensbruch, in: A. Cordes / H. Lück / D. Werkmüller (Hg.), Handwörterbuch zur deutschen Rechtsgeschichte, Schmidt, Berlin, Volume 3, 2nd edition, 2013, col. 505–509.

43 Compare the quantitative assessments of typical subject matters in the Court of Chancery by *M. E. Avery*, The History of the Equitable Jurisdiction of Chancery before 1460, Bulletin of the Institute of Historical Research, Volume 42 (1969), p. 129–144, especially p. 131, and *T. S. Haskett*, The Late Medieval Court of Chancery, Law and History Review, Volume 14 (1996), p. 245–313, especially p. 296.

44 For a parallel remedy in canon law, see *R. Perruso*, The iuramentum perhorrescentiae under Canon Law – An Influence on the Development of Early Chancery Jurisdiction?, Comparative Legal History, Volume 3 (2015), p. 2–37.

45 See above chapter V, 2.5.1.

2.2.4 *Oaths*

Oaths, while playing an enormous role in Chancery procedure, hardly appear as a ground for claims in the medieval Court of Chancery. In fact, the medieval Court of Chancery enforced contractual oral promises irrespective of the presence of an oath and relieved parties formally bound by oaths when these had been adhered to in conscience.[46] Although the influence of the Roman-canon law tradition (*pacta quantumcunque nuda sunt servanda*) was clearly tangible in this regard, the oath itself does not seem to have played a similarly important role as in *denunciatio evangelica* procedures.

2.2.5 *Failure of justice*

This leaves us with the two grounds for jurisdiction, which were further elaborated by Coing. The central reason for invoking either the *denunciatio evangelica* or the jurisdiction of the Court of Chancery was a 'failure of justice' (*defectus justitiae*). This strongly underlines the supplementary character of both institutions, which I have addressed above.[47] As my examination of the jurisdiction of the Court of Chancery has shown, however, a failure or defect of justice can be construed in a variety of circumstances – be it in the absence of a legal claim or of a suitable procedure, remedy or enforcement mechanism.[48] The legal landscape of secular and spiritual courts, which was commonly supplemented by the *denunciatio evangelica*, did not leave the necessary room for a similar invocation of this ground. This is especially true since the *denunciatio evangelica* offered essentially the same procedures as civilian and canonical courts.[49] It could thus hardly provide relief in cases of defective procedure. While we can identify important parallels regarding the justification for the respective jurisdictions, reference to defects of justice in both cases tells us very little about the practical scope of the proceedings.

46 Compare *J. L. Barton*, Equity in the Medieval Common Law, in: R. A. Newman (ed.), Equity in the World's Legal Systems – A Comparative Study, Emile Bruylant, Bruxelles, 1973, p. 139–155, p. 149–150; *J. H. Langbein / R. T. Lerner / B. P. Smith*, History of the Common Law – The Development of Anglo-American Legal Institutions, Aspen Publishers, New York, NY, 2009, p. 311–314.

47 See above chapter V, 2.5.

48 See above chapter V, 2.5.7.

49 *H. Coing*, English Equity and the Denunciatio Evangelica of the Canon Law, Law Quarterly Review, Volume 71 (1955), p. 223–241, p. 228.

2.2.6 *Natural obligations*

Coing strongly emphasised the possibility to enforce natural obligations unenforceable in other regular courts in both the Court of Chancery and through the *denunciatio evangelica*. It is certainly true that the Court of Chancery was called to enforce contracts, which did not meet the formal requirements of the common law – commonly because they were agreed orally.[50] However, the same could generally be said about ecclesiastical courts at the time.[51] Reliance upon the *demonstratio evangelica* was thus unnecessary in parallel cases.

Coing instead proposed that the enforcement of *nuda pacta* without *quid pro quo* or consideration represented a shared feature of both jurisdictions.[52] However, *nuda pacta* without consideration were apparently not recognised in the Court of Chancery, at least from the 15th century onwards.[53] This leaves us with Coing's example of the use as a natural obligation towards the beneficiary.[54] Such an understanding is certainly arguable but the elaborated structure of the use, resting on feudal property concepts, calls the classification under a general category of natural obligations into question. The use therefore seems unsuited as general proof for the acceptance of *nuda pacta* without consideration in the Court of Chancery. In relation to the enforcement of *nuda pacta* without consideration, the *denunciatio evangelica* thus apparently went further than the Court of Chancery.

2.3 Substance

Coing relied heavily on Paul Vinogradoff's *Conscience and Reason*[55] in addressing the problematic issue of substantive law in the late medieval Court of Chancery. In this article, Vinogradoff undertook one of the earliest comprehensive attempts to identify Roman-canon law roots of the Court of Chancery. The title was

50 Compare *J. L. Barton*, Equity in the Medieval Common Law, in: R. A. Newman (ed.), Equity in the World's Legal Systems – A Comparative Study, , p. 139–155, p. 149–150; *J. H Langbein / R. T. Lerner / B. P. Smith*, History of the Common Law – The Development of Anglo-American Legal Institutions, p. 311–312.

51 Remember again the maxim *pacta quantumcunque nuda sunt servanda.*

52 *H. Coing*, English Equity and the Denunciatio Evangelica of the Canon Law, Law Quarterly Review, Volume 71 (1955), p. 223–241, p. 234–235.

53 Compare *J. L. Barton*, Roman Law in England, in: Société d'Histoire des Droits de L'Antiquité (ed.), Ius Romanum Medii Aevi, Volume 5, 13a, p. 67. The 14th century practice remains opaque.

54 *H. Coing*, English Equity and the Denunciatio Evangelica of the Canon Law, Law Quarterly Review, Volume 71 (1955), p. 223–241, p. 235.

55 *P. Vinogradoff*, Reason and Conscience in Sixteenth Century Jurisprudence, Law Quarterly Review, Volume 24 (1908), p. 373–384.

clearly programmatic. Vinogradoff identified reason and conscience as the main sources for substantive decisions in the court. Coing considered this in line with the aspirations of the *denunciatio evangelica*.[56]

While we might identify reason with the secular and conscience with the spiritual world, no such differentiation had taken place in the late Middle Ages.[57] The overlap between reason and conscience might be most visible in St. German's *Doctor and Student*.[58] It was a central argument of the author that the common law of England, based upon reason, was mostly congruent with the demands of conscience and that a supplementary jurisdiction of a court of conscience was thus only necessary in exceptional cases. Indeed, reason and conscience were mentioned together all the time in both common law courts and the Court of Chancery.[59] Norman Doe impressively illustrated that legal debates in the late Middle Ages were characterised by a coincidence of references to what we today consider positivist and natural law arguments – or in other words reason and conscience.[60] In the light of this, it seems highly questionable in how far reliance on reason and conscience can be seen as a characteristic feature of the Court of Chancery. What Doe's studies actually suggest is that adjudication according to reason and conscience was the general ideal of the time. Every judge in secular and spiritual courts would gladly have professed to be deciding according to reason and conscience. Reason was considered as the embodiment of natural law, which in turn was the benchmark for decisions in conscience. Our modern understanding of reason and conscience thus creates a dichotomy, which did not exist in the minds of late medieval lawyers. Coing's suggestion that the emphasis on reason and conscience represented an idiosyncratic characteristic of the Court of Chancery and the *denunciatio evangelica* therefore appears highly questionable.

Laudably, Coing sought to underline his argument with examples of the practical application of the concepts of reason and conscience. He saw them embodied in both jurisdictions' provision of remedies against unjust enrichment and their enforcement of promises to third parties.[61] While the Court of

56 *H. Coing*, English Equity and the Denunciatio Evangelica of the Canon Law, Law Quarterly Review, Volume 71 (1955), p. 223–241, p. 231.

57 Compare also *D. Klinck*, Conscience, Equity and the Court of Chancery in Early Modern England, Ashgate, Farnham, 2010, p. 13–40.

58 T.F.T. Plucknett/J L. Barton (eds.), St. German's Doctor and Student, Selden Society, London, 1974.

59 See also *R. H. Helmholz*, 'Conscience' and the English Courts between 1500 and 1800, Presentation of 4 April 2014, Wittenberg (yet unpublished).

60 See *N. Doe*, Fundamental Authority in Late Medieval English Law, Cambridge University Press, Cambridge, 1990.

61 *H. Coing*, English Equity and the Denunciatio Evangelica of the Canon Law, Law Quarterly Review, Volume 71 (1955), p. 223–241, especially p. 235–236.

Chancery, throughout the centuries of its existence, never completely embraced a general concept of unjust enrichment, it is probably true that substantive parallels existed in both these areas of substantive law. However, since we have no evidence of elaborated substantive rules in the Court of Chancery, any more detailed comparison must fail.

Overall, the examination of substantive rules once again leaves us rather clueless. There is, after all, a reason why my examination on the 15th century Court of Chancery had to focus on procedure: While the work of St. German and the appeals to conscience clearly justify speculations, the available sources do not provide clear evidence for the practical application of elaborated rules of morality. The chance that the Lord Chancellors merely recognised the authoritative appeal of references to reason and conscience is significant. Indeed, the need for downplaying the existence of unfettered judicial discretion through reference to conscience might also have been a feature that the Court of Chancery shared with the *denunciatio evangelica* – but just as everything else in the area of substantive law, this remains purely speculative.

2.4 Procedure

Coing quoted Pope Innocent IV (1195–1254) for the general view that the *denunciatio evangelica* should follow the standard rules of canon law procedure (*de plano*) with some modifications.[62] It should be noted right away that 16th century evidence suggests that English equity courts were perceived to operate under a summary form of civil law rather than under the standard procedure.[63] Civil law summary procedure drew its origins from Roman-canon law summary procedure. The difference between the two might have seemed negligible. However, if we consider this evidence reliable, we can effectively dismiss the suggestion that the earlier Court of Chancery followed the standard (rather than the summary) rules of canon law procedure. This is also in line with my findings

62 *H. Coing*, English Equity and the Denunciatio Evangelica of the Canon Law, Law Quarterly Review, Volume 71 (1955), p. 223–241, p. 228. However, *G. Herouschek / D. Müller*, Die Ursprünge der Denunziation im Kanonischen Recht, in: H. Lück / B. Schildt (eds.), Recht – Idee – Geschichte – Beiträge zur Rechts- und Ideengeschichte für Rolf Lieberwirth anläßlich seines 80. Geburtstages, p. 3–24, p. 22, identified a movement towards the use of summary procedure in the late medieval *denunciatio evangelica*. My argument thus relates to *H. Coing*'s presentation of the *demonstratio* rather than its actual form by the time of the rise of the Court of Chancery.

63 See *J. Caesar*, in: L. M. Hill (ed.), The Ancient State Authoritie, and Proceedings of the Court of Requests by Sir Julius Caesar, Cambridge University Press, Cambridge, 1975, p. 8.

from the Chancery documentation. What could be more 'summary' than the 15th century procedure presented above? I will devote the third part of this chapter to a closer comparison between the procedure in the 15th century Court of Chancery and in contemporary Roman-canon law. With regard to Coing's arguments, I will therefore limit myself to a discussion of specific features of the *denunciatio evangelica* and to the timing of the introduction of Roman-canon law elements into Chancery procedure.

The *denunciatio evangelica* was opened with a libel (libellous) alleging the wrongdoing of the defendant.[64] While its function was undoubtedly similar to that of the original bill, it required the adherence to stricter formal standards. Most notably, Coing claimed that the plaintiff had to allege and prove the bad faith of the other party in order to establish jurisdiction.[65] While the majority of Chancery cases involved defendants acting in bad faith, no such formal requirement is deducible from their documentation.

As was the case in the Court of Chancery, the *denunciatio evangelica* required the defendants to answer to the allegations under oath.[66] Instead of the opportunity to present their view freely in an open format and from both a legal and factual viewpoint,[67] however, they were required to answer with positions (*positiones*).[68] These consisted of a point-by-point enumeration of their own factual claims.[69] A movement towards similar formal requirements was only noticeable in the early modern phase of the Court of Chancery. The question why the Court of Chancery would only adhere to the standards of its alleged origin gradually remains open.

Coing further alleged that facts submitted in the course of the trial of the *denunciatio evangelica* procedure, which were not expressly denied, were considered as established.[70] This was a familiar feature of common law pleadings.[71] However, it was incompatible with Chancery's claim to judge according to the truth of the matter rather than according to formalities. Since this was also a

64 *H. Coing*, English Equity and the Denunciatio Evangelica of the Canon Law, Law Quarterly Review, Volume 71 (1955), p. 223–241, p. 228.

65 *H. Coing*, English Equity and the Denunciatio Evangelica of the Canon Law, Law Quarterly Review, Volume 71 (1955), p. 223–241, p. 228.

66 *H. Coing*, English Equity and the Denunciatio Evangelica of the Canon Law, Law Quarterly Review, Volume 71 (1955), p. 223–241, p. 229.

67 As was the case in the late medieval Court of Chancery, see above chapter V, 3.1.

68 *H. Coing*, English Equity and the Denunciatio Evangelica of the Canon Law, Law Quarterly Review, Volume 71 (1955), p. 223–241, p. 229.

69 *K. W. Nörr*, Römisch-Kanonisches Prozessrecht – Erkenntnisverfahren erster Instanz in civilibus, p. 118–120.

70 *H. Coing*, English Equity and the Denunciatio Evangelica of the Canon Law, Law Quarterly Review, Volume 71 (1955), p. 223–241, p. 229.

71 See above chapter V, 3.1.7.

widely accepted definition of judgments in conscience across Europe, it remains open why, according to Coing at least, the *denunciatio evangelica* deviated from this principle.

At the stage of evidence, the use of delegates for the collection of witness testimony can be considered an important common feature of both the *denunciatio evangelica* and the Court of Chancery. Coing introduced the use of interrogatories as another example of a procedural parallel.[72] As I have shown above, the Court of Chancery only started adopting interrogatories from the very end of the 15th century.[73] This again speaks against a complete adoption of *denunciatio evangelica* procedure at an early date. If anything, we might thus consider an unsystematic and progressive adoption.

For further evidence of parallelisms, Coing referred to a more active role of the judge in comparison to standard Roman-canon law or common law procedures.[74] Undoubtedly, the Lord Chancellor had huge personal authority and large discretion in relation to the trial. Nevertheless, the examination of the standard process has clearly shown that his involvement in the actual proceedings was comparatively small and that he generally tended to delegate the earlier stages of the proceedings to his staff.[75]

The decree in *denunciatio evangelica* procedures commanded the defendant to go out of his sin.[76] Coing identified the same motivation underlying Chancery decisions. The reliance on conscience seems to confirm this understanding. On the other hand, the fact that there was no place for such terminology in Chancery decrees from the 15th century should not be neglected. Chancery decrees ordered well-defined acts and refrained from discussing the defendants' spiritual well-being. The consideration of the moral implications was indeed left to the *forum internum* – the place where the *denunciatio evangelica* sought to intervene.

At last, Coing mentioned the use of specific performance as the standard remedy in both jurisdictions as further evidence for his origin thesis.[77] While this parallel is well-established, it should not be forgotten that specific performance was the standard remedy of Roman-canon law generally. It thus hardly

72 *H. Coing*, English Equity and the Denunciatio Evangelica of the Canon Law, Law Quarterly Review, Volume 71 (1955), p. 223–241, p. 229.

73 See above chapter V, 4.1.6.

74 *H. Coing*, English Equity and the Denunciatio Evangelica of the Canon Law, Law Quarterly Review, Volume 71 (1955), p. 223–241, p. 229.

75 Compare above chapter V, 5.2.1.2.

76 *H. Coing*, English Equity and the Denunciatio Evangelica of the Canon Law, Law Quarterly Review, Volume 71 (1955), p. 223–241, p. 229.

77 *H. Coing*, English Equity and the Denunciatio Evangelica of the Canon Law, Law Quarterly Review, Volume 71 (1955), p. 223–241. p. 236–237.

qualifies as an example for the origin of the equitable jurisdiction of the Court of Chancery in the *denunciatio evangelica* specifically.

2.5 Conclusion

Admittedly, I have almost exclusively focused on stressing the weak points in Coing's argumentation. As should become clear from the following comparison of Roman-canon law and Chancery procedure, the parallels between the jurisdictions were generally substantial. The focus of my argumentation, however, lay on the features, which distinguished both the *demonstratio evangelica* and the Court of Chancery from the (summary) procedure of Roman-canon law. What I hope to have shown is that Coing's identification of the specific *demonstratio evangelica* procedure as the origin of the jurisdiction of the Court of Chancery remains problematic. Clear similarities between the *denunciatio evangelica* and the Court of Chancery appear incidental rather than structural. Coing's origin thesis is further undermined by the fact that some parallels appear earlier, some later in the history of the Court of Chancery. Of course, the fact that evidence for possible substantive similarities remains unavailable condemns the comparison to the state of incompleteness.

For criticism of Coing's thesis, we might furthermore adduce evidence from the 16th century. No contemporary writer ever brought up the suggested parallel between the *denunciatio evangelica* and the Court of Chancery, even when writing about the *denunciatio evangelica* from an English perspective.[78] In the concluding part of his article, Coing advanced the correct caveat that the Court of Chancery could only be understood as a supplementary device for the common law.[79] The *denunciatio evangelica* and the Court of Chancery constituted reactions towards different legal systems. The effect of this finding seems to me far more important than Coing was willing to acknowledge. It effectively already disqualifies the *denunciatio evangelica* as a comprehensive model for the Court of Chancery. This is not to say that it might not have inspired canonists in the Court of Chancery to adopt some of its features. All in all, however – and despite the supplementary and arguably penitentiary character of both jurisdictions – their parallels appear too incidental to establish an origin relationship.

78 *M. R. T. Macnair*, Equity and Conscience, Oxford Journal of Legal Studies, Volume 27 (2007), p. 659–681, p. 671–672, relying on *R. Cosin*, An Apologie for Sundrie Proceedings by Iurisdiction Ecclesiasticall, Barker, London, Part 2, 1593, p. 61. Of course, the fundamental parallel – the adjudication in conscience – was identified for both jurisdictions separately.

79 *H. Coing*, English Equity and the Denunciatio Evangelica of the Canon Law, Law Quarterly Review, Volume 71 (1955), p. 223–241, p. 238–240.

It might be suggested that Coing's initial dissatisfaction with the state of Chancery scholarship came back to haunt him: His hypothesis represented a convenient escape from the complicated task of explaining the transfer of legal ideas and institutions through practical application.

3. Comparison of Roman-canon law and Chancery procedure

It is my conclusion that the question about the relationship between Roman-canon law and the origins of the Court of Chancery has not been answered satisfactorily. Arguably, it cannot be answered conclusively on the basis of the available sources. What we nevertheless can achieve is a better identification of parallels between the jurisdictions, which will allow a more precise assessment of the degree of Roman-canon law influence in the late medieval Court of Chancery. For this purpose, I will follow the structure of my discussion of the 15th century process: bill, further pleadings, evidence and resolution. My examination has shown both the existence of an established procedure but also the absence of sophisticated procedural rules limiting judicial discretion. Since we lack evidence about the concrete use of this discretion, the comparison will necessarily have to remain selective.

Everyone familiar with Roman-canon law will know the degree of sophistication reached, at least in theory, by the end of the Middle Ages. For the purpose of understanding the late medieval Court of Chancery, it will be unnecessary to provide a complete presentation of Roman-canon law procedure at the time. I will rather focus on the identification of similarities and differences to what happened in the Court of Chancery. This comparison will generally be based on the standard works on the Roman-canon law process as it was developed and studied in the universities in the late Middle Ages. As far as the limited availability of local studies allows, however, I will also try to afford a view to the peculiarities of procedure in English ecclesiastical courts.[80]

80 *R. H. Helmholz*, The Oxford History of the Laws of England, Volume 1: The Canon Law and Ecclesiastical Jurisdiction from 567 to the 1640s, Oxford University Press, Oxford, 2004, provided the best introduction to the application of Roman-canon law in England. Reference will regularly be made in the footnotes. An excellent but thematically limited account was earlier provided by *C. Donahue*, Proof by Witnesses in the Church Courts of Medieval England – An Imperfect Reception of the Learned Laws, in: M. S. Arnold / T. A. Green (eds.), On the Laws and Customs of England: Essays in Honor of Samuel E. Thorne, University of North Carolina Press, Chapel Hill, NC, 1983, p. 127–158.

3.1 Bill

As shown above, proceedings in the Court of Chancery were initiated through the plaintiff's bill, which included *inter alia* a presentation of the factual dispute and a request to summon the defendant by subpoena.[81] The opening of the Roman-canon law process fulfilled essentially the same functions through a slightly more elaborated process. The request for summons and the presentation of the plaintiff's case were separated into two documents: the citation (*citatio*) and the libel (*libellus*). Plaintiffs commonly approached the court, presented their case orally and asked for the issuance of the citation before a formal libel, which put the allegations into writing had been drafted.[82] It was, however, equally possibly to present the elaborated libel when approaching the court for the first time.[83] This could accelerate the further process.

The citation itself ordered the defendant to answer to the allegations.[84] For this purpose, it included date and place for a return.[85] The defendant could be ordered to answer personally (*viva voce*) or in writing (*per litteras*).[86] Despite the general shift from oral to written trial, we can identify no such clear distinction in the practice of the 15th century Court of Chancery. Personal appearance in front of the court seems to have remained a necessity throughout the late medieval phase of the court. The citation furthermore included information about the parties and, depending on local customs, the grounds for the claim (*causa*).[87] No such information was provided in the subpoena.

Just like the bill, the libel presented the plaintiffs with the opportunity to portray the facts underlying the dispute from their perspective and establish their claim for relief. The libel defined the further process by establishing its

81 See above chapter V, 2.

82 *K. W. Nörr*, Römisch-Kanonisches Prozessrecht – Erkenntnisverfahren erster Instanz in civilibus, p. 68.

83 *K. W. Nörr*, Römisch-Kanonisches Prozessrecht – Erkenntnisverfahren erster Instanz in civilibus, p. 68.

84 Consider *K. Pennington*, Due Process, Community, and the Prince in the Evolution of the Ordo Iudiciarius, Revista internazionale di diritto commune, Volume 9 (1998), S. 9–47, for the importance of the right to answer to allegations in the development of due process.

85 *W. Litewski*, Der römisch-kanonische Zivilprozeß nach den älteren ordines iudiciarii, Jagiellonian University Press, Krakow, Volume 1, 1999, p. 262; *K. W. Nörr*, Römisch-Kanonisches Prozessrecht – Erkenntnisverfahren erster Instanz in civilibus, p. 70–71.

86 *K. W. Nörr*, Römisch-Kanonisches Prozessrecht – Erkenntnisverfahren erster Instanz in civilibus, p. 69. Compare also *W. Litewski*, Der römisch-kanonische Zivilprozeß nach den älteren ordines iudiciarii, Volume 1, p. 272.

87 *K. W. Nörr*, Römisch-Kanonisches Prozessrecht – Erkenntnisverfahren erster Instanz in civilibus, p. 71.

content (*quid*) and its legal basis (*quo iure*).[88] While the legal basis did not have to be addressed explicitly, the plaintiffs were required to present the reasons of their appeal in a way which would allow jurists to identify the legal basis of their claim.[89] Even though the bill in the late medieval Court of Chancery fulfilled similar functions, it looked different. Most importantly, the insistence on conscience and the appeal for charity stood out.

Libels differed significantly with regard to the respective claim. For possessory, proprietary and contractual claims, standard forms appeared.[90] The substantive literature on the drafting of libels shows a degree of differentiation and elaboration unmatched in the increasingly standardised, yet comparatively informal Chancery bills.[91] However, both bills and libels could be revised in case of formal inadequacy, thus lessening the impact of formal ignorance.[92]

By the end of the 13th century, libels commonly identified and enumerated the factual claims, which the plaintiffs intended to prove in the course of the process (*articuli*).[93] While Chancery bills also (maybe incidentally) prejudiced the scope of the factual dispute through their presentation of facts, no such far-sighted preparation of the process is discernible from the bills.

This short comparison of the opening stage of the process in both jurisdictions renders an equivocal result. I have repeatedly stressed the importance of the plaintiffs' opportunity to present their case freely, including both the factual and the legal dimension. This constitutes a parallel between the two jurisdictions compared here and a significant deviation from the writ system of the common law. On the other hand, the libel already provides a first impression of the fact that the degree of professionalization reached in the Roman-canon law process of the late Middle Ages was unparalleled in the contemporary Court of Chancery. The litigants might have been unable to predict the further process with sufficient certainty to justify the preparation of a list of provable facts. In

88 *K. W. Nörr*, Römisch-Kanonisches Prozessrecht – Erkenntnisverfahren erster Instanz in civilibus, p. 88.

89 Compare *W. Litewski*, Der römisch-kanonische Zivilprozeß nach den älteren ordines iudiciarii, Volume 1, p. 234; 237–242; *K. W. Nörr*, Römisch-Kanonisches Prozessrecht – Erkenntnisverfahren erster Instanz in civilibus, p. 89–92.

90 *K. W. Nörr*, Römisch-Kanonisches Prozessrecht – Erkenntnisverfahren erster Instanz in civilibus, S. 92.

91 Compare *W. Litewski*, Der römisch-kanonische Zivilprozeß nach den älteren ordines iudiciarii, Volume 1, p. 228; *K. W. Nörr*, Römisch-Kanonisches Prozessrecht – Erkenntnisverfahren erster Instanz in civilibus, S. 92.

92 *W. Litewski*, Der römisch-kanonische Zivilprozeß nach den älteren ordines iudiciarii, Volume 1, p. 242; *K. W. Nörr*, Römisch-Kanonisches Prozessrecht – Erkenntnisverfahren erster Instanz in civilibus, S. 93.

93 *K. W. Nörr*, Römisch-Kanonisches Prozessrecht – Erkenntnisverfahren erster Instanz in civilibus S. 95–96.

this regard, the procedure in the Court of Chancery was arguably closer to the summary procedure of the Roman-canon law, in which formal requirements were dispensed with. It was only there that a petition (*petitio*) informing the court of the basic facts underlying the case sufficed for the opening of proceedings.[94]

3.2 Further pleadings

3.2.1 Answer

In the late medieval Court of Chancery, the answer provided the defendant with the opportunity to react comprehensively to the plaintiff's original bill. All the allegations advanced in the bill could be addressed from both a factual and a legal perspective. Since the answer represented the defendants with far-ranging opportunities to stress what they considered the weaknesses of the claim, it was noticeably less standardised than the bill.[95]

Arguably, the contemporary Roman-canon law provided not one but two procedural instruments with distinctive consequences in reaction to the libel: exceptions (*exceptiones*) and the *litis contestatio*. Exceptions brought forward at this early stage of the proceedings were meant to either end or halt the process before the opening of the actual trial.[96] They were accordingly distinguished into peremptory (*exceptio peremptoria*) and dilatory (*exceptio dilatoria*) exceptions.[97] Peremptory exceptions were advanced whenever the defendant believed that the plaintiff's action was altogether excluded by law – for example because the matter was not justiciable or had already been settled.[98] Dilatory exceptions, on the other hand, were those, which would bar the immediate advancement of the process but not preclude it altogether.[99] They could for example address the

94 It seems noteworthy that Chancery writs and decrees referred to the original bill as *petitio*, see for example *Ardern v Ardern* (1465/1466), Calendars I, p. lxxii; *Revelle v Gower* (1471), Select Cases, p. 155.

95 See above chapter V, 3.1 introduction.

96 For an introduction to the different forms of exceptions, see *W. Litewski*, Der römisch-kanonische Zivilprozeß nach den älteren ordines iudiciarii, Volume 1, p. 299–317. For the English context specifically, see *R. H. Helmholz*, The Oxford History of the Laws of England, Volume 1: The Canon Law and Ecclesiastical Jurisdiction from 567 to the 1640s, p. 323.

97 *W. Litewski*, Der römisch-kanonische Zivilprozeß nach den älteren ordines iudiciarii, Volume 1, p. 305.

98 *R. H. Helmholz*, The Oxford History of the Laws of England, Volume 1: The Canon Law and Ecclesiastical Jurisdiction from 567 to the 1640s, p. 323.

99 *R. H. Helmholz*, The Oxford History of the Laws of England, Volume 1: The Canon Law and Ecclesiastical Jurisdiction from 567 to the 1640s, p. 323.

jurisdiction of the court, the standing of the parties or the evident lack of a legal claim from the libel.[100] These exceptions could generally be remedied through a timely adjustment or reintroduction of the libel.[101]

While exceptions were only raised if applicable, the *litis contestatio* was a necessary element of standard Roman-canon law proceedings.[102] In the *litis contestatio*, the defendants declared their readiness to contest the claim. The formal answer in England usually included the defendants' assertion "that the matters as they are narrated in the libel are not true and therefore the matters prayed for should not be done".[103] Procedurally, the *litis contestatio* precluded the introduction of further peremptory and dilatory exceptions.[104] It thus marked the end of the pre-trial and the opening of the trial stage.[105] Instead of contesting the claim, the defendant could obviously also acknowledge the plaintiff's allegations. In such a case, the decree followed immediately.[106]

In contrast to Chancery procedure, the defendants were generally not put on oath at this pre-trial stage. The oath was nevertheless an important feature of Roman-canon law procedure. It was commonly administered upon both parties after the *litis contestatio* at the beginning of the actual trial.[107] It was also at this stage that the parties advanced their positions (*positiones*) and responses (*responsiones*) for the purpose of identifying the contested facts.

3.2.2 Replication and rejoinder

As explained above, bill and answer in the Court of Chancery could be followed by replication, rejoinder and possibly further party exchange.[108] However, none

100 *R. H. Helmholz*, The Oxford History of the Laws of England, Volume 1: The Canon Law and Ecclesiastical Jurisdiction from 567 to the 1640s, p. 324.

101 *K. W. Nörr*, Römisch-Kanonisches Prozessrecht – Erkenntnisverfahren erster Instanz in civilibus, S. 99.

102 *W. Litewski*, Der römisch-kanonische Zivilprozeß nach den älteren ordines iudiciarii, Volume 1, p. 330; *K. W. Nörr*, Römisch-Kanonisches Prozessrecht – Erkenntnisverfahren erster Instanz in civilibus, p. 109.

103 *R. H. Helmholz*, The Oxford History of the Laws of England, Volume 1: The Canon Law and Ecclesiastical Jurisdiction from 567 to the 1640s, p. 326.

104 Compare *W. Litewski*, Der römisch-kanonische Zivilprozeß nach den älteren ordines iudiciarii, Volume 1, p. 333.

105 *R. H. Helmholz*, The Oxford History of the Laws of England, Volume 1: The Canon Law and Ecclesiastical Jurisdiction from 567 to the 1640s, p. 326.

106 *K. W. Nörr*, Römisch-Kanonisches Prozessrecht – Erkenntnisverfahren erster Instanz in civilibus, p. 111.

107 *W. Litewski*, Der römisch-kanonische Zivilprozeß nach den älteren ordines iudiciarii, Volume 1, p. 340; *K. W. Nörr*, Römisch-Kanonisches Prozessrecht – Erkenntnisverfahren erster Instanz in civilibus, p. 113.

108 See above chapter V, 3.2.

of the documents following the answer really fulfilled a distinctive function. They merely clarified earlier pleadings or advanced additional arguments.

It has been suggested that the positions and responses constituted a "unique and distinctive feature of the Roman-canon law process"[109] – a somewhat discouraging statement for a comparative analysis. They nevertheless addressed a problem that any elaborated legal process is faced with. The positions, which were often already presented in the libel,[110] constituted a one-by-one account of the alleged facts, often in the most detailed fashion.[111] In return, the responses addressed every one of the allegations accordingly.[112] The parallelisation of position and response helped immensely with the identification of the disputed issues.[113] This, in turn, gave structure to the trial and facilitated the concerted assignment of the courts' resources at the stage of proof.

This is almost reminiscent of late medieval common law pleading, which of course went much further in requiring the elimination of legal issues and the reduction to a single issue triable by jury.[114] If nothing else, the common law pleadings were effective in guaranteeing that the focus of the trial lay on justiciable facts – and that the trial could thus come to a timely conclusion. How did the late medieval Court of Chancery address this issue? The answer is probably not at all. We have seen numerous incidents of repetition and evasion in Chancery pleadings.[115] This might be considered a real methodological deficiency. The case of *Ardern v Ardern*[116] proves the point: The only truly contested issue was whether the condition reserving the profits of the land for the plaintiff actually existed and yet the evidence mostly failed to address this question. It is only at the beginning of the early modern period that we can find detailed factual submissions in bills and answers, which appear somehow modelled upon positions and responses.

109 *K. W. Nörr*, Römisch-Kanonisches Prozessrecht – Erkenntnisverfahren erster Instanz in civilibus, p. 116 [translation by the author].
110 See above 3.1.
111 *W. Litewski*, Der römisch-kanonische Zivilprozeß nach den älteren ordines iudiciarii, Jagiellonian University Press, Krakow, Volume 2, 1999, p. 358; *K. W. Nörr*, Römisch-Kanonisches Prozessrecht – Erkenntnisverfahren erster Instanz in civilibus, p. 116.
112 The responses were often called *interrogationes*. See *W. Litewski*, Der römisch-kanonische Zivilprozeß nach den älteren ordines iudiciarii, Volume 2, p. 356. In order to avoid confusion with interrogatories, which showed up later in both Chancery and Roman-canon law process, I will nonetheless use the term responses.
113 Compare *W. Litewski*, Der römisch-kanonische Zivilprozeß nach den älteren ordines iudiciarii, Volume 2, p. 356.
114 See above chapter V, 3.1.7.
115 See above chapter V, 3.1.5.
116 (1465/1466), Calendars I, p. lxxii, see the detailed discussion in chapter V above.

For an explanation of the unregulated character of Chancery pleadings, it seems sensible to shift the view from Roman-canon to the English common law. The technicality of the pleadings, which distorted the dispute underlying a claim, was a feature that the Court of Chancery sought to overcome. It might thus have allowed a maximum of party freedom in the pleadings in order to guarantee a more accurate portrayal of the circumstances underlying the dispute. This can only be qualified as an over-reaction, which the Roman-canon law avoided.

3.3 Evidence

In the Roman-canon law process, the exchange of positions and responses was followed by the stage of proof. The law of proof carried the function of resolving the disputed issues in a formalised manner. The burden of proof generally lay on the party asserting the relevant fact.[117] Exceptions applied where presumptions shifted the burden towards the opposing party.[118]

It seems doubtful whether a similar categorisation of the evidence process in the late medieval Court of Chancery is possible. The declared aim of the court was truth-finding rather than mere conflict resolution.[119] Accordingly, the examination of the sources has shown that formalities were largely absent from the 15th century process of evidence-gathering.[120] It is also unclear whether the late medieval court strictly attributed a burden of proof. While it seems certainly intuitive to delegate the responsibility to justify the original claim to the plaintiff, this is not clearly expressed in the sources. In the absence of positions and responses, it was also difficult to establish which facts had to be proved and who advanced the original allegation. As Michael Macnair has shown, the early modern Court of Chancery developed a law of proof, which largely followed Roman-canon law standards.[121] The 15th century sources, however, might merely show the roots of this development.

117 *W. Litewski*, Der römisch-kanonische Zivilprozeß nach den älteren ordines iudiciarii, Volume 2, p. 362; *R. H. Helmholz*, The Oxford History of the Laws of England, Volume 1: The Canon Law and Ecclesiastical Jurisdiction from 567 to the 1640s, p. 328; *K. W. Nörr*, Römisch-Kanonisches Prozessrecht – Erkenntnisverfahren erster Instanz in civilibus, p. 127.

118 *W. Litewski*, Der römisch-kanonische Zivilprozeß nach den älteren ordines iudiciarii, Volume 2, p. 364; *K. W. Nörr*, Römisch-Kanonisches Prozessrecht – Erkenntnisverfahren erster Instanz in civilibus, p. 128.

119 This was in line with the demands of the *forum internum* rather than with those of the *forum externum* in church courts.

120 See above chapter V, 4.

121 *M. R. T. Macnair*, The Law of Proof in Early Modern Equity, especially p. 289–295.

No account of Roman-canon concepts of proof could be complete without the discussion of the different grades of proof attributed to the respective means of proof. In order to establish a certain fact, the respective party had to provide 'full proof'.[122] The most famous incident of 'full proof' was the requirement to present two witnesses in support of a certain factual claim.[123] A casuistic literature developed the countless evidentiary constellations, which could establish full or half proof.[124] This seemingly mathematic approach presents a continuous source of academic fascination. In the light of the vast literature, it should not be necessary to describe the practice in more detail.[125] This is especially true because the documentation of the 15th century Court of Chancery presents only scarce evidence of similar considerations. While the desirability of the support of two witnesses for a factual claim was once mentioned in the Year Books,[126] the absence of further debates on this issue suggests that the Lord Chancellors evaluated the evidence according to certain guidelines but without seemingly mathematical precision.

Given the lack of a comparable theoretical framework for matters of proof in the Court of Chancery, it might be worthwhile to compare the practical approach to evidence-gathering in both jurisdictions. The available means of proof can serve as a starting point. Literature on Roman-canon law procedure routinely identified confessions, presumptions, physical evidence, party oaths, witness testimony and documents as means of proof.[127] The latter two – witness

122 *W. Litewski*, Der römisch-kanonische Zivilprozeß nach den älteren ordines iudiciarii, Volume 2, p. 369; *K. W. Nörr*, Römisch-Kanonisches Prozessrecht – Erkenntnisverfahren erster Instanz in civilibus, p. 129.

123 *K. W. Nörr*, Römisch-Kanonisches Prozessrecht – Erkenntnisverfahren erster Instanz in civilibus, p. 150–154.

124 Compare *K. W. Nörr*, Römisch-Kanonisches Prozessrecht – Erkenntnisverfahren erster Instanz in civilibus, p. 190.

125 See for example *J. P. Lévy*, La Hiérarchie des Preuves dans le Droit Savant du Moyen Age, depuis la Renaissance du droit romain jusqu'à la fin du XIVe siècle, Recueil Sirey, Paris, 1939; *C. Donahue*, Proof by Witnesses in the Church Courts of Medieval England – An Imperfect Reception of the Learned Laws, in: M. S. Arnold / T. A. Green (eds.), On the Laws and Customs of England: Essays in Honor of Samuel E. Thorne, p. 127–158; *M. Schmoeckel*, Humanität und Staatsraison – Die Abschaffung der Folter in Europa und die Entwicklung des gemeinen Strafprozeß- und Beweisrechts seit dem hohen Mittelalter, Böhlau, Cologne, 2000, especially p. 187–236; *S. Lepsius*, Von Zweifeln zur Überzeugung – Der Zeugenbeweis im gelehrten Recht ausgehend von der Abhandlung des Bartolus von Sassoferrato, Klostermann, Frankfurt / Main, 2003; *Y. Mausen*, Veritatis adiutur – La Procédure du Témoignage dans le Droit Savant et la Pratique Française, Giuffrè, Milan, 2006.

126 (1482), Y. B. 22 Edw. IV, Pasch., pl. 18, f. 6.

127 *R. H. Helmholz*, The Oxford History of the Laws of England, Volume 1: The Canon Law and Ecclesiastical Jurisdiction from 567 to the 1640s, p. 336–338,

testimony and documents – represented by far the most common type of evidence in procedures following Roman-canon law.[128] Since they also appear regularly in the 15th century Chancery sources, I will compare their regulation in both jurisdictions.

3.3.1 Witnesses

In Roman-canon law, witnesses were generally summoned upon the application of the parties – and usually also at their costs.[129] The parties thus remained very much in control of the proceedings. A similar approach was visible in the 15th century Court of Chancery, where the parties generally seem to have brought their own witnesses. I have described the practice of delegating the examination of witnesses in the Court of Chancery either to the masters or to local dignitaries following the issuance of a writ of *dedimus potestatem*.[130] Equally, Roman-canon law procedure provided ample opportunity for the examination of witnesses outside of the court through local auditors, notaries or judges.[131] It should be noted, however, that members of these groups had undergone some training in the law, whereas Chancery delegates were commonly 'lay lawyers'.[132]

The practice of conducting examinations outside of the court immediately raises questions about the requirements for the immediacy of proof. The 15th century Court of Chancery set no meaningful restrictions on the introduction of testimony: As *Ardern v Ardern* shows, oaths could even be taken in front of third parties who would then present their hearsay to the court.[133] This was unthinkable in Roman-canon law procedure. The witnesses had to swear their oath and testify directly in front of the examining authority.[134] The examination

showed that English ecclesiastical courts also heavily relied on group inquests as a means of proof. This procedure might have been modelled upon the common law jury.

128 Compare *W. Litewski*, Der römisch-kanonische Zivilprozeß nach den älteren ordines iudiciarii, Volume 2, p. 417; 419.

129 *R. H. Helmholz*, The Oxford History of the Laws of England, Volume 1: The Canon Law and Ecclesiastical Jurisdiction from 567 to the 1640s, p. 339.

130 See above chapter V, 4.1.1.

131 Compare *W. Litewski*, Der römisch-kanonische Zivilprozeß nach den älteren ordines iudiciarii, Volume 2, p. 399; *K. W. Nörr*, Römisch-Kanonisches Prozessrecht – Erkenntnisverfahren erster Instanz in civilibus, p. 134.

132 Thus their appearance in *J. P. Dawson*, A History of Lay Judges, Harvard University Press, Cambridge, Ma., 1960.

133 (1465/1466), Calendars I, p. lxxii.

134 *W. Litewski*, Der römisch-kanonische Zivilprozeß nach den älteren ordines iudiciarii, Volume 2, p. 134; *K. W. Nörr*, Römisch-Kanonisches Prozessrecht – Erkenntnisverfahren erster Instanz in civilibus, p. 140.

itself was conducted individually and privately in order to prevent collusion.[135] In another remarkable contrast, Chancery delegates could still examine witnesses in public and in the presence of the parties in the 15th century.[136]

Examiners in Roman-canon law procedure generally relied on party-prepared interrogatories and articles, which resulted from the open positions, when questioning witnesses.[137] While the examination officially remained in their hands, it was effectively guided by the parties. The answers were then summarised in depositions or transcribed in protocols.[138] It was unclear whether the examiners could always forward their own questions and provide personal comments with the depositions.[139] As I have explained in the last chapter, the Court of Chancery merely started introducing the use of interrogatories at the end of the 15th century.[140] Before that, the examination lay exclusively in the hands of the examiner, who would investigate upon the allegations in the bill and summarise the results in the deposition.[141] The extent of discretion in a lay delegate carried serious risks. The passivity of the abbot in *Ardern v Ardern* serves as an illustrative example.[142]

The Roman-canon law of proof provided countless opportunities to contest witness testimony after publication. Parties regularly raised objections to the content of the testimony or demanded the complete disqualification of a witness on personal grounds.[143] The courts, at least in England, apparently preferred the

135 This was at least increasingly the case in the late Middle Ages. Compare *W. Litewski*, Der römisch-kanonische Zivilprozeß nach den älteren ordines iudiciarii, Volume 2, p. 364, p. 401; *K. W. Nörr*, Römisch-Kanonisches Prozessrecht – Erkenntnisverfahren erster Instanz in civilibus, p. 143.

136 See above chapter V, 4.1.2, especially *Ardern v Ardern* (1465/1466), Calendars I, p. lxxii.

137 *W. Litewski*, Der römisch-kanonische Zivilprozeß nach den älteren ordines iudiciarii, Volume 2, p. 402–403; *K. W. Nörr*, Römisch-Kanonisches Prozessrecht – Erkenntnisverfahren erster Instanz in civilibus, p. 140–142.

138 *R. H. Helmholz*, The Oxford History of the Laws of England, Volume 1: The Canon Law and Ecclesiastical Jurisdiction from 567 to the 1640s, p. 341; *K. W. Nörr*, Römisch-Kanonisches Prozessrecht – Erkenntnisverfahren erster Instanz in civilibus, p. 144–145.

139 Against such discretion, see *W. Litewski*, Der römisch-kanonische Zivilprozeß nach den älteren ordines iudiciarii, Volume 2, p. 403. *R. H. Helmholz*, The Oxford History of the Laws of England, Volume 1: The Canon Law and Ecclesiastical Jurisdiction from 567 to the 1640s, p. 339, on the other hand, reported of a discretionary practice in England.

140 See above chapter V, 4.1.6.

141 See above chapter V, 4.1.4.

142 (1465/1466), Calendars I, p. lxxii.

143 *W. Litewski*, Der römisch-kanonische Zivilprozeß nach den älteren ordines iudiciarii, Volume 2, p. 382–398; *K. W. Nörr*, Römisch-Kanonisches Prozessrecht – Erkenntnisverfahren erster Instanz in civilibus, p. 135–138.

adjustment of the weight of evidence rather than its complete disqualification, thus reserving a degree of discretion in the regulated area of proof.[144] The formal publication of witness depositions in the Court of Chancery only became a necessity when witnesses were examined individually and privately.[145] No such evidence exists for the 15th century. Objections against witness testimony might have been raised at the hearing stage and have thus remained undocumented. Given the absence of technical rules of proof in the late medieval Court of Chancery, however, it seems likely that the Lord Chancellors attributed different weight to witness testimony rather than disqualifying it altogether and thereby limiting their own discretion.

3.3.2 Documents

Documentary evidence constituted the second most common means of proof in the Roman-canon law process.[146] In line with their love for classifications, the jurists distinguished strictly between public and private documents.[147] The former could generally establish full proof, while the latter generally merely represented half proof.[148] Public documents, for example, included notarised papers and those under public seal as well as court protocols.[149] The most common private documents were contracts and acquittances.[150] Specific rules, most notably for their contestation by witnesses, applied to each of these types of documents.[151] No such distinctions between different classes of documents are visible in Chancery sources from the 15th century. What we can instead observe is a seemingly indiscriminate introduction of any document with potential evidentiary value. It is evident that official documents must also have carried a

144 Compare *R. H. Helmholz*, The Oxford History of the Laws of England, Volume 1: The Canon Law and Ecclesiastical Jurisdiction from 567 to the 1640s, p. 341.

145 See above XX.

146 *K. W. Nörr*, Römisch-Kanonisches Prozessrecht – Erkenntnisverfahren erster Instanz in civilibus, p. 131.

147 On this distinction, see *W. Litewski*, Der römisch-kanonische Zivilprozeß nach den älteren ordines iudiciarii, Volume 2, p. 420.

148 *K. W. Nörr*, Römisch-Kanonisches Prozessrecht – Erkenntnisverfahren erster Instanz in civilibus, p. 154.

149 *W. Litewski*, Der römisch-kanonische Zivilprozeß nach den älteren ordines iudiciarii, Volume 2, p. 420; *K. W. Nörr*, Römisch-Kanonisches Prozessrecht – Erkenntnisverfahren erster Instanz in civilibus, p. 154.

150 Compare *K. W. Nörr*, Römisch-Kanonisches Prozessrecht – Erkenntnisverfahren erster Instanz in civilibus, p. 157.

151 *W. Litewski*, Der römisch-kanonische Zivilprozeß nach den älteren ordines iudiciarii, Volume 2, p. 424–426; *K. W. Nörr*, Römisch-Kanonisches Prozessrecht – Erkenntnisverfahren erster Instanz in civilibus, p. 156–157; 158–160.

greater weight than private documents in the judge's consideration of evidence in the Court of Chancery. This should, however, not distract us from the decisive distinction that he was – in contrast to colleagues following Roman-canon law procedure – exercising a wider discretion.

In a final parallel, both jurisdictions offered the opportunity to advance a claim for the discovery of documents in possession of the other party after the opening of the suit.[152]

Given the degree of technicality and professionalization reached in Roman-canon law procedure by the end of the Middle Ages, the two jurisdictions look far apart in the 15th century. However, a large part of the Roman-canon law of proof could be dispensed in summary procedures. Furthermore, the development in Chancery towards a greater openness for Roman-canon law principles had already set in. I have identified the use of interrogatories and the publication of testimony after private examination as noticeable examples. Perhaps more importantly, Macnair's study has shown that the early modern Court of Chancery developed a comprehensive idea of a law of proof, which appears in large parts modelled upon Roman-canon law procedure.[153]

In order to identify important similarities between the 15th century Court of Chancery and Roman-canon law, it might be necessary to take a step back and integrate the contemporary common law into the comparison. What clearly distinguished both jurisdictions from the common law was the availability of a theoretically unlimited range of means of proofs between which the litigants could actively choose. Whereas the common law writ system prescribed certain means of proof for specific causes of action and limited the role of witnesses to membership in an inscrutable jury, Roman-canon law and the Court of Chancery commonly (most importantly) incorporated the testimony of individual witnesses. With regard to the development of the English legal system, this constituted a real innovation. From this perspective, Roman-canon law and Chancery procedure shared the most decisive feature on the stage of evidence – irrespective of the substantial differences in concrete practice.

152 See for the Court of Chancery above chapter V, 4.2.2 and for roman-canon law procedure *K. W. Nörr*, Römisch-Kanonisches Prozessrecht – Erkenntnisverfahren erster Instanz in civilibus, p. 161.

153 *M. R. T. Macnair*, The Law of Proof in Early Modern Equity.

3.4 Determination

3.4.1 'Extra-judicial' conflict resolution

Due to its geographical and chronological scope of application, it is impossible to make quantitative assessments about the frequency of extra-judicial conflict resolution under Roman-canon law procedure. Richard Helmholz, however, noted that a large number of cases in medieval English ecclesiastical courts were resolved extra-judicially after the stage of evidence.[154] This was also a normative expectation expressed by classical canon lawyers.[155] A large share of extra-judicial settlements would be in line with my argumentation from the last chapter.[156] With its superior mechanism for issue identification and a relatively predictable system of proofs, the Roman-canon law procedure should have provided even greater incentives for timely settlement than the Court of Chancery. Since decisions became largely foreseeable, weaker parties should have been encouraged to settle in order to reduce the overall costs of the proceedings.[157] In the absence of quantitative data, however, this argumentation must remain hypothetical. My further comparison will be restricted to the judicial resolution of conflicts in both jurisdictions.

3.4.2 'Judicial' conflict resolution

The final stage of the process in the Court of Chancery was introduced by a judicial hearing, in which the parties' lawyers read out the case documentation and, potentially, advanced additional arguments in favour of their claims.[158] The practice under Roman-canon law procedure once again showed structural similarities. Advocates of both parties presented the allegations (*allegationes*) in front of the judge.[159] These generally included all legal and factual arguments, which might sway the judge towards a favourable decision.[160] Evidence of

154 *R. H. Helmholz*, The Oxford History of the Laws of England, Volume 1: The Canon Law and Ecclesiastical Jurisdiction from 567 to the 1640s, p. 341–343.

155 This was regularly based on the Decretal Ex parte tua (X 1.36.11).

156 See above chapter V, 5.1.2.

157 Compare above chapter V, 5.1.2.

158 See above chapter V, 5.2.1.2.

159 *W. Litewski*, Der römisch-kanonische Zivilprozeß nach den älteren ordines iudiciarii, Volume 2, p. 446; *K. W. Nörr*, Römisch-Kanonisches Prozessrecht – Erkenntnisverfahren erster Instanz in civilibus, p. 177–180.

160 *W. Litewski*, Der römisch-kanonische Zivilprozeß nach den älteren ordines iudiciarii, Volume 2, p. 446; *K. W. Nörr*, Römisch-Kanonisches Prozessrecht – Erkenntnisverfahren erster Instanz in civilibus, p. 177.

recorded allegations is lacking.[161] An exact comparison is thus rendered difficult. What seems clear, however, is that the lawyers in the Court of Chancery could hardly raise 'legal' arguments in the absence of an elaborated substantive law and were thus limited to factual considerations, which generally seems to have lead to a mere recitation of pleadings and depositions. In Roman-canon law procedure, the trial stage terminated with *renunciatio* and *conclusio in causa*: The parties and the court agreed officially to end the exchange of arguments.[162] No such formal act is proliferated through the Chancery sources.

At the stage of decision-making, it seems noteworthy that the judges following Roman-canon law procedure frequently sought the advice (*consilium*) of third parties.[163] This group included jurists, the court's assessors, colleagues, experts in extra-legal fields or even lay people.[164] A framework of duties and rules guided the integration of third parties into the deliberation process. While the advice was obligatory and binding on the judge in some cases, it could be purely discretionary in others.[165] I have referred to the practice of deliberating Chancery decisions with common law justices, the King's council or the court's masters.[166] This represented not only a sensible practice for the avoidance of jurisdictional conflicts but also a clear parallelism to Roman-canon law procedure. In the Court of Chancery, however, the practice seems to have remained entirely discretionary. Another significant distinction lay in the possibility to delegate important matters for decision to a higher court under Roman-canon law procedure,[167] whereas the Court of Chancery remained a court of first and last instance.

161 *K. W. Nörr*, Römisch-Kanonisches Prozessrecht – Erkenntnisverfahren erster Instanz in civilibus, p. 178. *W. Litewski*, Der römisch-kanonische Zivilprozeß nach den älteren ordines iudiciarii, Volume 2, p. 447, however, claimed that the oral allegations were commonly protocolled.

162 *K. W. Nörr*, Römisch-Kanonisches Prozessrecht – Erkenntnisverfahren erster Instanz in civilibus, p. 180–182.

163 *W. Litewski*, Der römisch-kanonische Zivilprozeß nach den älteren ordines iudiciarii, Volume 2, p. 455.

164 *K. W. Nörr*, Römisch-Kanonisches Prozessrecht – Erkenntnisverfahren erster Instanz in civilibus, p. 182–183. For an elaboration on the role of experts at this stage, see *Y. Mausen*, Ex scientia et arte sua testificatur, Rechtsgeschichte, Volume 10 (2007), p. 127–135.

165 *K. W. Nörr*, Römisch-Kanonisches Prozessrecht – Erkenntnisverfahren erster Instanz in civilibus, p. 183–185.

166 See above chapter V, 5.2.1.3.

167 *W. Litewski*, Der römisch-kanonische Zivilprozeß nach den älteren ordines iudiciarii, Volume 2, p. 561–563; *K. W. Nörr*, Römisch-Kanonisches Prozessrecht – Erkenntnisverfahren erster Instanz in civilibus, p. 185–186.

The adversarial element of Roman-canon law proceedings was emphasised by the maxims that the judge's decision should not exceed the scope of the libel (*sententia conformis libello*) and that it should be based on what was actually alleged and proved, not on conscience (*secundam allegata et probate, non secundum conscientiam*).[168] In this maxim, conscience was understood as the private knowledge or suspicion of the judge – in line with Macnair's suggested meaning of conscience in Chancery.[169] As I have shown above, the late medieval Court of Chancery explicitly rejected such limitations of judicial discretion.[170] It remains open whether this assertion rendered any practical effect.

Once the final decision had been made, Roman-canon law procedure generally required a reading in open court and a formalisation in writing.[171] Whether the same requirement existed in the late medieval Court of Chancery is unclear. The low number of decrees preserved on the back of Chancery bills raises doubts about the regular documentation of decisions in the 15th century. The few preserved decrees, however, show remarkable similarities with Roman-canon law decisions.

Naturally, ecclesiastical courts invoked the name of God rather than that of the king but the mentioning of the nature of the case and the names of the parties, the assertion of the rectitude of the judge and the recitation of all procedural steps constituted common elements.[172] At last, both jurisdictions merely provided a conclusion in the most general terms and an order towards one of the parties.[173] While Roman-canon law procedure generally allowed for the publication of legal grounds for the decision (*causae*), this was largely avoided in practice – not least because it offered potential grounds for appeal.[174] The absence of a reasoned opinion thus constituted another parallelism.

168 *K. W. Nörr*, Römisch-Kanonisches Prozessrecht – Erkenntnisverfahren erster Instanz in civilibus, p. 187–190.

169 See above chapter V, 2.7.5.

170 See above chapter V, 5.2.2.2.

171 *W. Litewski*, Der römisch-kanonische Zivilprozeß nach den älteren ordines iudiciarii, Volume 2, p. 459; 461; *R. H. Helmholz*, The Oxford History of the Laws of England, Volume 1: The Canon Law and Ecclesiastical Jurisdiction from 567 to the 1640s, p. 343.

172 *R. H. Helmholz*, The Oxford History of the Laws of England, Volume 1: The Canon Law and Ecclesiastical Jurisdiction from 567 to the 1640s, p. 343, has identified these elements as typical for English ecclesiastical courts.

173 For Roman-canon law procedure, see *R. H. Helmholz*, The Oxford History of the Laws of England, Volume 1: The Canon Law and Ecclesiastical Jurisdiction from 567 to the 1640s, p. 343.

174 Compare *K. W. Nörr*, Römisch-Kanonisches Prozessrecht – Erkenntnisverfahren erster Instanz in civilibus, p. 200. Similarly, *W. Litewski*, Der römisch-kanonische Zivilprozeß nach den älteren ordines iudiciarii, Volume 2, p. 465.

Equally, both jurisdictions could order any act or omission from the parties as an interlocutory or final remedy. It was merely the execution of the decision, which reminds us of the different roles of ecclesiastical courts operating under Roman-canon law procedure and the Court of Chancery in the late medieval normative world. While the ecclesiastical courts had to rely on the threat of excommunication for contumacy in order to compel adherence to their decisions,[175] the Court of Chancery could employ the comparatively advanced royal administrative machinery.[176]

Overall, the resolution of cases showed noticeable similarities between Roman-canon law and Chancery procedure. Indeed, the formal parallels of the documented decisions seem so substantial that we might rule out a mere coincidence. The relative similarity of decision-making in both jurisdictions is again underlined by a comparison to the contemporary common law, which relied exclusively on the inscrutable verdict of a local jury.

4. Conclusion

The similarities between Roman-canon law and Chancery procedure in the late Middle Ages appear highly significant and yet hardly systematic. It seems necessary to emphasise at this stage that I deliberately focused on the presentation of corresponding procedures in Roman-canon law and the Court of Chancery. Elements of Roman-canon law procedure, which remained entirely unparalleled in the Court of Chancery, have been avoided, since an object of comparison was missing. One such element was the system of appeals in Roman-canon law. Its impact on the process can hardly be overestimated. The regular threat of an appeal effectively requires the documentation of every step of the proceedings and enforces professionalization in the lower courts. The high degree of judicial discretion in the Court of Chancery would probably not have persisted throughout the late Middle Ages in a system allowing for appeals.

In order to avoid a common misunderstanding in the search for the origins of the Court of Chancery, it is necessary to abandon the strict division between common law and Roman-canon law origins. My comparisons clearly show

175 *R. H. Helmholz*, The Oxford History of the Laws of England, Volume 1: The Canon Law and Ecclesiastical Jurisdiction from 567 to the 1640s, p. 345.

176 Compare *R. H. Helmholz*, The Oxford History of the Laws of England, Volume 1: The Canon Law and Ecclesiastical Jurisdiction from 567 to the 1640s, p. 345, for the situation at common law.

elements of both jurisdictions in 15th century Chancery practice. Nevertheless, in its structure – but not necessarily in detail[177] – the Chancery process was much closer to Roman-canon law than to the common law. Reference to its main elements bill/libel, answer, witness testimony, documentary evidence, hearing/allegations, judicial decision-making and decree should suffice to reinforce this point. On the other hand – and despite incidental parallels in detail – the sophistication found not only in academic treatments of Roman-canon law but also in its application in other European supreme courts[178] was unparalleled in the late medieval Court of Chancery. The examination of Chancery documentation clearly shows that the Lord Chancellors and their staff were first and foremost practitioners. They undoubtedly borrowed extensively from what they knew from ecclesiastical adjudication or what they had studied at the universities. In contrast to the jurists, however, they had absolutely no academic ambitions: They were practical borrowers rather than devoted followers of roman-canon law.[179]

That is also why we must give up the hope of finding a convenient and comprehensive explanation for the similarities between Roman-canon law and the Court of Chancery, and instead accept the more differentiated reality. The adoption of principles of Roman-canon law procedure in the Court of Chancery was a practical process, in which legal ideas from one place met the legal and cultural reality of another place. They were thereby transformed through practice and experience – not least from the common law –, so that the result constituted a new normative order. No matter how used we are to considering the dichotomy between the common law and equity courts as an identity-defining element of the common law tradition, we should not overlook that its roots lie in a 'transfer' of legal ideas not unlike many others.[180]

What does this conclusion tell us about the question brought up at the beginning of this chapter? Was the rise of the Court of Chancery only one part of a general European development, possibly even of a 'reception' of Roman-canon or civil law ideas? I believe this question requires a broader scope and cannot be answered by a mere identification of Roman-canon law elements in Chancery

177 An interesting point of distinction lay in the terminology of Roman-canon law and the Court of Chancery, which rarely coincided despite the fact that Chancery issued all official documents in Latin.

178 See below chapter VIII.

179 This is, of course, not to say that local decision-makers in ecclesiastical courts were always strict followers of the academic Roman-canon law procedure. Their adherence to the technical rules of the learned laws in England offers potential for further research.

180 For a theoretical introduction, see *A. Watson*, Legal Transplants, University of Georgia Press, Athens, Ga., 2nd edition, 1993.

procedure. What is necessary instead is an identification of the court's role in the context of the developing English legal system. It is only then that we can establish whether the English legal system faced similar problems and found similar answers as other European legal systems.

Chapter VII

Functions of the Court of Chancery

The knowledge of the 15th Chancery process and its origins should now allow us to draw first conclusions about the role of the Court of Chancery in the developing English legal system of the late Middle Ages. A caveat might be in order: The (hi)story identified from the sources is told from the perspective of the litigants. It strictly revolves around individual conflicts brought before the court as an institution for conflict resolution. Arguably, this fact limits the potential of my research for a complete explanation of the rise of the Court of Chancery.

It is certainly true that the sources tell us very little about the institution of Chancery itself, about its political standing and about its role in the centralisation of royal power. Few would doubt that the late medieval and early modern monarchs either passively favoured or actively encouraged the expansion of the Court of Chancery as a counterbalance to an increasingly confident and independent common law jurisdiction. The rise of the court cannot be understood without recognition of its close ties to the monarchy through the person of the Lord Chancellor and the royal administration. Yet, none of this is directly visible in the sources I have analysed. At best, we might draw inferences from the acceptance for trial of cases directly encroaching upon established common law jurisdiction.[1] Even then, however, the sources tell us nothing about the Lord Chancellors' motives, about their political role and about potential encouragement from the monarchs.

I would, however, also consider this limitation an opportunity. As I have outlined above, the institutional history of the Court of Chancery has been researched thoroughly.[2] Likewise, political histories have already identified the role of Chancery in the expansion of the centralised monarchy successfully.[3] What earlier research has merely touched upon marginally, however, is the

1 See for example *Qwyncy v Landasdale* (1432–1443), Calendars I, p. xxxii; *Abbot of Burton v Stanley* (1432–1443), Calendars I, p. xxxiii; *Trewonwall v Bodrugan* (1450–1454), Calendars I, p. xlvii. For a discussion of the delineation of common law and Chancery jurisdiction, see above chapter V, 2.5.2.

2 See chapter III.

3 See for example *S. B. Chrimes*, An Introduction to the Administrative History of Medieval England, Blackwell, Oxford, Volume 7, 3rd edition, 1966. The author, however, admitted that few studies of the fifteenth century existed, *ibid.*, p. 241.

question how the Court of Chancery concretely contributed to the development of the legal system through its process. It is in this very area that the documentation of Chancery cases from the 15th century – from the litigants' perspective – promises most valuable insights.

Relying upon my previous analysis of the sources, it is my hypothesis that the late medieval Chancery process provided the potential cure for two central deficiencies of royal conflict resolution in the common law courts at the time: an inability to integrate societal change and a corresponding lack of legitimacy. This chapter will be devoted to an identification of these deficiencies and of the answers provided by Chancery procedure in order to facilitate a development towards a more integrative (1.) and legitimate (2.) legal system. It will be my conclusion (3.) that the late medieval Court of Chancery should be considered a catalyst for the modernisation of the English legal system.

1. Integration

1.1 Equity

On a first look, the analysis of late medieval Chancery procedure has reinforced a common perception of the equitable jurisdiction amongst scholars and practitioners alike: It offered far-ranging flexibility to address perceived individual injustice through the means of judicial discretion. This finding is indeed fully in line with most conventional accounts of equity in general.[4] A need for equity in order to overcome the injustices of a strict law or to promote the law's 'true' intention[5] has been a common feature of literature on justice from Aristotle to Aquinas and beyond. Equity is, in short, a universal answer to a universal problem.[6] A formalised system of laws tends to over-regulate some and under-regulate other potential conflict situations. Equity represents the abstract remedy.

For our purposes, it is of utmost importance to remember that St. German, relying on the scholastic tradition, introduced this concept into the practical

4 For an introduction to *St. German*'s 'conventional' understanding of equity and its roots in Aristotelian thought, see *D. Klinck*, Conscience, Equity and the Court of Chancery in Early Modern England, Ashgate, Farnham, 2010, p. 46–50.

5 The identification of a 'true' intention of the law is now considered a standard method of interpretation (teleological interpretation). It is, however, difficult to apply to more formalised and potentially sacred legal texts. Equity often offered the justification for such a potentially dangerous exercise.

6 Compare also *H. S. Maine*, Ancient Law (1866), Transaction Publishers, New Brunswick, NJ, 2002, especially p. 24–25; 44–72.

discourse of the English courts.[7] It could thus hardly be considered an exaggeration to perceive of him as the father of the equitable jurisdiction in England. However, it was the very point of my historical introduction and my portrayal of the late medieval process that the late medieval Court of Chancery was not (yet) St. German's idealised court of equity.[8] Quite to the contrary, the term equity was not commonly in use in relation to the Court of Chancery before St. German's *Doctor and Student*. An explanation of the rise of the court, which relies too heavily on notions of equity, thus has to answer to criticisms of anachronism.

While I have little doubt that equitable ideas in this sense inspired decision-making in the Court of Chancery, they were never expressed explicitly or even implied in the exchanges between the parties. What is instead visible in the sources is practical conflict resolution. The question that can finally be answered after the analysis of the sources is not how the intervention of the Court of Chancery was justified. That might actually be classified as a typical medieval or early modern debate with little relevance for the modern reader. It is rather how the Court of Chancery managed to remedy the problems it was faced with on a daily basis and why this required the existence of a separate jurisdiction. It will be my argument that the court offered a procedure which not merely remedied minor injustices at the edges or in the gaps of the law in an otherwise functioning system – as St. Germans's equity was supposed to[9] – but that it rather offered a vehicle for a (potentially) continuous adaptation of the law to the demands of society. It thus transformed the English legal system in a way that contemporary discussions of equity never foresaw.

7 See also *J. L. Barton*, Equity in the Medieval Common Law, in: R. A. Newman (ed.), Equity in the World's Legal Systems – A Comparative Study, Emile Bruylant, Bruxelles, 1973, p. 139–155, p. 152; *J. L. Barton*, Introduction, in: T. F.T. Plucknett / J. L. Barton (eds.), St. German's Doctor and Student, Selden Society, London, 1974, p. xlvii. *D. Klinck*, Imaging Equity in Early Modern England, La Revue Du Barreau Canadien, Volume 84 (2005), p. 217–247, describes the early modern understanding of equity in the Court of Chancery.

8 Also *J. Getzler*, Patterns of Fusion, in: P. Birks (ed.), The Classification of Obligations, Clarendon Press, Oxford, 1997, p. 157–192, p. 178, contended that "St German's Doctor and Student, which propounds the canonist concept of conscience as the foundation of the discretion to vary legal justice in equitable cases, may have had the purpose of giving intellectual structure to practice rather than reflecting the way in which equity lawyers actually thought".

9 Compare T. F.T. Plucknett / J. L. Barton (eds.), St. German's Doctor and Student, S. 97.

1.2 Royal adjudication before the Court of Chancery

The starting point for this discussion is the state of royal conflict resolution before or – considering the impossibility of marking the beginning of the court in light of its gradual evolution – without the Court of Chancery. For this purpose, our look has to revert back to the late medieval common law. I have already identified numerous problems of the common law process, which the Court of Chancery sought to cure. For an identification of the role of the Court of Chancery, however, it will be necessary to analyse the overall state of the common law as the centrepiece of the royal system of justice at the time.

1.2.1 Formalism and inflexibility

The common perception of late medieval common law is one of routinized formalities and inflexibility.[10] While this view might not adequately reflect the complexity of the common law at the time, it is generally reaffirmed by comparisons, for example with Roman-canon law procedure. The main reasons for this assessment have been identified before: The limited number of writs complicated access to the courts in cases lying outside of pre-established fact-patterns.[11] Pleading was a highly technical exercise for the elimination of those contingencies, which had overcome the writ-selection process.[12] The respective courses of actions prescribed the admissible methods of proof[13] and the judges effectively limited their role to that of legal advisers.[14] The limited role of bill procedure at common law could not remedy any of these restrictions.[15] It should be noted that this degree of formalism not merely removed adjudication in the royal courts from the world of lay people. Arguably, the delegation of responsibility to a professionalised elite of adjudicators – and the sergeants appearing in common law trials were just that – was well-suited for guaranteeing non-violent conflict resolution. More importantly, however, the degree of formalism present in late medieval common law also inhibited reformative interventions by the parties involved in the trial – either the parties or the judge. Since the program of the trial was entirely preconceived by the respective courses of action, no opportunity arose for the integration of new arguments.

10 See above, especially chapter II, 1.5.3.
11 See above chapter V, 2.4.4.
12 See above chapter V, 3.1.7.
13 See above chapter V, 4.
14 See above chapter V, 5.2.1.5.
15 See above chapter II, 1.5.3.

A qualification seems necessary: The common law possessed one important element of informality and uncertainty in the form of the jury.[16] Naturally, the work of the jury is hardly represented in the sources. Studies on the early modern period have suggested that the common law judges exercised significant control over the jury and thereby effectively cloaked their own interventions as jury decisions.[17] The decision-making processes of late medieval juries must remain a mystery. However, the creative potential of a largely uncontrolled jury is clear. The jury did not need to justify its findings and could therefore effectively integrate its own – officially extra-legal[18] – considerations into the common law process.[19] The formal hostility towards the integration of standards of morality or character judgments could thus, at least potentially, partly be remedied.

Irrespective of possible jury intervention, the common law process did not provide any formally accepted opportunities for the parties or the judge to influence or even shape the process. Quite to the contrary, the procedures leading up to the verdict were defined by the respective courses of action and were thus perceived as static, even if the final result remained unpredictable. It is this public impression of the unalterability of the common law process that is also reflected in the late medieval Chancery bills:

The case of *Ardern v Ardern*[20] represents but one example of the public perception of the common law process. Since the common law provided no course of action for the enforcement of oral conditions on formalised agreements, the plaintiff knew that he "may have no remedy in this case by the course of the common law"[21] and thus turned to the Court of Chancery. The same rationale lay behind the earliest use or trust cases.[22] The case of *White v White*[23]

16 See above chapter V, 5.2.1.5.

17 Compare *T. A. Green*, Verdict According to Conscience – Perspectives on the English Criminal Trial Jury 1200–1800, University of Chicago Press, Chicago, Il., 1985, especially p. 139–140; *J. H. Langbein / R. T. Lerner / B. P. Smith*, History of the Common Law – The Development of Anglo-American Legal Institutions, Aspen Publishers, New York, NY, 2009, p. 431–434.

18 Offcially, of course, the role of the jury was restricted to answering questions of fact, see above chapter V, 3.1.7; 5.2.1.5.

19 *J. H. Langbein / R. T. Lerner / B. P. Smith*, History of the Common Law – The Development of Anglo-American Legal Institutions, p. 424–427, relying on the precedent in *Bushell's Case* (1670) 124 English Reports 1006.

20 (1465/1466), Calendars I, p. lxxii.

21 *Ardern v Ardern* (1465/1466), Calendars I, p. lxxii.

22 See for example *Groos v Depeham* (1454–1455), Calendars I, p. xlviii; *Fitz Harry v Lyngeyn* (1454–1455), Calendars I, p. xlviii; *Duke of Gloucester v Bishop of Ely* (1472–1473), Calendars I, p. xc; *Neville v Osborn* (1473), Calendars I, p. xciv; *Tryppe v Chevyn* (1484), Calendars I, p. cxvi.

23 (1399–1413) Select Cases, S. 95.

might serve as an illustrative example: The plaintiff complained that her deceased husband had transferred all his property to the defendants for them to hold it for the benefit of herself and her daughter. Since the defendants had failed to honour this alleged agreement, she appealed to the Court of Chancery. The bill did not even mention the common law jurisdiction. This is hardly a surprise. It was simply well established that there was no common law action for what would later be called a breach of trust.

The limitations of the effective *numerus clausus* of writs were thus well known at the time. They have also been much discussed in all later scholarship on the common law. However, centuries of experience with a transsubstantive process carry the risk of underestimating the enormous impact of these limitations: As long as common law judges followed the traditional writ structure consistently and prevented its reform, it was impossible to widen the scope of the common law from within. Litigants were effectively helpless when facing yet unregulated conflict situations.

The perceived unalterability of the common law is furthermore visible in Chancery cases, in which the litigants tried to evade the evidentiary restrictions of the common law.[24] In *Haryngton v Haryngton*,[25] described in greater detail above, the plaintiff sought release from a sealed bond. Since a knight he employed under a contract had deserted his service, he refused payment under the terms of the bond. The fact that the knight had switched allegiances, however, could not be pleaded at common law because the bond was considered irrefutable proof of the obligation. The famous cases, discussed by St. German,[26] in which the common law denied relief upon payment of a contractual obligation without acquittance, provide another illustrative example.[27] As shown above, the truth-finding mechanisms of the common law, prescribed by the respective courses of actions, were wholly inadequate. They privileged certainty over truth to a degree hardly acceptable to the common litigant, let alone those versed in concepts of moral theology. Once again, the parties were left without any effective remedy, no matter how far the evidentiary restrictions were removed from their perceptions of fairness.

Perhaps less obviously, the early trespass cases in the Court of Chancery represent another example of the stasis and perceived unalterability of the

24 For cases discussing evidence that would not have been admissible or could not be obtained under common law, see for example *Sharp v Temper* (1461–1467), Calendars I, p. lxiii; *Baker v Parson* (1465–1467), Calendars II, p. l; *Fowler v Iwardby* (1466), Calendars I, p. ixviii; *Blower v Luke* (1470), Calendars II, p. li.

25 (1432–1443), Calendars I, p. xxxiv. The facts of the case are presented in greater detail above chapter V, 2.5.1.

26 T. F.T. Plucknett / J. L. Barton (eds.), St. German's Doctor and Student, p. 77–79.

27 See for example *Brampton v Seymour* (1386), Select Cases, p. 2; (1482); Y. B. 22 Edw. IV, Pasch.,pl. 18, f. 6.

common law.[28] In cases like *Pykworth v Sambroke*,[29] the plaintiffs did not complain about the common law process as such but rather about its seemingly guaranteed outcome. In the face of possible retaliation from defendants known as "notorious and common extortioners and oppressors of the people in their country",[30] local common law juries were perceived as compromised. Thus, the plaintiffs feared that even if they made their case and the jury knew about the truth of the allegations, their arguments might have no weight in the outcome of the trial. The common law provided no safeguards against improper influence on local juries. The connection with the stasis of the common law might not be immediately visible. However, underlying these disputes was the impression that the common law courts effectively supported established power structures and left litigants seeking what they considered justice without a remedy.

The three classes of cases illustrate the common perception of the common law process in the late Middle Ages: It was conceived as static and inflexible. It will be helpful for a characterisation of the Court of Chancery's response to the perceived state of the common law to remember how and why it was brought about.

As we have seen, the stasis reached by the common law in the 14th century was not one of its original features. During its formative period, the council and Chancery regularly introduced new courses of action and refined existing ones in order to accommodate demand for royal conflict resolution.[31] From this perspective, the development towards fixed and immutable forms of actions seems like a regression. Scholars have advanced various explanations for the increasing stasis of the common law in the late Middle Ages.[32] The debate about the early evolution of the common law generally lies outside the scope of my study. Nevertheless, it seems advisable to consider two possible explanations –

28 Examples for such early trespass cases include *Bokelond v Bount* (1394), Select Cases, p. 12; *Beaufort v Puncherdon* (1410–1412), Select Cases, S. 97; *Appleton v Aleyn* (1432–1443), Calendars I, p. xxxi; *Quyncy v Londasdale* (1432–1443), Calendars I, xxxii; *Saxby v Laurence* (1432–1443), Calendars I, p. xxxiii; *Burton v Yerbaugh* (1432–1443), Calendars I, p. xxv.

29 (1407) Select Cases, p. 87.

30 *Pykworth v Sambroke* (1407), Select Cases, p. 87.

31 See above chapter II, 1.5.2.

32 For a short summary of the debate, see *J. H. Langbein / R. T. Lerner / B. P. Smith*, History of the Common Law – The Development of Anglo-American Legal Institutions, p. 272–274. *J. H. Langbein* presents *F. W. Maitland* as a main proponent of what I will call 'constitutionalism' – the thesis that Parliament became sufficiently powerful to block unwanted reform attempts in an alliance with common lawyers and *G. O. Sayles* as a proponent of what I will call 'professionalisation' – the thesis that the elaborated structure of the common law at the time rendered the key players of the legal system adverse to change.

which I will call professionalisation and constitutionalisation[33] – in order to better understand the state of the royal conflict resolution at the time. In the end, this reflection will also help to highlight not only the opportunities but also the risks of the rise of the Court of Chancery in the face of an already established central court system.

1.2.2 Professionalisation

With its focus on feudal law and its ritualised procedure, medieval common law looks suspiciously arcane to the modern day observer. Such an assessment, however, carries the risk of overlooking its central achievements. By the 14th century, when first evidence of the Court of Chancery emerges, clerics and laymen had lost their dominant position in common law proceedings.[34] Instead, the common law was dominated by an elite group of professional lawyers educated within the courts.[35] More than most lay lawyers, they had both the time and the mind to systematise conflict resolution in the common law courts. The incentive was clear: Formalised adjudication allowed for the monopolisation of the legal process and its income streams in the hands of the privileged legal elite. Thus, it is arguable that professionalisation and formalisation were mutually reinforcing developments.[36]

On the one hand, the advantages of formalisation are plain to see: By providing standard ways of settling complex conflict situations through the application of routinized procedures, formality can reduce the complexity of the conflict and thereby the costs for its resolution – financially but possibly also emotionally.[37] On the other hand, a possible downside becomes visible in the

33 A definition is provided in the footnote above.

34 Compare *A. Musson*, The English Common Law and Chancery Jurisdiction, Late Middle Ages and Early-Modern Times, in: A. Wijffels/C.H. van Rhee (eds.), European Supreme Courts – A Portrait through History, Third Millennium Publishing, London, 2013, p. 172–181, p. 176.

35 For a full history of this development, see *P. Brand*, The Origins of the English Legal Profession, Blackwell, Oxford, 1992; *C. Donahue*, The Legal Professions of Fourteenth-Century England: Serjeants of the Common Bench and Advocates of the Courts of Arches, in: S. Jenks/J. Rose/C. Whittick (eds.), Laws, Lawyers and Texts – Studies in Medieval Legal History in Honour of Paul Brand, Brill, Leiden, 2012, p. 227–251.

36 Compare for parallel developments on the European continent *M. Stolleis*, Römisches Recht und die Entstehung des modernen Staates, Akademie-Journal, Vol. 2/2002, p. 53–57, p. 53.

37 Compare *N. Luhmann*, Ausdifferenzierung des Rechts, Suhrkamp, Frankfurt/Main, 1981, p. 57, who contended that modern legal systems block the argumentative escape to love, belief, power or art.

Chancery bills presented above: inflexibility due to the overregulation of every step of the process. Given the advantages of formality for the legal profession, it is hardly surprising that it often tends towards conservativeness.[38] The development of the common law in the late Middle Ages merely provides a particularly strong example.

1.2.3 Constitutionalisation

The inflexibility of late medieval common law can also be understood as a safeguard against excessive royal intervention. In this sense, it was the result of a constitutional development. I have identified Chancery and the *curia regis* as the central institutions for inserting flexibility into the common law in the first centuries after the conquest.[39] Chancery was a royal department under the supervision of the king's closest adviser, the Lord Chancellor, and the *curia regis* constituted of the magnates and other advisors at the royal court. Both institutions were thus located in closest proximity to the king. Containing their influence over the legal process, therefore also meant withdrawing it from royal reach. While the judges at common law, at this stage, served at the will of the king, the inflexible process also naturally limited their discretion.[40]

The classical history of the exclusion of royal influence over the common law relies on a 17th century narrative.[41] Not least inspired by Coke's ideas about an ancient common law constitution, it goes like this: Parliament and common lawyers formed a century-long alliance.[42] Under this narrative, such illustrious

38 Compare *L. M. Friedman*, Lawyers in Cross-Cultural Perspective, in: R. L. Abel/ P. S. C. Lewis (eds.), Lawyers in Society – Comparative Theories, University of California Press, Berkeley, Ca., 1988 (repr. 2005), p. 1–26, p. 20–21, who, of course, also questioned this common perception. Empirical evidence across a representative number of jurisdictions seems to be lacking.

39 See above chapter II, 1.5.2.

40 Arguably, the common law judges, who had risen from the ranks of the common lawyers, were quite content to raise the impression of their own impotence, thereby avoiding constitutional struggles.

41 For brief introductions, see *H. J. Berman*, The Origins of Historical Jurisprudence – Coke, Selden, Hale, Yale Law Journal, Volume 102 (1994), p. 1651–1738, p. 1673–1694; *J. Goldsworthy*, The Myth of the Common Law Constitution, in: D. E. Edlin (ed.), Common Law Theory, Cambridge University Press, Cambridge, 2007, p. 204–236.

42 Compare for example *W. Holdsworth*, A History of English Law, Methuen, London, Volume 1, 7th edition, 1956, p. 210–211; *D. E. C. Yale* in: D. E. C. Yale (ed.), Lord Nottingham's 'Manual of Chancery Practice' and 'Prolegomena of Chancery and Equity', Cambridge University Press, Cambridge, 1965, (repr. 1986), p. 7–8.

constitutional milestones as the Magna Charta,[43] Coke's limitations on the royal prerogative[44] or the abolition of prerogative courts during the English Revolution[45] can all be attributed to the strength of this bond. The local noblemen sitting in parliament feared royal intervention against their own interests and saw the common lawyers, who relied on their payments, as natural allies. From this perspective, the inflexibility of the common law was arguably not much more than the price to pay for the establishment of first incidents of a separation of powers. It is clear that the prerogative courts like the Court of Chancery, with their supposed unity – and factually close relationship – of judge and king, were a natural enemy of this development. With some pride, John Fortescue noted that the king of England at the end of the 15th century was "not able to change the laws of his kingdom at pleasure, for he rule[d] his people with a government not only royal but also political".[46] Despite all justified scepticism, the narrative arguably offers a valuable perspective for the understanding of the late medieval common law.

On the one hand, common law was highly professionalised for its time and had reached a remarkable independence from the king. On the other hand, this came at the cost of narrowing its scope and stifling all innovation. The stage for the Court of Chancery was set. While it faced a difficult legal and political landscape, it was also offered with an enormous potential for expansion.

1.3 Role of Chancery procedure

It is my argument that the procedure of the Court of Chancery – outlined above – provided the perfect framework for the expansion of royal conflict resolution into the areas yet uncovered by common law procedure. The Court of Chancery developed as a necessary complement to the common law and as such also constituted a counter-reaction to its stasis in the late Middle Ages.

43 See above chapter II, 1.3, especially fn. 10.

44 See especially *Case of Prohibitions* [1607] EWHC J23 (KB) and *Case of Proclamations* (1610) EWHC J22 (KB), which denied the king the role as an ultimate judge and held that the monarch could only create law through parliament.

45 See *D. E. C. Yale* in: D. E. C. Yale (ed.), Lord Nottingham's 'Manual of Chancery Practice' and 'Prolegomena of Chancery and Equity', Cambridge University Press, Cambridge, 1965, (repr. 1986), p. 7–8. The Court of Chancery, of course, withstood parliamentary attempts at an abolition during the revolutionary period.

46 *J. Fortescue*, in: S. Lockwood (ed.), On the Laws and Governance of England, Cambridge University Press, Cambridge, 1997, p. 17.

1.3.1 Bill

The first – and possibly most important – contribution of Chancery procedure to the development of the royal legal system was the systematic provision of a bill procedure for the opening of the process. While bills were exceptionally accepted first in the *curia regis*, then in Parliament and later also in common law courts,[47] the Court of Chancery finally provided an institutionalised non-writ procedure in a central court. This allowed plaintiffs to advance their claims irrespective of the pre-envisaged forms of action. The importance of this development should not be underestimated. It is true that litigants never lacked forums for conflict resolution. After all, ecclesiastical courts or local tribunals did not exhibit comparable access barriers as the common law.[48] However, the Court of Chancery provided all the additional advantages of the centralised royal machinery of justice – most importantly its authority and its enforcement mechanisms – without the earlier restrictions.

The writ procedure effectively guaranteed that the common law could merely resolve a finite number of specific conflict constellations. On the other hand, the opportunities for conflicts were endless – however familiar the underlying interests. This meant that a substantial share of conflicts in late medieval England remained outside the scope of royal adjudication.

The problem naturally grew larger the further societal conflicts differed from the times when the writ system originally developed. Facilitating the opening of a legal process in a royal court through formalised yet substantively open bills provided a way out of this dilemma. The bills allowed litigants to bring conflicts, which had not been reflected in the adjudication of the common law courts, into the system of royal adjudication through the Court of Chancery. They thereby represented a first step towards contingency, which has been characterised as a characteristic feature of modern Western legal systems:[49] When every kind of conflict constellation can be brought to the attention of the court, the development of procedural and substantive rules, which allow for adjudication, follows almost naturally.

The integration of all varieties of societal conflicts was further aided by the fact that the bills allowed for the presentation of both legal and factual

47 See *T. F. T. Plucknett*, A Concise History of the Common Law, Butterworth, London, 5th edition, 1956, p. 386–387; *J. H. Langbein / R. T. Lerner / B. P. Smith*, History of the Common Law – The Development of Anglo-American Legal Institutions, p. 105–111. An introduction to bill procedure in medieval England is provided above chapter II, 1.5.3.

48 For the opening of procedures in ecclesiastical courts under Roman-canon law procedure, see above chapter VI, 3.1.

49 *N. Luhmann*, Ausdifferenzierung des Rechts, esp. p. 200–210.

arguments.[50] In contrast to the common law, litigants were not required to draw artificial distinctions or to distort the factual circumstances in order to allow for classification under one or more of the existing writs. Instead, they could present the conflict as it emerged from their perspective. This must have substantially reduced the barriers of access to the royal courts – if only because it required less professional assistance.

Overall, the bill procedure thus represented a first step towards a comprehensive integration of societal conflicts into the royal legal system.

1.3.2 Further pleadings

The open process was also reflected in the exchange of documents between the parties in the Court of Chancery. In contrast to common law pleading, the litigants did not have to reduce the complexities of the case to a yes-or-no question that would be answerable by a jury.[51] Instead, both parties could introduce additional legal or factual arguments into the process, thus providing the court with an all-encompassing overview over the actual conflict situation. As outlined above, they were not even precluded from supplementing or varying their own arguments for the sake of truth-finding.[52] Chancery pleading therefore represented another incident of integration of factual and legal arguments into the legal process.

Naturally, the acceptance of cases in all their complexity comes with certain risks. Common law pleading – even considering all its flaws – was a highly professionalised mechanism to resolve complicated fact patterns into a binary yes-or-no question. The essentially unstructured Chancery process, which had not established a similar translation process, soon resulted in overly long and tedious litigation.[53]

1.3.3 Evidence

The lack of evidentiary restrictions in the late medieval Court of Chancery added another dimension to its integrative process. The parties were provided with the opportunity to introduce all available documents and witness statements into the process, thereby broadening the factual basis of the later decision.[54] Additionally, the examination under oath could extract relevant information, which

50 See above chapter V, 2.4.
51 See above chapter V, 3.1.
52 See chapter V, 3.2.4.
53 See above chapter II, 5.
54 See above chapter V, 4.

would have remained hidden from a common law court, from the knowledge of the defendants.[55] On the other hand, it potentially limited the freedom of the parties to shape the process according to their own wishes.

The integration of all the available evidence arguably facilitated a better representation of the actual facts underlying the case at trial. The conclusive number of available means of proof in different forms of action at common law could easily distort the image of the actual conflict at trial: Important facts could be barred form the legal process since evidence establishing them was inadmissible. Under these conditions, less important facts could then assume an undue importance for lack of other sources of information. This is not to say that the Chancery process of the 15th century struck the right balance when it came to the acceptance of proof. My examination of witness testimony has exposed a high degree of irrelevant information, which must have impeded decision-making in the court.[56] However, the Court of Chancery clearly broke the chains of the restrictive common law system of proof, even if it went potentially too far in facilitating integration.

1.3.4 Determination

All the facts and arguments presented during the course of the trial had to be processed by the court – the Lord Chancellor and his staff – for decision-making. This was certainly no easy task. Effectively, the court had to resolve what I have described as an overly complex process through a single act of judgment. Since the 15th century Chancery process up to this point provided no mechanisms for the reduction of the complexities of the case, the court was charged with what we might consider the ultimate act of integration: It had to translate the broad range of facts and arguments into a legal decision – a simple royal decree in favour of either the plaintiffs or the defendants. While the Court of Chancery provided a much broader scope of discretionary remedies than the common law courts,[57] decision-making still required differentiating important from unimportant facts, evaluating the validity of arguments and identifying the correct result. These tasks require the assistance of a professionalised staff. It is only logical that the judicial branch of Chancery became staffed with civil lawyers from the second half of the 15th century onwards.[58]

55 See above chapter V, 3.1.
56 See above chapter V, 4.1.3.
57 See above chapter V, 5.2.3.
58 *N. Pronay*, The Chancellor, the Chancery, and the Council at the End of the Fifteenth Century, in: H. Hearder/H. R. Loyn (eds.), British Government and Administration – Studies Presented to S. B. Chrimes, University of Wales Press, Cardiff, 1974, p. 87–103.

In contrast to the earlier stages of the process, decision-making in the Court of Chancery reflected a higher degree of professionalization than it did at common law, where laymen remained responsible for the final verdicts. This, however, brought with it a high concentration of power in the hands of the Lord Chancellor. From the perspective of the constitutional struggles between parliament and common lawyers on the one hand and the king and central administration on the other hand, the Court of Chancery arguably shifted the power over the legal process to the latter: The final decision-maker was, after all, the most prominent representative of the king. Even if we reject modern American interpretations of the jury as a democratic element in legal proceedings,[59] the Chancery process clearly exhibited a tendency towards centralisation – and in effect towards royal absolutism.[60]

1.4 Subjects of integration

Integration was not merely a theoretical possibility provided by the 15th century Chancery process. It was an actual development reflected in the cases. Chancery documentation offers an insight into numerous conflicts, which the common law process – adjusted to the needs of the first two centuries after the conquest – was unable to deal with. It suggests that it was a prime function of the Court of Chancery to bring adjudication in the royal courts in line with the realities of late medieval property and business requirements.[61]

A discussion of the societal and economic changes in late medieval England lies outside the scope of my study. Indeed, these developments – including their impact on the law – have already been researched intensively.[62] What I would like to do instead is to present a brief impression of how the most common classes of cases in the Court of Chancery were related to these changes.

59 The Seventh Amendment of the Constitution guarantees jury trial: "In Suits at common law, where the value in controversy shall exceed twenty dollars, the right of trial by jury shall be preserved, and no fact tried by a jury, shall be otherwise reexamined in any Court of the United States, than according to the rules of the common law." For an example of the literature, see *J. Abramson*, The Jury System and the Ideal of Democracy, Harvard University Press, Cambridge, Ma., 2001.

60 Compare *J. Getzler*, Patterns of Fusion, in: P. Birks (ed.), The Classification of Obligations, p. 157–192, p. 180.

61 For a critical view on this development from a contemporary perspective, see *K. Akuffo*, A Subaltern Theory of Equity, African Journal of International and Comparative Law, Volume 24 (2016), p. 12–44.

62 For a great exploration of societal changes and their impact on the law in late medieval England, see *R. C. Palmer*, English Law in the Age of the Black Death – A Transformation of Governance and Law, The University of North Carolina Press, Chapel Hill, NC, 1993.

1.4.1 Use

Maitland identified first regular incidents of a separation of legal title and the 'use' of property in England at the beginning of the 13th century.[63] Privileged Englishmen intending to devote parts of their property to Franciscan monks, who were forbidden to own any property themselves, ingeniously transferred land to the local community for the use of the friars.[64] That is not to say that problem or solution were distinctively English. The Franciscan poverty controversy occupied lawyers across Europe.[65] Either way, a regular use practice was established almost two centuries before the Court of Chancery came to adjudicate similar cases.

It has been suggested that the feoffment to uses became popular beyond the limited scope of monasteries during the middle of the 14th century.[66] The rationale for its growing popularity is indirectly related to the cases of the Franciscan friars. The use was employed to guarantee the enjoyment of property to groups of persons the common law failed to recognise.

It grew out of the understandable wish to dispose of land upon death.[67] Feudal law, reclining in its coherence and yet a lasting influence for centuries to come, foresaw that land passed upon the death of the title-holder under the rules of primogeniture.[68] The transfer was furthermore heavily taxed.[69] When land holding and military service were interdependent in the first centuries after the conquest, this arrangement was sensible. However, when military service as a condition for land holding was superseded by fiscal duties, it simply lost its rationale.

63 *F. Pollock / F. W. Maitland*, The History of English Law before the Time of Edward I, Cambridge University Press, Cambridge, Volume 2, 2nd edition reissue, 1968, p. 230–232. Similar constructs, however, had been in use from as early as the conquest, *ibid.*

64 *F. Pollock / F. W. Maitland*, The History of English Law before the Time of Edward I, Volume 2, p. 231.

65 For an introduction, see *V. Mäkinen*, Property Rights in the Late Medieval Discussion on Franciscan Property, Peeters, Leuven, 2001.

66 *R. H. Helmholz*, The Early Enforcement of Uses, Columbia Law Review, Volume 79 (1979), p. 1503–1513, p. 1503.

67 Compare *J. Biancalana*, Testamentary Cases in Fifteenth-Century Chancery, The Legal History Review, Volume 76 (2008), p. 283–306, p. 285; *J. H. Langbein / R. T. Lerner / B. P. Smith*, History of the Common Law – The Development of Anglo-American Legal Institutions, p. 304-306.

68 For an overview, see *T. F. T. Plucknett*, A Concise History of the Common Law, p. 527–530.

69 See *E. W. Ives*, The Genesis of the Statute of Uses, The English Historical Review, Volume 82 (1967), p. 673–697, p. 674; *J. H. Langbein / R. T. Lerner / B. P. Smith*, History of the Common Law – The Development of Anglo-American Legal Institutions, p. 304.

Title-holders, especially those without a son of age, took an active interest in transferring their land freely upon their death. Yet, that transfer was exclusively regulated by feudal law. Furthermore, the most common intended beneficiaries – wives, underage children or monasteries – could not hold the title at common law anyway.[70] The solution was essentially the same as in the case of the Franciscan monks, except that the local community was exchanged with friends and local dignitaries who acted as feoffees (later trustees). The use thus developed as a will substitute.[71]

Given its low prominence before the 14th century, however, the use had not been recognised by the medieval common law writ system.[72] Richard Helmholz has identified first incidents of the enforcement of uses in ecclesiastical courts.[73] He furthermore suggested that they might have acted as part of their auxiliary jurisdiction in cases of a failure of justice.[74] Either way, it was only a few decades later that the Court of Chancery offered the first systematic recognition of the use from a royal court.

The case of *White v White*[75] serves as a straight-forward example of an early use case from the reign of Henry IV. (1399–1413). The main facts have been summarised above.[76] Addressing the Court of Chancery, the plaintiff complained that the defendants, instead of honouring the agreement, took all the profits of the land. The plaintiff described a typical use or trust constellation and the alleged behaviour of the defendants accordingly constituted what we might call a breach of trust. Naturally, we do not know about the outcome of the trial

70 Compare *L. Holcombe*, Wives and Property – Reform of the Married Women's Property Law in Nineteenth-Century England, University of Toronto Press, Toronto, 1983, p. 18–36; the equitable approach is presented *ibid.*, p. 37–47; *S. F. C. Milsom*, Historical Foundations of the Common Law, Butterworths, London, 2nd edition, 1981, p. 86–87.

71 Also *E. W. Ives*, The Genesis of the Statute of Uses, The English Historical Review, Volume 82 (1967), p. 673–697, p. 673; *J. H. Langbein / R. T. Lerner / B. P. Smith*, History of the Common Law – The Development of Anglo-American Legal Institutions, p. 304.

72 *F. Pollock / F. W. Maitland*, The History of English Law before the Time of Edward I, Volume 2, p. 232.

73 *R. H. Helmholz*, The Early Enforcement of Uses, Columbia Law Review, Volume 79 (1979), p. 1503–1513.

74 *R. H. Helmholz*, The Early Enforcement of Uses, Columbia Law Review, Volume 79 (1979), p. 1503–1513, p. 1507–1508. It has been suggested above chapter V, 2.5.7 that the late medieval Court of Chancery, just like the ecclesiastical courts, might have reserved jurisdiction for failures of justice.

75 (1399–1413) Select Cases, S. 95.

76 See 1.2.1.

but similar cases soon became numerous,[77] suggesting the protection of uses by the Court of Chancery at this early stage. The societal interest in disposing of property upon death was thus recognised for the first time in a royal court.

1.4.2 Contract

The protracted legal regime for the exchange of goods in late medieval common law has been referred to above.[78] The actions of debt and covenant provided the framework within which promises could be enforced in common law courts.[79] Both forms effectively offered little more than an enforcement mechanism for the parties' written obligations. They did not impose mutual duties and thus acknowledge the underlying exchange relationship. Both actions furthermore required compliance with strict formalities, usually including proof of the existence of a sealed deed.[80]

This regime was quickly stretched to its limits when commercial exchange expanded beyond the narrow scope of the upper and higher middle classes.[81] It goes without saying that the production of sealed deeds enforceable in common law courts demanded experience or the involvement of lawyers. As a result of the urbanisation following the Black Death and the dissolution of many master and serf relationships in the middle of the 14th century, more and more members of lower classes became dependant upon the exchange of goods for sustaining themselves in the growing cities.[82] They could hardly be expected to safeguard their everyday exchanges by the costly and time-consuming formalities required by common law.

77 Compare for example *Groos v Depeham* (1454–1455), Calendars I, p. xlviii; *Fitz Harry v Lyngeyn* (1454–1455), Calendars I, p. xlviii; *Duke of Gloucester v Bishop of Ely* (1472–1473), Calendars I, p. xc; *Neville v Osborn* (1473), Calendars I, p. xciv; *Tryppe v Chevyn* (1484), Calendars I, p. cxvi.

78 See for example chapter V, 4.2.3 and 1.2.1 in this chapter.

79 For an introduction to medieval contract substitutes and a characterisation of further developments, see *A. W. B. Simpson*, A History of the Common Law of Contract – The Rise of the Action of Assumpsit, Clarendon Press, Oxford, 1975, p. 3–196.

80 *A. W. B. Simpson*, A History of the Common Law of Contract – The Rise of the Action of Assumpsit, p. 10–13, 73. A writ of debt did not formally require a sealed instrument. The plaintiff, however, would have been challenged to prove the existence of a debt in absence of written evidence.

81 Compare *R. C. Palmer*, English Law in the Age of the Black Death – A Transformation of Governance and Law, p. 5, especially fn. 15.

82 Compare *J. H. Langbein / R. T. Lerner / B. P. Smith*, History of the Common Law – The Development of Anglo-American Legal Institutions, p. 227.

Additionally, even within the scope of application of the common law actions, tensions arose. The inflexible obligations did not contemplate cases of fraud. For example, parties could demand renewed payment or delivery in the absence of a formal acquittance and deny the existence of any condition not stipulated in writing.[83] The greater the variety of exchange relationships, the more difficult it was to hold the other party to account for such fraudulent behaviour without the aid of a legal action (i. e. by a boycott).

The ecclesiastical courts provided some legal protection for exchange relationships outside of the scope of the common law by enforcing parole contracts – at least those entered into upon oath.[84] Overall, however, English courts and tribunals were unfit to deal with the demands of a society increasingly built upon exchange relationships.[85] The Court of Chancery not only accepted these 'contract' cases for adjudication. It also offered a procedure well suited to the private character of many everyday exchanges. Like the ecclesiastical courts, the Court of Chancery examined the defendant under oath.[86] It could thereby, at least potentially, overcome the evidentiary difficulties, which were responsible for the strict stance of the common law courts.

The late 14th century case of *Brampton v Seymour*[87] provides an early example of a case, in which the Court of Chancery was petitioned over a contract case. The plaintiff reported that he had met the defendant for the exchange of the latter's payment against a written relief from his obligations. He then alleged that he had been deceived to pass over the relief in the expectation of payment. The defendant, however, disappeared with the written relief and refused to honour his obligations. An action at common law was precluded by the formal acquittance in the hands of the defendants; the plaintiff thus turned to the Court of Chancery.

While we cannot know about the outcome of this early case, Year Book reports from the second half of the 15th century prove that the Court of Chancery by this time enforced promises in the absence of sealed deeds[88] and

83 The topic has been addressed above chapter V, 4.2.3. Reference can again be made to our exemplary case of *Ardern v Ardern* (1465/1466), Calendars I, p. lxxii and to T.F.T. Plucknett/J.L. Barton (eds.), St. German's Doctor and Student, p. 77–79. See also *S.F.C. Milsom*, Historical Foundations of the Common Law, p. 86.

84 *R.H. Helmholz*, The Oxford History of the Laws of England, Volume 1: The Canon Law and Ecclesiastical Jurisdiction from 567 to the 1640s, Oxford University Press, Oxford, 2004, p-358–368.

85 Compare *R.C. Palmer*, English Law in the Age of the Black Death – A Transformation of Governance and Law, p. 5.

86 See above chapter VI, 3.2.1.

87 (1386) Select Cases, p. 2.

88 (1468), Y. B. 8 Edw. IV, Pasch., pl. 11, f. 4.

relieved from the obligation to double payment in the absence of a formal acquittance.[89] The court thereby responded to a societal need for a less formal and manipulable contract law.

1.4.3 Merchants' law

The growing importance of the exchange economy also led to an increased presence of foreign merchants in England.[90] The developing merchant community of the late Middle Ages and the normative framework, in which it operated, have been the object of numerous studies.[91] In this context, it should suffice to draw out the specific role of the Court of Chancery in regulating this community.

Chancery documentation from the 15th century provides ample evidence of Spanish,[92] Dutch[93] or Italian[94] merchants appealing to the Court of Chancery. What characterises their petitions is a sense of precariousness in a foreign legal system. The case of *Damico v Burdican*,[95] presented in greater detail above,[96] is

89 (1482), Y. B. 22 Edw. IV, Pasch., pl. 18, f. 6.

90 The role of the mercantile community in the growth of the Court of Chancery was especially emphasised by *J. A. Guy*, The Development of Equitable Jurisdictions, 1450–1550, in: E. W. Ives/A. H. Manchester (eds.), Law, Litigants, and the Legal Profession, Royal Historical Society, London, 1983, p. 80–86, p. 82; *M. Beilby*, The Profits of Expertise: The Rise of the Civil Lawyers in Chancery Equity, in: M. Hicks (ed.), Profit, Piety and the Professions in Later Medieval England, Sutton, Gloucester, 1990, p. 72–90, p. 78.

91 That is not to say that a clear consensus on the form and contents of this normative framework has emerged. A classical introduction was provided by *H. J. Berman*, Law and Revolution – The Formation of the Western Legal Tradition, Harvard University Press, Cambridge, Ma., 1983, p. 333–356. For critical assessments of the classical view, which also reference earlier works on the subject, see *A. Cordes*, Auf der Suche nach der Rechtswirklichkeit der mittelalterlichen Lex mercatoria, Zeitschrift der Savigny-Stiftung für Rechtsgeschichte – Germanistische Abteilung, Volume 118 (2001), p. 168–184 (for an English version see: *A. Cordes*, The search for a medieval Lex mercatoria, in: V. Piergiovanni (ed.), From lex mercatoria to commercial law, Duncker & Humblot, Berlin, 2005, p. 53–68); *E. Kadens*, Order within Law, Variety within Custom: The Character of the Medieval Merchant Law, Chicago Journal of International Law, Volume 5 (2004), p. 39–65. For a closer examination of the regulatory framework in England, see *F. Eichler*, Lex Mercatoria – das englische Marktrecht des Mittelalters, Mauke, Hamburg, 2008.

92 See *de Castro v Narbone* (1474–1480), Calendars I, p. ci.

93 See *le Leche v Courtney* (1474–1480), Calendars I, p. civ.

94 See *Damico v Burdican* (1474–1480), Calendars I, p. ciii; *Giglis v Welby* (1491–1492), Calendars I, p. ccxx.

95 (1474–1480), Calendars I, p. ciii.

96 See chapter V, 2.4.2.

especially illustrative. The plaintiff, an Italian weaver, sought protection from the Court of Chancery against his imprisonment on what he perceived to be forged allegations. He explicitly referred to the difficulty of defending himself at common law and of raising bail in the absence of local contacts.

In the event of legal disputes in domestic courts, the foreign merchants seemingly sought the help of what they considered an unbiased institution in the face of a common law, which, from the outside, appeared inscrutable and potentially prejudiced towards foreigners. The Court of Chancery must have looked like the ideal answer to their pleas. Chancery as a governmental department was responsible for diplomatic relations and as such not only approachable in Latin but also aware of the interests of the foreign community in England.[97] Furthermore, the procedure administered in the Court of Chancery exhibited – as shown above[98] – many similarities to the Roman-canon law procedure continental merchants were familiar with. Whether the court at this stage also administered a substantive law in line with the general usages of merchants must again remain open.

The role of the Court of Chancery in cases involving foreign merchants was guaranteed by statutes from the 14th and 15th century establishing a supervisory jurisdiction over staple towns – largely autonomous aggregations of foreign merchants in London or other cities[99] – and designating the Lord Chancellor the official protector of foreigners.[100] It remains unclear whether the statutes merely codified existing practices or actively caused the influx of foreign merchants into the court.

All this has led J. A. Guy to the conclusion that the rise of the Court of Chancery in the second half of the 15th century must be understood as a "response to the needs of the Yorkist mercantile community".[101] Given the variety of cases, this statement might be considered an exaggeration. Never-

97 Compare *N. Pronay*, The Chancellor, the Chancery, and the Council at the End of the Fifteenth Century, in: H. Hearder / H. R. Loyn (eds.), British Government and Administration – Studies Presented to S. B. Chrimes, University of Wales Press, Cardiff, 1974, p. 87–103, S. 96.

98 See chapter VI.

99 For an early introduction, see *S. Brodhurst*, The Merchants of the Staple, Law Quarterly Review, Volume 17 (1901), p. 56–76.

100 Most notably in the Statute of the Staple 1353, 27 Edw. III. For a summary of the Lord Chancellor's role in relation to foreign merchants, see *N. Pronay*, The Chancellor, the Chancery, and the Council at the End of the Fifteenth Century, in: H. Hearder / H. R. Loyn (eds.), British Government and Administration – Studies Presented to S. B. Chrimes, p. 87–103, S. 96.

101 *J. A. Guy*, The Development of Equitable Jurisdictions, 1450–1550, in: E. W. Ives / A. H. Manchester (eds.), Law, Litigants, and the Legal Profession, p. 80–86, p. 82.

theless, the role of foreign merchants reflects another incident of the integration of existing societal interests into the royal legal system by the Court of Chancery.

1.5 Conclusion

Both the theory and the practice evidenced by the sources suggest that the late medieval Court of Chancery acted as an integrative force between life and law.

By opening up the legal process through the different stages of procedure and leaving behind the restrictive formality characteristic of contemporary common law, the Court of Chancery allowed the complexities of everyday life into the royal legal system. It thus greatly expanded the scope of the central legal system.

On the other hand, it is certainly arguable that, in its early phase, the court failed to recognise the advantages of the formalised common law system and went too far in embracing informality. The effectively limitless opportunities for informational input crippled the Chancery process in later centuries and made further reforms a necessity. Both common law and Chancery procedure still had a long a way to go before approximating an 'adequate complexity' – a state in which information from the outside is processed effectively within the legal system.[102]

The findings confirm the precaution I have advocated towards the use of the term 'equity' in relation to the late medieval Court of Chancery.[103] Equity naturally establishes certain connotations: if not about general considerations of justice, then about the Aristotelian and Scholastic concept or even about St. German's English approximation.[104] I do not want to belittle the potential influence of such substantive considerations on the actual decision-making of the Court of Chancery – especially not for the early modern period.[105] However, my examination of the surviving sources has clearly shown that the evidence from the first centuries of the court mandates a focus on its procedure. Speculations on the admittedly fascinating topic of substantive equity in the

102 *N. Luhmann*, Ausdifferenzierung des Rechts, p. 388, proposed that a legal system was just when it reflected an 'adequate complexity'.

103 See above chapter I.

104 A classical account, which stresses the substantive role of equity and downplays the role of procedure is provided by *P. A. Ryan*, Equity: System or Process?, The Catholoc Lawyer, Volume 3 (1957), p. 59–66. For a short introduction to the substantive content of equity, see again *D. Klinck*, Conscience, Equity and the Court of Chancery in Early Modern England, p. 46–50.

105 For the role of conscience in the early modern Court of Chancery, see *D. Klinck*, Conscience, Equity and the Court of Chancery in Early Modern England, especially p. 62–67; 80–88.

late medieval Court of Chancery risk overlooking the great procedural innovations at the heart of the early Court of Chancery.

Interestingly, sociological literature on law has often charged the term equity with an additional (yet related) meaning. In the context of this scholarship, equity is a common stage in the evolution of a legal system towards modernity. In contrast to this branch of scholarship, I do not wish to make claims beyond the English situation in the late Middle Ages. However, a brief introduction to two eminent proponents of this strand of thought from two centuries – Henry S. Maine and Niklas Luhmann – will show that such an understanding of equity comes much closer to the integration function I have identified above.

In his evolutionary theory of the law, which mainly builds upon experience and knowledge of Roman, Indian and English law, Maine advanced the thesis that "social opinions and social necessities are always more or less in advance of Law"[106] – a statement in line with my characterisation of late medieval English society and the common law. Advocating that the happiness of the people depended on the promptitude "by which Law is brought into harmony with society",[107] Maine identified three typical instruments for this harmonisation in their historical order: legal fictions, equity and legislation.[108] The severity of an archaic and formulaic law is thus lessened by equity, which allows a closer integration of law and society.

Similarly, Niklas Luhmann characterised equity as an ancient facilitator of legal change in systems, which are generally adverse to change.[109] In his view, equity served as a tool for the integration of extra-legal – most notably religious – expectations of normativity into the legal system in societies, which did not yet clearly differentiate between law, religion and morality. In line with Maine's argument, Luhmann considered equity a pre-modern predecessor of a differentiated system of laws, which has translated moral judgments into legislation.[110]

The integrative function of the Court of Chancery, which I have identified above, is generally in line with these sociological accounts of the role of equity in the modernization of the law. Both Maine's and Luhmann's explanations, however, remain solely theoretical and lack empirical evidence. Given the ambition of their respective projects, the authors surely cannot be faulted for this omission. However, the lack of empirical evidence also obscures what Maine

106 *H. S. Maine*, Ancient Law, p. 24.
107 *H. S. Maine*, Ancient Law, p. 25.
108 Compare *H. S. Maine*, Ancient Law, p. 25.
109 Compare *N. Luhmann*, Ausdifferenzierung des Rechts, p. 25.
110 See *N. Luhmann*, Das Recht der Gesellschaft, Suhrkamp, Frankfurt / Main, 1991, p. 228.

and Luhmann actually meant by equity. Maine merely suggested that equity reflected a system of "distinct principles" claiming a "superior sanctity",[111] whereas Luhmann seems to have characterised equity as an entrance gate for moral considerations.[112]

What I hope to have shown through my examination of the 15th century cases is that the integration of societal interests – contemporary morality included – depended on the provision of an open procedure. My examination of contemporary documentation thus shows how exactly the Court of Chancery could become an 'entrance gate' for a modernization of the English legal system.

Following these findings, it also becomes clear that the equity theses advanced by Maine and Luhmann do not do justice to the lasting modernising impact of the Court of Chancery. The decisive innovation of the court – its integrative procedure – remains a vital part of a modern legal system up to this day. In contrast to the substantive equity that was characterised by St. German and that Maine and Luhmann might have had in mind, it was in no way superseded by legislation but rather remains a necessary instrument for the integration of life and law in modern legal systems.

2. Legitimacy

The role of the late medieval Court of Chancery was not limited to integration. In the following, I will argue that the court also provided an added legitimacy to the developing royal legal system. The use of the term legitimacy might require further explanation. Indeed, the characteristics of a legal process that I aim to identify below are more commonly discussed under the subjects of justice[113] or even equity.[114] The use of these terms, however, can easily create the expectation

111 *H. S. Maine*, Ancient Law, p. 28.

112 Compare *N. Luhmann*, Das Recht der Gesellschaft, p. 228.

113 This is especially true for the procedural dimension of my following examination. The defining research on this issue commonly employs the term 'procedural justice'. For an introduction, see *E. A. Lind / T. R. Tyler*, The Social Psychology of Procedural Justice, Plenum Press, New York, NY, 1988; *K. F. Röhl*, Verfahrensgerechtigkeit (Procedural Justice), Zeitschrift für Rechtssoziologie, Volume 14 (1993), p. 1–34.

114 This is the case in the defining study of *G. S. Leventhal*, What Should Be Done with Equity Theory? New Approaches to the Study of Fairness in Social Relationships, in K. J. Gergen / M. S. Greenberg / R. H. Willis (eds.), Social Exchange – Advances in Theory and Research, Plenum Press, New York, NY, 1980, p. 27–55. In this context, equity is defined as "justice based on merit or contributions", *ibid.* p. 29 – a definition, which is clearly of limited help in our search for the correct understanding of equity in relation to the late medieval Court of Chancery.

of an evaluation of the legal system upon certain external – and typically metaphysical – standards.[115] The examination of the 15th century documentation has shown the futility of such an undertaking. What the sources can tell us is how the Court of Chancery was perceived by the litigants and why they sought its help for conflict resolution. This evidence can be considered the key to the increase in litigation and the following rise in status. Understood in this way, legitimacy is not measured by conformity with objective standards but with the individual expectations of actual or potential litigants.

Following this definition, it seems possible to distinguish two dimensions of the legitimacy of the legal process in the eyes of litigants.[116] The first dimension is result-orientated. It thus focuses on the outcome of the legal process. This substantive legitimacy might be evaluated by an "individual's belief that it is fair and appropriate when rewards, punishments, or resources are distributed in accordance with certain criteria".[117] Naturally, discussing legitimacy from this perspective requires some knowledge of the substantive rules underlying adjudication. Given our limited knowledge of the late medieval Court of Chancery, the insights offered by such an approach must remain limited.

The second dimension, on the other hand, is input-oriented. It focuses on the capacity of the legal process to provide mutually acceptable standards for conflict resolution, irrespective of the later outcome. From this perspective, the legal process is evaluated by an "individual's belief that allocative procedures which satisfy certain criteria are fair and appropriate".[118] This requires knowledge of the procedural rules governing adjudication. These, of course, are the rules, which have been identified above. As the further discussion will show, the procedural elements providing legitimacy largely correspond with those facilitating integration. Effectively, integration and legitimacy could be understood as two sides of the same coin: Integrating societal realities into the legal system might have raised its legitimacy, while procedures, which were conceived as legitimate might have encouraged integration through litigation in the Court of Chancery.

115 This is well-reflected in the litarature on moral theology in the Court of Chancery. An overview is presented above chapter III, 4.

116 *G. S. Leventhal*, What Should Be Done with Equity Theory? New Approaches to the Study of Fairness in Social Relationships, in K. J. Gergen / M. S. Greenberg / R. H. Willis (eds.), Social Exchange – Advances in Theory and Research, p. 27–55, p. 30.

117 *G. S. Leventhal*, What Should Be Done with Equity Theory? New Approaches to the Study of Fairness in Social Relationships, in K. J. Gergen / M. S. Greenberg / R. H. Willis (eds.), Social Exchange – Advances in Theory and Research, p. 27–55, p. 30, speaks of a "distribution rule".

118 *G. S. Leventhal*, What Should Be Done with Equity Theory? New Approaches to the Study of Fairness in Social Relationships, in K. J. Gergen / M. S. Greenberg / R. H. Willis (eds.), Social Exchange – Advances in Theory and Research, p. 27–55, p. 30, speaks of a "procedural rule".

2.1 Outcome-oriented legitimacy

It might be considered a necessary requirement for the functioning of a legal system that its outcomes conform with basic expectations of fairness. Indeed, it is hardly conceivable that the increasing demand for litigation in the 15th century Court of Chancery was not also related to the expectation that the outcome of its adjudication conformed to certain substantive principles.

However, it nevertheless remains extremely difficult to characterise – let alone generalise – the substantive expectations of the litigants. Did they simply trust the court to share their innate suspicions of what is right and what is wrong? Maybe that superficial description is closer to the truth than we might initially believe. After all, a similar understanding is reflected in the central importance of *synderesis* – that "natural power or motive force of the rational soul" that is "moving and steering [the person] to good & abhorring evil"[119] – in St. German's 16th century theory of justice. In our modern individualised societies, following such 'instincts' in adjudication sounds like a recipe for tyranny. In pre-Reformation thought, however, the collective belief was that these 'instincts' were universal – at least with regard to the dominant religious community.[120]

When evaluating the legitimacy of the results of the legal process today, we commonly examine either only its internal coherence or also its conformity with external standards of justice – whether we call these universal human rights or natural law.[121] Internal coherence was illusory under the fragmented legal regime of the late Middle Ages.[122] Conformity with standards of a higher law, on the other hand, was a central question of scholarly discussions of the law.[123] What the documentation of the Court of Chancery suggests is that it was also a central question in the regular litigation of a secular court. The centrality of conscience in Chancery adjudication has been discussed equally thoroughly as the fact that conscience was understood objectively.[124] Litigants clearly stressed and relied on conscience in their bills, the court presented itself as a court of conscience in its hearings and everyone considered conscience an objective standard.[125] A first look suggests a perfect congruence of expectations and reality, which in turn promises a high degree of outcome-oriented legitimacy.

119 T. F. T. Plucknett / J. L. Barton (eds.), St. German's Doctor and Student, p. 81.

120 Compare *D. Klinck*, Conscience, Equity and the Court of Chancery in Early Modern England, p. 17.

121 *K. F. Röhl*, Verfahrensgerechtigkeit (Procedural Justice), Zeitschrift für Rechtssoziologie, Volume 14 (1993), p. 1–34, p. 6.

122 Compare above chapter II, 1.1.

123 Once more, the English discussion is best reflected in T. F. T. Plucknett / J. L. Barton (eds.), St. German's Doctor and Student.

124 See above chapter V, 2.7.

125 See above chapter V, 2.7.

Yet, experience tells us that two parties often use the same term, while talking about completely different things. What did litigants expect concretely and were their expectations commonly fulfilled? The appeal to conscience was a common feature of almost all Chancery bills as was the plea to the Lord Chancellor to decide "for the love of God and in the way of charity".[126] This, however, does not mean that the plaintiffs necessarily had a clear notion of what conscience would mean in all circumstances. The bills do not reflect a deduction from first principles but rather argumentation around concrete facts.[127]

From the style of argumentation in the bills and from the professional background of the (common) lawyers involved in Chancery adjudication, it seems highly unlikely that litigants were immediately aware of the confessional literature that could have provided a template for the application of the concept of conscience to everyday conflict constellations.[128] The bills present no evidence of direct citations and their concise style left no room for scholastic arguments.[129] The continuous invocation of conscience nevertheless must have carried outcome-oriented expectations. At the very least, it seems to have conveyed the trust that the court generally shared the litigants' moral values and that these values guided decision-making. Even though we cannot identify direct evidence of the court following confessional literature either, that trust seems justified. Both the civilian-trained staff and the Lord Chancellor with his religious background must have had a basic knowledge of confessional literature.[130] Whether this was actively employed for decision-making or merely represented background knowledge that influenced their discretionary rulings remains unclear but the court certainly tried to provide the impression of adjudicating to the demands of conscience.[131]

126 See above chapter V, 2.7.

127 See above chapter V, 2.7.1.

128 For an introduction to the contemporary confessional literature with further references, see for example *O. I Langholm*, The Merchants in the Confessional – Trade and Price in the Pre-Reformation Penitential Handbooks, Brill, Leiden 2003; *J. Goering*, The Internal Forum and the Literature of Penance and Confession, Traditio, Volume 50 (2004), p. 175–227; *W. Decock*, Moral Theologians and Contract Law – The Moral Transformation of the Ius Commune, Martinus Nijhoff, Leiden, 2013, especially p. 44.

129 See above chapter V, 2.4.1 and chapter V, 1.1.

130 For the professional background of Chancery clerks, see *N. Pronay*, The Chancellor, the Chancery, and the Council at the End of the Fifteenth Century, in: H. Hearder/H.R. Loyn (eds.), British Government and Administration – Studies Presented to S.B. Chrimes, p. 87–103; *M. Beilby*, The Profits of Expertise: The Rise of the Civil Lawyers in Chancery Equity, in: M. Hicks (ed.), Profit, Piety and the Professions in Later Medieval England, p. 72–90.

131 See above chapter V, 2.7.2.

In order to ascertain whether the late medieval Court of Chancery provided an added outcome-oriented legitimacy to the royal legal system, a comparative look at the contemporary common law is in order. The characteristics of the common law identified above – conservatism and formality[132]– suggest a lack of recognition of outcome-oriented expectations.

The actual perception of the common law, however, might have been mitigated by other factors: Most importantly, litigants seem to have accepted the limited scope of the common law. In the Chancery bills, a lack of common law jurisdiction was presented as a simple fact rather than an injustice in itself.[133] The availability of alternative local and ecclesiastical jurisdictions as well as of the limited bill procedure might have lessened the impact of the limitations of the common law. Additionally, the common law provided basic stability. While it could not guarantee equal treatment, it provided equal rules for conflict resolution.[134] This was clearly an outcome-oriented achievement in the conflicted legal landscape of the late Middle Ages. After judgment, the decisions of the courts were also regularly enforced.[135] The common law thus offered a security largely unheard of in other jurisdictions. Indeed, contemporary literature suggests that insiders at least felt a certain pride in the provision of a functioning legal system.[136]

This mild look at the outcome-oriented legitimacy of the common law courts is supported by contemporary theorisations of the secular jurisdiction. Theologians commonly assumed that man-made laws not violating natural law were legitimate and indeed necessary for the functioning of society.[137] Much common law litigation focused on property, which was considered in need of secular regulation.[138] It should be remembered that the questions of outcome-oriented legitimacy of the common law prompted St. German to write *Doctor and Student*.[139] His judgment was clear: The common law largely conformed to

132 See 1.2.1.

133 Compare above chapter V, 2.5.1.

134 See above 1.2.

135 *J. H. Baker*, An Introduction to English Legal History, Butterworths, London, 4th edition, 2002, p. 66–67, described the standard instruments for enforcement at common law.

136 *J. Fortescue*, in: S. Lockwood (ed.), On the Laws and Governance of England, p. 38, at the very least, asked the apparently rhetorical question: "Now, is not this procedure for revealing the truth better and more effective than the process which the civil laws devise?" (ca. 1470).

137 Compare *J. L. Barton*, Introduction, in: T. F.T. Plucknett / J. L. Barton (eds.), St. German's Doctor and Student, p. xxv, with reference to St. German's primary inspiration *J. Gerson*.

138 T. F.T. Plucknett / J. L. Barton (eds.), St. German's Doctor and Student, p. 19.

139 See above chapter V, 2.7.4.

the requirements of natural law and conscience. Its strict application merely gave rise to a number of hardships, which required the existence of a separate jurisdiction in conscience.[140] As a common lawyer himself, St. German might be considered a natural apologist of the jurisdiction. Yet, the evidence of a general dissatisfaction with the outcomes of the common law is scant. It rather left space for improvement, which the Court of Chancery, with its emphasis on conscience, was able to fill.

2.2 Input-oriented legitimacy

The second dimension of legitimacy addresses the serving function of procedure for a fair trial. It is not immediately concerned with procedures for allocation (for example each party receives half)[141] but merely with those procedures leading towards decision-making. In the last decades, these topics have commonly been discussed under the headline 'procedural justice'.[142] The idea that procedural justice might provide legitimacy rests on an important assumption: If the procedure regulating a process is seen as fair, its outcomes will likely be accepted, even if it they are disadvantageous to one of the parties.[143]

Literature on procedural justice often alleges a direct correlation between an emphasis on procedural justice and the absence of standards for substantive justice within a legal process:[144] When the outcome of a conflict is hardly regulated by substantive rules, procedural rules gain additional importance. Evidence of this can be found in medieval common law as well as in modern constitutional law.[145]

140 *J. L. Barton*, Introduction, in: T. F.T. Plucknett / J. L. Barton (eds.), St. German's Doctor and Student, p. xlvi-xlvii, arrived at the same conclusion.

141 Compare *K. F. Röhl*, Verfahrensgerechtigkeit (Procedural Justice), Zeitschrift für Rechtssoziologie, Volume 14 (1993), p. 1–34, p. 6.

142 For introductory literature, see above fn. 990.

143 *G. S. Leventhal*, What Should Be Done with Equity Theory? New Approaches to the Study of Fairness in Social Relationships, in K. J. Gergen / M. S. Greenberg / R. H. Willis (eds.), Social Exchange – Advances in Theory and Research, p. 27–55, p. 36.

144 This thesis has been called 'substitution theory (Substitutionstheorie)' by *K. F. Röhl*, Verfahrensgerechtigkeit (Procedural Justice), Zeitschrift für Rechtssoziologie, Volume 14 (1993), p. 1–34, p. 17.

145 For the absence of clearly identifiable substantive elements in medieval common law, compare for example *J. H. Baker*, An Introduction to English Legal History, p. 53. The growing importance of procedural considerations in elements of modern constitutional law can be seen in the expanding jurisprudence of the European Court of Human Rights on Art. 6 of the European Convention on Human Rights. It might also be worth remembering that much of modern

In the Court of Chancery, the absence of identifiable substantive rules is hardly correlating with detailed procedural rules. As we have seen, late medieval Chancery procedure was actually unregulated to a fault.[146] However, a slight modification of the aforementioned thesis might be helpful for the further evaluation of the court: The lack of substance might have been remedied with additional opportunities for participation.

In order to provide a clearer image of the participative opportunities provided by Chancery procedure, I will quickly revisit the different stages of procedure.

The thesis underlying my argumentation is simple: Procedure dominated the late medieval Chancery process; by offering numerous opportunities to be heard and to enter into regulated discussions about the conflict, it added legitimacy to the complete process.

2.2.1 *Bill*

The bill procedure provided the plaintiffs with the opportunity to present their hardships in an open forum, which represented the authority of the king. It guaranteed that their legal and factual arguments were at least acknowledged in their entirety. In contrast to the technical writ purchase, which initiated proceedings at common law, the bill left room for the address of perceived individual injustices. This is even reflected in the wording of the bills: The self-portrayal as 'poor servants' might hardly have reflected the economical realities of most plaintiffs in the court, yet it underlines the expectation that personal struggles can be addressed in front of the court.[147] Another typical feature of Chancery bills again reveals the central importance of procedure: Instead of asking for concrete remedies, the plaintiffs commonly appealed for a subpoena that ordered the defendants to answer.[148] While this appeal soon became a mere formality, it might first have expressed and then symbolised the plaintiffs' trust that an examination of the defendant in front of the court will result in justice.

2.2.2 *Further pleadings*

The answer provided the defendants with the opportunity to be heard. Being examined under oath might have put them under considerable pressure. On the other hand, however, it also constituted the clearest possible evidence that their

American constitutional law is built upon the originally procedural concept of 'due process'.

146 See for example above chapter V, 4.1.3.

147 See above chapter V, 2.3.

148 See above chapter V, 2.6.1.

testimony was taken seriously. The defendants thus either literally had their 'day in court' or at least a great responsibility in preparing the (written) answer.[149] The fact that they could not only respond to the allegations but were also free to present their own version of the events must have contributed to a favourable impression of the process. Replication and rejoinder even provided the litigants with the opportunity to adjust their initial arguments in reaction to the other parties' statements.[150] A comparison to the common law, where the pleading process was dominated by technicalities argued between lawyers,[151] suggests that the parties had a stronger influence on the process, which should have increased its legitimacy.

2.2.3 Evidence

Few elements of a legal process provide more potential for frustration than the inability to prove an (allegedly) justified claim. Naturally, that risk also existed in the Court of Chancery. In contrast to the strict common law system of proofs,[152] however, the inability to prove a case was not an inherent feature of the jurisdiction. As explained above, the medieval Court of Chancery provided low barriers for the introduction of evidence.[153] It thus offered the parties with the opportunity to present the full range of evidence they considered relevant.[154] The frustration of being subjected to irrelevant evidence from the other party might have undermined the legitimacy of the court from the other party's perspective. It certainly complicated Chancery proceedings to a worrisome degree.[155] Yet, the advantages of the openness for evidence might have outweighed the potential dangers in the eyes of the litigants.

2.2.4 Determination

When looking at the participative dimension at the final stages of the Chancery process, it is important to not only consider judgments but also extra-judicial conflict resolution. I have illustrated the large share of settlements and identified elements of Chancery procedure conducive to such outcomes.[156] A negotiated

149 Compare above chapter V, 3.1, introduction.
150 See above chapter V, 3.2, especially 3.2.4.
151 See above chapter V, 3.1.7.
152 See above chapter V, 4.
153 See above chapter V, 4.
154 The evidence from the sources suggests that parties focused on documents and witness testimony in making their case, see above chapter V, 4.
155 See above chapter V, 4.1.3.
156 See above chapter V, 5.1.

settlement usually falls short of the expectations of either party but the agreement guarantees the acceptance of the final result. This might be considered the ideal representation of procedural input from the parties generating legitimacy.

In the event of the case going to a formal judgment, the contributions of the respective parties to the process ended with the final hearing. In this way, Chancery procedure resembled common law procedure.[157] However, the parties' efforts in argumentation suggest some trust in the rational decision-making capabilities of the trained Chancery staff, which was supposed to build upon the arguments presented at trial by the parties themselves. The decision-making process was thus not entirely removed from the parties' sphere of influence. This can be contrasted with the image of corrupted or compromised juries conveyed by some bills.[158]

2.2.5 *Adversarial structure*

Empirical research on procedural justice in our time has consistently shown that greater party control over the legal process increases the perception of fairness.[159] Several early studies on procedural justice have developed this finding into the hypothesis that adversarial models of trial were preferable to inquisitorial models.[160] The look at the late medieval Court of Chancery reinforces the former finding while further undermining the latter hypothesis. By traditional standards, the Court of Chancery showed more elements of inquisitorial adjudication than the common law.[161] Not only did it exhibit numerous features of continental inquisitorial procedure, it also provided the judge with

157 For parallels between the final hearings at common law and in the Court of Chancery, see above chapter V, 5.2.1.5.

158 Of course, plaintiffs in the Court of Chancery had a specific interest in conveying this image. After all, they sought access to the Court of Chancery in cases of established common law jurisdiction.

159 *G. S. Leventhal*, What Should Be Done with Equity Theory? New Approaches to the Study of Fairness in Social Relationships, in K. J. Gergen / M. S. Greenberg / R. H. Willis (eds.), Social Exchange – Advances in Theory and Research, p. 27–55, p. 36.

160 See for example *J. Thibaut / L. Walker*, Procedural Justice: A Psychological Analysis, Laurence Erlbaum Associates, Hillsdale, NJ, 1975; *E. A. Lind / B. E. Erickson / N. Friedland / M. Dickenberger*, Reactions to Procedural Models for Adjudicative Conflict Resolution – A Cross-National Study, Journal of Conflict Resolution, Volume 22 (1978), p. 318–339.

161 The distinction between an 'adversarial' common law and an 'inquisitorial' Chancery procedure can for example be found in *A. D. Kessler*, Our Inquisitorial Tradition: Equity Procedure, Due Process and the Search for an Alternative to the Adversarial, Cornell Law Review, Volume 90 (2005), p. 1181–1275.

broad discretionary powers: As such, he could theoretically entertain his own investigations. Factually, however, the parties were granted extensive freedoms in conducting the trial. Their control over the process was thus not significantly lower than it was under the 'adversarial' common law.[162]

2.2.6 *Comparative evaluation*

In one of the defining studies on procedural justice, Gerald S. Leventhal proposed seven criteria for the evaluation of procedural fairness.[163] These criteria should not be considered ultimate standards for the input-oriented legitimacy discussed above. Nevertheless, a comparison between Chancery and common law procedure from this perspective might be considered an interesting experiment, which could ultimately prove helpful for a better characterisation of the perception of both jurisdictions. An evaluation based on Leventhal's study comes with one important limitation: Both his selection of criteria and their understanding rely on studies of modern legal systems. It would be anachronistic to simply assume that late medieval litigants showed the same perceptions of the legal process as litigants in modern Western legal systems. The application of modern procedural justice scholarship, however, suggests some fascinating parallels between modern and late medieval perceptions of legal procedures. In the context of late medieval litigation, the findings of this scholarship should not be understood as empirical evidence but rather as helpful hypotheses.

(1) Selection of agents

The first criterion addresses the decision-making agents.[164] In this regard, the Court of Chancery and the common law courts differed fundamentally. While the Lord Chancellor, who represented the highest authority of the realm, took final decisions in Chancery, the common law employed juries from the

162 This might lead us to question the artificial distinction between 'adversarial' and 'inquisitorial' models altogether. It rather obscures the specific characteristics of a legal process than providing a helpful characterisation. From my experience, this has often led to misunderstandings of the continental European civil process or the role of the judge in the Anglo-American legal system.

163 *G. S. Leventhal*, What Should Be Done with Equity Theory? New Approaches to the Study of Fairness in Social Relationships, in K. J. Gergen / M. S. Greenberg / R. H. Willis (eds.), Social Exchange – Advances in Theory and Research, p. 27–55, p. 37–38.

164 *G. S. Leventhal*, What Should Be Done with Equity Theory? New Approaches to the Study of Fairness in Social Relationships, in K. J. Gergen / M. S. Greenberg / R. H. Willis (eds.), Social Exchange – Advances in Theory and Research, p. 27–55, p. 37.

neighbourhood of the parties, who represented self-determination. Modern empirical studies have shown that parties consider far-removed authorities more believable.[165] The reason might lie in the absence of a suspicion of personal bias. The fear of a partial jury is also represented in the Chancery bills.[166] Overall, the advantages and disadvantages of a civil and local decision-making body on the one hand and a royal and central decision-making body on the other hand are difficult to weigh. It should be clear, however, that the Court of Chancery provided a convincing alternative to those struggling with jury intervention in common law courts.

(2) Setting ground rules

Second, procedural justice is allegedly advanced by fixed ground rules, which provide the parties with the opportunity to reasonably foresee the further development of the trial.[167] My examination of 15th century Chancery cases has shown that the court hardly operated under fixed ground rules. The only thing the parties could expect was that they would not be inhibited by technicalities in the presentation of their cases.[168] The common law was much clearer in this regard. While the procedural framework provided by the respective courses of action must have irritated most litigants, it was largely predictable from the perspective of their lawyers. Naturally, the consistency of legal rules was a main concern for professional lawyers in the late Middle Ages and still is today.[169] However, surveys conducted with lay participants of legal processes have shown that consistency has a comparatively low impact on the evaluation of a legal process – litigants commonly do not look beyond their individual case.[170] This modern finding might be in line with the lack of concern about legal certainty visible in late medieval Chancery documentation.

165 *K. F. Röhl*, Verfahrensgerechtigkeit (Procedural Justice), Zeitschrift für Rechtssoziologie, Volume 14 (1993), p. 1–34, p. 15, relying on *J. L. Gibson*, Institutional Legitimacy, Procedural Justice, and Compliance with Supreme Court Decisions – A Question of Causality, Law and Society Review, Volume 25 (1991), p. 631–636.

166 See for example the case of *White v White* (1399–1413) Select Cases, S. 95, presented in greater detail above 1.2.1.

167 *G. S. Leventhal*, What Should Be Done with Equity Theory? New Approaches to the Study of Fairness in Social Relationships, in K. J. Gergen / M. S. Greenberg / R. H. Willis (eds.), Social Exchange – Advances in Theory and Research, p. 27–55, p. 38.

168 See above throughout chapter V.

169 As exemplified by the rigidity of the common law. For a reflection on the importance of consistency in modern legal systems, see *N. Luhmann*, Das Recht der Gesellschaft, p. 214–238.

170 *K. F. Röhl*, Verfahrensgerechtigkeit (Procedural Justice), Zeitschrift für Rechtssoziologie, Volume 14 (1993), p. 1–34, p. 12, relying on *T. R. Tyler*, Why People Obey the Law, Yale University Press, New Haven, CT, 1990.

(3) Gathering information

A further criterion for evaluation lies in the capability of a legal process to gather and integrate external information.[171] Both the limits of the common law in this regard and the superior truth-finding mechanisms of the Court of Chancery have been discussed extensively above.[172] Interestingly, studies have continuously shown a high regard for witness testimony amongst litigants – despite its well-documented flaws.[173] The examination of Chancery documentation has equally exposed the potential dangers of witness testimony.[174] Nevertheless, witness testimony was imported into the common law trial from as early as the second half of the 15th century.[175] This clearly speaks for the perceived success of Chancery procedure.

(4) Decision structure

Furthermore, the perception of procedural justice can be influenced by the way the final decision is made – especially under whose advice or influence.[176] The Court of Chancery cleverly gained additional authority from the integration of key players of the legal and political process in decision-making.[177] This partly obscured the enormous judicial discretion and helped to create an impression of professionalised decision-making. The procedures at common law must have appeared comparatively obscure. While the professional judge could guide the course of the trial, the final decision-making process remained behind closed curtains – thus provoking suspicions from the losing party.

(5) Appeals

Another factor proposed for the evaluation of procedural fairness is the existence of a system of appeals, which provides dissatisfied litigants with a hope of

171 *G. S. Leventhal*, What Should Be Done with Equity Theory? New Approaches to the Study of Fairness in Social Relationships, in K. J. Gergen / M. S. Greenberg / R. H. Willis (eds.), Social Exchange – Advances in Theory and Research, p. 27–55, p. 38.

172 See chapter V, 4.1.5; 4.2.3.

173 *K. F. Röhl*, Verfahrensgerechtigkeit (Procedural Justice), Zeitschrift für Rechtssoziologie, Volume 14 (1993), p. 1–34, p. 16, relying on *J. Thibaut / L. Walker*, Procedural Justice: A Psychological Analysis.

174 See above chapter V, 4.1.3.

175 Compare the report by *J. Fortescue*, in: S. Lockwood (ed.), On the Laws and Governance of England, Cambridge University Press, Cambridge, 1997, p. 38–40.

176 *G. S. Leventhal*, What Should Be Done with Equity Theory? New Approaches to the Study of Fairness in Social Relationships, in K. J. Gergen / M. S. Greenberg / R. H. Willis (eds.), Social Exchange – Advances in Theory and Research, p. 27–55, p. 38.

177 See above chapter V, 5.2.1.3.

redress.[178] Clearly, such a system was lacking in late medieval England.[179] As pointed out earlier, the absence of an established hierarchy of courts could result in the re-adjudication of a single issue in several distinct forums.[180] The Chancery bills suggest that the court sometimes effectively acted like a court of appeal in accepting cases that had been adjudicated before in local, ecclesiastical or common law courts.[181] Given the multitude of jurisdictions and the continuous risk of further litigation, the absence of opportunities for appeal might not have hurt the legitimacy of the Court of Chancery as much as the modern lawyer might expect.

(6) Safeguards

Another criterion identified by Leventhal is the existence of safeguards, which guarantee that the institutional actors perform their duties "with honesty and integrity".[182] Once again, neither the common law courts nor Chancery provided regular oversight mechanisms. Both common law judges and the Lord Chancellor served at the will of the king. It is hard to imagine that a late medieval monarch based the allocation of offices on the quality of adjudication in civil matters. The Court of Chancery, however, possessed a smart alternative for the creation of an image of "honesty and integrity": It portrayed itself as a court of conscience.[183] Questioning the integrity of a bishop adjudicating on the basis of conscience must have been a daring task for late medieval litigants.

(7) Change mechanisms

The last important criterion for the perception of procedural fairness is the possibility to change – potentially unfair – procedures.[184] An obvious mecha-

178 *G. S. Leventhal*, What Should Be Done with Equity Theory? New Approaches to the Study of Fairness in Social Relationships, in K. J. Gergen / M. S. Greenberg / R. H. Willis (eds.), Social Exchange – Advances in Theory and Research, p. 27–55, p. 38.

179 For an introduction to the pluralism of medieval conflict resolution in England, see above chapter II, 1.1.

180 See chapter V, 2.5.

181 See above chapter V, 2.5.

182 *G. S. Leventhal*, What Should Be Done with Equity Theory? New Approaches to the Study of Fairness in Social Relationships, in K. J. Gergen / M. S. Greenberg / R. H. Willis (eds.), Social Exchange – Advances in Theory and Research, p. 27–55, p. 38.

183 See above chapter V, 2.7.2.

184 *G. S. Leventhal*, What Should Be Done with Equity Theory? New Approaches to the Study of Fairness in Social Relationships, in K. J. Gergen / M. S. Greenberg / R. H. Willis (eds.), Social Exchange – Advances in Theory and Research, p. 27–55, p. 38.

nism for change from our modern perspective is legislation.[185] In late medieval England, legislation failed almost entirely as a tool for procedural change.[186] In the context of integration, I have discussed the stasis that consequently beset common law procedure in the late Middle Ages.[187] 15th century Chancery procedure was almost equally free from external, parliamentary interventions.[188] As shown above, however, the Court of Chancery provided the litigants with a much greater opportunity to influence and thus develop the process. This might have been considered an especially effective remedy for procedures, which were perceived as unfair.

2.3 Conclusion

My evaluation has revealed that the late medieval Court of Chancery process largely conformed to the expectations of litigants – both regarding the opportunities for input and the rationale for its outcomes. Participative elements like unrestricted pleading and a broad array of means of proof allowed litigants to influence the process according to their preferences. The emphasis on conscience by both litigants and the court itself conformed to the often moralistic attitude of the time – expressed in theological justifications of the secular jurisdiction as well as in confessional literature.

The Chancery process thus effectively provided potential for discursive elements:[189] It offered a forum for a largely rational exchange of arguments based upon a foundation of commonly shared values.[190]

How does conformity with the expectations of litigants add to the overall legitimacy of the legal system? First of all, it encouraged individual litigants to participate in the legal process. The routinized recourse to this individual opportunity then contributed to collective acceptance.[191] When everyone

185 Compare for example *H. S. Maine*, Ancient Law, p. 25; 29–30; *N. Luhmann*, Das Recht der Gesellschaft, p. 228. The question has also been addressed above 1.5.

186 See above 1.2.1.

187 See above 1.2.1.

188 For an exception, see chapter V, 2.8 above.

189 Compare modern theorisations of the legal process from the perspective of discursive theory, most notably *J. Habermas*, Faktizität und Geltung – Beiträge zur Diskurstheorie des Rechts und des demokratischen Rechtsstaats, Suhrkamp, Frankfurt / Main, 4th edition, 1994.

190 Compare also *K. F. Röhl*, Verfahrensgerechtigkeit (Procedural Justice), Zeitschrift für Rechtssoziologie, Volume 14 (1993), p. 1–34, p. 27, for an integration of discursive theory and procedural justice.

191 Compare *K. F. Röhl*, Verfahrensgerechtigkeit (Procedural Justice), Zeitschrift für Rechtssoziologie, Volume 14 (1993), p. 1–34, p. 20 with reference to *N. Luhmann*, Legitimation durch Verfahren, Suhrkamp, Frankfurt / Main, 9th edition, 1983.

around you agrees to the legitimacy of a legal process, you will equally seek the legitimisation of your claims within that legal process. The development is thus self-reinforcing: In an adaptable process, legitimacy is gained through the mere participation of litigants.

The initial question remains open: Did the late medieval Court of Chancery add legitimacy to the royal system of adjudication as a whole? From the perspective of the established common law jurisdiction, the risk of the Court of Chancery largely conforming to litigants' expectations is apparent. It might, in turn, undermine the legitimacy of the common law. Theoretically, late medieval litigants should have been discouraged to rely on a jurisdiction that often disregarded their expectations when a superior alternative existed in the same location (albeit not always in the same cases). The risk was thus that the royal courts might have suffered overall. However, it should not be forgotten that the common law featured desirable qualities like predictability or professionalism, which conceivably also qualified as sources of legitimacy.[192]

The miniscule decline of the caseload in the common law courts further proves their continuous popularity.[193] A strict juxtaposition of both jurisdictions might also reflect a misunderstanding of the relationship between the common law and the Court of Chancery. Chancery was a complimentary, not an alternative jurisdiction. While it provided the mechanisms to remedy weaknesses of the common law, it never sought to replace it. The Lord Chancellors neither showed the ambition nor the expertise to supersede the existing regulatory frameworks in areas like property law. The necessity of the common law and of its qualities was thus never really in question – and neither was its legitimacy.[194] On the contrary, Chancery could remedy perceived injustices of the common law and thus also lessen the potential for criticism.

That is not to say that the inter-dependence between common law and what became the equitable jurisdiction in the Court of Chancery was an ideal solution. The necessity of continuous adaptations to both jurisdictions remained and the expectable competitive dissonances soon appeared.[195] Yet, the establishment of the Court of Chancery provided a gradual increase in legitimacy for the

192 See above 1.2.2–1.2.3.

193 See *J. H. Baker*, An Introduction to English Legal History, p. 40.

194 This is, of course, the question that has been raised by *F. W. Maitland*, English Law and the Renaissance (with some Notes), Cambridge University Press, Cambridge, 1901. My conclusion is in line with most more recent assessments, compare *J. H. Baker*, Introduction, in: J. H. Baker (ed.), The Reports of John Spelman, Selden Society, London, Volume 2, 1978, p. 24–28; *D. Jenkins*, English Law and the Renaissance Eighty Years on: In Defence of Maitland, The Journal of Legal History, Volume 2 (1981), p. 107–142.

195 See above chapter V, 4.2.

English legal system as a whole while avoiding the greater adaptive challenges of radical reform.

3. Modernisation

Ideally, the findings on integration and legitimacy should leave us with a better understanding of the function of the Court of Chancery for the English legal system of the late Middle Ages. They should also help us to correct misconceptions about the antiquity of the English equitable jurisdiction. From today's point of view, the term equity and a court in the governmental department of Chancery have a thoroughly archaic ring to them. The history of the court, plagued with uncertainties, delay and mounting costs seems to confirm this impression. A look at the dark history of the court, however, carries the risk of misunderstanding the initial function of its jurisdiction.

That risk is only further increased by adopting a broader European perspective. The persistence of the late medieval Court of Chancery throughout centuries of great legal innovation in universities and courts across Europe looks like an anachronism: While formalisation, unification of jurisdictions and secularisation were the supposed trends of the following centuries,[196] the Court of Chancery instead offered an absence of articulated substance, a lasting bifurcation of central adjudication and a moralisation of the legal discourse. A closer look at each of these trends, however, should reduce some of the distance between the late medieval institution that was the Court of Chancery and the early modern legal developments across Europe.

3.1 Formalisation

An isolated look at the late medieval Court of Chancery certainly confirms the impression of a decidedly informal jurisdiction. Irrespective of the values and ideas underlying Chancery judgments, the fact that the Lord Chancellors adjudicated in the absence of fixed substantive rules allowed for wide discretion. However, this isolated look obscures the comparatively strong early elements of formality in English common law, which remained an essential part of the English legal system.[197] After all, the rise of the court was a reaction to the over-

196 Compare the popular works on the development of the law from the late Middle Ages by *H.J. Berman*, Law and Revolution – The Formation of the Western Legal Tradition, and *P. Prodi,* Eine Geschichte der Gerechtigkeit: Vom Recht Gottes zum modernen Rechtsstaat, C.H. Beck, Munich, 2003, transl. by A. Seemann.

197 *N. Doe*, Fundamental Authority in Late Medieval English Law, Cambridge University Press, Cambridge, 1990, especially p. 33–59, who nevertheless also identified elements of natural law thinking in the common law courts.

emphasis on stability at common law. It thus provided a remedy to some excesses of strict formalism. Even in densely regulated areas of the law, the need for some flexibility is commonly acknowledged up to today. The rise of the court should thus rather be understood as a corrective movement in an on-going development towards formalism.

3.2 Unification

Similar considerations apply to the topic of the unification of the legal system. First of all, it seems necessary to remember that the common law represented a comparatively strong central legal system from as early as the 12th century.[198] The Court of Chancery merely added to the dominance of central royal adjudication in England. Both jurisdictions formed part of the royal administration, were subject to royal oversight and largely employed the same lawyers. They were thus elements of a concentration of power in Westminster. As pointed out above, their ascent partly came at the cost of local and ecclesiastical jurisdictions across England.[199] Acknowledging the additional centralising force of the Court of Chancery leaves us with the irritant of a separate jurisdiction under the same roof. However, the expectation of a single hierarchical structure can be considered a result of unity paradigms of the 19th century.[200] Parallel jurisdictions were a common element of the law before and have actually never truly disappeared.[201] The establishment and continuous existence of a new jurisdiction can thus hardly be considered an anachronistic development.

198 *R. C. van Caenegem*, The Birth of the English Common Law, Cambridge University Press, Cambridge, 2nd edition, 1988 (repr. 1989), S. 92–93, p. 107–110.

199 See above chapter V, 2.5.

200 Compare *T. Duve*, German Legal History: National Traditions and Transnational Perspectives, Rechtsgeschichte, Volume 22 (2014), p. 16–48; p. 18–22, for the state of German scholarship in the late 19th century.

201 Compare *A. Wijffels*, Introduction: European Legal History and the Diversity of Supreme Judicatures, in: A. Wijffels / C. H. van Rhee (eds.), European Supreme Courts – A Portrait through History, Third Millennium Publishing, London, 2013, p. 14–37, p. 31: "After the 18th century rationalist and 19th-century positivistic attempts to establish a more or less exclusive national pyramid hierarchy of courts, modern practitioners are thus once again confronted with forms of legal pluralism and jurisdictional diversity which, albeit based on different societal interests, are reminiscent of the situation which prevailed during the late-medieval and early modern periods." For evidence of the continued existence of parallel normative orders, we might also think of the lasting presence of religious legal orders. Compare also *T. Duve*, German Legal History: National Traditions and Transnational Perspectives, Rechtsgeschichte, Volume 22 (2014), p. 16–48.

3.3 Secularisation

It would be another mistake to consider the Court of Chancery an obstacle in the process of the increasing monopolisation of the legal process by the state. Despite the early presence of bishops and further clerics, Chancery was a secular authority under the direct supervision of the king. The Court of Chancery even expanded royal jurisdiction at the cost of the ecclesiastical courts.[202] The emphasis on conscience in Chancery should be understood differently: It simply reflected the societal attitudes of the time. As I have discussed above, the import of societal values carried with it the potential to strengthen the legitimacy of the court.[203] Furthermore, the intervention of Chancery often proved economically sensible.[204] Recent scholarship has emphasised the lasting impact of the integration of theological considerations into the *ius commune* and the common law.[205] In the Court of Chancery as well as in other jurisdictions, this was actually a feature of secularisation. The moralisation of the law strengthened the state's claim for legal authority against the church.

3.4 Conclusion

By analysing the process and identifying the function of the Court of Chancery in the late medieval English legal system, I hope to have refuted anachronistic preconceptions. At the heart of the development of the equitable jurisdiction in the Court of Chancery was progress rather than regress.

Given the stasis and formality of the common law, the royal system of adjudication required new integrative and legitimating impulses. The modernisation of the English legal system was a necessity and the Court of Chancery provided decisive tools to adjust the legal system to the needs of the times. Modernisation did not stop with the establishment of Court of Chancery or in the 15th century. On the contrary, the 16th century was a time of great innovation in both common law and Chancery. However, the early phase of the Court of Chancery laid out the roots for all further developments. Chancery was at the same time a model and a cautionary tale: What worked well in the Court of

202 Compare *R. H. Helmholz*, The Oxford History of the Laws of England, Volume 1: The Canon Law and Ecclesiastical Jurisdiction from 567 to the 1640s, p. 228–236.

203 See 2.

204 See above, especially 1.4.

205 See *J. Q. Whitman*, The Origins of Reasonable Doubt – Theological Roots of the Criminal Trial, Yale University Press, New Haven, Ct., 2008; *W. Decock*, Moral Theologians and Contract Law – The Moral Transformation of the Ius Commune.

Chancery could be adopted at common law and what did not work could be rejected. The existence of an equitable jurisdiction in the Court of Chancery with its similarities to Roman-canon law procedure also provided a continuously open entrance gate for continental European ideas.[206]

Overall, the institutionalised duopoly of formality and flexibility in common law and Chancery created the potential for the on-going adjustment of both jurisdictions upon the experiences of and the challenges from each other – which finally lead to their unification. The existence of a separate equitable jurisdiction allowed for a modernisation through constant adaptation. It merely underlines the importance of the jurisdiction of the Court of Chancery that this is classically acknowledged as a main feature of the common law legal tradition.

206 Compare for example the adoption of a law of proof identified by *M. R. T. Macnair*, The Law of Proof in Early Modern Equity, Duncker & Humblot, Berlin, 1999.

Chapter VIII

The rise of the Court of Chancery in the European Perspective

Having identified the Chancery process in the 15th century, its roots in Roman-canon law and its function in the developing English legal system, it is time to return to the initial question: Why did the development of a second parallel jurisdiction in the Court of Chancery remain an idiosyncratic feature of the English legal system – a feature which came to characterise the common law legal tradition for centuries and yet remains largely elusive to outsiders up to this day? It is my strong belief that a comparative look, integrating the findings of my functional assessment above, will allow for a better understanding of this development.

The idea of comparing the Court of Chancery with other European courts established in the late Middle Ages is not new. Recent literature on centralised supreme courts in Europe commonly identifies the late medieval Court of Chancery as one example of a wider European development. Indeed, the emergence of central courts from the royal council, endowed with the residual judicial powers of the monarch, is observable in numerous jurisdictions across Europe. Alain Wijffels even characterised the dualism between customary and conciliar courts[1] as being typical for the late medieval period[2] and Mark Godfrey suggested that in jurisdictions where no central court existed yet, it developed out of the *curia*.[3] The latter assessment, of course, does not capture the English development adequately, since the most characteristic feature of the English legal system was the early establishment of a central jurisdiction in the common law courts.[4] These authors have not solely commented on the shared origins of

1 The terminology might require further clarification. However, this is hardly the place to address fundamental questions about the meaning or existence of customary law. It should suffice to say that, in this context and in the following chapter, customary courts are traditional local courts administrating medieval feudal law, whereas conciliar courts are courts originating from royal councils.

2 *A. Wijffels*, Introduction: European Legal History and the Diversity of Supreme Judicatures, in: A. Wijffels / C. H. van Rhee (eds.), European Supreme Courts – A Portrait through History, Third Millennium Publishing, London, 2013, p. 14–37, p 31.

3 *A. M. Godfrey*, Civil Justice in Renaissance Scotland – The Origins of a Central Court, Brill, Leiden, 2009, p. 4.

4 See below. The historical development has been presented above chapter II, 1.3.

the Court of Chancery and other conciliar courts. Alain Wijffels also suggested that "the organisation and functioning of the Court of Chancery, for example, was in many ways comparable to the late-medieval higher courts on the Continent".[5]

However, the existing literature rarely went beyond mentioning possible similarities in passing. More detailed comparisons are still missing, not least because comprehensive literature on the respective European courts has been lacking until very recently. Based upon the latest literature on the procedure of several late medieval and early modern European supreme courts, Michael Macnair has suggested a comparison with three European courts evolving at the end of the Middle Ages: the *Reichskammergericht* in the Holy Roman Empire, the *Grand Conseil de Malines* in the Low Countries and the Court of Session in Scotland.[6] As the further discussion will show, the history of the latter two courts provides excellent material for direct comparisons, not merely because of their similar institutional roots. The situation in the Holy Roman Empire, on the other hand, was complicated by the parallel emergence of two central courts, the *Reichskammergericht* and the *Reichshofrat*. It was arguably the latter that shared more features with the Court of Chancery. I will integrate both courts into my comparison insofar as their distinct characteristics allow. In addition to Macnair's suggested comparisons, I will also refer to the *Parlement de Paris* because of its model character for other European courts and of its geographical and political proximity to England. However, it needs to be borne in mind that the French court predated the Court of Chancery by more than one and the other aforementioned courts by more than two centuries.

The selection of these courts for comparison requires a short explanation. My comparison is supposed to present an overview over parallel developments in neighbouring jurisdictions in the late Middle Ages based on available secondary literature. This is why this chapter will focus on relatively well-researched Northwestern European supreme courts. Given the central economic and academic importance of Southern European jurisdictions at the time, a further expansion of the comparison seems desirable.[7] However, this task must be left to future researchers.

5 *A. Wijffels*, Introduction: European Legal History and the Diversity of Supreme Judicatures, in: A. Wijffels / C. H. van Rhee (eds.), European Supreme Courts – A Portrait through History, p. 14–37, p. 33.

6 *M. R. T. Macnair*, Equity and Conscience, Oxford Journal of Legal Studies, Volume 27 (2007), p. 659–681, p. 668.

7 It might for example be worthwhile to integrate the Portuguese *Tribunal de Grace* or the Venetian merchants' courts, which also professed to judge in equity or conscience rather than law into the comparison.

In a work focused on the identification of the Chancery process and its role in the development of the English legal system, such as this, it will not be possible to offer an in-depth comparison between the respective origins and procedures of the aforementioned courts. Rather than a purely comparative work in itself, this book should be considered as another foundation upon which more detailed comparisons can be built. However, from the existing secondary literature and my own research, it should be possible to identify basic similarities and differences between the aforementioned jurisdictions as well as to highlight the potential for further research.

The look beyond the English borders will also provide further support for an explanation of the rise of the Court of Chancery without recourse to debates about the nature of 'equity' – that most mysterious element of English law. As we will see, equity – despite its prominence in contemporary legal theory and its invocation in adjudication all across Europe – did not gain an equally prominent role in the emergence of the supreme courts in surrounding jurisdictions: While they also administered equity, they did not do so exclusively.

Before embarking upon the comparison, it might be necessary to address one of its potential risks. It requires little knowledge of European legal history to acknowledge the fact that the true singularity of the English development lies in the continuity of the common law jurisdiction from the 12th century onwards up to this day rather than in the later rise of conciliar courts operating under Roman-canon law procedure. Indeed, the late Middle Ages have been characterised as "the age of the chancellor and Council"[8] in the light of the growing influence of conciliar courts across Europe. What remained unparalleled in surrounding jurisdictions was not the rise of the Court of Chancery but rather the resistance of an existing national legal system. An isolated look at the rise of the Court of Chancery thus carries the risk of conveniently smoothing central differences between the common law and the civil law tradition. The European perspective therefore mandates that a comparative analysis addresses the question why the emerging jurisdiction in the Court of Chancery did not replace the antiquated system of the common law rather than establishing itself as a parallel jurisdiction.

This has been a commonplace in historical research on the common law tradition for more than a century. Since Maitland's famous lecture on *Law and the Renaissance* academic controversies have revolved around the 'risk' of a supersession of the common law by institutions based upon civil or Roman-canon law in the wake of the rise of the Court of Chancery. Modern scholarly treatments largely agree that Maitland overestimated the 'risk' of such a

8 *B. Guenée*, States and Rulers in Later Medieval Europe, Blackwell, Oxford, 1985, p. 122.

reception,[9] if it ever existed at all. The professional class of common lawyers, bound through the homogenous education in the Inns of Courts, was firmly in charge of the process in all central courts and thus indispensable. On top of that, alleged sympathies of the absolutist Tudor monarchy for the 'imperial' civil law have been convincingly refuted.[10] Henry VIII not only surrounded himself with common lawyers as his chief advisers, he even installed one of them, Thomas More, as Lord Chancellor, thus breaking the long-standing episcopal tradition.

The continuous institutional stability of the common law may thus be considered well established. My research, however, proposes a shift of perspective towards the Court of Chancery and its institutional design. In the structures it had developed in the 14th and 15th century, the court lacked the potential of other European courts to monopolise central adjudication at the highest level.

It will be my argument that while the Court of Chancery shared numerous parallels with other developing European supreme courts in the 15th century, most notably in its origins (1.) and its procedures (2), it was, from the very outset, jurisdictionally (3.) and functionally (4.) limited. My assessment will rest on the identification of the functions of the Court of Chancery in the last chapter. The comparative approach will allow for a better understanding of the respective developments in England and in surrounding jurisdictions. It will lead into a critical reassessment of the alleged singularity of the jurisdictional bifurcation in the common law tradition.

1. Origins

The most striking similarity between the Court of Chancery and the aforementioned European courts lies in their origin. It is the development of central judicial institutions from royal and imperial councils in the late Middle Ages that created the image of a uniform European development despite the widely diverging political and constitutional landscapes in Western Europe.[11] This

9 Remember also that the idea of a systematic 'reception' of Roman law in continental Europe has largely been debunked in the literature of the last few decades. For a brief summary from an English perspective, see *J. H. Baker*, Introduction, in: J. H. Baker (ed.), The Reports of John Spelman, Selden Society, London, Volume 2, 1978, especially p. 23–51.

10 *W. Holdsworth*, A History of English Law, Methuen, London, Volume 4, 3rd edition, 1945 (repr. 1966), p. 252–293.

11 A discussion of the constitutional constellations in the respective territories – however central to the understanding of the respective legal systems – lies outside the scope of this study. Reference should be made to the numerous works on the constitutional history of the late Middle Ages. A succinct introduction into developments across Europe is provided by *B. Guenée*, States and Rulers in Later Medieval Europe.

section should provide a short introduction into the emergence of the courts, which constitute the objects for my comparison.

1.1 Grand Conseil de Malines

In the 14th and 15th century, the Low Countries consisted of several largely independent provinces under a single rule.[12] These individual provinces also developed their own superior courts during the course of the 15th century.[13] The focus of this comparison, however, will lie on the first central court of law in the Low Countries. Following the Burgundian acquisition of territories, the consolidation of a unitary rule over the provinces allowed for the establishment of first central government structures.[14] As everywhere else in medieval Europe, the administration of justice was considered a key responsibility of the sovereign – a responsibility, which required delegation in the face of monarchical time constraints.[15] In the Low Countries, it was the *curia comitis*, the sovereign's council that dispensed justice on behalf of the respective ruler.[16] With the growing number of appeals to the council, the resolution of legal conflicts became the sole domain of a specialised group of councillors with legal expertise.[17] This '*Grand Conseil*' (Great Council) became distinguishable as a separate entity from the *curia comitis* in the decade between 1435 and 1445.[18]

As the origin in the *curia comitis* would suggest, the *Grand Conseil* was originally an itinerant court, following the sovereign's household.[19] Given provincial opposition to a supra-provincial supreme court, the role of the *Grand*

12 *C. H. van Rhee*, The Low Countries until 1800, in: A. Wijffels / C. H. van Rhee (eds.), European Supreme Courts – A Portrait through History, Third Millennium Publishing, London, 2013, p. 204–219, p. 204.

13 *C. H. van Rhee*, The Low Countries until 1800, in: A. Wijffels / C. H. van Rhee (eds.), European Supreme Courts – A Portrait through History, p. 204–219, p. 204.

14 *C. H. van Rhee*, The Low Countries until 1800, in: A. Wijffels / C. H. van Rhee (eds.), European Supreme Courts – A Portrait through History, p. 204–219, p. 204.

15 *C. H. van Rhee*, Litigation and Legislation – Civil Procedure at First Instance in the Great Council for the Netherlands in Malines (1522–1559), Archives Générales du Royaune, Brussels, 1997, S. 9.

16 *C. H. van Rhee*, Litigation and Legislation – Civil Procedure at First Instance in the Great Council for the Netherlands in Malines (1522–1559), S. 9.

17 *C. H. van Rhee*, Litigation and Legislation – Civil Procedure at First Instance in the Great Council for the Netherlands in Malines (1522–1559), S. 9.

18 *C. H. van Rhee*, Litigation and Legislation – Civil Procedure at First Instance in the Great Council for the Netherlands in Malines (1522–1559), S. 9.

19 *C. H. van Rhee*, The Low Countries until 1800, in: A. Wijffels / C. H. van Rhee (eds.), European Supreme Courts – A Portrait through History, p. 204–219, p. 204.

Conseil was highly contested in the first century of its existence. This might be demonstrated best by the first attempts to establish a permanently fixed seat for the *Grand Conseil*. The court first settled as a *parlement* in Malines in 1473 but the seat was abolished following provincial opposition only four years later.[20] The fixed establishment of the *Grand Conseil* in Malines in 1504 finally ended another period as an itinerant court.[21]

1.2 Court of Session

From the English perspective, the Scottish legal development might present the most intuitive object for comparison. Arguably, no other jurisdiction was 'closer to home' in the late Middle Ages. After all, judicial conflict resolution in Scotland was largely based upon Scottish common law, which showed significant similarities to contemporary English law.[22] This common law, however, was exclusively administered in local courts.[23] A central court – like the Court of Common Pleas or King's Bench – was missing.

Despite the existence of common law courts all across Scotland, the king retained an extraordinary jurisdiction, which was administered interchangeably by parliament, the king's council and the monarch himself.[24] It was this jurisdiction that also provided the source for the development of the Court of Session.

The term 'session' was first coined for a judicial decision-making body mentioned in parliamentary legislation from 1426.[25] While the exact membership structure of this early session remains unclear, the legislation mandated the integration of the Lord Chancellor and the estates – nobility, clergy and the cities – in the decision-making process.[26] Later acts of Parliament extended the competencies and established permanent sessions irrespective of the meetings of

20 *C. H. van Rhee*, Litigation and Legislation – Civil Procedure at First Instance in the Great Council for the Netherlands in Malines (1522–1559), S. 9.

21 *C. H. van Rhee*, Litigation and Legislation – Civil Procedure at First Instance in the Great Council for the Netherlands in Malines (1522–1559), S. 9.

22 *A. M. Godfrey*, Civil Justice in Renaissance Scotland – The Origins of a Central Court, p. 42.

23 *A. M. Godfrey*, Civil Justice in Renaissance Scotland – The Origins of a Central Court, p. 42.

24 *A. M. Godfrey*, Civil Justice in Renaissance Scotland – The Origins of a Central Court, p. 42.

25 *A. M. Godfrey*, Civil Justice in Renaissance Scotland – The Origins of a Central Court, p. 43.

26 *A. M. Godfrey*, Civil Justice in Renaissance Scotland – The Origins of a Central Court, p. 43–44.

parliament.[27] From the 1460s, the king's council increasingly monopolised adjudication under the residual jurisdiction of the king:[28] While central royal adjudication remained on the rise, the first 'session' disappeared.[29] It was not before the 1480s that the name 'session' reappeared, this time for the gatherings of the king's council in its judicial capacity.[30] The residual role of parliament as a court was finally subsumed by the 1490s.[31] In the following decades, the judicial work was delegated to specialised Lords of Session: council members with legal experience and trained parliamentary appointees.[32] The Lord Chancellor remained involved in adjudication. The statutory institution of the Session as a College of Justice in 1532 arguably marked its final settlement as the central Scottish court.[33]

1.3 Reichskammergericht / Reichshofrat

The strong role of largely sovereign territories in the Holy Roman Empire complicates comparisons with other European jurisdictions. Heinz Duchhardt has claimed that the German states simultaneously developed on two – the territorial and the imperial – levels.[34] This naturally also impacted the emergence of a central jurisdiction.

27 *A. M. Godfrey*, Civil Justice in Renaissance Scotland – The Origins of a Central Court, p. 48–58.

28 *A. M. Godfrey*, Civil Justice in Renaissance Scotland – The Origins of a Central Court, p. 61–66; *A. M. Godfrey*, Scotland: the Court of Session from its Foundation to 1800, in: A. Wijffels / C. H. van Rhee (eds.), European Supreme Courts – A Portrait through History, Third Millennium Publishing, London, 2013, p. 190–197, p. 192.

29 Compare *A. M. Godfrey*, Scotland: the Court of Session from its Foundation to 1800, in: A. Wijffels / C. H. van Rhee (eds.), European Supreme Courts – A Portrait through History, p. 190–197, p. 193.

30 *A. M. Godfrey*, Civil Justice in Renaissance Scotland – The Origins of a Central Court, p. 61.

31 *A. M. Godfrey*, Civil Justice in Renaissance Scotland – The Origins of a Central Court, p. 67; *A. M. Godfrey*, Scotland: the Court of Session from its Foundation to 1800, in: A. Wijffels / C. H. van Rhee (eds.), European Supreme Courts – A Portrait through History, p. 190–197, p. 192.

32 *A. M. Godfrey*, Civil Justice in Renaissance Scotland – The Origins of a Central Court, p. 67.

33 This constitutes the main argument of *A. M. Godfrey*'s excellent investigation into the origins of the Court of Session.

34 *H. Duchhardt*, Das Reichskammergericht, in: B. Diestelkamp (ed.), Oberste Gerichtsbarkeit und Zentrale Gewalt, Böhlau, Cologne, 1996, p. 1–13, p. 1 ("*doppelte Staatlichkeit*").

Michael Macnair has suggested the *Reichskammergericht* (Royal Chamber Court) as an object for comparison with the Court of Chancery.[35] This choice seems intuitive not least for the amount of scholarly attention the court has received.[36] However, in contrast to the aforementioned European courts, the *Reichskammergericht* did not originate from a sovereign's council. Despite its name, it seems indeed questionable whether it can be attributed to the imperial level at all. Rather than an element of central state-building, the *Reichskammergericht* has often been characterised as a safeguard for individual territories against overbearing imperial control.[37]

A *Kammergericht* (Chamber Court) directly attached to the king's court existed for the larger part of the 15th century.[38] After opposition against this court from the localities, the establishment of the *Reichskammergericht* in 1495 then represented a compromise between the estates and the emperor.[39] As a part of its responsibility, it acted as an umpire between the different territories and the empire.[40] It thus rather embodied opposition to central power than an imperial jurisdiction.[41] Durchhardt thus found that it should be categorised as a supreme court but not as a royal court[42] – in contrast to the aforementioned courts in England, Scotland and the Low Countries.

Both the personnel and the seat of the court confirm this classification: The judges were nominated proportionately by the estates rather than solely by the

35 *M. R. T. Macnair*, Equity and Conscience, Oxford Journal of Legal Studies, Volume 27 (2007), p. 659–681, p. 668.

36 Consider as introductory examples *B. Diestelkamp*, Das Reichskammergericht im Rechtsleben des Heiligen Römischen Reicher Deutscher Nation, Böhlau, Cologne, 1985; *V. Press*, Das Reichskammergericht in der deutschen Geschichte, Böhlau, Cologne, 1987; *F. Ranieri*, Die Arbeit des Reichskammergerichts in Wetzlar – Kontinuität und Diskontinuität im Vergleich zur Speyerer Zeit, Böhlau, Cologne, 1988; *G. Schmidt-von Rhein*, Das Reichskammergericht in Wetzlar, Böhlau, Cologne, 3rd century edition, 2000.

37 *H. Duchhardt*, Das Reichskammergericht, in: B. Diestelkamp (ed.), Oberste Gerichtsbarkeit und Zentrale Gewalt, p. 1–13, p. 3.

38 *E. Ortlieb*, The Holy Roman Empire: the Imperial Courts' System and the Reichshofrat, in: A. Wijffels / C. H. van Rhee (eds.), European Supreme Courts – A Portrait though History, Third Millennium Publishing, London, 2013, p. 86–96, S. 90.

39 *H. Duchhardt*, Das Reichskammergericht, in: B. Diestelkamp (ed.), Oberste Gerichtsbarkeit und Zentrale Gewalt, p. 1–13, p. 3–4.

40 *A. Baumann*, The Holy Roman Empire: the Reichskammergericht, in: A. Wijffels / C. H. van Rhee (eds.), European Supreme Courts – A Portrait though History, Third Millennium Publishing, London, 2013, S. 96–103, S. 96.

41 Compare *H. Duchhardt*, Das Reichskammergericht, in: B. Diestelkamp (ed.), Oberste Gerichtsbarkeit und Zentrale Gewalt, p. 1–13, p. 10.

42 *H. Duchhardt*, Das Reichskammergericht, in: B. Diestelkamp (ed.), Oberste Gerichtsbarkeit und Zentrale Gewalt, p. 1–13, p. 10.

royal (and imperial) administration.[43] They were commonly trained lawyers or nobles who had acquired legal knowledge.[44] In the first decades of its existence, the *Reichskammergericht* usually sat in free cities outside any territorial sphere of influence and far removed from the royal (and imperial) court in Vienna.

Given the peculiar origins of the *Reichskammergericht*, it might be helpful to take the second central supreme court of the Holy Roman Empire into view for a comparison with the Court of Chancery. Indeed, the origins of the *Reichshofrat* (Court Council of the Empire), which developed as a competing central jurisdiction at the imperial court in Vienna, will sound more familiar to a reader of this book.

The *Reichshofrat* originated in the royal council of the Habsburg monarchs.[45] Just like the other councils across late medieval Europe, the tasks of the *Hofrat* (Court Council) in the late Middle Ages included the complete spectrum of what we would now consider legislative, administrative and judicial functions.[46] Even after the establishment of the *Reichskammergericht*, the council continued to adjudicate when appealed to, thereby relying on the residual jurisdiction of the king.[47] Like other conciliar courts across Europe, the judicial role of the *Hofrat* only evolved gradually.

The establishment of the *Reichskammergericht* might actually have provided the decisive motivation for the development of the *Hofrat* into a court of law.[48] Opposition to territorial influence at the *Reichskammergericht* might have encouraged the specialisation, which allowed the *Hofrat* to compete with the existing central court of the realm. However, this also means that the *Reichshofrat* is only commonly acknowledged as a central court from the second half of the 16th century onwards – and thus a century later than the other courts discussed above.[49]

43 *A. Baumann*, The Holy Roman Empire: the Reichskammergericht, in: A. Wijffels/C. H. van Rhee (eds.), European Supreme Courts – A Portrait through History, S. 96–103, S. 96–97.

44 *A. Baumann*, The Holy Roman Empire: the Reichskammergericht, in: A. Wijffels/C. H. van Rhee (eds.), European Supreme Courts – A Portrait through History, S. 96–103, S. 96–97.

45 *E. Ortlieb*, The Holy Roman Empire: the Imperial Courts' System and the Reichshofrat, in: A. Wijffels/C. H. van Rhee (eds.), European Supreme Courts – A Portrait through History, p. 86–96, S. 91.

46 *W. Sellert*, Der Reichshofrat, in: B. Diestelkamp (ed.), Oberste Gerichtsbarkeit und Zentrale Gewalt, Böhlau, Cologne, 1996, p. 15–44, p. 21–23.

47 *E. Ortlieb*, The Holy Roman Empire: the Imperial Courts' System and the Reichshofrat, in: A. Wijffels/C. H. van Rhee (eds.), European Supreme Courts – A Portrait through History, p. 86–96, S. 90–91.

48 *W. Sellert*, Der Reichshofrat, in: B. Diestelkamp (ed.), Oberste Gerichtsbarkeit und Zentrale Gewalt, p. 15–44, p. 16–21.

49 Compare *W. Sellert*, Der Reichshofrat, in: B. Diestelkamp (ed.), Oberste Gerichtsbarkeit und Zentrale Gewalt, p. 15–44, p. 16.

Despite greater specialisation, the judges at the *Reichshofrat* were not necessarily trained lawyers.[50] Their appointment remained the sole responsibility of the emperor, who – on the other hand – quickly became bound by certain conventions guaranteeing the integration of both confessions and academic expertise.[51] The Chancellor was a constitutive member of the council in the late Middle Ages but largely refrained from judicial tasks in the early modern period.[52]

1.4 Parlement de Paris

In this comparison, the *Parlement de Paris* will necessarily remain an outsider. Its early development clearly distinguishes it from the surrounding supreme courts, which saw the main impulses for their evolution around the 15th century. A look at the *Parlement de Paris* nevertheless appears indispensible for two concrete reasons: First, with evidence of its existence dating back to the 12th century, the *Parlement de Paris* represents the only court in the comparison with the potential to serve as a model for the Court of Chancery. Second, the ties between England and France during the time of the establishment of the Court of Chancery were intense and the potential for mutual influences thus significant.[53]

The development of the *Parlement de Paris* followed the establishment of the French monarchy in Paris.[54] It is impossible to attribute a concrete starting date to the exercise of judicial functions by the *Parlement*.[55] Its origins, on the other hand, are firmly established. Following medieval conceptions about the role of the sovereign as the ultimate secular judge, the judicial tasks of the monarchy were originally discharged by the king in his council.[56] Given the increasing preoccupation of the king with other governmental functions, first signs of a

50 *W. Sellert*, Der Reichshofrat, in: B. Diestelkamp (ed.), Oberste Gerichtsbarkeit und Zentrale Gewalt, p. 15–44, p. 38–40.

51 *W. Sellert*, Der Reichshofrat, in: B. Diestelkamp (ed.), Oberste Gerichtsbarkeit und Zentrale Gewalt, p. 15–44, p. 33–40.

52 Compare *E. Ortlieb*, The Holy Roman Empire: the Imperial Courts' System and the Reichshofrat, in: A. Wijffels/C. H. van Rhee (eds.), European Supreme Courts – A Portrait through History, p. 86–96, S. 91.

53 This is, of course, not least exemplified by the 100 Years' War (1337–1453) between the two countries.

54 *S. Dauchy*, Cours souveraines et genèse de l'état – Le Parlement de Paris, in: B. Diestelkamp (ed.), Oberste Gerichtsbarkeit und Zentrale Gewalt, Böhlau, Cologne, 1996, p. 45–72, p. 46.

55 *S. Dauchy*, Cours souveraines et genèse de l'état – Le Parlement de Paris, in: B. Diestelkamp (ed.), Oberste Gerichtsbarkeit und Zentrale Gewalt, p. 45–72, p. 47.

56 *S. Dauchy*, Cours souveraines et genèse de l'état – Le Parlement de Paris, in: B. Diestelkamp (ed.), Oberste Gerichtsbarkeit und Zentrale Gewalt, p. 45–72, p. 47.

judicial specialisation of certain councillors became visible during the 12th century.[57] However, the settlement of the *Parlement de Paris* as a permanent institution for conflict resolution to which the king delegated his jurisdiction over regular civil conflicts is commonly attributed to the reign of Louis IX (1226–1270).[58] The court settled in Paris and soon established an appellate jurisdiction over most parts of France.[59] Local courts were thus largely relegated to first-instance adjudication. At first, the *Parlement de Paris* showed significant personnel continuity with the *curia regis* but the role of its members was characterised by increasing judicial independence and specialisation by the 14th century.[60] While the judgments of the court were continuously pronounced in the name of the king, the monarch became less and less involved in adjudication despite retaining a residual jurisdiction for exceptional cases.[61]

By the 15th century, the *Parlement de Paris* was not only fully established as the supreme central court. It had also gained significant personnel independence from the monarchy, assumed a central role in the review of legislation and served as a model for appellate courts in the provinces.

1.5 Conclusion

The origins of the courts show remarkable parallels: The Court of Chancery, the *Grand Conseil de Malines*, the Court of Session, the *Reichshofrat* and the *Parlement de Paris* all originated in the councils of the respective central monarchies. They drew their legitimisation from the (residual) jurisdiction of the sovereign. Originally, following late medieval conceptions about the comprehensive powers of the sovereign, the sovereign was perceived as the ultimate 'fountain of justice' – he was not only empowered but also obliged to intervene when the regular course of justice had failed. The intervention of the king and his council – and later of the Court of Chancery – in cases, where the common law allegedly failed to provide justice, may thus be considered as characteristic for late medieval Europe.

57 *S. Dauchy*, Cours souveraines et genèse de l'état – Le Parlement de Paris, in: B. Diestelkamp (ed.), Oberste Gerichtsbarkeit und Zentrale Gewalt, p. 45–72, p. 47.

58 *R. C. van Caenegem*, History of European Civil Procedure, in: M. Cappelletti (ed.), International Encyclopedia of Comparative Law, Volume 14: Civil Procedure, Mohr, Tübingen, 1973, p. 33.

59 *S. Dauchy*, Cours souveraines et genèse de l'état – Le Parlement de Paris, in: B. Diestelkamp (ed.), Oberste Gerichtsbarkeit und Zentrale Gewalt, p. 45–72, p. 57.

60 Compare *S. Dauchy*, Cours souveraines et genèse de l'état – Le Parlement de Paris, in: B. Diestelkamp (ed.), Oberste Gerichtsbarkeit und Zentrale Gewalt, p. 45–72, p. 52–54.

61 *S. Dauchy*, Cours souveraines et genèse de l'état – Le Parlement de Paris, in: B. Diestelkamp (ed.), Oberste Gerichtsbarkeit und Zentrale Gewalt, p. 45–72, p. 56.

The evolution of more specialised courts of justice from the councils marks a step in the differentiation of state functions: The adjudicative tasks of the sovereign were delegated to a group of councillors, who quickly developed legal expertise. Whereas the king could eventually seize jurisdiction personally and otherwise retained influence on the courts through the appointment process, routine adjudication was largely removed from his duties and thus also from his interests.

1.5.1 Single-judge vs. collegiate courts

While the institutional origins of the respective courts were clearly similar, the substantive differences should not fall from view. Indeed, it might be all too tempting to ignore the substantive differences for the establishment of a broader European narrative. For once, the *Grand Conseil de Malines*, the Court of Session, the *Reichshofrat* and the *Parlement de Paris* all remained collegiate courts due to their roots in the councils. The Court of Chancery, on the other hand, quickly developed into a single-judge court. By the middle of the 15th century, the Lord Chancellor had exclusive responsibility for the decisions in Chancery.[62] One reason for this might lie in the distinctively English tradition of employing a low number of judges. It would have been a serious competitive disadvantage of the supplementary jurisdiction in the Court of Chancery if it had employed more judges than the established common law. The other reason, of course, lies in the delegation of the adjudicative tasks to the existing governmental department of Chancery. Its hierarchical structure practically mandated that the Lord Chancellor also retained the final say in judicial matters. Despite the involvement of Chancellors in the development of the judicial councils in the other European jurisdictions, a similar integration into an existing hierarchy did not exist. The conciliar origins in the other European courts thus also remained more visible.

1.5.2 13th vs. 14th vs. 15th century

A second important distinction has already been mentioned above. The conciliar courts developed over a timeframe of more than three centuries. They thus faced different political and legal landscapes in their formative periods. The Parlement de Paris was settled as a central court by the 13th century. The Court of Chancery

62 The Master of the Rolls eventually acted as a substitute during the absence of the Lord Chancellor, see above chapter II, 5.1. Additionally, my evaluation of Chancery decrees has shown that the Lord Chancellor regularly discussed the implications of decisions with lawyers and other experts, see above chapter V, 5.2.1.3.

was firmly established as a separate institution, although not functionally clearly differentiated from the *curia regis*, by the second half of the 14th century. The Session and the *Grand Conseil de Malines* were only mentioned as separate institutions by the 1420s and 1440s – and even then their design still differed substantially from their structure at the beginning of the 16th century. The development towards the duopoly of *Reichskammergericht* and *Reichshofrat* was only set in motion by the founding of the former in 1495.

1.5.3 Central vs. local authorities

As mentioned above, the courts developed in significantly diverging constitutional landscapes. This is not the place to trace the respective constitutional developments in the Low Countries, Scotland, the Holy Roman Empire, France and England in the late Middle Ages – that task should be left to political histories. Nevertheless, it should have become clear from the short introduction into the establishment of the respective courts that competition between central and local power-holders was a key factor in the development of the conciliar courts. The Court of Chancery arguably faced the least opposition: The timid attempts to control its expansion through parliamentary petitions never questioned the new jurisdiction itself. After all, adjudication was already largely centralised in the common law courts. The Holy Roman Empire represents the opposite end of the spectrum. While the *Reichskammergericht* was formally the result of a compromise between the central imperial powers and the estates of the realm, its formation is commonly perceived as a safeguard for the respective territories against expansionist ambitions by the imperial crown. Since the establishment of the *Reichshofrat* was arguably a counter-reaction to this development, local rulers often contested its jurisdiction. In Scotland and in the Low Countries, the development of the conciliar courts was at least delayed by local opposition against an expanding central jurisdiction in the monarchical sphere of influence.

1.5.4 Origins of the common law

One more caveat is in order: The similarities in the institutional origins of the respective courts should be treated with caution. In order to highlight the risks of all too convenient comparisons, it might be helpful to remember the origins of the common law courts. While their roots lay in the 12th century, they also originated from the *curia regis*. Just like the conciliar courts mentioned above, they represent an instance of the differentiation of state functions – of a king effectively delegating certain judicial tasks to a professionalised tribunal. The number of late medieval courts with conciliar origins in Europe is far too high to allow for enumeration. This is not to say that the common law courts should also be classified as further incidents of the conciliar courts identified above. It merely means that a meaningful comparison of the respective courts also mandates an evaluation of their procedures and their jurisdiction.

2. Procedure

The procedure of the respective courts offers another promising field for comparison. It was arguably the growing presence of Roman-canon law procedure in English courts in the late Middle Ages that led Maitland to the discussion of an English 'reception' as part of a wider European movement. The most influential of these courts was, of course, the Court of Chancery. I have identified the Roman-canon law-inspired structure as well as numerous common law elements of Chancery proceedings. A closer comparison of the role of Roman-canon law procedure and the integration of local procedural traditions in the surrounding jurisdictions would help to clarify the position of the Court of Chancery in the wider framework of developing conciliar courts in late medieval Europe.

The existing literature hardly provides concrete procedural comparisons between the European courts.[63] This is not least for the fact that the first comprehensive accounts of the respective procedural regimes have only appeared recently or are still lacking. A comparison is furthermore complicated by the procedural evolution in the courts. I have identified significant changes in Chancery procedure between my research period in the second half of the 15th century and the early modern phase of the court. Research on the procedure of the Dutch, Scottish and imperial courts largely relies on sources from the 16th century onwards – not least because of the asynchronous development of the courts. Any comparison based on the existing studies must therefore remain somewhat asynchronous. I hope that this book will provide further encouragement for more detailed studies. Indeed, a look through the literature almost mandates a research focus on the procedure of the aforementioned courts, since the absence of substantive standards of law was felt equally across all jurisdictions.[64]

63 For a rare exception, see *R. C. van Caenegem*, History of European Civil Procedure, in: M. Cappelletti (ed.), International Encyclopedia of Comparative Law, Volume 14: Civil Procedure.

64 For a most impressive attempt to overcome this problem with regards to the Holy Roman Empire, see *P. Oestmann*, Rechtsvielfalt vor Gericht – Rechtsanwendung und Partikularrecht im Alten Reich, Klostermann, Frankfurt / Main, 2002.

2.1 Grand Conseil de Malines

C. H. van Rhee characterised the procedure in the *Grand Conseil de Malines* as Romano-canonical with a strong French influence.[65] This French influence may have been due to the role of the *Parlements de Paris* as a model supreme court and the shared language.[66] The court nevertheless also showed distinctive local features. As other supreme courts across Europe, it developed its own distinctive style, which, however, required relatively little adaptation from trained Roman-canon lawyers.[67] In contrast to the Court of Chancery, the procedure can largely be identified from codified statements of the rules – so called ordinances.[68]

A quick summary of the main stages of the process will sound extremely familiar to every reader of the former chapters: Proceedings were initiated through open-ended petitions.[69] The defendant was then summoned to answer to the allegations.[70] The further exchange of arguments was meant to delineate the scope of the dispute.[71] At the stage of proof, the parties could introduce available evidence, preferably documents.[72] Witnesses were examined either by a court official or by a local commissioner.[73] The decision-making process was initiated by a final hearing, which was then followed by deliberations of the court.[74] The judgment was published without reasons and the process appa-

65 Compare *C. H. van Rhee*, Litigation and Legislation – Civil Procedure at First Instance in the Great Council for the Netherlands in Malines (1522–1559), p. 12–13, with further references. For an introduction to this French style of procedure, see below 2.4.

66 *C. H. van Rhee*, Litigation and Legislation – Civil Procedure at First Instance in the Great Council for the Netherlands in Malines (1522–1559), p. 12.

67 *C. H. van Rhee*, Litigation and Legislation – Civil Procedure at First Instance in the Great Council for the Netherlands in Malines (1522–1559), p. 13.

68 On those ordinances, see *C. H. van Rhee*, Litigation and Legislation – Civil Procedure at First Instance in the Great Council for the Netherlands in Malines (1522–1559), p. 15–25.

69 *C. H. van Rhee*, Litigation and Legislation – Civil Procedure at First Instance in the Great Council for the Netherlands in Malines (1522–1559), p. 53–56.

70 *C. H. van Rhee*, Litigation and Legislation – Civil Procedure at First Instance in the Great Council for the Netherlands in Malines (1522–1559), p. 73–81.

71 Compare *C. H. van Rhee*, Litigation and Legislation – Civil Procedure at First Instance in the Great Council for the Netherlands in Malines (1522–1559), p. 343.

72 *C. H. van Rhee*, Litigation and Legislation – Civil Procedure at First Instance in the Great Council for the Netherlands in Malines (1522–1559), p. 147–186, especially p. 175–177.

73 *C. H. van Rhee*, Litigation and Legislation – Civil Procedure at First Instance in the Great Council for the Netherlands in Malines (1522–1559), p. 166–175.

74 *C. H. van Rhee*, Litigation and Legislation – Civil Procedure at First Instance in the Great Council for the Netherlands in Malines (1522–1559), p. 187–223, especially p. 194–196.

rently contributed to a large number of settlements before judgment.[75] What thus characterised the procedure at the *Grand Conseil de Malines* was the strong role of the parties, which allowed them to shape the process according to their interests.[76] The parallels to the Court of Chancery are apparent.

All the aforementioned elements are characteristic for Roman-canon law procedure. It is in the details where proceedings differed. A few examples should suffice: Since the *Grand Conseil* was a collegiate court, judgment had to be passed unanimously or by mere majority by a group of judges.[77] Furthermore, the court, from its very beginning, recognised a large number of exceptions against the testimony of witnesses and applied the publication rule, which guaranteed the secrecy of evidence.[78] As mentioned above, this rule was only introduced in Chancery in the 16th century.[79] Progress to the next stage of the proceedings in the *Grand Conseil* also required a motion by the parties.[80] This naturally delayed the process. Overall, van Rhee characterised the procedure as "formal and occasionally cumbersome"[81] – a judgment hardly applicable to the late medieval but all the more so to the early modern Court of Chancery. This merely underlines the problem of the asynchronous comparison.

What should be kept in mind is that the *Grand Conseil de Malines*, like *Reichskammergericht*, *Reichshofrat* and the *Parlement de Paris* mostly acted as a court of appeal. Naturally, this required the adaptation of the procedure. It should be sufficient to note that a system of appeals imposes additional weight on documentation. Since the Court of Chancery did not officially consider appeals, however, I will refrain from a closer examination of specific appeal procedures.

75 Compare *C. H. van Rhee*, Litigation and Legislation – Civil Procedure at First Instance in the Great Council for the Netherlands in Malines (1522–1559), p. 344, 351.

76 Compare *C. H. van Rhee*, Litigation and Legislation – Civil Procedure at First Instance in the Great Council for the Netherlands in Malines (1522–1559), p. 349, who employed the German procedural concept of '*Verhandlungs- und Dispositionsmaximen*' for the illustration of substantive party influence over the process.

77 *C. H. van Rhee*, Litigation and Legislation – Civil Procedure at First Instance in the Great Council for the Netherlands in Malines (1522–1559), p. 196.

78 *C. H. van Rhee*, Litigation and Legislation – Civil Procedure at First Instance in the Great Council for the Netherlands in Malines (1522–1559), p. 178–185.

79 See above chapter V, 5.2.1.1.

80 *C. H. van Rhee*, Litigation and Legislation – Civil Procedure at First Instance in the Great Council for the Netherlands in Malines (1522–1559), p. 353.

81 *C. H. van Rhee*, Litigation and Legislation – Civil Procedure at First Instance in the Great Council for the Netherlands in Malines (1522–1559), p. 354.

2.2 Court of Session

The Scottish development once more provides the closest object for comparison: Local courts in Scotland had been operating under a fully developed procedure, which showed strong parallels to that of the English common law. The establishment of the central Court of Session thus theoretically carried the potential for a procedural dualism of the kind we have identified in England.[82] Furthermore, Mark Godfrey has convincingly argued that the procedure of the Court of Session must have largely developed during the 15th century,[83] which he considered a period of "experiment and reform".[84] From the discussion above, a similar characterisation of Chancery procedure in the 15th century seems legitimate.

According to Godfrey's study, Roman-canon law procedure was dominant in the king's council by 1500, if not before.[85] By then, the forms of the common law had mainly disappeared from discussion in the council. The main difference to England obviously lay in the fact that Roman-canon law procedure was extended to all other courts within a few years after the official recognition of the Court of Session in 1532. While Roman-canon law procedure shaped the trial, the court nevertheless insisted on following its own native 'practick' or style – fully in line with continental European courts.[86] The practical consequences of these adjustments remain hard to identify.

It will be unnecessary to repeat the typical elements of Roman-canon law procedure that the Court of Session shared with the Court of Chancery. It might, however, be all the more interesting to identify shared deviations from Roman-canon law procedure in both courts and incidents of the application of Roman-canon law procedure in the Court of Session, which were unparalleled in the Court of Chancery. The former include the general absence of a formal libel, which carried enumerated positions and articles. Like the bill in the Court of Chancery, petitions to the Court of Session provided space for a free exposition of the facts underlying the claim. A further parallel between Chancery and Session was the existence of a relatively open process of oral or written pleading

82 This dualism, however, did not materialise since the Court of Session monopolised jurisdiction and thereby ousted common law procedure.

83 *A. M. Godfrey*, Civil Justice in Renaissance Scotland – The Origins of a Central Court, p. 161.

84 *A. M. Godfrey*, Civil Justice in Renaissance Scotland – The Origins of a Central Court, p. 163.

85 *A. M. Godfrey*, Civil Justice in Renaissance Scotland – The Origins of a Central Court, p. 168.

86 *A. M. Godfrey*, Civil Justice in Renaissance Scotland – The Origins of a Central Court, p. 162.

for the clarification of the issues underlying the dispute. Incidents, in which the procedure of the Scottish king's council sided with classical Roman-canon law rather than with the 15th century Chancery include the explicit pleading of exceptions,[87] the use of interrogatories and the application of the publication rule. Since Chancery procedure adopted the latter techniques from the beginning of the 16th century, it is difficult to tell whether these differences are not once again the result of an asynchronous comparison.

Given its collegiate character, the decision-making in the Scottish Session naturally differed from that in the Court of Chancery. While the Scottish Chancellor usually presided over adjudication by the council in the 15th century, he was merely one of several (usually 15) judges. The presence of churchmen in the council guaranteed further expertise in Roman-canon law procedure.[88] The collegiate structure even allowed for dissent in exceptional cases.[89] Just like the Court of Chancery, the Court of Session generally published decrees rather than judgments. Mark Godfrey's hypothesis that this represented a mere technicality characteristic for late medieval law rather than a substantive difference is in line with my findings about the Court of Chancery.[90]

Overall, the procedural parallels between the Court of Chancery and the Session can hardly be overstated. Both courts' procedures were praised as positive alternatives to the old forms of common law.[91] The use of exceptions, interrogatories and the application of the publication rule might suggest that the Session was more consistent in the application of Roman-canon law procedure from the outset. However, a closer examination of the stages of development of the Scottish court in the 15th century could potentially reduce the differences even further.

2.3 Reichskammergericht / Reichshofrat

The central courts of the Holy Roman Empire provide a much more difficult object for comparison. While both the *Reichskammergericht* and the *Reichshofrat* certainly shared the general use of a written procedure based upon principles of

87 *A. M. Godfrey*, Civil Justice in Renaissance Scotland – The Origins of a Central Court, p. 183–185.

88 *A. M. Godfrey*, Civil Justice in Renaissance Scotland – The Origins of a Central Court, p. 172.

89 *A. M. Godfrey*, Civil Justice in Renaissance Scotland – The Origins of a Central Court, p. 174.

90 *A. M. Godfrey*, Civil Justice in Renaissance Scotland – The Origins of a Central Court, p. 181. For my discussion, see above chapter V, 5.2.2.4.

91 *A. M. Godfrey*, Civil Justice in Renaissance Scotland – The Origins of a Central Court, p. 164.

Roman-canon law with the three aforementioned courts, a comparison with late medieval Chancery procedure is complicated by the fact that both courts only came into operation and developed their procedure from the 16th century onwards.[92] Given the substantial procedural changes in Chancery procedure in the 16th century,[93] which lie outside of my research period, a concrete comparison might be of little use, if not misleading. I will therefore limit myself to identifying general procedural trends in the development of the central imperial courts, which might be of interest for the integration of the Court of Chancery into a broader European narrative.

The fact that the *Reichskammergericht* was founded upon a compromise between the empire and the estates as a new institution also meant that it was less inhibited by earlier customs than the other courts presented above and, most importantly, the Court of Chancery. Since it had no traditions to build on, its emphasis from the outset lay on professionalism rather than tradition. This is merely underlined by the academic background of lawyers and most judges.[94] The main protagonists of the trial were largely aware of the delicacies of Roman-canon law procedure and no earlier practice or style prevented its adoption.

While the court did not disclose its reasoning in its judgments, anonymised opinions were commonly published in order to foster academic discussion.[95] It goes without saying that such an approach lay far outside the ambition of the late medieval Court of Chancery with its practical approach to individual justice. From the courts examined in this chapter, the *Reichskammergericht* was arguably the most faithful follower of Roman-canon law procedure.

The *Reichshofrat* consciously sought to distance itself from the *Reichskammergericht* and the procedure provided ample opportunity in this regard. The parallel to the Court of Chancery, which offered a flexible alternative to the professionalised common law, is apparent. Before the 17th century, lawyers were rarely involved in adjudication before the *Reichshofrat*.[96] The parties instead presented their case themselves. This is arguably only possible in the absence of strict procedural rules.

92 See the introduction to this chapter above.

93 See above chapter VI, 1.

94 Compare *A. Baumann*, The Holy Roman Empire: the Reichskammergericht, in: A. Wijffels/C. H. van Rhee (eds.), European Supreme Courts – A Portrait through History, S. 96–103, S. 96–97.

95 *H. Duchhardt*, Das Reichskammergericht, in: B. Diestelkamp (ed.), Oberste Gerichtsbarkeit und Zentrale Gewalt, p. 1–13, S. 9.

96 *E. Ortlieb*, The Holy Roman Empire: the Imperial Courts' System and the Reichshofrat, in: A. Wijffels/C. H. van Rhee (eds.), European Supreme Courts – A Portrait through History, p. 86–96, S. 92.

Proceedings in the *Reichshofrat* were thus generally less formal and substantially quicker than those in the *Reichskammergericht*.[97] The absence of official ordinances codifying the procedure at the *Reichshofrat* throughout the 16th century lead to numerous complaints from the estates, who feared imperial discretion.[98] It has even been alleged that the 16th century court lacked a common procedure altogether.[99] However, the look across the Channel to the Court of Chancery and the Court of Session has shown that a procedural practice could easily develop through practice and without codification. It is clear that the design of the process in the *Reichshofrat* largely followed Roman-canon law.[100] After all, the Roman-canon law model was virtually uncontested from the continental European perspective.

The diplomatic expertise of the imperial council, potentially coupled with the informality of the process, also seems to have encouraged settlements in the *Reichshofrat*.[101] This constitutes another interesting parallel to the Court of Chancery.

2.4 Parlement de Paris

By the time of the final settlement of the *Parlement de Paris* in the 13th century, Roman-canon law procedure had already been fully developed and taught at Italian universities as well as in Paris.[102] It thus comes as no surprise that the French central court also largely operated under Roman-canon law procedure. However, contemporary practitioners of the court as well as later commentators have habitually stressed the existence of a distinct local style.[103] Supposedly, the French style integrated elements of earlier local customs. A stronger focus on

97 *W. Sellert*, Der Reichshofrat, in: B. Diestelkamp (ed.), Oberste Gerichtsbarkeit und Zentrale Gewalt, p. 15–44, p. 42.

98 *W. Sellert*, Der Reichshofrat, in: B. Diestelkamp (ed.), Oberste Gerichtsbarkeit und Zentrale Gewalt, p. 15–44, p. 41.

99 *W. Sellert*, Der Reichshofrat, in: B. Diestelkamp (ed.), Oberste Gerichtsbarkeit und Zentrale Gewalt, p. 15–44, p. 40.

100 Compare *E. Ortlieb*, The Holy Roman Empire: the Imperial Courts' System and the Reichshofrat, in: A. Wijffels/C.H. van Rhee (eds.), European Supreme Courts – A Portrait through History, p. 86–96, S. 92.

101 Compare *W. Sellert*, Der Reichshofrat, in: B. Diestelkamp (ed.), Oberste Gerichtsbarkeit und Zentrale Gewalt, p. 15–44, p. 40.

102 Compare *R. C. van Caenegem*, History of European Civil Procedure, in: M. Cappelletti (ed.), International Encyclopedia of Comparative Law, Volume 14: Civil Procedure, p. 33.

103 For an introduction, see *R. C. van Caenegem*, History of European Civil Procedure, in: M. Cappelletti (ed.), International Encyclopedia of Comparative Law, Volume 14: Civil Procedure, p. 33.

orality has been identified as the key mark of distinction.[104] This was especially visible in the examination of witnesses. From the end of the 13th century onwards, witnesses were examined under oath publically and in the presence of the parties.[105]

I have identified the existence of a distinct style integrating local customs,[106] a strong focus on orality[107] and the public examination of witnesses in the localities[108] as typical elements of the Chancery process in the 15th century. However, a first comparative look at the respective procedures suggests that the parallels end here. In contrast to the Court of Chancery, the *Parlement de Paris* lacked the model of an existing central court, in whose shadow it could develop. Its procedure was furthermore heavily influenced by royal ordinances.[109] Indeed, a closer examination suggests that the *Parlement de Paris* followed Roman-canon law procedure significantly more closely than the Court of Chancery. The classical technique for the exchange of arguments in Roman-canon law, which remained largely absent from the late medieval Court of Chancery, proves the point: The litigants in the *Parlement de Paris* made extensive use of positions, articles and exceptions.[110] The look across the Channel might indeed leave us with the impression that the insistence on a national French style reflected a political project rather than the reality of the late medieval procedure in the *Parlement de Paris*.

In the procedural context, it is important to remember that the *Parlement de Paris* operated almost exclusively as a court of appeal. Since the scope of the proceedings commonly extended to both matters of law and matters of fact, a comparison to first-instance proceedings in other courts arguably remains possible. However, the status of the *Parlement de Paris* as a court of appeal

104 *A. Wijffels*, Late-Medieval and Early-Modern France, in: A. Wijffels / C. H. van Rhee (eds.), European Supreme Courts – A Portrait through History, Third Millennium Publishing, London, 2013, p. 62–73, p. 68.

105 *R. C. van Caenegem*, History of European Civil Procedure, in: M. Cappelletti (ed.), International Encyclopedia of Comparative Law, Volume 14: Civil Procedure, p. 34.

106 See above throughout chapter V and chapter VI, 4.

107 See above chapter V, 3.1 introduction.

108 See above chapter V, 4.1.1.

109 *R. C. van Caenegem*, History of European Civil Procedure, in: M. Cappelletti (ed.), International Encyclopedia of Comparative Law, Volume 14: Civil Procedure, p. 35; *S. Dauchy*, Cours souveraines et genèse de l'état – Le Parlement de Paris, in: B. Diestelkamp (ed.), Oberste Gerichtsbarkeit und Zentrale Gewalt, p. 45–72, p. 71.

110 Compare *R. C. van Caenegem*, History of European Civil Procedure, in: M. Cappelletti (ed.), International Encyclopedia of Comparative Law, Volume 14: Civil Procedure, p. 33–35.

nevertheless clearly left its mark on the process. This is perhaps best evidenced by the institutional separation of the court into three chambers, which remained a distinct element of the French system of *parlements*: The plaintiff first addressed the *Chambre des Requêtes* with a request for an appeal against an earlier decision.[111] This represented an additional step at the pre-trial stage before the drafting of the libel. The trial itself could then be held in the *Grand'Chambre* before the collegiate court. It was from there that the judges delegated fact-finding, most notably the examination of witnesses, to the *Chambre des Enquêtes*.[112] This distribution of judicial functions became characteristic for the French legal system.

Judgments in the *Parlement de Paris* followed the opinion of the majority of the collegiate court. They were typically prepared by one of the judges, who was appointed as a *rapporteur* for the specific case.[113] Throughout the late Middle Ages, the Chancellor commonly sat with the court. Rather than getting involved with its daily business in addition to his other governmental functions, however, he merely represented the link with the monarchy and its interests.[114]

2.5 Conclusion

The *Grand Conseil de Malines*, the Court of Session, the *Reichskammergericht* and the *Parlement de Paris* all adopted Roman-canon law procedure with distinctive, yet hardly defining local styles. Within certain limitations, the same might be said about the *Reichshofrat*. This is a well-known fact that hardly needs further elaboration. The popularity of Roman-canon law procedure was based upon its academic prestige as well as its practicability. It offered widely acknowledged instruments for the push for modernisation, which stood behind the establishment of the European supreme courts. In this sense, a European development is clearly identifiable. It would represent truly insular thinking to exclude the Court of Chancery from this development, which consisted of "a wave of

111 *R. C. van Caenegem*, History of European Civil Procedure, in: M. Cappelletti (ed.), International Encyclopedia of Comparative Law, Volume 14: Civil Procedure, p. 33.

112 *R. C. van Caenegem*, History of European Civil Procedure, in: M. Cappelletti (ed.), International Encyclopedia of Comparative Law, Volume 14: Civil Procedure, p. 34.

113 *R. C. van Caenegem*, History of European Civil Procedure, in: M. Cappelletti (ed.), International Encyclopedia of Comparative Law, Volume 14: Civil Procedure, p. 35.

114 Compare *S. Dauchy*, Cours souveraines et genèse de l'état – Le Parlement de Paris, in: B. Diestelkamp (ed.), Oberste Gerichtsbarkeit und Zentrale Gewalt, p. 45–72, p. 53.

procedural and professional changes which brought about an increasingly scientific approach to decision-making".[115]

Nevertheless, it follows from my examination of Roman-canon law influence in the 15th century that the Court of Chancery distanced itself further from the academic model of Roman-canon law procedure than the surrounding jurisdictions. Arguably, this was because it was most strongly influenced by another existing procedural culture, namely that of the common law. The opposition to the common law was directedly reflected in the rejection of the technicalities of Roman-canon law procedure in the late medieval court. Since the Court of Chancery was, at least in large parts, a reaction to the fully functioning but overly formal common law jurisdiction, it could not develop the same degree of technicality as the *Grand Conseil de Malines*. In this regard, its procedural development rather shows a parallel with the *Reichshofrat*, which, more than a century later, represented a similarly informal alternative to the *Reichskammergericht*.

The comparison with the Scottish Court of Session remains most interesting because it operated under similar conditions: It equally represented a response to the formalism of the common law, which is also reflected its procedure. Yet, the Court of Session did not face central common law courts with a comparable structural security and professional identity. The late medieval Court of Chancery thus stood within a European procedural movement[116] but nevertheless remained securely grounded in the English legal tradition.

3. Jurisdiction

The jurisdictional landscape in the respective territories offers a highly fragmented image. The variety of competing and complimentary jurisdictions, which I have identified in England, was typical for late medieval Europe. Considering the stronger role of local power-holders, especially in the Low Countries and the Holy Roman Empire, we might indeed expect an even greater degree of fragmentation than in comparatively centralised England. It would be impossible to present to a detailed picture of the respective developments. My short overview over the jurisdiction of the *Grand Conseil de Malines*, the Court of Session, the two imperial courts of the Holy Roman Empire and the *Parlement de Paris* will therefore be limited to the identification of the role of the courts

115 *J. H. Baker*, The Oxford History of the Laws of England, Volume 6: 1483–1558, Oxford University Press, Oxford, 2003, p. 10.

116 With its beginnings in the middle of the 14th century, the Court of Chancery was arguably even at the forefront of this procedural development as far as the central level is concerned.

within the legal landscape and the concrete grounds which allowed for the opening of a suit. The former will include the placement in the court hierarchy (if existing) as well as the identification of competing courts both on the central level and the local level. The latter will focus on the personal and subject-matter jurisdictions of the respective courts. This discussion should allow introductory insights into the respective potential of the courts and the obstacles in the way of their expansion.

3.1 Grand Conseil de Malines

Throughout the first centuries of its existence, the *Grand Conseil de Malines* remained at the centre of countless jurisdictional conflicts.[117] As a result of the court's organic growth from the *curia*, its jurisdiction was never clearly delineated and thus frequently overlapped with the jurisdiction of other courts at the royal court and in the territories.[118] R. C. van Rhee has argued that the uncertainty arising from the jurisdictional competition might have been in the interest of the sovereign, who retained the opportunity to intervene in cases of interest without alienating local power-holders, who in turn remained invested in everyday business.[119] The – from our modern perspective remarkable – indifference towards jurisdictional uncertainty was equally visible in English legal circles in the late Middle Ages.[120] It might have been a typical feature of the time.

The *Grand Conseil* was established in the face of opposition from the territories, who considered central adjudication a threat to the existence of their own judicial powers. As a result of negotiations between the central court and the provinces, Brabant, Hainaut, Utrecht and Gelders were granted jurisdictional privileges, which precluded appeals from their local supreme courts to Malines.[121] First-instance cases from these provinces could nevertheless be adjudicated in the *Grand Conseil de Malines*, when they were covered by the subject-matter jurisdiction of the court.[122] The cohesion of the territories under

117 *C. H. van Rhee*, Litigation and Legislation – Civil Procedure at First Instance in the Great Council for the Netherlands in Malines (1522–1559), p. 27.
118 *C. H. van Rhee*, Litigation and Legislation – Civil Procedure at First Instance in the Great Council for the Netherlands in Malines (1522–1559), p. 27.
119 *C. H. van Rhee*, Litigation and Legislation – Civil Procedure at First Instance in the Great Council for the Netherlands in Malines (1522–1559), p. 28.
120 See above chapter VII, 2.1; 2.2.6.
121 *C. H. van Rhee*, Litigation and Legislation – Civil Procedure at First Instance in the Great Council for the Netherlands in Malines (1522–1559), p. 11.
122 *C. H. van Rhee*, Litigation and Legislation – Civil Procedure at First Instance in the Great Council for the Netherlands in Malines (1522–1559), p. 11.

the rule of the *Grand Conseil* still remained low throughout the early existence of the court and the Northern territories (what is now the Netherlands) left the jurisdiction of the court in 1581.[123] On the central level, the court faced additional competition from the Privy Council, which also originated form the royal court, from 16th century onwards.[124]

Despite its oversight function as a court of appeal, the *Grand Conseil de Malines* also adjudicated a wide array of first-instance cases:[125] Certain privileged individuals, usually nobles, could appeal directly to the court irrespective of the subject-matter at hand. The court furthermore claimed exclusive jurisdiction over what we would consider matters of constitutional and administrative law. Naturally, these cases were of special interest for the crown. The role of the *Grand Conseil* as supervisory judicial institution was underlined by its intervention in cases, in which several local courts were already involved or in which the regular course of justice had failed. Parallels to the role of the Court of Chancery as a last resort against failures of justice come to mind. The *Grand Conseil de Malines* could also adjudicate on the basis of a mutual submission by the parties.

This general overview over the jurisdiction of the *Grand Conseil* should suffice to identify the main differences with regard to the Court of Chancery. The *Grand Conseil* heard very different classes of cases. Its focus lay on appeals as well as on matters of public law. Apart from these cases, access was largely restricted to privileged individuals. The large majority of cases in the Court of Chancery, on the other hand, were civil cases in first instance. It is arguable that the political origins of the *Grand Conseil* remained more visible in its practice.

3.2 Court of Session

A reflection on the respective jurisdictional limitations of the Court of Session and the Court of Chancery goes to the heart of the diverging developments in Scotland and England. Originally, the jurisdiction of the common law courts constrained the residual role of the council in adjudication in Scotland as well as in England. The early Session in the king's council operated in respect of the

123 Compare *C. H. van Rhee*, Litigation and Legislation – Civil Procedure at First Instance in the Great Council for the Netherlands in Malines (1522–1559), p. 12.

124 *C. H. van Rhee*, Litigation and Legislation – Civil Procedure at First Instance in the Great Council for the Netherlands in Malines (1522–1559), p. 28.

125 The concrete grounds for the jurisdiction of the *Grand Conseil de Malines* were enumerated, followed by a deeper explanation, in *C. H. van Rhee*, Litigation and Legislation – Civil Procedure at First Instance in the Great Council for the Netherlands in Malines (1522–1559), p. 35–36.

confinements and procedures of the common law.[126] The question why Scotland did not follow the English model of jurisdictional bifurcation therefore imposes itself on any discussion about the two courts: Why did the Court of Session become a supreme rather than a supplementary jurisdiction? By the middle of the 16th century, the Court of Session was firmly established at the top of a Scottish judicial hierarchy[127] – and in contrast to England it sat there all alone.

In the middle of the 15th century, the Session already functioned as a central court despite the lack of institutional autonomy as part of the king's council.[128] Jurisdictional competition came from eventual interventions of parliament as well as from local common law and ecclesiastical courts. The latter were assimilated into the secular legal order in the 1560s[129] – long before the corresponding 19th century reforms in England.

The jurisdiction of the Session was not restricted by subject matter or personal status. Like the Court of Chancery, the Session acted as a regular first-instance court. Its tasks nevertheless included a strong supervisory jurisdiction over local courts.[130] By the middle of the 15th century already, adjudication in the Session was merely constrained by the exclusive jurisdiction of ecclesiastical courts and the jurisdiction of local common law courts over crimes and title to land (fee simple).[131] The parallels to England could hardly be closer. Formally, at least, the Court of Chancery operated under the same limitations. Most importantly, the common law courts strictly defended their exclusive jurisdiction over fee simple despite all inroads by Chancery through the acceptance of possessory claims and the recognition of the use.[132] It is certainly arguable that the strong role of the central common law courts in England also guaranteed that the role of the Court of Chancery in other areas of law remained more limited than that of the Session. However, as we have seen, the boundaries in other areas often became

126 *A. M. Godfrey*, Civil Justice in Renaissance Scotland – The Origins of a Central Court, p. 269.

127 Compare *A. M. Godfrey*, Civil Justice in Renaissance Scotland – The Origins of a Central Court, p. 5.

128 *A. M. Godfrey*, Civil Justice in Renaissance Scotland – The Origins of a Central Court, p. 268.

129 *A. M. Godfrey*, Scotland: the Court of Session from its Foundation to 1800, in: A. Wijffels/C. H. van Rhee (eds.), European Supreme Courts – A Portrait through History, p. 190–197, p. 195.

130 *A. M. Godfrey*, Civil Justice in Renaissance Scotland – The Origins of a Central Court, p. 211.

131 Compare *A. M. Godfrey*, Civil Justice in Renaissance Scotland – The Origins of a Central Court, p. 207.

132 Compare above chapter V, 2.5.2.

blurred and the jurisdiction over fee simple stands out as the only concrete demarcation line.

This might be one of the reasons why Mark Godfrey has dedicated large parts of his book on the origins of the Court of Session on the question how it gained jurisdiction over fee simple – in contrast to the Court of Chancery.[133] After all, the procedures of the common law in both kingdoms were modelled to suit the common law title and the adjudication of title under a Roman-canon law inspired procedure constituted a huge break of tradition.[134] Both the Session and Chancery adjudicated a large share of property cases in the 15th century, while respecting the limitation on title.[135] However, the increasing number of possessory actions effectively undermined the exclusive jurisdiction of the common law courts. In England, the King's Bench, the second central common law court, stepped in with the action of ejectment and thereby largely re-established the common law monopoly on property claims.[136] In Scotland, on the other hand, the only institution capable of offering a reformed procedure was the Session.[137] Its growing status as well as the inability of the common law courts to provide a functioning alternative then also allowed the Session to extend its jurisdiction to title over land by the beginning of the 16th century.[138] The explanation for the diverging developments is simple: Scotland lacked a central institution capable of rivalling the Session.[139] In contrast to England, it also had no professional elite protective of the existing system. It thus seems correct to conclude, "in Scotland, the Court of Session came to fill the place of both a Chancery and a King's Bench".[140] The lack of central competition allowed the monopolisation of jurisdiction in the Court of Session.

133 *A. M. Godfrey*, Civil Justice in Renaissance Scotland – The Origins of a Central Court, p. 208.

134 *A. M. Godfrey*, Civil Justice in Renaissance Scotland – The Origins of a Central Court, p. 271.

135 *A. M. Godfrey*, Civil Justice in Renaissance Scotland – The Origins of a Central Court, p. 272.

136 *A. M. Godfrey*, Civil Justice in Renaissance Scotland – The Origins of a Central Court, p. 272.

137 Compare *A. M. Godfrey*, Civil Justice in Renaissance Scotland – The Origins of a Central Court, p. 272.

138 The development has been explained in detail in *A. M. Godfrey*, Civil Justice in Renaissance Scotland – The Origins of a Central Court, p. 268–354.

139 Also *A. M. Godfrey*, Civil Justice in Renaissance Scotland – The Origins of a Central Court, p. 272.

140 *A. Harding*, The Medieval Brieves of Protection and the Development of the Common Law, Juridical Review, Volume 11 (1966), p. 115–149, p. 148.

3.3 Reichskammergericht / Reichshofrat

The Holy Roman Empire arguably exhibited the most challenging legal landscape: Jurisdictional competition existed not only between the imperial level and the territories (and the church) but also between the two imperial courts. It has often been argued that the relationship between the *Reichskammergericht* and the *Reichshofrat* was defined by competition rather than complementation.[141] Neither court developed clear rules for a delineation of the respective jurisdictions.[142] The basic standard operative in the collaboration between the two courts was the rule of 'prevention' (*Prävention*). According to this rule, both courts refrained from adjudicating cases, which were already under consideration of the other court.[143] However, the sources show numerous examples, in which the *Reichshofrat* ignored this rule.[144] Indeed, the conciliar court claimed certain privileges in matters of importance to the imperial household.[145] It thus rejected the equality of both courts. The emperor accordingly advocated the *Reichshofrat*'s 'preeminence' (*Präeminenz*).[146]

Regarding the relationship of the central courts to the territories, their oversight function remained restricted. As a result of numerous negotiations between the emperor and territorial leaders, certain territories were granted privileges *de non appellando*.[147] Appeals against decisions from the respective territories were thus generally excluded, although the restrictions were often circumvented with reliance on other jurisdictional grounds.[148] In return for

141 Compare *W. Sellert*, Der Reichshofrat, in: B. Diestelkamp (ed.), Oberste Gerichtsbarkeit und Zentrale Gewalt, p. 15–44, p. 17.

142 *W. Sellert*, Der Reichshofrat, in: B. Diestelkamp (ed.), Oberste Gerichtsbarkeit und Zentrale Gewalt, p. 15–44, p. 17.

143 *W. Sellert*, Der Reichshofrat, in: B. Diestelkamp (ed.), Oberste Gerichtsbarkeit und Zentrale Gewalt, p. 15–44, p. 20.

144 *W. Sellert*, Der Reichshofrat, in: B. Diestelkamp (ed.), Oberste Gerichtsbarkeit und Zentrale Gewalt, p. 15–44, p. 20.

145 *W. Sellert*, Der Reichshofrat, in: B. Diestelkamp (ed.), Oberste Gerichtsbarkeit und Zentrale Gewalt, p. 15–44, p. 20.

146 *W. Sellert*, Der Reichshofrat, in: B. Diestelkamp (ed.), Oberste Gerichtsbarkeit und Zentrale Gewalt, p. 15–44, p. 21.

147 *E. Ortlieb*, The Holy Roman Empire: the Imperial Courts' System and the Reichshofrat, in: A. Wijffels / C. H. van Rhee (eds.), European Supreme Courts – A Portrait through History, p. 86–96, S. 93. For an impression of the practical impact of these privileges, see the numerous references in *P. Oestmann*, Geistliche und weltliche Gerichtsbarkeit – Zuständigkeitsstreitigkeiten und Instanzenzüge, Böhlau, Köln, 2012.

148 *E. Ortlieb*, The Holy Roman Empire: the Imperial Courts' System and the Reichshofrat, in: A. Wijffels / C. H. van Rhee (eds.), European Supreme Courts – A Portrait through History, p. 86–96, S. 93.

these privileges, the emperor mandated the availability of three-tier proceedings in the territories, thus raising the costs for judicial independence.[149] It is interesting to see how the imperial courts in the face of strong local opposition tried to secure their grasp on the developing legal system through greater professionalism and imperial influence, respectively.

Both the *Reichskammergericht* and the *Reichshofrat* accepted first-instance as well as appeal proceedings.[150] First-instance litigation, however, was restricted to limited classes of cases. Most importantly, litigants, who were recognised as directly subject to the emperor – princes, earls, bishops, imperial cities and imperial convents – were privileged to appeal to the imperial courts in first-instance.[151] The imperial jurisdiction furthermore covered breaches of the peace, which were considered an offence against the emperor.[152] While first-instance proceedings often concerned matters of public law, appeal proceedings usually addressed matters of civil law, which were the domain of local courts in the first instance. In the first century of the existence of the *Reichskammergericht*, the appeal proceedings dominated the work of the court.[153]

The role of the imperial courts in the Holy Roman Empire appears idiosyncratic. It might be doubted whether a closer comparison with the Court of Chancery will prove illuminating. At this stage, it should suffice to state that the territorial opposition to the central courts in the Holy Roman Empire stands in stark contrast to the centralised structure of the English monarchy. The Court of Chancery thus faced very different – and arguably easier identifiable – jurisdictional competition.

149 *E. Ortlieb*, The Holy Roman Empire: the Imperial Courts' System and the Reichshofrat, in: A. Wijffels/C. H. van Rhee (eds.), European Supreme Courts – A Portrait through History, p. 86–96, S. 93.

150 *E. Ortlieb*, The Holy Roman Empire: the Imperial Courts' System and the Reichshofrat, in: A. Wijffels/C. H. van Rhee (eds.), European Supreme Courts – A Portrait through History, p. 86–96, S. 93.

151 *E. Ortlieb*, The Holy Roman Empire: the Imperial Courts' System and the Reichshofrat, in: A. Wijffels/C. H. van Rhee (eds.), European Supreme Courts – A Portrait through History, p. 86–96, S. 93.

152 Compare *E. Ortlieb*, The Holy Roman Empire: the Imperial Courts' System and the Reichshofrat, in: A. Wijffels/C. H. van Rhee (eds.), European Supreme Courts – A Portrait through History, p. 86–96, S. 93.

153 The appeal business culminated at around 75 percent of the overall workload of the court, *A. Baumann*, The Holy Roman Empire: the Reichskammergericht, in: A. Wijffels/C. H. van Rhee (eds.), European Supreme Courts – A Portrait through History, S. 96–103, S. 98.

3.4 Parlement de Paris

The *Parlement des Paris* played a significant role in the centralisation of the state that has characterised France since the late Middle Ages. After its permanent settlement in the 13th century, it quickly established itself at the top of the hierarchy of regular courts in France.[154] While an appeal to the king in his council remained possible throughout the Middle Ages as an expression of his residual jurisdiction,[155] the *Parlement de Paris* was thus established as the supreme regular court. This was mainly achieved through the acceptance of appeals from local courts and the formulation of regulations for their operation.[156] Not unlike the Court of Chancery two centuries later, the *Parlement de Paris* thus assumed a supervisory function over the secular legal system.

In contrast to the Court of Chancery, however, the *Parlement de Paris* faced no existing central jurisdiction during the time of its expansion. The fragmented opposition of local power-holders operating secular courts in the periphery hardly delayed its rise to the top of the judicial hierarchy. Either way, the local courts could not match the degree of professionalisation in the *Parlement de Paris*. Effectively, the rise of the *Parlement de Paris* thus came at the cost of seignoral and municipal courts.[157] While they largely retained their jurisdiction in first instance cases, they had to cede the last word to the Paris court. On the other hand, the *Parlement de Paris* employed specialists from the localities in order to guarantee the adherence to local customs.[158] This can be seen as compensation to the increasing centralisation of adjudication in Paris – a policy fully in line with the recurring emphasis on the protection of French traditions despite the far-reaching introduction of Roman-canon law.

The *Parlement de Paris* remained the central court of appeal for most of France throughout the late Middle Ages. It was only from the 15th century onwards that

154 Compare *A. Wijffels*, Late-Medieval and Early-Modern France, in: A. Wijffels / C. H. van Rhee (eds.), European Supreme Courts – A Portrait through History, p. 62–73, p. 62.

155 *S. Dauchy*, Cours souveraines et genèse de l'état – Le Parlement de Paris, in: B. Diestelkamp (ed.), Oberste Gerichtsbarkeit und Zentrale Gewalt, p. 45–72, p. 56.

156 Compare *S. Dauchy*, Cours souveraines et genèse de l'état – Le Parlement de Paris, in: B. Diestelkamp (ed.), Oberste Gerichtsbarkeit und Zentrale Gewalt, p. 45–72, p. 47; 51.

157 Compare *S. Dauchy*, Cours souveraines et genèse de l'état – Le Parlement de Paris, in: B. Diestelkamp (ed.), Oberste Gerichtsbarkeit und Zentrale Gewalt, p. 45–72, p. 48.

158 *S. Dauchy*, Cours souveraines et genèse de l'état – Le Parlement de Paris, in: B. Diestelkamp (ed.), Oberste Gerichtsbarkeit und Zentrale Gewalt, p. 45–72, p. 61–62.

the monarchy founded local *parlements* after the Paris model.[159] This relieved the *Parlement de Paris* of appeal duties. Both its practical oversight as well as its continuous prestige, however, guaranteed that its centralising function remained intact.

The oversight function of the *Parlement de Paris* also effectively extended to the ecclesiastical jurisdiction. Litigants could challenge the abuse of church courts in an appeal to the *Parlement*.[160] The necessary procedure might remind us of the common law's writs of prohibition rather than of the continuous – and largely unregulated – inroads of the Court of Chancery in the ecclesiastical jurisdiction. The result, however, was the same: Secular authorities in England and France successfully limited the scope of the ecclesiastical jurisdiction.

I have repeatedly stressed the role of the *Parlement de Paris* as a court of appeal. As such, it was generally open to litigants in all civil and criminal cases. On the other hand, the *Parlement* rarely adjudicated cases at first instance. Matters directly relating to the royal household represented the only noticeable exception.[161] In this sense, the *Parlement de Paris* arguably showed the least parallels to the Court of Chancery, which only provided first instance adjudication in civil matters and fulfilled no official appeal function. This naturally limits the potential for comparisons between the two courts.

3.5 Conclusion

It is hardly a surprise that the different constitutional surroundings strongly reflected upon the respective jurisdiction of the courts. It will be unnecessary to reiterate the situation in Scotland, the Low Countries, the Holy Roman Empire and France. What the discussion has shown is that the jurisdictional constellation in England was unique: It was only in England that the judicial system had already been centralised in common law courts with a claim to comprehensive judicial authority. The lack of a powerful local opposition against the establishment of a conciliar court was equally distinctive. Despite the absence of central common law courts, the Scottish comparison remains the closest.

This is reflected in the classes of cases, which were adjudicated by the respective courts. Both the Court of Chancery and the Court of Session received

159 For an overview, see *A. Wijffels*, Late-Medieval and Early-Modern France, in: A. Wijffels/C.H. van Rhee (eds.), European Supreme Courts – A Portrait through History, p. 62–73, p. 62–63.

160 *S. Dauchy*, Cours souveraines et genèse de l'état – Le Parlement de Paris, in: B. Diestelkamp (ed.), Oberste Gerichtsbarkeit und Zentrale Gewalt, p. 45–72, p. 51.

161 *S. Dauchy*, Cours souveraines et genèse de l'état – Le Parlement de Paris, in: B. Diestelkamp (ed.), Oberste Gerichtsbarkeit und Zentrale Gewalt, p. 45–72, p. 51.

first-instance litigation in civil matters. Although neither court could claim universal jurisdiction, at least at the outset, litigants did not have to invoke certain privileges in order to appear before the two courts. While access to the courts naturally remained a question of resources, they were both theoretically open to any free man – and woman. Access to the *Grand Conseil de Malines*, the imperial courts of the Holy Roman Empire and the *Parlement de Paris* at first-instance, on the other hand, either required additional justification or was entirely barred for the common litigant. It was, from the very outset, restricted to limited classes of cases largely defined by personal status and royal and imperial interest.

4. Function

Having established an overview over the origins, procedures and jurisdiction of comparable conciliar courts across late medieval Europe, it is time to return to the findings on the functions of the Court of Chancery in the developing English legal system in the last chapter. What can these findings tell us about the peculiarity or the comparability of the Court of Chancery? The discussion will focus on the functions identified and defined above: I will thus discuss the role of professionalization and constitutionalisation, which I have mentioned as significant features of the late medieval common law, in the development of the European supreme courts as well as the importance of integration and legitimacy – the functions I have attributed to the late medieval Court of Chancery.[162]

It would be presumptuous to characterise the respective functions of the *Grand Conseil de Malines*, the Court of Session, the imperial courts of the Holy Roman Empire and the *Parlement de Paris* based upon the limited insights gained from secondary literature. Such a task would require detailed knowledge of the primary sources from the respective courts. The comparative overview, based upon the examination of the origins, procedures and jurisdiction of the courts, might nevertheless allow a more modest illustration of some notable differences. A short reiteration of the English situation will be helpful:

What stood out out in the developing English legal system of the late Middle Ages was the distribution of roles. On the one hand, the established common law jurisdiction provided a forum for centralised and professionalised adjudication. It had started to emancipate itself from the royal court and thus already showed tender roots of constitutional opposition to the monarchy. This jurisdiction was, on the other hand, complemented by the Court of Chancery. It arguably stepped in where the common law left an open door. It thus countered

162 See chapter VII.

the rigidity of common law procedure with a strong focus on integration. Furthermore, it reacted to dissatisfaction with the seemingly unalterable common law by drawing legitimacy from a broad conformity with the expectations of the parties. Naturally, the contrast between the two jurisdictions was not entirely clear-cut. The common law possessed some integrative elements like the action of trespass on the case and the Court of Chancery consciously drew its legitimacy from royal authority rather than popular support. The attribution of different functions to the common law courts and the Court of Chancery nevertheless helps to understand the developing bifurcation of the English legal system as well as its remarkable persistence. It renders the fact that the Court of Chancery, on an initial view, seems like an anachronistic development against the background of the late medieval modernisation of European law largely unproblematic. It is true that the court operated under deliberately informal procedures[163] and concentrated judicial power in closest vicinity to the king.[164] However, since the Court of Chancery was limited to an auxiliary role in the developing English legal system, these anachronisms could not stand in the way of its establishment. On the contrary, the Court of Chancery had a specific role and could excel in it. Due to its limited aspirations, the conflicts with other jurisdictions remained manageable. The court could focus its energies on adjudication and quickly establish itself as an indispensible part of the English legal system.

It is obvious that the other courts presented above were not in a comparably comfortable position. Their roles were hardly limited in similar ways. On the contrary, the *Grand Conseil de Malines*, the Court of Session, the *Reichskammergericht*, the *Reichskammergericht* and the *Parlement de Paris* were political as much as legal projects. They reflected attempts to centralise adjudication in professionalised courts under the influence of the respective rulers, which naturally caused added opposition. A similar problem could not arise in England, where professionalised central courts already existed. The potential for increased royal influence over Chancery represented the only parallel in this regard. A brief comparative overview over the functions identified for common law courts and the Court of Chancery respectively will clarify the differences:

163 This arguably questioned the professionalisation of the judiciary, which was visible in the common law courts. See above chapter VII, 1.2.2.

164 This, in turn, questioned first elements of a separation of powers and thus of a constitutionalisation of the English political system. See above chapter VII, 1.2.3.

4.1 Constitutionalisation

The conciliar courts in the Low Countries, Scotland, the Holy Roman Empire and France can be seen as an expression of the expansion of central monarchical power. Jurisdictional privileges for several territories aside, one main task of the developing conciliar courts was the establishment of oversight over local adjudication. The originally residual jurisdiction of the sovereign thereby served as the vehicle for increasingly regular interventions. The rise of the respective courts thus resulted in a rearrangement of powers at the local and the central level.

The English development cannot be explained in similar terms. While the rise of the Court of Chancery might have led to a further increase in central adjudication, local adjudication was already diminished through the status of the common law. The greater potential for constitutional conflicts in England presented itself within the central administration – on a horizontal rather than a vertical level. Royal influence over the Lord Chancellor endangered the first traces of judicial independence from the monarchy, which were developing in the common law courts. A similar constellation might only be visible in the emperor's attempts at strengthening the *Reichshofrat* in the face of an increasingly independent *Reichskammergericht*.

4.2 Professionalisation

My evaluation of the 15th century sources has clearly established the anti-formalist character of Chancery procedure. Since the Court of Chancery represents an ideal-type of anti-formalist jurisprudence, this hardly comes as a surprise.[165] Even today, the promise of adjudication based on simple standards of justice rather than incomprehensible legal technicalities offers a certain charm. However, this promise only becomes truly attractive in the face of a well-defined formalistic counterpart. While the common law courts filled this role exemplarily, the same can hardly be said for the pre-existing courts in the surrounding jurisdictions.

165 Compare *S. N. Subrin*, How Equity Conquered Common Law: The Federal Rules of Civil Procedure in Historical Perspective, University of Pennsylvania Law Review, Volume 135 (1987), S. 909–1002, on the roots of modern American civil procedure in equity procedure and *D. Marcus*, The Federal Rules of Civil Procedure and Legal Realism as a Jurisprudence of Law Reform, Georgia Law Review, Volume 44 (2010), p. 433–510, on the centrality of anti-formalist procedural reforms for American Legal Realists.

As mentioned in relation to the Scottish example,[166] local courts in other jurisdictions could be equally trapped in archaic procedures as the English common law. However, the dedication to these procedures could hardly rival that of English common lawyers, who had spent years learning the intricacies of pleading to different actions at the Inns of Court. The fact that the common law had largely monopolised litigation over significant issues added to the misery. Trained lawyers outside of England, on the other hand, were university graduates in civil and canon law. The greater openness and adaptability of Roman-canon law procedure has become visible from the discussions above. The attitude towards professionalization was thus a different one: A look at the *Reichskammergericht* or the *Parlement de Paris* suggests that, outside of England, increased professionalism was perceived as an opportunity rather than a threat. The formalisation of judicial conflicts could thus set an example for lower courts and thereby provide a vehicle for the professionalization of adjudication throughout the realm.

4.3 Integration

The Court of Chancery reacted to the perceived inalienability of the common law by offering an open procedure, which facilitated the integration of societal interests into the developing legal system. As explained above, the institutional design and the basic procedural rules largely followed Roman-canon law procedure.[167] The rationale behind this adoption hardly requires an explanation. Roman-canon law procedure, developed in universities and practically modified to the respective needs of continental secular courts as well as ecclesiastical courts all across Europe, offered an attractive model for a flexible system of judicial administration.

The other European courts, of course, employed similar procedures. Even though greater adherence to the formalities of Roman-canon law procedure might have eventually restricted the litigants' impact on the proceedings, their procedures generally provided a similar potential for the integration of societal interests into the legal system. The artificial barriers to the provision of justice set up by common law procedure were clearly unparalleled in the surrounding supreme courts. With the possible exception of Scotland, however, the provision of an open procedure that promised the cure to individual hardships hardly represented the defining feature of the developing courts. The general advantages of Roman-canon law procedure were not in dispute on the continent.

166 See above 2.2.
167 See chapter VI.

While its integrative features might have been valued, they were hardly associated with the developing conciliar courts concretely.

4.4 Legitimacy

The term legitimacy opens a wide array of topics for discussion. The newly created central courts in late medieval Europe commonly sought justification for their existence in the powers of the sovereign. The idea that the king was the ultimate fountain of justice and thus had both a right and a duty to dispense justice was largely uncontested. A delegation from the sovereign was thus considered as sufficient legitimisation for adjudication between the subjects. This thinking existed in England and Scotland as well as on the continent. However, this is not the kind of legitimacy I have discussed with regard to the Court of Chancery above. From the late medieval perspective, it may have been unthinkable to seek legitimisation from the people rather than from the sovereign but they were the ones who carried their conflicts into the courts and thereby decided about their respective success. The question in how far the respective European courts conformed to expectations of litigants thus remains valid.

I have distinguished between conformity to procedural and substantive expectations. As far as the procedural dimension is concerned, it might suffice to reiterate to substantial similarities between the procedural regimes in the respective courts.[168] The question whether and in how far the courts responded to the substantive expectations of the parties might be more interesting. A concrete assessment would require the study of the sources from the respective jurisdictions. Nevertheless, there is no doubt that the judges in all European courts perceived the observance of higher – religiously inspired – standards of justice as their duty. However, the distinctive focus on conscience in the Court of Chancery was unparalleled in the surrounding jurisdictions. Neither the *Grand Conseil de Malines*, nor the Court of Session nor the imperial courts of the Holy Roman Empire, nor the *Parlement de Paris* considered themselves courts of conscience. This was a concept they would have attributed to the spiritual courts. It might be considered another reflection of the reaction of the Court of Chancery towards the common law that it felt the need to explicitly invoke a

168 The concrete procedural elements, which allowed the parties in the Court of Chancery greater control over the process and thereby favored their acceptance of the proceedings have been explained in some detail above in chapter VII. Following this argumentation, it seems possible that the greater degree of informality in the Court of Chancery – in comparison to the other conciliar courts – also led to greater acceptance by the litigants.

language of justice familiar to the common litigant. After all – and in contrast to the surrounding supreme courts – it could not offer the exclusive authority of central royal adjudication.

4.5 Equity

In this context, a return to the term equity might provide further clarification. Just like the self-declaration as a court of conscience in the 15th century, the label of an equitable jurisdiction remained exclusive to the Court of Chancery. This is not to say that the other conciliar courts did not consider equity a guiding principle in adjudication. In fact, the 1532 legislation codifying the Court of Session in Scotland explicitly stated that all proceedings in the court were to "conform to reason, equity and justice".[169] This was the rhetoric of the time. However, it seems like these three concepts were not even clearly distinguished – let alone defined. As mentioned above, the absence of identifiable rules of substantive law was a common feature of the developing conciliar courts. Why, then, should we assume that the Court of Chancery was the place to fill the term equity with meaning by strictly adjudicating upon certain standards of morality?

The legal sociological understanding of equity captures the English development in the Court of Chancery with far greater precision. Irrespective of the labels of conscience and equity, the main innovation of the Court of Chancery in the late Middle Ages lay in its open-ended procedure, which allowed modernisation at the heart of the English legal system. Since the *Grand Conseil de Malines*, the Court of Session, the *Reichskammergericht*[170] and the *Parlement de Paris* did not exist in similar opposition to an established central court, their functions could not be equally limited. The label equity – understood from the perspective of legal sociology – could not apply similarly.

4.6 Conclusion

In this regard, the limited scope of the "judicial procedure derived from the *ius commune*" in England was hardly "decided on the battlefields of the 1640s and by

169 Quoted from *A. M. Godfrey*, Civil Justice in Renaissance Scotland – The Origins of a Central Court, p. 170. I have modernised the language in order to allow better readability.

170 The *Reichshofrat*, which, at least in part, constituted a response to the success of the *Reichskammergericht* has consciously been neglected in this enumeration. It might be worthwhile to consider its contribution to the evolution of the imperial legal system from the perspective of legal sociology.

the 'Protestant Wind' of 1688", as Michael Macnair has suggested.[171] It was rather the result of the functional limitations of the Court of Chancery, which were clearly visible by the late Middle Ages. By the time the professional elites of the common law dominated Chancery proceedings, a monopolisation of central adjudication in the Court of Chancery or under its procedures was illusory.

The look at the European conciliar courts from the functional perspective offers ambiguous results. The characteristic functions of the Court of Chancery – although partly identifiable in the other European conciliar courts – fail to explain their development. Instead, it has become clear that the functions I have associated with the medieval common law – namely constitutional reform and professionalization – played a significant role in the rise of the *Grand Conseil de Malines* as well as in the Court of Session, the imperial courts of the Holy Roman Empire and the *Parlement de Paris*. This further underlines the hypothesis that the attribution of different roles to the two central jurisdictions was the distinctive feature of the English legal system. The Court of Chancery was arguably charged with less responsibility for the development of the legal system than the other European courts.

171 *M. R. T. Macnair*, Equity and Conscience, Oxford Journal of Legal Studies, Volume 27 (2007), p. 659–681, p. 669.

Chapter IX

Conclusion

The Court of Chancery represented the institutional basis for the procedural modernisation of the English legal system in the late Middle Ages. The lasting success of this modernisation is visible in the longevity of the jurisdictional bifurcation in the common law legal tradition. In contrast to most other European jurisdictions, the future shape of the English legal system was already recognisable in the 15th century. Undoubtedly, the remarkable persistence of English judicial institutions was a result of general constitutional stability as much as of the ingenuity of their design. However, this book has shown that the Court of Chancery of the late Middle Ages became the main facilitator of the adjustment of the English legal system to the changing societal needs of the time. It was the resulting adaptability of the legal system that guaranteed its lasting stability.

The development of a separate jurisdiction with functional limitations was specifically English and must be understood as a reaction to the existing common law jurisdiction – and yet an isolated view at the domestic legal system only tells half of the story. The rise of the Court of Chancery would have been unthinkable without the strong influence of Roman-canon law upon its procedure. It was the adaptation of Roman-canon law procedure to the characteristic requirements of late medieval English law that opened the process towards a stronger participation of the litigants. Under these conditions, the Court of Chancery could develop its integrative force and strengthen the legitimacy of the legal system. The court furthermore stood in the wider European tradition of central courts emanating from royal councils in the late Middle Ages. The diverging outcomes are best explained by the clearly defined role of the Court of Chancery in the English legal system, which was unparalleled in other European jurisdictions.

The Court of Chancery was thus a response to a domestic problem – deeply grounded though it may have been in the procedural and institutional developments of late medieval Europe. As a whole, the evolution of the English legal system in the late Middle Ages formed a part – and was arguably a secular forerunner – of the modernisation of 'Western' legal culture identifiable across Europe.[1] However, the distinctive element that separated the English develop-

1 In addition to *H. J. Berman*, Law and Revolution – The Formation of the Western Legal Tradition, Harvard University Press, Cambridge, Ma., 1983, who famously

ment from that of the surrounding jurisdictions was the establishment of a second, separate jurisdiction for the adaptation of the law to the requirements of early modernity. The comparison with other developing European supreme courts has shown that the functional division between the common law courts and the Court of Chancery justifies the classification of the English equitable jurisdiction as an idiosyncratic feature in the history of the common law legal tradition. It might be considered ironic that the rise of the most European of superior English courts established a lasting jurisdictional division so foreign to lawyers outside of the common law tradition.

advocated this thesis, consider also *van Caenegem*'s conclusion about the development of the common and civil law traditions – firmly in the spirit of European legal unification: "The ingredients are the same, the rhythm of their impact, the succession of their ups and downs was different" (*R. C. van Caenegem*, The Birth of the English Common Law, Cambridge University Press, Cambridge, 2nd edition, 1988, p. 109).

Bibliography

1. Editions

W. P. Baildon (ed.), Select Cases in Chancery A. D. 1364 to 1471, Selden Society, London, 1896

J. H. Baker / S. F. C. Milsom (eds.), Sources of English Legal History – Private Law to 1750, Butterworths, London, 1986

W. H. Bryson (ed.), Reports of Cases in the Court of Chancery in the Middle Ages (1325–1508), Dog Ear Publishing, Indianapolis, In., 2016

R. C. van Caenegem (ed.), Royal Writs in England from the Conquest to Glanvill, Selden Society, London, 1959

Calendars of the Proceedings in Chancery in the Reign of Queen Elizabeth, To Which are Prefixed Examples of Earlier Proceedings from the Reign of Richard the Second to that of Queen Elizabeth, Inclusive, Public Record Office, London, Volume 1, 1827

Calendars of the Proceedings in Chancery in the Reign of Queen Elizabeth, To Which are Prefixed Examples of Earlier Proceedings from the Reign of Richard the Second to that of Queen Elizabeth, Inclusive, Public Record Office, London, Volume 2, 1830

D. C. Douglas / G. W. Greenaway (eds.), English Historical Documents, Volume 2: 1042–1189, Eyre &Spottiswoode, London, 1968

G. D. G. Hall (ed.), The Treatise on the Laws and Customs of England Commonly Called Glanvill, Nelson, London, 1965

F. Hargrave (ed.), A Collection of Tracts Relative to the Law of England from Manuscripts, Lynch & Co. Dublin, 1787 (repr. 1982)

L. M. Hill (ed.), The Ancient State Authoritie, and Proceedings of the Court of Requests by Sir Julius Caesar, Cambridge University Press, Cambridge, 1975

M. C. Klingelsmith (ed.), Statham's Abridgment of the Law, The Lawbook Exchange, Clark, NJ, Volume 1, 2007

S. Lockwood (ed.), On the Laws and Governance of England, Cambridge University Press, Cambridge, 1997

F. W. Maitland (ed.), Pleas of the Crown for the Country of Gloucester A. D. 1221, Macmillan, London, 1884

T. F. T. Plucknett / J. L. Barton (eds.), St German's Doctor and Student, Selden Society, London, 1974

F. Pollock (ed.), Table Talk of John Selden, Quaritch London, 1927

G. O. Sayles (ed.), Select Cases in the Court of King's Bench under Edward III, Selden Society, London, Volume 5, 1958

Some Proceedings in Chancery under Wolsey, Bulletin of the Institute of Historical Research, Volume 8 (1931), p. 17–20

H. J. Schröder (ed.), Disciplinary Decrees of the General Councils – Text, Translation, and Commentary, Herder, St. Louis, Mo., 1937

D. E. C. Yale (ed.), Epieikeia: A Dialogue on Equity in Three Parts, Yale Law School Library Publications, New Haven, Ct., 1953

D. E. C. Yale (ed.), Lord Nottingham's Chancery Cases, Selden Society, London, Volume 2, 1961

D. E. C. Yale (ed.), Lord Nottingham's Chancery Cases, Selden Society, London, Volume 1, 1957

D. E. C. Yale: Lord Nottingham's 'Manual of Chancery Practice' and 'Prolegomena of Chancery and Equity', Cambridge University Press, Cambridge, 1965, (repr. 1986)

2. Literature

J. Abramson, The Jury System and the Ideal of Democracy, Harvard University Press, Cambridge, Ma., 2001

H. Adams et al., Essays in Anglo-Saxon Law, Rothman, South Hackensack, NJ, 1972

K. Akuffo, A Subaltern Theory of Equity, African Journal of International and Comparative Law, Volume 24 (2016), p. 12–44

J. B. Ames, The Origin of Uses and Trusts, in: Select Essays in Anglo-American Legal History, Little, Brown, and Company, Boston, Ma., Volume 2, 1908, p. 737–752

M. E Avery, An Evaluation of the Effectiveness of the Court of Chancery under the Lancastrian Kings, The Law Quarterly Review, Volume 86 (1970), p. 84–97

M. E. Avery, The History of the Equitable Jurisdiction of Chancery before 1460, Bulletin of the Institute of Historical Research, Volume 42 (1969), p. 129–144

J. H. Baker, An Introduction to English Legal History, Butterworths, London, 4th edition, 2002

J. H. Baker, English Law and the Renaissance, The Cambridge Law Journal, Volume 44 (1985), p. 46–61

J. H. Baker, Manual of Law French, Avebury, Letchworth, 1979

J. H. Baker, The Common Lawyers and the Chancery: 1616, The Irish Jurist, Volume 4 (1969), p. 368–392

J. H. Baker, The Common Law Tradition – Lawyers, Books and the Law, Hambledon Press, London, 2000

J. H. Baker (ed.), The Reports of John Spelman, Selden Society, London, Volume 2, 1978

J. H. Baker, The Oxford History of the Laws of England, Volume 6: 1483–1558, Oxford University Press, Oxford, 2003

W. Barbour, Some Aspects of Fifteenth-Century Chancery, Harvard Law Review, Volume 31 (1918), p. 834–859

W. T. Barbour, The History of Contract in Early English Equity, in: P. Vinogradoff (ed.), Oxford Studies in Social and Legal History, Clarendon Press, Oxford, Volume 4, 1914, p. 1–237

J. L. Barton, Equity in the Medieval Common Law, in: R. A. Newman (ed.), Equity in the World's Legal Systems – A Comparative Study, Emile Bruylant, Bruxelles, 1973

J. L. Barton, Roman Law in England, in: Société d'Histoire des Droits de L'Antiquité (ed.), Ius Romanum Medii Aevi, Giuffrè, Milan, Volume 5, 13a, 1971

A. Baumann, The Holy Roman Empire: the Reichskammergericht, in: A. Wijffels / C. H. van Rhee (eds.), European Supreme Courts – A Portrait through History, Third Millennium Publishing, London, 2013, S. 96–103

G. Behrens, An Early Tudor Debate on the Relation between Law and Equity, Legal History, Volume 19 (1998), p. 143–161

M. Beilby, The Profits of Expertise: The Rise of the Civil Lawyers and Chancery Equity, in: M. Hicks (ed.), Profit, Piety and the Professions in Later Medieval England, Sutton, Gloucester, 1990, p. 72–90

P. Bellini, 'Denunciatio Evangelica' e 'Denunciatio Iudicialis Privata' – Un Capitolo di Storia Disciplinare della Chiesa, Giuffrè, Milan, 1986

J. Bentham, Indications Respecting Lord Eldon, Including History of the Pending Judges'-Salary-Raising Matter, in: P. Schofield (ed.), Official Aptitude Maximized; Expenses Minimized, Clarendon Press, Oxford, 1993 (repr. 2008), p. 203–289

H. J. Berman, Law and Revolution – The Formation of the Western Legal Tradition, Harvard University Press, Cambridge, Ma., 1983

H. J. Berman, The Origins of Historical Jurisprudence – Coke, Selden, Hale, Yale Law Journal, Volume 102 (1994), p. 1651–1738

J. Biancalana, Testamentary Cases in Fifteenth-Century Chancery, The Legal History Review, Volume 76 (2008), p. 283–306

M. Blatcher, The Court of King's Bench 1450–1550 – A Study in Self Help, Athlone Press, London, 1978
W. Blackstone, Commentaries on the Laws of England, Clarendon Press, Oxford, Volume 3, 1768 (repr. 1966)
A. Boureau, La Loi du Royaume – Les Moines, le Droit et la Construction de la Nation Anglaise (XIè-XIIIè siècles), Les Belles Lettres, Paris, 2001
P. Brand, The Formation of the English Legal System, 1150–1400, in A. Padoa-Schioppa (ed.), Legislation and Justice, Clarendon Press, Oxford, 1997, p. 103–121
P. Brand, The Origins of the English Legal Profession, Blackwell, Oxford, 1992
S. Brodhurst, The Merchants of the Staple, Law Quarterly Review, Volume 17 (1901), p. 56–76
R. C. van Caenegem, History of European Civil Procedure, in: M. Cappelletti (ed.), International Encyclopedia of Comparative Law, Volume 14: Civil Procedure, Mohr, Tübingen, 1973
R. C. van Caenegem, The Birth of the English Common Law, Cambridge University Press, Cambridge, 2nd edition, 1988 (repr. 1989)
W. F. Cahill, Development by the Medieval Canonists of the Concept of Equity, The Catholic Lawyer, Volume 7 (1961), p. 112–120
M. Campbell, The English Yeomen under Elizabeth and the Early Stuarts, Yale University Press, New Haven, Ct., 1942
J. Carroll, The Role of Guilt in the Formation of Modern Society – England 1350–1800, The British Journal of Sociology, Volume 32 (1981), p. 459–503
Certaine Observations Concerning the Office of the Lord Chancellor. Composed by the Right Honorable, and most Learned, Thomas Lord Ellesmere, late Lord Chancellor of England, Printed for Matthew Walbanck, Henry Twyford and John Place, London, 1651
Z. Chafee, Coming Into Equity with Clean Hands, Michigan Law Review, Volume 47 (1949), p. 877–906
S. B. Chrimes, An Introduction to the Administrative History of Medieval England, Blackwell, Oxford, Volume 7, 3rd edition, 1966
C. S. Christopher, Progress in the Administration of Justice during the Victorian Period, Select Essays in Anglo-American Legal History, Little, Brown, and Company, Boston, Ma., Volume 1, 1907, p. 516–557
H. Coing, English Equity and the Denunciatio Evangelica of the Canon Law, Law Quarterly Review, Volume 71 (1955), p. 223–241
A. Cordes, Auf der Suche nach der Rechtswirklichkeit der mittelalterlichen Lex mercatoria, Zeitschrift der Savigny-Stiftung für Rechtsgeschichte – Germanistische Abteilung, Volume 118 (2001), p. 168–184
A. Cordes, The Search for a Medieval Lex mercatoria, in: V. Piergiovanni (ed.), From lex mercatoria to Commercial Law, Duncker & Humblot, Berlin, 2005, p. 53–68
R. Cosin, An Apologie for Sundrie Proceedings by Iurisdiction Ecclesiasticall, Barker, London, 1593
S. Dauchy, Cours souveraines et genèse de l'état – Le Parlement de Paris, in: B. Diestelkamp (ed.), Oberste Gerichtsbarkeit und Zentrale Gewalt, Böhlau, Cologne, 1996, p. 45–72
J. P. Dawson, A History of Lay Judges, Harvard University Press, Cambridge, Ma., 1960
J. P. Dawson, Coke and Ellesmere Disinterred: The Attack on the Chancery in 1616, Illinois Law Review, Volume 36 (1941/42), p. 127–152
L. De Luca, Aequitas Canonica ed Equity Inglese alla Luce del Pensiero di C. Saint Germain, Ephemerides Iuris Canonici, Volume 3 (1947), p. 46–66
W. Decock, The Judge's Conscience and the Protection of the Criminal Defendant: Moral Safeguards against Judicial Arbitrariness, in: G. Martyn / A. Musson / H. Pih-

lamajäki (eds.), From the Judge's Arbitrium to the Legality Principle – Legislation as a Source of Law in Criminal Trials, Duncker & Humblot, Berlin, 2013, p. 69–94

W. Decock, Theologians and Contract Law – The Moral Transformation of the Ius Commune (ca. 1500–1650), Martinus Nijhoff, Leiden, 2013

B. Diestelkamp, Das Reichskammergericht im Rechtsleben des Heiligen Römischen Reicher Deutscher Nation, Böhlau, Cologne, 1985

J. Dietrich, Attempting Fusion: Professor Worthington's 'Equity' and Its Integration with the Common Law, Common Law World Review, Volume 34 (2005), p. 62–84

S. K. Dobbins, Equity: The Court of Conscience or the King's Command, the Dialogues of St. German and Hobbes Compared, Journal of Law and Religion, Volume 9 (1991), p. 113–149

N. Doe, Fundamental Authority in Late Medieval English Law, Cambridge University Press, Cambridge, 1990

C. Donahue, Proof by Witnesses in the Church Courts of Medieval England – An Imperfect Reception of the Learned Laws, in: M. S. Arnold / T. A. Green (eds.), On the Laws and Customs of England: Essays in Honor of Samuel E. Thorne, University of North Carolina Press, Chapel Hill, NC, 1983, p. 127–158

C. Donahue, The Legal Professions of Fourteenth-Century England: Serjeants of the Common Bench and Advocates of the Courts of Arches, in: S. Jenks / J. Rose / C. Whittick (eds.), Laws, Lawyers and Texts – Studies in Medieval Legal History in Honour of Paul Brand, Brill, Leiden, 2012, p. 227–251

H. Duchhardt, Das Reichskammergericht, in: B. Diestelkamp (ed.), Oberste Gerichtsbarkeit und Zentrale Gewalt, Böhlau, Cologne, 1996, p. 1–13

T. Duve, European Legal History – Global Perspectives. Working Paper for the Colloquium European Normativity – Global Historical Perspectives, Max Planck Institute for European Legal History Research Paper Series 2013-06 (2012), http://ssrn.com/abstract=2292666

T. Duve, German Legal History: National Traditions and Transnational Perspectives, Rechtsgeschichte, Volume 22 (2014), p. 16–48

F. Eichler, Lex Mercatoria – das englische Marktrecht des Mittelalters, Mauke, Hamburg, 2008

E. D. Elliott, The Evolutionary Tradition in Jurisprudence, Columbia Law Review, Volume 85 (1985), p. 38–94

G. R. Elton, F. W. Maitland, Weidenfeld and Nicolson, London, 1985

T. A. O. Endicott, The Conscience of the King: Christopher St. German and Thomas More and the Development of English Equity, University of Toronto Faculty Law Review, Volume 47 (1989), p. 549–570

C. H. S. Fifoot, Frederic William Maitland – A Life, Harvard University Press, Cambridge, Ma., 1971

A. Fiori, Il giuramento di innocenza nel processo canonico medievale – Storia e disciplina della purgatio canonica, Klostermann, Frankfurt / Main, 2013

M. Fortier, Equity and Ideas: Coke, Ellesmere, and James I, Renaissance Quarterly, Volume 51 (1998), p. 1255–1281

M. Fortier, The Culture of Equity in Early Modern England, Ashgate, Farnham, 2005

L. M. Friedman, Lawyers in Cross-Cultural Perspective, in: R. L. Abel / P. S. C. Lewis (eds.), Lawyers in Society – Comparative Theories, University of California Press, Berkeley, Ca., 1988 (repr. 2005), p. 1–26

K. Funk, Equity Without Chancery: The Fusion of Law and Equity in the Field Code of Civil Procedure, New York 1846–76, The Journal of Legal History, Volume 36 (2015), p. 152–191

M. Galanter, The Vanishing Trial: An Examination of Trials and Related Matters in Federal and State Courts, Journal of Empirical Legal Studies, Volume 1 (2004), p. 459–570

J. Getzler, Patterns of Fusion, in: P. Birks (ed.), The Classification of Obligations, Clarendon, Oxford, 1997, p. 157–192

J. L. Gibson, Institutional Legitimacy, Procedural Justice, and Compliance with Supreme Court Decisions: A Question of Causality, Law and Society Review, Volume 25 (1991), p. 631–636

A. M. Godfrey, Civil Justice in Renaissance Scotland – The Origins of a Central Court, Brill, Leiden, 2009

A. M. Godfrey, Scotland: the Court of Session from its Foundation to 1800, in: A. Wijffels / C. H. van Rhee (eds.), European Supreme Courts – A Portrait through History, Third Millennium Publishing, London, 2013, p. 190–197

J. Goering, The Internal Forum and the Literature of Penance and Confession, Traditio, Volume 59 (2004), p. 175–227

J. Goldsworthy, The Myth of the Common Law Constitution, in: D. E. Edlin (ed.), Common Law Theory, Cambridge University Press, Cambridge, 2007, p. 204–236

R. W. Gordon, Critical Legal Histories, Stanford Law Review, Volume 57 (1984), p. 57–125

R. W. Gordon, Historicism in Legal Scholarship, Yale Law Journal, Volume 90 (1981), p. 1017–1024

R. W. Gordon, J. Willard Hurst and the Common Law Tradition in American Legal Historiography, Law and Society, Volume 10 (1975), S. 9–55

C. M. Gray, The Boundaries of the Equitable Function, The American Journal of Legal History, Volume 20 (1976), p. 192–226

T. A. Green, Verdict According to Conscience – Perspectives on the English Criminal Trial Jury 1200–1800, University of Chicago Press, Chicago, Il., 1985

R. Griffith-Hill / M. Jones (eds.), Magna Carta, Religion and the Rule of Law, Cambridge University Press, Cambridge, 2015

R. D. Groot, The Jury of Presentment before 1215, The American Journal of Legal History, Volume 26 (1982), p. 1–24

B. Guenée, States and Rulers in Later Medieval Europe, Blackwell, Oxford, 1985

J. A. Guy (ed.), Christopher St German on Chancery and Statute, Selden Society, London, 1985

J. A. Guy, Law, Equity and Conscience in Henrician Juristic Thought, in: A. Fox / J. A. Guy (eds.), Reassessing the Henrician Age – Humanism, Politics and Reform 1500–1550, Blackwell, Oxford, 1986, p. 179–220

J. A. Guy, The Development of Equitable Jurisdictions, 1450–1550, in: E: W. Ives / A. H. Manchester (eds.), Law, Litigants, and the Legal Profession, Royal Historical Society, London, 1983, p. 80–86

J. Habermas, Faktizität und Geltung – Beiträge zur Diskurstheorie des Rechts und des demokratischen Rechtsstaats, Suhrkamp, Frankfurt / Main, 4th edition, 1994

A. Harding, The Medieval Brieves of Protection and the Development of the Common Law, Juridical Review, Volume 11 (1966), p. 115–149

A. D. Hargreaves, Equity and the Latin Side of Chancery, Law Quarterly Review, Volume 68 (1952), p. 481–499

T. S. Haskett, Access to Grace – Bills, Justice, and Governance in England, 1300–1500, in: H. Millet (ed.), Suppliques et Requêtes – Le Gouvernement par la Grâce en Occident (XIIème à XVème Siècle), École française de Rome, Rome, 2003, p. 297–317

T. S. Haskett, Conscience, Justice and Authority in the Late-Medieval English Court of Chancery, in: A. Musson (ed.), Expectations of the Law in the Middle Ages, Boydell Press, Woodbridge, 2001, p. 151–163

T. S. Haskett, Country Lawyers? The Composers of English Chancery Bills, in: P. Birks (ed.), The Life of the Law, Proceedings of the Tenth British Legal History Conference, Oxford, 1991, Hambledon Press, London, 1993, S. 9–23

T. S. Haskett, The Presentation of Cases in Medieval Chancery Bills, in: W. M. Gordon / T. D. Fergus (eds.), Legal History in the Making – Proceedings of the Ninth Legal History Conference, Glasgow, 1989, Hambledon Press, London, 1991, p. 11–28

T. S. Haskett, The Late Medieval Court of Chancery, Law and History Review, Volume 14 (1996), p. 245–313

H. D. Hazeltine, The Early History of English Equity, in: P. Vinogradoff (ed.), Essays in Legal History, Oxford University Press, Oxford, 1913, p. 261–285

R. H. Helmholz, Canon Law as a Means of Legal Integration in the Development of English Law, in: H. Scholler (ed.), Die Bedeutung des kanonischen Rechts für die Entwicklung einheitlicher Rechtsprinzipien, Nomos, Baden-Baden, 1996, p. 49–68

R. H. Helmholz, 'Conscience' and the English Courts between 1500 and 1800, Presentation of 4 April 2014, Wittenberg

R. H. Helmholz, Natural Law in Court – A History of Legal Theory in Practice, Harvard University Press, Cambridge, Ma., 2015

R. H. Helmholz, The Early Enforcement of Uses, Columbia Law Review, Volume 79 (1979), p. 1503–1513

R. H. Helmholz, The Oxford History of the Laws of England, Volume 1: The Canon Law and Ecclesiastical Jurisdiction from 567 to the 1640s, Oxford University Press, Oxford, 2004

R. H. Helmholz, The Privilege and the Ius Commune, in: *R. H. Helmholz et al.*, The Privilege against Self-incrimination, University of Chicago Press, Chicago, Il., 1997, p. 17–46

R. H. Helmholz, The Spirit of Classical Canon Law, University of Georgia Press, Athens, Ga., 1996

R. H. Helmholz, Views of Trust and Treuhand, in: R. H. Helmholz / R. Zimmermann (eds.), Itinera fiduciae – Trust and Treuhand in historical perspective, Duncker & Humblot, Berlin, 1998, p. 27–44

E. G. Henderson, Legal Rights to Land in the Early Chancery, American Journal of Legal History, Volume 26 (1982), S. 97–122

G. Herouschek / D. Müller, Die Ursprünge der Denunziation im Kanonischen Recht, in: H. Lück / B. Schildt (eds.), Recht – Idee – Geschichte – Beiträge zur Rechts- und Ideengeschichte für Rolf Lieberwirth anläßlich seines 80. Geburtstages, Böhlau, Cologne, 2000, p. 3–24

L. Holcombe, Wives and Property – Reform of the Married Women's Property Law in Nineteenth-Century England, University of Toronto Press, Toronto, 1983

W. Holdsworth, A History of English Law, Methuen, London, Volume 1, 7th edition, 1956

W. Holdsworth, A History of English Law, Methuen, London, Volume 4, 3rd edition, 1945 (repr. 1966)

W. Holdsworth, A History of English Law, Methuen, London, Volume 5, 3rd edition, 1945 (repr. 1966)

W. Holdsworth, A History of English Law, Methuen, London, Volume 6, 2nd edition, 1937 (repr. 1966)

W. Holdsworth, A History of English Law, Methuen, London, Volume 9, 1925

W. Holdsworth, The Reception of Roman Law in the Sixteenth Century, The Law Quarterly Review, Volume 28 (1912), p. 236–254

O. W. Holmes, Early English Equity, in: Select Essays in Anglo-American Legal History, Little, Brown, and Company, Boston, Ma., Volume 2, 1908, p. 705–721

O. W. Holmes, The Common Law, Transaction Publishers, New Brunswick, NJ, 2005

J. C. Holt, Magna Charta, Cambridge University Press, Cambridge, 3rd edition, 2015

M. J. Horwitz, The Historical Contingency of the Role of History, Yale Law Journal, Volume 90 (1981), p. 1057–1059

A. Hudson, Conscience as the Organising Concept of Equity, Canadian Journal of Comparative and Contemporary Law, Volume 2 (2016), p. 261–299

D. Ibbetson, The Earl of Oxford's Case (1615), in: C. Mitchell / P. Mitchell (eds.), Landmark Cases in Equity, Hart, Oxford, 2012, p. 1–32

E. W. Ives, The Genesis of the Statute of Uses, The English Historical Review, Volume 82 (1967), p. 673–697

D. Jenkins, English Law and the Renaissance Eighty Years on: In Defence of Maitland, The Journal of Legal History, Volume 2 (1981), p. 107–142

W. J. Jones, The Elizabethan Court of Chancery, Clarendon Press, Oxford, 1967

N. Jones, Trusts in England after the Statute of Uses, in: R. H. Helmholz / R. Zimmermann (eds.), Itinera fiduciae – Trust and Treuhand in historical perspective, Duncker & Humblot, Berlin, 1998, p. 173–205

N. Jones, Wills, Trusts and Trusting from the Statute of Uses to Lord Nottingham, The Journal of Legal History, Volume 31 (2010), p. 273–298

W. Jowitt / C. Walsh (eds.), The Dictionary of English Law, Sweet & Maxwell, London, Volume 1, 1959

E. Kadens, Order within Law, Variety within Custom: The Character of the Medieval Merchant Law, Chicago Journal of International Law, Volume 5 (2004), p. 39–65

D. M. Kerly, An Historical Sketch of the Equitable Jurisdiction of the Court of Chancery, Cambridge University Press, Cambridge, 1890 (repr. 2011)

A. D. Kessler, Our Inquisitorial Tradition: Equity Procedure, Due Process and the Search for an Alternative to the Adversarial, Cornell Law Review, Volume 90 (2005), p. 1181–1275

G. Klass, Efficient Breach, in: G. Klass / G. Letsas / P. Saprai (eds.), The Philosophical Foundations of Contract Law, Oxford University Press, Oxford, 2014, p. 362–387

D. Klinck, Conscience, Equity and the Court of Chancery in Early Modern England, Ashgate, Farnham, 2010

D. Klinck, Imaging Equity in Early Modern England, La Revue Du Barreau Canadien, Volume 84 (2005), p. 217–247

W. N. Knight, Shakespeare's Court Case, Law and Critique, Volume 2 (1991), p. 103–112

A. Krey, Inquisitionsprozess, in: A. Cordes / H. Lück / D. Werkmüller (eds.), Handwörterbuch zur deutschen Rechtsgeschichte, Schmidt, Berlin, Volume 2, 2nd edition, 2012, col. 1243–1248.

J. H. Langbein / R. T. Lerner / B. P. Smith, History of the Common Law – The Development of Anglo-American Legal Institutions, Aspen Publishers, New York, NY, 2009

J. H. Langbein, The Disappearance of Civil Trial in the United States, Yale Law Journal, Volume 122 (2012), p. 522–572

J. H. Langbein, The Historical Origins of the Privilege against Self-incrimination at Common Law, Michigan Law Review, Volume 92 (1994), p. 1047–1085

J. H. Langbein, Torture and the Law of Proof – Europe and England in the Ancien Régime, The University of Chicago Press, Chicago, Il., 1977

C. C. Langdell, The Development of Equity Pleading from Canon Law Procedure, in: Select Essays in Anglo-American Legal History, Little, Brown, and Company, Boston, Ma., Volume 2, 1908, p. 753–778

O. I Langholm, The Merchants in the Confessional – Trade and Price in the Pre-Reformation Penitential Handbooks, Brill, Leiden 2003

C. Lefebvre, Gratien et les origins de la 'denunciatio evangelica' en droit canonique, Ephemerides iuris canonici, Volume 6 (1950), p. 60–93

S. Lepsius, Von Zweifeln zur Überzeugung – Der Zeugenbeweis im gelehrten Recht ausgehend von der Abhandlung des Bartolus von Sassoferrato, Klostermann, Frankfurt / Main, 2003

G. S. Leventhal, What Should Be Done with Equity Theory? New Approaches to the Study of Fairness in Social Relationships, in K. J. Gergen / M. S. Greenberg / R. H. Willis (eds.), Social Exchange – Advances in Theory and Research, Plenum Press, New York, NY, 1980, p. 27–55

J. P. Lévy, La Hiérarchie des Preuves dans le Droit Savant du Moyen Age, depuis la Renaissance du droit romain jusqu'à la fin du XIVe siècle, Recueil Sirey, Paris, 1939

E. A. Lind / B. E. Erickson / N. Friedland / M. Dickenberger, Reactions to Procedural Models for Adjudicative Conflict Resolution – A Cross-National Study, Journal of Conflict Resolution, Volume 22 (1978), p. 318–339

E. A. Lind / T. R. Tyler, The Social Psychology of Procedural Justice, Plenum Press, New York, NY, 1988

W. Litewski, Der römisch-kanonische Zivilprozeß nach den älteren ordines iudiciarii, Jagiellonian University Press, Krakow, Volume 1, 1999

W. Litewski, Der römisch-kanonische Zivilprozeß nach den älteren ordines iudiciarii, Jagiellonian University Press, Krakow, Volume 2, 1999

M. Lobban, Preparing for Fusion: Reforming the Nineteenth-Century Court of Chancery, Part I, Law and History Review, Volume 22 (2004), p. 389–427

M. Lobban, Preparing for Fusion: Reforming the Nineteenth-Century Court of Chancery, Part II, Law and History Review, Volume 22 (2004), p. 565–599

N. Luhmann, Ausdifferenzierung des Rechts, Suhrkamp, Frankfurt / Main, 1981

N. Luhmann, Das Recht der Gesellschaft, Suhrkamp, Frankfurt / Main, 1991

N. Luhmann, Legitimation durch Verfahren, Suhrkamp, Frankfurt / Main, 9th edition, 1983

M. R. T. Macnair, Arbitrary Chancellors and the Problem of Predictability, in: E. Koops / W. J. Zwalve (eds.), Law & Equity – Approaches in Roman Law and Common Law, p. 79–104

M. R. T. Macnair, Equity and Conscience, Oxford Journal of Legal Studies, Volume 27 (2007), p. 659–681

M. R. T. Macnair, The Law of Proof in Early Modern Equity, Duncker & Humblot, Berlin, 1999

H. S. Maine, Ancient Law (1866), Transaction Publishers, New Brunswick, NJ, 2002

F. W. Maitland, English Law and the Renaissance (with some Notes), Cambridge University Press, Cambridge, 1901

F. W. Maitland, Equity – A Course of Lectures, Cambridge University Press, Cambridge, 1936 (repr. 1969)

F. W. Maitland, The Forms of Action at Common Law – A Course of Lectures, Cambridge University Press, Cambridge, 1909 (repr. 1968)

F. W. Maitland, Why the History of English Law is not Written, in: H. A. L. Fisher (ed.), The Collected Papers of Frederic William Maitland, Cambridge University Press, Cambridge, Volume 1, 1911, p. 480–497

V. Mäkinen, Property Rights in the Late Medieval Discussion on Franciscan Property, Peeters, Leuven, 2001

D. Marcus, The Federal Rules of Civil Procedure and Legal Realism as a Jurisprudence of Law Reform, Georgia Law Review, Volume 44 (2010), p. 433–510

Y. Mausen, Ex scientia et arte sua testificatur, Rechtsgeschichte, Volume 10 (2007), p. 127–135

Y. Mausen, Veritatis adiutur – La Procédure du Témoignage dans le Droit Savant et la Pratique Française, Giuffrè, Milan, 2006

P. M. McDermott, Jurisdiction of the Court of Chancery to Award Damages, The Law Quarterly Review, Volume 109 (1992), p. 652–673

M. Meccarelli, Arbitrium – Un'aspetto sistematico degli ornamenti giuridici in età di diretto comune, Giuffrè, Milan, 1998

F. Metzger, Das englische Kanzleigericht unter Kardinal Wolsey, Promotion an der Friedrich-Alexander-Universität Erlangen-Nürnberg, 1977
F. Metzger, The Last Phase of the Medieval Chancery, in: A. Harding (ed.), Law-Making and Law-Makers in British History – Papers Presented to the Edinburgh Legal History Conference 1977, Royal Historical Society, London, 1980, p. 79–89
S. F. C. Milsom, Historical Foundations of the Common Law, Butterworths, London, 2nd edition, 1981
A. Musson, The English Common Law and Chancery Jurisdiction, Late Middle Ages and Early-Modern Times, in: A. Wijffels / C. H. van Rhee (eds.), European Supreme Courts – A Portrait through History, Third Millennium Publishing, London, 2013, p. 172–181
K. W. Nörr, Römisch-Kanonisches Prozessrecht – Erkenntnisverfahren erster Instanz in civilibus, Springer, Berlin, 2012
K. W. Nörr, Zur Stellung des Richters im Gelehrten Prozeß der Frühzeit: Iudex secundum allegata non secundum conscientiam iudicat, C. H. Beck, Munich, 1967
P. Oestmann, Geistliche und weltliche Gerichtsbarkeit – Zuständigkeitsstreitigkeiten und Instanzenzüge, Böhlau, Köln, 2012
P. Oestmann, Rechtsvielfalt vor Gericht – Rechtsanwendung und Partikularrecht im Alten Reich, Klostermann, Frankfurt / Main, 2002
E. Ortlieb, The Holy Roman Empire: the Imperial Courts' System and the Reichshofrat, in: A. Wijffels / C. H. van Rhee (eds.), European Supreme Courts – A Portrait through History, Third Millennium Publishing, London, 2013, p. 86–96
C. S. Orwin / C. S. Orwin, The Open Fields, The Clarendon Press, Oxford, 3rd edition, 1967
R. C. Palmer, English Law in the Age of the Black Death – A Transformation of Governance and Law, The University of North Carolina Press, Chapel Hill, NC, 1993
K. Pennington, Due Process, Community, and the Prince in the Evolution of the Ordo Iudiciarius, Revista internazionale di diritto commune, Volume 9 (1998), S. 9–47
R. Perruso, The iuramentum perhorrescentiae under Canon Law – An Influence on the Development of Early Chancery Jurisdiction?, Comparative Legal History, Volume 3 (2015), p. 2–37
L. O. Pike, Common Law and Conscience in the Ancient Court of Chancery, in: Select Essays in Anglo-American Legal History, Little, Brown, and Company, Boston, Ma., Volume 2, 1908, p. 722–736
T. F. T. Plucknett, A Concise History of the Common Law, Butterworth, London, 5thedition, 1956
T. F. T. Plucknett, Frederic William Maitland, New York University Law Review, Volume 26 (1951), p. 1–9
F. Pollock / F. W. Maitland, The History of English Law before the Time of Edward I, Cambridge University Press, Cambridge, Volume 1, 2nd edition reissue, 1968
F. Pollock / F. W. Maitland, The History of English Law before the Time of Edward I, Cambridge University Press, Cambridge, Volume 2, 2nd edition reissue, 1968
F. Pollock, The Transformation of Equity, in: P. Vinogradoff (ed.), Essays in Legal History, Oxford University Press, Oxford, 1913, p. 286–296
R. A. Posner, Economic Approach to Legal Procedure and Judicial Administration, Journal of Legal Studies, Volume 2 (1972), p. 399–458
J. B. Post, Equitable Resorts before 1450, in: E. W. Ives / A. H. Manchester (eds.), Law, Litigants, and the Legal Profession, Royal Historical Society, London, 1983, p. 68–79
E. Powell, Arbitration and the Law in England in the Late Middle Ages, Transactions of the Royal Historical Society, Volume 33 (1983), p. 49–67
S. E. Prall, Chancery Reform and the Puritan Revolution, American Journal of Legal History, Volume 6 (1962), p. 28–44
V. Press, Das Reichskammergericht in der deutschen Geschichte, Böhlau, Cologne, 1987

P. Prodi, Eine Geschichte der Gerechtigkeit: Vom Recht Gottes zum modernen Rechtsstaat, C. H. Beck, Munich, 2003, transl. by A. Seemann

N. Pronay, The Chancellor, the Chancery, and the Council at the End of the Fifteenth Century, in: H. Hearder / H. R. Loyn (eds.), British Government and Administration – Studies Presented to S. B. Chrimes, University of Wales Press, Cardiff, 1974, p. 87–103

D. Rabban, From Maine to Maitland via America, Cambridge Law Journal, Volume 68 (2009), p. 410–435

D. Rabban, Law's History – American Legal Thought and the Transatlantic Turn to History, Cambridge University Press, Cambridge, 2013

D. Rabban, The Historiography of the Common Law, Law and Society, Volume 28 (2003), p. 1161–1201

F. Ranieri, Die Arbeit des Reichskammergerichts in Wetzlar – Kontinuität und Diskontinuität im Vergleich zur Speyerer Zeit, Böhlau, Cologne, 1988

D. Rendleman, The Triumph of Equity Revisited: The Stages of Equitable Discretion, Nevada Law Journal, Volume 15 (2015), p. 1397–1453

C. H. van Rhee, Litigation and Legislation – Civil Procedure at First Instance in the Great Council for the Netherlands in Malines (1522–1559), Archives Générales du Royaune, Brussels, 1997

C. H. van Rhee, The Low Countries until 1800, in: A. Wijffels / C. H. van Rhee (eds.), European Supreme Courts – A Portrait through History, Third Millennium Publishing, London, 2013, p. 204–219

K. F. Röhl, Verfahrensgerechtigkeit (Procedural Justice), Zeitschrift für Rechtssoziologie, Volume 14 (1993), p. 1–34

J. Rose, Studying the Past: the Nature and Development of Legal History as an Academic Discipline, The Journal of Legal History, Volume 31 (2010), pp. 101–128

A. Roth, Landfriedensbruch, in: A. Cordes / H. Lück / D. Werkmüller (Hg.), Handwörterbuch zur deutschen Rechtsgeschichte, Schmidt, Berlin, Volume 3, 2nd edition, 2013, col. 505–509

Z. Rueger, Gerson's Concept of Equity and Christopher St. German, History of Political Thought, Volume 3 (1982), p. 1–30

P. A. Ryan, Equity: System or Process?, The Catholoc Lawyer, Volume 3 (1957), p. 59–66

G. Schmidt-von Rhein, Das Reichskammergericht in Wetzlar, Böhlau, Cologne, 3rd edition, 2000

M. Schmoeckel, Humanität und Staatsraison – Die Abschaffung der Folter in Europa und die Entwicklung des gemeinen Strafprozeß- und Beweisrechts seit dem hohen Mittelalter, Böhlau, Cologne, 2000

D. J. Seipp, Jurors, Evidences and the Tempest of 1499, in: J. W. Cairns / G. McLeod (eds.), The Dearest Birth Right of the People of England – The Jury in the History of the Common Law, Hart, Oxford, 2002, p. 75–92

W. Sellert, Der Reichshofrat, in: B. Diestelkamp (ed.), Oberste Gerichtsbarkeit und Zentrale Gewalt, Böhlau, Cologne, 1996, p. 15–44

A. W. B. Simpson, A History of the Common Law of Contract – The Rise of the Action of Assumpsit, Clarendon Press, Oxford, 1975

G. Spence, The Equitable Jurisdiction of the Court of Chancery, Lee and Blanchard, Philadelphia, Pa., Volume 1, 1846 (repr. 1981)

G. Spence, The Equitable Jurisdiction of the Court of Chancery, Lee and Blanchard, Philadelphia, Pa., Volume 2, 1850 (repr. 1981)

M. Stolleis, Römisches Recht und die Entstehung des modernen Staates, Akademie-Journal, Vol.2/2002, p. 53–57

J. Story, Commentaries on Equity Jurisprudence as Administered in England and America, Little, Brown &Co., Boston, Ma., Volume 1, 12th edition, 1877

J. Story, Commentaries on Equity Jurisprudence, Little, Brown, & Co., Company, Boston, Ma., Volume 2, 12th edition, 1877
S. N. Subrin, How Equity Conquered Common Law: The Federal Rules of Civil Procedure in Historical Perspective, University of Pennsylvania Law Review, Volume 135 (1987), S. 909–1002
T. P. Taswell-Langmead, in: T. F. T. Plucknett (ed.), English Constitutional History – From the Teutonic Conquest to the Present Time, Sweet & Maxwell, London, 10th edition, 1946
T. N. Tentler, The Summa for Confessors as an Instrument of Social Control, in: C. Trinkaus / H. A. Oberman (eds.), The Pursuit of Holiness in Late Medieval and Renaissance Religion, Brill, Leiden, 1974, p. 103–126
J. Thibaut / L. Walker, Procedural Justice: A Psychological Analysis, Laurence Erlbaum Associates, Hillsdale, NJ, 1975
B. Tierney, Religion, Law, and the Growth of Constitutional Thought, Cambridge University Press, Cambridge, 1982
C. Tomlins, What is Left of the Law and Society Paradigm after Critique? Revisiting Gordon's "Critical Legal Histories", Law & Society Inquiry, Volume 37 (2012), p. 155–166
P. Tucker, The Early History of the Court of Chancery: A Comparative Study, The English Historical Review, Volume 115 (2000), p. 791–811
T. R. Tyler, Why People Obey the Law, Yale University Press, New Haven, Ct., 1990
P. Vinogradoff, Reason and Conscience in Sixteenth Century Jurisprudence, Law Quarterly Review, Volume 24 (1908), p. 373–384
A. Watson, Legal Transplants, University of Georgia Press, Athens, Ga., 2nd edition, 1993
M. Weber, Grundriss der Sozialökonomik, Band 3: Wirtschaft und Gesellschaft, Mohr Siebeck, Tübingen, 1922
J. Q. Whitman, The Origins of Reasonable Doubt – Theological Roots of the Criminal Trial, Yale University Press, New Haven, Ct., 2008
A. Wijffels, Introduction: European Legal History and the Diversity of Supreme Judicatures, in: A. Wijffels / C. H. van Rhee (eds.), European Supreme Courts – A Portrait through History, Third Millennium Publishing, London, 2013, p. 14–37
A. Wijffels, Late-Medieval and Early-Modern France, in: A. Wijffels / C. H. van Rhee (eds.), European Supreme Courts – A Portrait through History, Third Millennium Publishing, London, 2013, p. 62–73
B. Wilkinson, Constitutional History of Medieval England 1216–1399, Longmans, Green and Co., London, Volume 3, 1958
I. Williams, Christopher St German – Religion, Conscience and Law in Reformation England, in: M. Hill / R. H. Helmholz (eds.), Great Christian Jurists in English History, Cambridge University Press, Cambridge, 2017, p. 69–92
S. Worthington, Equity, Oxford University Press, Oxford, 2nd edition, 2006
W. Zeydel, American and British Law, The Quarterly Journal of the Library of Congress, Volume 21 (1964), p. 285–292
R. Zimmermann, The Law of Obligations – Roman Foundations of the Civilian Tradition, Juta & Co., Cape Town, 1990